CAMBRIDGE STUDIES IN INTERNATIONAL RELATIONS: 98

Power in Global Governance

CAMBRIDGE STUDIES IN INTERNATIONAL RELATIONS: 98

Power in Global Governance

Edited by

Michael Barnett and Raymond Duvall
University of Minnesota

CAMBRIDGE
UNIVERSITY PRESS

PUBLISHED BY THE PRESS SYNDICATE OF THE UNIVERSITY OF CAMBRIDGE
The Pitt Building, Trumpington Street, Cambridge, United Kingdom

CAMBRIDGE UNIVERSITY PRESS
The Edinburgh Building, Cambridge, CB2 2RU, UK
40 West 20th Street, New York, NY 10011-4211, USA
477 Williamstown Road, Port Melbourne, VIC 3207, Australia
Ruiz de Alarcón 13, 28014 Madrid, Spain
Dock House, The Waterfront, Cape Town 8001, South Africa

http://www.cambridge.org

First published 2005
Reprinted 2006

Printed in the United Kingdom at the University Press, Cambridge

Typeface Palatino 10/12.5 pt.   *System* LaTeX 2$_\varepsilon$ [TB]

A catalogue record for this book is available from the British Library

Library of Congress Cataloguing in Publication data

Power in global governance / edited by Michael Barnett, Raymond Duvall.
    p.   cm. – (Cambridge studies in international relations; 98)
Chiefly papers presented at a conference held at the University of Wisconsin in
April 2003.
Includes bibliographical references and index.
ISBN 0 521 84024 4 – ISBN 0 521 54952 3 (pb.)
1. Power (Social sciences) – Congresses. 2. International organization –
Congresses. 3. International relations – Congresses. I. Barnett, Michael N.,
1960– II. Duvall, Raymond. III. Series.
JC330.P6949 2004
327.1'01. – dc22   2004049735

ISBN 0 521 84024 4 hardback
ISBN 0 521 54952 3 paperback

Contents

Contents

Notes on the contributors

EMANUEL ADLER is Professor of International Relations at the Hebrew University of Jerusalem and the Andrea and Charles Bronfman Chair of Israeli Studies at the University of Toronto. The author of numerous books and articles – including *The Power of Ideology* (University of California Press, 1987); *Progress in Postwar International Relations* (Columbia University Press, 1991), coedited with Beverly Crawford; *Security Communities* (Cambridge University Press, 1998), coedited with Michael Barnett; and "Seizing the Middle Ground: Constructivism in World Politics," *European Journal of International Relations* (1997) – he is best known for his contribution to the subjects of epistemic communities, security communities, and, more generally, constructivism in international relations.

MICHAEL BARNETT is the Harold Stassen Professor of International Affairs at the Hubert H. Humphrey School and Adjunct Professor of Political Science at the University of Minnesota. He previously taught at the University of Wisconsin-Madison. He teaches and publishes in the areas of international relations, international organizations, and Middle Eastern politics. Among his books are *Dialogues in Arab Politics: Negotiations in Regional Order* (Columbia University Press, 1998); *Eyewitness to a Genocide: The United Nations and Rwanda* (Cornell University Press, 2002); and, with Martha Finnemore, *Rules for the World: International Organizations in Global Politics* (Cornell University Press, 2004).

STEVEN BERNSTEIN is Associate Professor of International Relations at the University of Toronto. His current research focuses on global governance and the problem of legitimacy. His book, *The Compromise of Liberal Environmentalism* (Columbia University Press), was runner-up for the 2002 Sprout Award, given annually by the International Studies Association to the best book in international environmental studies. His other published work includes articles in *European Journal of International Relations, Canadian Journal of Political Science, Policy Sciences,* and *Global Environmental Politics.*

RAYMOND DUVALL is Morse-Alumni Distinguished Teaching Professor of Political Science and Associate Director of the Interdisciplinary Center for the Study of Global Change at the University of Minnesota. His recent publications include *Cultures of Insecurity: States, Communities and the Production of Danger* (University of Minnesota Press, 1999), coedited with Jutta Weldes, Mark Laffey, and Hugh Gusterson. His earlier research focused on theories of the capitalist state, dependency theory, and civil conflict, including revolutionary struggles, and was published in various journals, including *American Political Science Review, International Organization, International Studies Quarterly,* and *Comparative Political Studies.*

MARTHA FINNEMORE is Associate Professor of Political Science and International Affairs at George Washington University in Washington, DC. From 1994 to 1996 she was a Social Science Research Council/MacArthur Foundation Fellow and guest scholar at the Brookings Institution in Washington, DC. Her books include *National Interests in International Society* (Cornell University Press, 1996); *The Purpose of Intervention: Changing Beliefs about the Use of Force* (Cornell University Press, 2003); and, with Michael Barnett, *Rules for the World: International Organizations in Global Politics* (Cornell University Press, 2004).

LLOYD GRUBER, Associate Professor at the University of Chicago's Irving B. Harris Graduate School of Public Policy Studies, is the author of *Ruling the World: Power Politics and the Rise of Supranational Institutions* (Princeton University Press, 2000). His current work examines the long-term political impact of economic openness and inequality in globalizing societies.

ANDREW HURRELL is University Lecturer in International Relations and Fellow of Nuffield College, Oxford. His publications include: *Inequality, Globalization, and World Politics* (Oxford University Press, 1999), coedited with Ngaire Woods; *Order and Justice in International Relations* (Oxford University Press, 2003), coedited with Rosemary Foot and John Gaddis; and *The Problem of World Order in the Twenty-First Century* (Oxford University Press, forthcoming).

IAN JOHNSTONE is Associate Professor of International Law at the Fletcher School of Law and Diplomacy, Tufts University. Prior to joining the Fletcher School, he was an aide in the Office of the Secretary-General of the United Nations, where he served from 1994 to 1995, and then again from January 1997 to July 2000. His UN career also includes positions in the Department of Peace-keeping Operations and Office of the Legal Counsel. His books include *Keeping the Peace: Multidimensional UN Operations in Cambodia and El Salvador*, coeditor and contributing author (Cambridge University Press, 1997); *Rights and Reconciliation: UN Strategies in El Salvador* (Lynne Rienner, 1995); and *Aftermath of the Gulf War: An Assessment of UN Action* (Lynne Rienner, 1994).

ETHAN B. KAPSTEIN is Paul Dubrule Professor of Sustainable Development at INSEAD, Fontainebleau, France, Research Associate at the French Institute for International Relations (IFRI) in Paris, and Visiting Fellow of the Center for Global Development in Washington, DC. He wrote this chapter while serving in 2003–04 as a Transatlantic Fellow of the German Marshall Fund of the United States.

HELEN M. KINSELLA is Assistant Professor of Political Science at the University of Wisconsin-Madison. She completed her Ph.D. at the University of Minnesota and held a postdoctoral fellowship at Harvard University's Kennedy School of Government.

MARK LAFFEY lectures on international politics in the Department of Politics and International Studies, School of Oriental and African Studies, University of London. He is coeditor of *Democracy, Liberalism and War: Rethinking the Democratic Peace Debate* (Lynne Rienner, 2001).

RONNIE D. LIPSCHUTZ is Professor of Politics and Associate Director of the Center for Global, International, and Regional Studies at the University of California, Santa Cruz. He is also Chair of the Politics Ph.D. program at UCSC. His most recent books include *Global Environmental Politics: Power, Perspectives and Practice* (CQ Press, 2004), *After Authority: War, Peace and Global Politics in the Twenty-First Century* (SUNY Press, 2000), and *Cold War Fantasies: Film, Fiction and Foreign Policy* (Rowman and Littlefield, 2001).

HIMADEEP MUPPIDI is Assistant Professor, Department of Political Science, Vassar College. He is the author of *The Politics of the Global* (University of Minnesota Press, 2004).

MARK RUPERT is Professor of Political Science at Syracuse University's Maxwell School of Citizenship and Public Affairs, and teaches in the areas of international relations and political economy. He is the author of *Producing Hegemony: The Politics of Mass Production and American Global Power* (Cambridge University Press, 1995); *Ideologies of Globalization: Contending Visions of a New World Order* (Routledge, 2000); and the coeditor (with Hazel Smith) of *Historical Materialism and Globalization* (Routledge, 2002).

GREGORY SHAFFER is Associate Professor of Law at the University of Wisconsin-Madison. His publications include *Defending Interests: Public–Private Partnerships in WTO Litigation* (Brookings Institution Press, 2003), *Transatlantic Governance in the Global Economy* (with Mark Pollack, Rowman and Littlefield, 2001), and over thirty articles and book chapters on international trade law, global governance, and globalization's impact on domestic regulation. He also is senior fellow at the UW Center on World Affairs and the Global Economy.

JUTTA WELDES is Senior Lecturer in International Relations at the University of Bristol. She is the author of *Constructing National Interests: The United States and the Cuban Missile Crisis* (University of Minnesota Press, 1999), coeditor of *Cultures of Insecurity: States, Communities, and the Production of Danger* (University of Minnesota Press, 1999), and editor of *To Seek Out New Worlds: Science Fiction and World Politics* (Palgrave, 2003).

Acknowledgements

Most of the contributions in this volume were originally presented at a conference, "Who Governs in Global Governance?" at the University of Wisconsin-Madison in April 2003. For generous financial support, we want to thank the University of Wisconsin's Global Studies Program and the Global Governance Research Circle, the Political Science Department at the University of Minnesota, and the MacArthur-funded consortium between the University of Wisconsin, University of Minnesota, and Stanford University. We owe tremendous thanks to all who were present. In addition to those who delivered papers, we also want to give special thanks to Helen M. Kinsella, Jon Pevehouse, Kathryn Sikkink, Bruce Cronin, Orfeo Fioretos, Duncan Snidal, Bob Keohane, John Ruggie, Neta Crawford, Alex Wendt, and Charles Kupchan. Particular thanks to Meghana Nayak and Patrick Cottrell, who did such a masterful job organizing the conference and then preparing the manuscript for review. Michael Barnett also wants to thank those who participated in his graduate seminar on international organizations, who read and commented on the early versions of these papers. We also want to acknowledge two anonymous reviewers at Cambridge University Press. Special thanks to John Haslam at Cambridge University Press for helping us with the process from its point of conception to its moment of birth. And a special thanks to Karen Anderson Howes, who did a masterful job of copyediting the manuscript; she rescued us from many unsightly errors and, in the end, helped to transform the manuscript into a book.

Bud Duvall dedicates this book to his wife Catherine, whose love and friendship sustain him, and to his three sons, Daegen, Matthew, and Ladley, for the joy that they generate. Michael Barnett dedicates this book, once again, to his wife, Victoria, and his daughters, Maya and Hannah. They are daily reminders that what was once unimaginable is, in fact, quite possible.

1   Power in global governance

Michael Barnett and Raymond Duvall

The idea of global governance has attained near-celebrity status. In little more than a decade the concept has gone from the ranks of the unknown to one of the central orienting themes in the practice and study of international affairs of the post-Cold War period. The intensifying connections between states and peoples, better known as globalization, are now frequently presumed to create the need for governance and rule-making at the global level. According to such a view, only with global governance will states and peoples be able to cooperate on economic, environmental, security, and political issues, settle their disputes in a nonviolent manner, and advance their common interests and values. Absent an adequate supply of global governance, states are likely to retreat behind protective barriers and re-create the conditions for enduring conflict. Global governance, then, is thought to bring out the best in the international community and rescue it from its worst instincts. Although the study of global governance has a long pedigree, its prominence increased dramatically after the Cold War. A scholarly journal now bears its name. Several presses now have series on the subject. Although scholars have been less likely to invest global governance with the same heroic qualities as do policymakers, they have tended to see it as capable of helping states overcome conflict and achieve their common aspirations. For policymakers and scholars, global governance is one of the defining characteristics of the current international moment.

We thank Neta Crawford, Kathryn Sikkink, Helen M. Kinsella, Jon Pevehouse, Mike Williams, Kurt Burch, Thomas Diez, Tom Donahue, William Duvall, Ayten Gundogdu, Colin Kahl, Amit Ron, Latha Varadarajan, Stefano Guzzini, and especially Duncan Snidal, Charles Kupchan, Alex Wendt and Bob Keohane. We also acknowledge the bibliographic assistance of Emilie Hafner-Burton and Jonathan Havercroft.

This impressive attention to the concept and workings of global governance, however, has not included a sustained consideration of power. This is paradoxical because governance and power are inextricably linked. Governance involves the rules, structures, and institutions that guide, regulate, and control social life, features that are fundamental elements of power. To account for how global activities are guided and how world orders are produced, therefore, requires careful and explicit analysis of the workings of power. Moreover, the classical questions of governance, particularly in the liberal tradition, are centrally concerned with power. Scholars and policymakers regularly address questions of who governs, how institutions might be designed to check the potential abuse of power, and how individual autonomy and liberty can be preserved. Certainly some of these issues have trickled into the conversation on global governance, but not nearly enough. There seems to be something about how global governance is understood, conceptually and empirically, that de-centers power as an analytical concept.

Yet injecting power into discussions of global governance is not as simple as it might seem because of the discipline's tunnel vision when identifying power. Ever since E. H. Carr delivered his devastating rhetorical blow against the "utopians" and claimed power for "realism," much of the discipline has tended to treat power as the ability of one state to use material resources to get another state to do what it otherwise would not do. The readiness to rely on this concept would be warranted if it captured the full range of ways in which actors are constrained in their ability to determine their policies and their fates. But it does not, which is hardly surprising. As famously noted by W. B. Gallie (1956), and as repeated by social theorists ever since, power is an essentially contested concept. Its status owes not only to the desire by scholars to "agree to disagree" but also to their awareness that power works in various forms and has various expressions that cannot be captured by a single formulation. Therefore, the tendency of the discipline to gravitate toward realism's view of power leads, ironically, to the underestimation of the importance of power in international politics.

This volume revisits power, offers a new conceptualization that captures the different forms it takes in global politics, and demonstrates how these different forms connect and intersect in global governance. This volume, then, makes two critical contributions. First, it offers a richer and more nuanced understanding of power in international relations. Such an undertaking at this historical moment is both propitious and necessary. September 11, the war on terrorism, the US invasion and occupation of Iraq, the perceived willingness of the United States to either use or abuse international organizations, law, and treaties, and the debate over American empire have fixated scholars on the most visible and destructive dimensions of power. We certainly need to know about the ability of actors to compel others to change their foreign policies. Analysis of power in international politics, then, must include a consideration of how, why, and when some actors have "power over" others. Yet we also need to consider the enduring structures and processes of global life that enable and constrain the ability of actors to shape their fates and their futures. For example, the extension of sovereignty from the West to the Third World gave decolonized states the authority to voice their interests and represent themselves, and the emergence of a human rights discourse helped to make possible the very category of human rights activists who articulate human rights norms. Analysis of power, then, also must include a consideration of the normative structures and discourses that generate differential social capacities for actors to define and pursue their interests and ideals.

To understand how global outcomes are produced and how actors are differentially enabled and constrained requires a consideration of different forms of power in international politics. Power is the production, in and through social relations, of effects that shape the capacities of actors to determine their own circumstances and fate.[1] But power does not have a single expression or form. It has several. In this volume we identify four. *Compulsory power* refers to relations of interaction that allow one actor to have direct control over another. It operates, for example, when one state threatens another and says, "change your policies, or else." *Institutional power* is in effect when actors exercise indirect control over others, such as when states design international institutions in ways that work to their long-term advantage and to the disadvantage of others. *Structural power* concerns the constitution of social capacities and interests of actors in direct relation to one another. One expression of this form of power is the workings of the capitalist world-economy in producing social positions of capital and labor with their respective differential abilities to alter their circumstances and fortunes. *Productive power* is the socially diffuse production of subjectivity in systems of meaning and signification. A particular meaning of development, for

---

[1] This definition slightly amends John Scott's (2001: 1–2).

instance, orients social activity in particular directions, defines what constitutes legitimate knowledge, and shapes whose knowledge matters. These different conceptualizations, then, provide distinct answers to the fundamental question: in what respects are actors able to determine their own fate, and how is that ability limited or enhanced through social relations with others? Later in this chapter we provide the conceptual groundwork for the taxonomy that generates these four forms of power.

This conceptualization offers several advantages for scholars of international relations theory. It detaches discussions of power from the limitations of realism, encourages scholars to see power's multiple forms, and discourages a presumptive dismissal of one form in favor of another. It provides a framework for integration. Taxonomies not only highlight distinct types but also point to connections between them. In this way, it discourages thinking about forms of power as competing and encourages the consideration of how these different forms interact and relate to one another. It does *not* map precisely onto different theories of international relations. To be sure, each theoretical tradition does favor an understanding of power that corresponds to one or another of the forms. As we will see, realists tend to focus on what we call compulsory power, and critical theorists on structural or productive power. Yet scholars can and frequently do draw from various conceptualizations of power that are sometimes associated with another theoretical school in international relations. We believe that such poaching and cross-fertilization is healthy, is needed, and might, in a small way, help scholars move away from perpetual rivalry in disciplinary "ism" wars and toward dialogue across theoretical perspectives. Indeed, the contributors to this volume, who come from very different wings of the discipline, demonstrate how a healthy recognition of power's polymorphous character, and a willingness to look for connections between these different forms, enhances and deepens our understanding of international politics.

Our second goal is to demonstrate how a consideration of power reshapes understanding of global governance. Global governance without power looks very different from global governance with power. With only slight exaggeration, much of the scholarship on global governance proceeds as if power either does not exist or is of minor importance. We suspect that this state of affairs exists because of how post-Cold War politics, organized around liberalism and globalization, imprinted the meaning, practice, and definition of global governance.

The vocabulary of "global governance" appeared at the very same moment that the Cold War receded from view.[2] The Cold War was not only a description of a bipolar threat system; it also represented a mode of organizing the analysis and practice of international politics. With the end of the Cold War, the issue became what would and should take its place. For many, global governance represented a way of organizing international politics in a more inclusive and consensual manner. In contrast to the Cold War and the Soviet–American rivalry that permeated all global institutions and injected them with principles of exclusivity and hierarchy, various commissions and inquiries into the post-Cold War order gravitated to this concept precisely because it offered to equalize and tame power relations, and create a more inclusive and egalitarian governance system. Alongside the eclipse of the Cold War was the emergence of globalization. Although globalization has various dimensions, a unifying claim was that intensifying transnational and interstate connections requires regulatory mechanisms – governance, although expressly *not* a government – at the global level.

To the extent that global governance entails only the mechanisms of coordination, it could appear to be merely a technical machine, but in fact there are strong values running this machine. Liberalism is the spirit in the machine. There are, of course, many different definitions of liberalism, but as a category in theory and in practice in international relations it has typically revolved around the belief: in the possibility, although not the inevitability, of progress; that modernization processes and interdependence (or, now, globalization) are transforming the character of global politics; that institutions can be established to help manage these changes; that democracy is a principled objective, as well as an issue of peace and security; and that states and international organizations have an obligation to protect individuals, promote universal values, and create conditions that encourage political and economic freedom (Doyle, 1997, 1995; Zacher and Matthews, 1995; Keohane, 1990; Deudney and Ikenberry, 1999a).[3]

The belief was that the end of the Cold War provided the opportunity to create a more desirable world. The very language of global governance conjures up the possibility and desirability of effecting progressive political change in global life through the establishment of a

---

[2] For a useful overview of the concept that also situates it in disciplinary and global context, see Hewson and Sinclair, 1999.
[3] For an interesting analysis of the different forms that liberalism can take, historically and conceptually, see Richardson, 1997.

normative consensus – a collective purpose – usually around fundamental liberal values. The language of interests is often married to the
language of values of the "international community," values such as
democracy, human rights, the rule of law, and markets. These values
are seen as desirable not only because of their inherent goodness but
also because they would help to create a more peaceful and prosperous world. Expanding the boundaries of the community, then, expands
the zones of peace and freedom. The end of the Cold War also created a new opportunity to foster and manage the growing interstate
and transnational connections. International organizations are central
to this enterprise. They could coordinate and regulate a more interdependent world, and thus help states and others further their interests.
But they also could help spread the fundamental values of the "international community." Indeed, the heads of many international organizations asserted that many ills could be cured with a liberal dose of
these liberal values. This emphasis on how the international community
could come together to advance their collective interests, solve collective
problems, and further the community's collective values has tended to
deflect attention away from power.

The prevailing definitions of global governance also have liberal
undertones and mask the presence of power. Most definitions revolve
around the coordination of people's activities in ways that achieve more
desirable outcomes.[4] Governance, in this view, is a matter of resolving
conflicts, finding common purpose, and/or overcoming inefficiencies
between actors in situations of interdependent choice. This definition
rests on liberal precepts, the analytics of social choice, and the claim
that political actors may have shared interests that require collaboration and coordination. Power rarely figures in these discussions. Certainly scholars are aware that power is frequently important for solving
collective-action problems (though sometimes this is called leadership);
that hard bargaining can take place between grossly unequal states;
that some actors are better positioned than others to affect outcomes
and influence the distribution of goods and services; and that causal

---

[4] The Commission on Global Governance (1995: 2) defined global governance as "the sum
of the many ways individuals and institutions, public and private, manage their common
affairs. It is the continuing process through which conflict or diverse interests may be
accommodated and cooperative action may be taken." Similarly Oran Young (1994: 53)
defines governance as the "establishment and operation of social institutions . . . capable
of resolving conflicts, facilitating cooperation, or more generally alleviating collective-
action problems in a world of interdependent actors." See also Prakash and Hart,
1999: 2; Gordenker and Weiss, 1996: 17; and Keohane and Nye, 2000a: 12.

effect is assigned to particular actors. But the choice-theoretic perspective frequently masks relations of imposition, domination, structural determination, or cultural hegemony.[5]

Scholarly developments over the last decade also reinforced the decoupling of global governance and power. Because Andrew Hurrell addresses this issue in chapter 2, we can be brief here. Although disciplinary attention to global governance is of recent vintage, the concept represents not fashion-mongering but rather accessorizing the wardrobe of international institutions. The field of international organization has long been concerned with the general question of international governance, the creation of international order from norms and rules rather than from coercion (Ruggie and Kratochwil, 1986). This general concern with international governance in the absence of a sovereign became a dominant feature of the post-Cold War literature, whether in the guise of "governance without government," international regimes and institutions, global civil society, transnational actors, or international law. Significantly, many of the theoretical rivals to realism, most notably neoliberal institutionalism, liberalism, and constructivism, have been drawn to these areas precisely because it potentially allows them to demonstrate the relevance of institutional, ideational, and normative variables and the limitations of a traditional realist, "power"-oriented analysis (Barnett and Duvall, 2005). Consequently, these scholars have tended to position their arguments regarding international governance against "power."[6] The result is that explicit and systematic attention to power disappears from their analyses of global governance.

By using the optics of power, we transform the image of global governance. No longer is it solely concerned with the creation and maintenance of institutional arrangements through consensual relations and voluntary choice. It now becomes a question of how global life is organized, structured, and regulated. Such a re-visioning of global governance not only reshapes understanding of global governance. It also forces us to consider basic normative issues of international relations theory. The concern with power, after all, brings attention to global structures, processes, and institutions that shape the fates and life chances

[5] Those who are more inclined to critical approaches have an easier time seeing power in governance. See Rosenau, 1995; Sewell and Salter, 1995: 377; Latham, 1999; and Wilkenson and Hughes, 2003.

[6] Because these rivals to realism have attempted to demonstrate just how limited a power-centric analysis is, realists have responded by insisting that power is quite alive and well in the international system and present in global governance (Grieco, 1997a; Waltz, 1999; Gilpin, 2002).

7

of actors around the world. We become concerned with the legitimacy of particular governing arrangements, who gets to participate, whose voice matters, and whose vote counts. An examination of international institutions, accordingly, concerns not only whether they are efficient but also whether they are fair and legitimate. The focus on power, in short, compels us to engage the analytics, the empirics, and the ethics of global governance.

Conceptualizing power

Although the discipline frequently adopts a realist conception of power, in fact there have been many attempts to modify, supplement, or displace it.[7] Yet the realist approach remains the industry standard. This is a problem. The failure to develop alternative conceptualizations of power limits the ability of international relations scholars to understand how global outcomes are produced and how actors are differentially enabled and constrained to determine their fates. Our alternative begins by identifying the critical dimensions of power, and then uses these dimensions to construct a taxonomy that captures the forms of power in international politics.[8]

Our starting point for opening the conceptual aperture is to identify the critical dimensions that generate different conceptualizations of power. In general terms, power is the production, in and through social relations, of effects that shape the capacities of actors to determine their own circumstances and fate. This definition informs our argument that conceptual distinctions of power should be represented in terms of two

[7] See Enloe, 1996; Hirst, 1998; Guzzini, 1993, 2000; Baldwin, 1980, 1989, 2002; Nye, 1990, 2002.

[8] This taxonomy bears some resemblance to, but is distinct from, the conventional "four-faces" approach to power because, we contend, ours is analytically more systematic and precise, and conceptually more general. Peter Digeser (1992: 980) nicely summarizes the differences among the four faces in the following way: "Under the first face of power the central question is, 'Who, if anyone, is exercising power?' Under the second face, 'What issues have been mobilized off the agenda and by whom?' Under the radical conception, 'Whose objective interests are being harmed?' Under the fourth face of power the critical issue is, 'What kind of subject is being produced?'" For other summaries of these faces, see Hayward 2000: chap. 1; Clegg, 1989; and Hay, 1997. Because the four faces developed sequentially through a progressive debate about gaps and absences in prior conceptions, they are not elements in a systematic typology. There are no analytical dimensions that distinguish across all four faces, and the faces overlap and blur into one another. While they point to crucially important issues in theorizing power, for the purposes of conceptual precision they can be improved upon with a systematic taxonomy that captures most of the key distinctions that the four-faces scholars seek to make, while sharpening the analytical differences that give rise to them.

analytical dimensions that are at the core of the general concept: the *kinds* of social relations through which power works; and the *specificity* of social relations through which effects on actors' capacities are produced. The first dimension – kinds – refers to the polar positions of social relations of interaction and social relations of constitution. Accordingly, power is either an attribute of particular actors and their interactions or a social process of constituting what actors are as social beings, that is, their social identities and capacities. It can operate, for example, by the pointing of a gun and the issuing of commands, or in underlying social structures and systems of knowledge that advantage some and disadvantage others. The second dimension – specificity – concerns the degree to which the social relations through which power works are direct and socially specific or indirect and socially diffuse. It can operate, for example, at the very instant when the gun is brandished or through diffuse processes embedded in international institutions that establish rules that determine who gets to participate in debates and make decisions. Below we explore each dimension, then show how the polar positions within each dimension combine to generate our taxonomy of power.

How power is expressed: interaction or constitution

The first dimension concerns whether power works in interactions or social constitution. One position on this dimension treats social relations as composed of the actions of pre-constituted social actors toward one another. Here, power works through behavioral relations or interactions, which, in turn, affect the ability of others to control the circumstances of their existence. In these conceptions, power nearly becomes an attribute that an actor possesses and may use knowingly as a resource to shape the actions and/or conditions of action of others.

The other position consists of social relations of constitution. Here, power works through social relations that analytically precede the social or subject positions of actors and that constitute them as social beings with their respective capacities and interests. Constitutive relations cannot be reduced to the attributes, actions, or interactions of given actors. Power, accordingly, is irreducibly social. In other words, constitutive arguments examine how particular *social* relations are responsible for producing particular kinds of actors. As Alexander Wendt (1998: 105) puts it, "Constitutive theories . . . account for the properties of things by reference to the structures in virtue of which they exist." Because these social relations, in effect, generate different social kinds that have different self- (and other-) understandings and capacities, they have real consequences for an actor's ability to shape the conditions and processes of its existence.

This conceptual distinction between power working through social relations of interaction or in social relations of constitution tracks fairly closely with a distinction that frequents the literature on power: "power over" and "power to." Concepts of power rooted in action and interaction point to actors' exercising control over others; they are, then, "power over" concepts. Concepts of power tied to social relations of constitution, in contrast, consider how social relations define who are the actors and what are the capacities and practices they are socially empowered to undertake; these concepts are, then, focused on the social production of actors' "power to." Some scholars, who examine how constitutive relations make possible certain types of action, focus on how community or collective action is facilitated, while others stress how the social relations of constitution can have a disciplining effect and therefore lead to self-regulation and internalized constraints.[9] In either case, though, the concern is with the effect of social relations of constitution on human capacity.

This interaction/constitutive distinction also foregrounds particular features of the *effects* of power. Because power is a property of actors' actions and interactions in behavioral conceptions, there is a strong tendency to see its effects primarily in terms of the action of the object of power. In contrast, constitutive power is generally seen as producing effects only in terms of the identities of the occupants of social positions. We want to stress, though, that there is no ontological or epistemological reason why scholars working with one of those concepts need exclude the effects identified by the other. If power works through the actions of specific actors in shaping the ways and the extent to which other actors exercise control over their own fate, it can have a variety of effects, ranging from directly affecting the behavior of others to setting the terms of their very self-understandings; behavioral power, then, can shape actors' subjectivities and self-understandings. Similarly, if power is in social relations of constitution, it works in fixing what actors are as social beings, which, in turn, defines the meaningful practices in which they are disposed to engage as subjects; constitutive power, then, shapes behavioral tendencies. Thus, scholars examining power through

---

[9] For the former, see Arendt, 1959; Habermas, 1984; and Barnes, 1988. For the latter, see Foucault, 1995; Isaac, 1987; and Hayward, 2000.

social interaction can see effects on social identities, and those examining power through constitutive relations can see effects on action.

The specificity of social relations of power: direct or diffuse

The second core analytical dimension concerns how specific – direct and immediate – are the social relations through which power works. Specific relations of power entail some immediate and generally tangible causal/constitutive connection between the subject and the object, or between two subjects. Scholars working with this conception tend to presume that connections between actors are mechanistic, flush with contact, direct, and/or logically necessary. A consequence of this dependence on social proximity is that it becomes more difficult to observe power in operation the greater is the social distance, the lag between stimulus and effect, or the absence of logical necessity between these connections.

This approach is nicely summarized by Robert Dahl's (1957: 204) famous claim that there is "no action at a distance." Although Dahl intentionally left vague both what counts as "distance" and the meaning of "connection" between two actors, he stressed that a relation of power was knowable if and only if there is an observable and traceable connection between A and B. Consequently, while his conceptualization did not preclude the idea of power as spatially, temporally, or socially indirect or diffuse, it did work against it. But it is not only Dahl's and related behavioral conceptions that operate with a specific and direct view of power. Some constitutive analyses do so, as well. For example, scholars such as Roy Bhaskar (1979), Anthony Giddens (1984), and Alexander Wendt (1999) point to the structured relationship of co-constitution between social roles or structural positions (such as Marxian class categories), and how their social capacities are defined in direct and specific relation to other roles or positions. In this way, they identify a direct and specific relationship between the social positions, which are jointly constituted structurally (Isaac, 1987). This is how Marxist approaches consider, for instance, the co-constitutive social relations of capital and labor in capitalism; the capitalist class structure generates distinctive social capacities and interests of the social positions of capital and labor. In general, specific relations concern the direct causal/constitutive connection between actors that are in physical, historical, or social-positional proximity.

Other approaches see power in indirect and socially diffuse relations. Instead of insisting that power work through an immediate, direct, and specific relationship, these conceptions allow for the possibility of power even if the connections are detached and mediated, or operate at a physical, temporal, and social distance. Scholars that locate power in the rules of institutions, whether formal or informal, frequently trace its operation to such indirect mechanisms. Those examining concrete institutions have shown how evolving rules and decision-making procedures can shape outcomes in ways that favor some groups over others; these effects can operate over time and at a distance, and often in ways that were not intended or anticipated by the architects of the institution (Pierson, 2000). Similarly, scholars influenced by post-structuralism examine how historically and contingently produced discourses shape the subjectivities of actors; the very reason for genealogical and discourse-analytic methods is to demonstrate how systems of knowledge and discursive practices produce subjects through social relations that are quite indirect, socially diffuse, and temporally distant (Fairclough, 1994; Kendall and Wickham, 1999). For instance, students of gender, race, and nation routinely recognize how socially diffuse discourses, and not isolated, direct, and proximate actions, produce the subjects of the modern world.

These two core dimensions – the kinds of social relations through which power works, and the specificity of the social relations through which power's effects are produced – generate a fourfold taxonomy of power. In table 1.1, each cell represents a different conceptual type. Compulsory power exists in the direct control by one actor over the conditions of existence and/or the actions of another. Institutional power exists in actors' indirect control over the conditions of action of socially distant others. Structural power operates as the constitutive relations of a direct and specific, hence, mutually constituting, kind. And, productive power works through diffuse constitutive relations to produce the situated subjectivities of actors.

Table 1.1 *Types of power*

		Relational specificity	
		Direct	Diffuse
	Interactions of specific actors	Compulsory	Institutional
Power works through			
	Social relations of constitution	Structural	Productive

Because concepts of power are partly distinguished by the conceptu-alized relationship between agency and structure, our taxonomy relates to the agent–structure duality to the extent that the generic concern is with the relationship between social context and human action. We want to stress, though, that because each type of power has at least an implicit view of both agency and structure, none simply reflects an entirely agen-tic or structural perspective (to the neglect of the other). Nevertheless, they do vary in specific ways. Compulsory and, to a lesser degree, institutional power emphasize agency to the point where structure be-comes the context in which A's actions and B's reactions are set and constrained, thereby leaning heavily on agency and treating structure as constraint. In contrast, concepts of structural and productive power emphasize structure relative to purposeful agency, even while recogniz-ing that meaningful practices and, hence, human agency are essential in producing, reproducing, and possibly transforming these structures.

Compulsory power: direct control over another

This first concept of power focuses on a range of relations between actors that allow one to shape directly the circumstances and/or actions of another. Some of the most famous and widely used definitions of power fall under this concept. Max Weber (1947: 52), for instance, defined power as the "probability that one actor within a social relationship will be in a position to carry out his own will despite resistance, regardless of the basis on which this probability exists."

In terms of sheer influence, especially for scholars of international relations, arguably no definition surpasses that of Robert Dahl's earliest formulation. For him, power is best understood as the ability of A to get B to do what B otherwise would not do (1957: 202–03). Dahl's concept has three defining features. One, there is *intentionality* on the part of Actor A. What counts is that A wants B to alter its actions in a particular direction. If B alters its actions under the mistaken impression that A wants it to, then that would not count as power because it was not A's intent that B do so. Two, there must be a *conflict* of desires to the extent that B now feels compelled to alter its behavior. A and B want different outcomes, and B loses. Three, A is successful because it has material and ideational *resources* at its disposal that lead B to alter its actions. Although theorists have debated whether the relevant resources are an intrinsic property of actors or are better understood as part of a relationship of dependence between two or more actors, the underlying claim is that

13

identifiable resources that are controlled and intentionally deployed by actors are what counts in thinking about power.[10]

Although Dahl's initial conceptualization usefully illustrates the concept of compulsory power, our taxonomy highlights how compulsory power need not hinge on intentionality. Compulsory power is present whenever A's actions control B's actions or circumstances, even if unintentionally. As Bachrach and Baratz (1962: 952) argue, power still exists even when those who dominate are not conscious of how their actions are producing unintended effects. The victims of "collateral damage" of bombing campaigns certainly experience the power of the deliverer even if it was not the latter's intention to create such damage. Because power is the production of effects, arguably compulsory power is best understood from the perspective of the recipient, not the deliverer, of the direct action.

Compulsory power is an obviously important form of power in international politics and global governance.[11] For many scholars – both realists and their critics – to study power in international relations is to consider how one state is able to use material resources to advance its interests in direct opposition to the interests of another state. This approach steers attention to the great powers. States, and especially the great powers, are able to determine the content and direction of global governance by using their decisive material advantages not only to determine what are the areas to be governed but also to directly "coordinate" the actions of lesser powers so that they align with their interests (Gilpin, 2002). Yet major powers are not alone in the ability to deploy resources to overcome the objections of actors. Multinational corporations can use their control over capital to shape the foreign economic policies of small states and global economic policies. International organizations also exhibit compulsory power.[12] The World Bank can shape the development policy of borrowing states. The United Nations High Commissioner for Refugees can shape the life chances of refugees and other displaced peoples (Harrell-Bond, 2002). In this volume, Laffey

---

[10] For the first claim, see Emerson, 1962; Blau, 1964; Wrong, 1988. For the second, see Lasswell and Kaplan, 1950; Bertrand Russell 1986: 19–20.

[11] See Claude, 1962; Knorr, 1973; and Baldwin, 1989 and 2002. For a discussion and critique of power-centered analysis, see Vasquez, 1998; Guzzini, 1993 and 1998.

[12] It is partly because of the recognition of the concentration of such resources for compulsory power in international organizations that many scholars and policymakers argue for a de-concentration of decisional authority, a substantial democratization of the institutions of global governance, or mechanisms of accountability (Stiglitz, 2002b; Dahl, 1957; Dahl and Stinebrickner, 2003; Wellens, 2002).

and Weldes (chap. 3) demonstrate dimensions of the policing of global governance.

Compulsory power is not limited to material resources and also includes symbolic and normative resources. Transnational activists, civil society organizations, and international nongovernmental organizations have demonstrated the ability to use rhetorical and symbolic tools, and shaming tactics, to get specific targeted states, multinational corporations, and others to comply with the values and norms that they advance (Keck and Sikkink, 1998). Various transnational activists successfully used symbolic means to press the Clinton administration to sign the landmine treaty (Price, 1998). Activists have formed associations and deployed branding and certification techniques to try to use consumer power to compel producers to comply with labor, environmental, and human rights standards (Broad, 2002). As Greg Shaffer (chap. 6) and Lloyd Gruber (chap. 5) observe, sometimes the most powerful states can directly use economic institutions to their advantage and against the interests of others. Ian Johnstone (chap. 8) shows how less powerful members of the Security Council are able to use legal norms to constrain the actions of the powerful. As Michael Barnett and Martha Finnemore (chap. 7) argue, international organizations are able to use their expert, moral, delegated, and rational-legal authority as a resource to compel state and nonstate actors to change their behavior. In general, scholars should be attentive to a range of technologies and mechanisms as they consider how one actor is able to directly control the conditions of behavior of another actor.

Institutional power: actors' control over socially distant others

Whereas compulsory power entails the direct control of one actor of the conditions and actions of another, institutional power is actors' control of others in indirect ways. Specifically, the conceptual focus here is on the formal and informal institutions that mediate between A and B, as A, working through the rules and procedures that define those institutions, guides, steers, and constrains the actions (or non-actions) and conditions of existence of others, sometimes even unknowingly.

Thus, compulsory and institutional power differ in the following ways. To begin, whereas compulsory power typically rests on the resources that are deployed by A to exercise power directly over B, A cannot necessarily be said to "possess" the institution that constrains and shapes B. It is certainly possible that a dominant actor maintains total control over an institution, which, in turn, lords over other actors. If so, then it is arguably best to conceptualize the institution as possessed by the actor, that is, as an instrument of compulsory power. But rare is the institution that is completely dominated by one actor. Instead, it is much more likely that an institution has some independence from specific resource-laden actors (Abbott and Snidal, 1998; Barnett and Finnemore, 2004). This provides the principal analytical grounds for making the move to the institutional context.

Second, the recognition of the importance of institutional arrangements highlights that A and B are socially removed from – only indirectly related to – one another. This distance can be spatial or temporal. Spatially, A's actions affect the behavior or conditions of others *only through* institutional arrangements (such as decisional rules, formalized lines of responsibility, divisions of labor, and structures of dependence); power is no longer a matter of A's direct effect on B, but works instead through socially extended, institutionally diffuse relations. In other words, A does not "possess" the resources of power, but because A stands in a particular relation to the relevant institutional arrangements its actions exercise power over B. Temporally, institutions established at one point in time can have ongoing and unintended effects at a later point. Long-established institutions represent frozen configurations of privilege and bias that can continue to shape the future choices of actors. Third, analyses of institutional power necessarily consider the decisions that were not made (the proverbial dogs that don't bark) because of institutional arrangements that limit some opportunities and bias directions, particularly of collective action (Bachrach and Baratz, 1962; 1975). Institutional arrangements can shape the agenda-setting process in ways that eliminate those very issues that are points of conflict.

International relations scholars have developed a range of arguments that examine how formal and informal institutions enable some actors to shape the behavior or circumstances of socially distant others. The literature on formal and informal agenda-setting focuses on who sets the agenda and how that agenda omits certain possibilities (Mansbach and Vasquez, 1981; Krasner, 1985; Pollack, 2003). Also of relevance is the literature that highlights traditional notions of dependence, that is, how material processes limit the choices available to dependent actors. Albert Hirschman (1945), for example, famously argued that market forces can create diffuse dependent relationships that limit weaker actors' choices. Others have considered how enduring systems of exchange and interdependence can be mechanisms of power (Keohane and Nye, 1977; Baldwin, 1980; Caporaso, 1978).

Also prominent here are neoliberal institutional approaches that focus on the behavioral constraints and governing biases of institutions. The general concern is with durable solutions to games of interdependent choice and how institutions help to solve coordination and cooperation dilemmas. Yet the institutional rules that establish a particular focal point also serve to generate unequal leverage in determining collective outcomes. In short, the institutions that are established to help actors achieve mutually acceptable, even Pareto-superior, outcomes also create "winners" and "losers" to the extent that the ability to use the institution and, accordingly, collective rewards – material and normative – is unevenly distributed long into the future and beyond the intentions of the creators (Gruber, 2000; Krasner, 1991). Indeed, many scholars examining how international institutions look from the vantage point of the weak tend to stress these very features (Murphy, 1984; Ayoob, 1995: chap. 7).

Global governance involves formal and informal institutional contexts that dispose that action in directions that advantage some while disadvantaging others. Understanding power in this way makes it much more difficult to approach global governance purely in terms of cooperation, coordination, consensus, and/or normative progress; governance is also a matter of institutional or systemic bias, privilege, and unequal constraints on action. Conversely, if global governance itself is conceptualized in terms of production, reproduction, and/or transformation of such asymmetries, then theorization and analysis must, by logical necessity, rest on a conception of power that sees power as interaction through diffuse social relations. In this volume several contributors illuminate aspects of these institutional features. Lloyd Gruber (chap. 5) identifies how the state architects of the European Monetary System intended not only to preserve their privileged position into the future but also to ensure that the international arrangements would sufficiently bind future domestic and governmental actors that might want to overhaul its rules. Greg Shaffer (chap. 6) shows how different institutional arrangements have very different consequences for not only who gets to determine what are fair trading practices but also what sorts of interests and values are preserved and secured. Ethan Kapstein (chap. 4) shows how institutional arrangements that have some element of consent nevertheless mobilize bias and allocate differential rewards to the participants.

Structural power: direct and mutual constitution of the capacities of actors

Structural power concerns the structures – or, more precisely, the co-constitutive, internal relations of structural positions – that define what kinds of social beings actors are. It produces the very social capacities of structural, or subject, positions in direct relation to one another, and the associated interests that underlie and dispose action. This makes it quite different from institutional power. Whereas institutional power focuses on the constraints on interest-seeking action, structural power concerns the determination of social capacities and interests. This important difference owes chiefly to their different theoretic understandings of structure. Scholars focusing on institutional power usually define institutions and structure in almost interchangeable terms, as sets of rules, procedures, and norms that constrain the action of already constituted actors with fixed preferences. Scholars focusing on structural power conceive structure as an internal relation – that is, a direct constitutive relation such that structural position A exists only by virtue of its relation to structural position B (Bhaskar, 1979; Isaac, 1987). The classic examples here are master–slave and capital–labor relations. From this perspective, the kinds of social beings that are mutually constituted are directly or internally related; that is, the social relational capacities, subjectivities, and interests of actors are directly shaped by the social positions that they occupy.

Structural power shapes the fates and conditions of existence of actors in two critical ways. One, structural positions do not generate equal social privileges; instead structures allocate differential capacities, and typically differential advantages, to different positions. Capital–labor and master–slave relations are obvious examples of how social structures constitute unequal social privileges and capacities. Two, the social structure not only constitutes actors and their capacities; it also shapes their self-understanding and subjective interests. In other words, structural power can work to constrain some actors from recognizing their own domination. To the degree that it does, actors' self-understandings and dispositions for action serve to reproduce, rather than to resist, the differential capacities and privileges of structure. As Steven Lukes (1974: 24) observed: "is it not the supreme and most insidious exercise of power to prevent people, to whatever degree, from having grievances shaping their perceptions, cognitions, and preferences in such a way that they accept their role in the existing order of things?"

In this way, structural power operates even when there are no instances of A acting to exercise control over B.[13]

Various international relations scholars have employed structural power in their analyses of the workings of international relations and global governance. Gramscians and historical materialists have examined how global institutions help to stabilize and spread a global governance that has a markedly liberal and capitalist character (Rupert and Smith, 2002; Murphy, 1994; Cox, 1992; Latham, 1999). Explicitly following Stephen Lukes and Antonio Gramsci, Stephen Gill and David Law (1989) argue that, while power exists in coercion and institutional arrangements, to understand the workings of the global capitalist economy requires a recognition of global production relations as constitutive structure. For them, as well as other Gramscians and historical materialists, the structure of global capitalism substantially determines the capacities and resources of actors. It also shapes their ideology, that is, the interpretive system through which they understand their interests and desires. This ideology is hegemonic in that it serves the objective interests of the capitalists and their fellow travelers at the direct expense of the objective (but not, then, recognized) interests of the world's producing classes, thereby disposing action toward the reproduction, rather than the substantial transformation, of the structure and its relations of domination. In the same spirit, Robert Cox (1992) draws on Machiavelli's notion of power as a centaur: it operates overtly to the extent that one actor will manipulate strategic constraints for the purposes of controlling the actions of actors (the beast of compulsory and institutional power), and it operates covertly to the extent that it generates the social powers, values, and interpretations of reality that deeply structure internal control (the man that is structural power). World-systems theorists also draw on this conception of power to the extent that they argue that: structures of production generate particular kinds of states identified as core, semi-periphery, and periphery; the positions in the world-system generate commensurate sets of identities and interests; and those in the subordinate positions adopt (ideologically generated) conceptions of interest that support their own domination and their lesser position in that world-system (Wallerstein, 1998). In this volume, Mark Rupert (chap. 9) analyzes the class basis of the contemporary form of economic globalization, namely,

---

[13] This concept of structural power thus permits a meaningful distinction between objective and subjective interests. See Benton, 1981.

neoliberalism, the class conflict that this form generates, and the establishment of international fora, such as the World Economic Forum, for
creating the ideological legitimacy for continued economic globalization. Ronnie Lipschutz (chap. 10) notes how the workings of global
capitalism have, in many ways, imprinted the meaning and function
of global civil society such that it helps to reproduce a politics that is
congenial to the class interests of the dominant classes.

Productive power: production of subjects through diffuse social relations

Productive power and structural power overlap in several important
respects. Both are attentive to constitutive social processes that are,
themselves, not controlled by specific actors, but that are effected only
through the meaningful practices of actors. Both concern how the social
capacities of actors are socially produced, and how these processes shape
actors' self-understandings, and perceived interests. And neither concept of power depends on the existence of expressed conflict (although
both view resistance as essential for understanding change).

Yet structural and productive power differ in a critical respect:
whereas the former works through direct structural relations, the latter
entails more generalized and diffuse social processes. Specifically, and
at the risk of gross simplification, structural power is *structural* constitution, that is, the production and reproduction of internally related positions of super- and subordination, or domination, that actors occupy.
Productive power, by contrast, is the constitution of all social subjects with various social powers through systems of knowledge and
discursive practices of broad and general social scope. Conceptually,
the move is away from structures, per se, to systems of signification
and meaning (which are structured, but not themselves structures),
and to networks of social forces perpetually shaping one another. In
that respect, attention to productive power looks beyond (or is post-)
structures.

This difference between direct and diffuse social relations of constitution has two important implications for thinking about productive
power. First, productive power concerns discourse, the social processes and the systems of knowledge through which meaning is produced, fixed, lived, experienced, and transformed (Macdonell, 1986).
Discourses are understood here not as dialogues among specific actors
or in terms of Habermasian notions of communicative action. Instead,

the concept refers to systems of signification – how "microfields" or the quotidian "define the (im)possible, the (im)probable, the natural, the normal, what counts as a problem" (Hayward, 2000: 35). In this way, discourses are sites of social relations of power, because they situate ordinary practices of life and define the social fields of action that are imaginable and possible (Foucault, 1984; 1983).

Second, discursive processes and practices produce social identities and capacities as they give meaning to them. In Michel Foucault's (1970: 170) archetypical formulation, humans are not only power's intended targets but also its effects. Discourse, therefore, is socially productive for all subjects, constituting the subjectivity of all social beings of diverse kinds with their contingent, though not entirely fluid, identities, practices, rights, responsibilities, and social capacities (Judith Butler, 1990). Productive power, therefore, differs from structural power in its approach to subjectivity. Because structural power concerns the co-constitution of subjects, it typically envisions hierarchical and binary relations of domination that work to the advantage of those structurally empowered to the disadvantage of the socially weak. In contrast, productive power concerns the boundaries of all social identity, and the capacity and inclination for action of the socially advantaged and disadvantaged alike, as well as the myriad social subjects that are not constituted in binary hierarchical relationships. Productive power, in this way, refuses "to assume that some essence is at the root of human subjectivity, [and raises] the possibility that *every* ordering of social relations, and *every* ordering of social selves (every inter- and intra-subjective power relation) bears some cost in the form of violence it does to 'what it might be "in the self and in the social world"'" (Hayward, 2000: 6; emphasis in original). In general, the bases and workings of productive power are the socially existing and, hence, historically contingent and changing understandings, meanings, norms, customs, and social identities that make possible, limit, and are drawn upon for action (ibid.: 30).

Some of the best examples of the analysis of productive power in international relations refer to the discursive production of the subjects, the fixing of meanings, and the terms of action, of world politics. One question concerns the kinds of subjects that are produced. Basic categories of classification, such as "civilized," "rogue," "European," "unstable," "Western," and "democratic" states, are representative of productive power, as they generate asymmetries of social capacities (Doty, 1996; Blaney and Inayatullah, 1994; 2003). A related theme is how the "other" comes to be defined and how that definition is associated with the practices and policies that are possible, imaginable, permissible, and desirable (Campbell, 1992; Neumann and Welsh, 1991). Also, socially contested efforts to set and fix meanings can be expressive of productive power (Williams, 1996; Neumann, 1999). A particular discourse of development orients action in one direction and away from others (James Ferguson, 1994; Sen, 1999). As Helen Kinsella demonstrates in this volume (chap. 11), the gendered categories of "civilian" and "combatant" in international humanitarian law have real consequences for those on the ground, protecting some while putting others at the risk of death. Ronnie Lipschutz (chap. 10) observes how the global civil society is constituted in a way that leads to the narrowing of politics. The question of "governing" global social life here is a matter of seeing how the articulations of particular discourses come to predominate. Scholars also become more attentive to how certain "problems" come to be constructed in the way they do, the knowledge that is authorized or legitimated in the construction of those problems, and how that knowledge can be productive and powerful. We become more attentive, in short, to what needs to be "governed," who is authorized to "govern," what counts as legitimate knowledge, and whose voices are marginalized, points specifically raised in the essays in this volume by Barnett and Finnemore (chap. 7), Adler and Bernstein (chap. 13), and Muppidi (chap. 12).

From power to resistance

Power and resistance are mutually implicated because the social relations that shape the ability of actors to control their own fates are frequently challenged and resisted by those on the "receiving end." This does not mean, of course, that all actors are continuously engaged in every circumstance to achieve that ultimately impossible condition that Foucault critiqued as the "fully sovereign subject." But there is a human inclination to resist in the face of power and to seek greater capacity to influence the social forces that define them and their parameters of action, at least in the modern condition.

Our taxonomy of power, in that respect, generates a taxonomy of resistance. Compulsory power fosters the inclination of directly controlled actors to possess those attributes that enable them to counter the actions of their controllers, and, in turn, themselves, to directly shape the behavior of others. Along these lines, contemporary observers of American unipolarity predict that there will emerge a counterbalancing coalition of like-minded European states. Institutional power is associated with resistance premised on altering the "rules of the game" and the agenda for social action, as well as altering the distribution of material and symbolic rewards that are generated through institutional (coordinated or collective) action. Challenges to the institutional power of the nuclear non-proliferation regime by states such as India and Pakistan are illustrative, as are efforts by various NGOs to extend international human rights law to include explicitly a recognition of women's rights as human rights.

Structural power generates resistance as attempts by those in subordinate structural positions to reduce the inequality that inheres in that relationship, as well as potentially to transform the structures that sustain it. However, because structures are not controlled by specific actors, resistance almost always takes the form of solidaristic action by occupants of subordinated structural positions. Suggestive examples of resistance to structural power include the transnationally coordinated labor and anti-globalization campaigns of recent years, and the decolonization and new international economic order movements of the middle decades of the 1900s.

Productive power fosters resistance as attempts by actors to destabilize, even to remake, their subjectivities, and, thereby, to transform, or at least to disrupt, the broader social processes and practices through which those subjectivities are produced, normalized, and naturalized. Transnational religious "fundamentalist" movements, and the violent organizations that they occasionally spawn, are sometimes interpreted as illustrating resistance to discourses of Enlightenment modernity or to global capitalism (Djait, 1985; Juergensmeyer, 2000). Resistance also can include how knowledgeable actors become aware of discursive tensions and fissures, and use that knowledge in strategic ways (e.g., deconstructing or inverting the discourse) to increase their sovereignty, control their own fate, and remake their very identities (Hayward, 2000: 34–35). Opposition to decolonization drew from liberal discourses of equality, autonomy, liberty, and national self-determination to destabilize the discourse of colonialism and to argue for independence (Crawford, 2002). In general, resistance is a multifaceted conceptual field, ranging from direct response to the actions and inactions of powerful actors to the subtle changes in practices through which dominant discursive understandings are altered. Because power in world politics is complex and takes many forms, so, too, is resistance.

Organization of the volume

The contributors to this volume explore the variety of ways in which power is in global governance. They examine a range of different sites of global governance, including international organizations, transnational policing, international humanitarian law, the World Economic Forum, the European Union, and global civil society. In these disparate locations governance activities are taking place. Sometimes there is a "who" that is doing the governing. For some of the contributors, states are directly compelling others to alter their foreign policies or establishing international organizations that bias outcomes in ways that safeguard their interests. For other contributors, international organizations and international institutions are concrete actors that have authority over various transnational spaces and activities. Sometimes, though, there is not a "who" but rather a structure and discourse that constitute actors and define what are legitimate practices that steer global activities in particular directions. For some of the contributors, arenas such as global civil society are not composed of a "who" with agency but rather are discourses that make possible certain kinds of actors, practices, and possibilities.

The common thread linking these different sites and structures of global governance is liberalism. Putting power back into analysis, the authors identify how international relations scholars need to be more attentive to the many ways in which power exists in the liberal practices and liberal institutions of global governance. The practices of liberalism are sometimes supported by outright coercion of the sort found in compulsory power. Global institutions, such as the World Trade Organization, that support free trade contain rules that shape present and future behavior, bias outcomes in some directions over others, and generate winners and losers in the way identified in institutional power. Liberalism also has structures, most obvious in capitalist relations of production and the democratic political relationship of state and citizen, that directly shape subjectivities and interests in ways that encourage actors to be complicit in their own domination in the way found in structural power. And, it can be understood as discursive and indirectly producing particular kinds of subjects such as global civil society in the way found in productive power.

The contributors also look for connections between the different forms of power. To understand the European Monetary System requires attention to compulsory and institutional power. To see the power in global policing requires attention to how the discourses of global capitalism produce what are viewed as threats to that order, and how police are deployed to compel others to stay silent. To understand the power of international organizations requires attention to productive, institutional, and compulsory power. To understand the gendered nature of international humanitarian law requires a consideration of the relationship between structural and productive power. By examining the connections between different forms of power, the contributors deepen understanding of power in global governance.

In chapter 2, Andrew Hurrell asks how power has been neglected in liberal-inflected international relations scholarship on global governance. He identifies three varieties of liberal writing in international relations theory. The first is liberal institutionalism. It is so focused on showing how international institutions help to ameliorate disputes and enhance collective welfare that it frequently neglects both how power exists in a variety of ways, driving the selection of institutions, giving actors very little choice regarding their participation, shaping the content of international norms and law; and how dependence lurks below interdependence. Liberal constructivism emphasizes how institutions are the place where new norms are created and modified and where states change their identities and interests. Yet liberal constructivism overlooks power when it fails to appreciate how states frequently determine which NGOs are born, succeed, and live to lobby for another day; how transnational civil society contains a set of values that privilege some voices over others; how international norms shape the balance of power within societies; and how these international norms are largely those that are consistent with the powerful North. Liberal hegemony focuses on the special characteristics of American hegemony and how those characteristics have shaped the liberal international order. Although this school sees a clear relationship between power and the international liberal order, it exaggerates the degree of freely chosen consent on the part of weaker actors; and it fails to appreciate just how illiberal and illegitimate many of these institutions actually are.

Hurrell then considers how international relations scholars might bridge the divide between, on the one hand, realists who stress power but fail to recognize the importance of international institutions and, on the other hand, liberals who see international institutions without power. He considers a range of different resolutions that highlight the relationship between culture and hegemony as a way of reaching across the consensus–coercion spectrum. He concludes by considering

25

the normative implications of a pluralized world that is governed by a growing number of liberal international institutions.

In chapter 3, Mark Laffey and Jutta Weldes shift the angle of vision away from interstate relations and international institutions narrowly conceived. They explore power in global governance by examining the increase in and transformation of policing that accompanies and helps to produce the globalization of a neoliberal form of capitalist restructuring. These policing practices are a highly visible form of compulsory power and, they argue, are integral to contemporary global governance, but have been overlooked or misunderstood as a result of the liberal assumption that global governance is essentially peaceful and cooperative. They claim that neoliberal globalization is a form of productive power and examine mundane practices of policing long ignored within a discipline more attentive to the upper reaches of state power. This claim enables them to show where and how different forms of power – structural and institutional as well as productive and compulsory – are implicated in the policing practices that both enable and reinforce the practices of commodification and privatization at the heart of neoliberalism. Out of the contested processes through which neoliberalization takes place, they argue, there emerges a new structure of global governance, one nowhere more apparent than in contemporary practices of policing. The argument is then illuminated in two case studies: the policing of privatization and of "anti-globalization" protests.

In chapter 4, Ethan Kapstein examines the relationship between compulsory power, institutional power, and norms of fairness in the international trading system. The theory of international institutions has been largely shaped by two competing traditions. Rational choice theorists hold that international institutions respond to market failures in world politics. Power-oriented theorists, in contrast, emphasize the distributive character of international arrangements. Neither of these perspectives, however, has taken seriously the role of fairness considerations in institutional design. The challenge is to show why those that can exhibit compulsory power might want to ensure that international institutions are invested with a sense of "fairness" and legitimacy, and how these seemingly fair and legitimate institutions nevertheless continue to mobilize bias in ways that give even the "losers" a reason to stay within the regime. Kapstein opens by discussing the concept of fairness and some of the evidence from experimental economics that highlights its importance. This discussion allows him to reformulate how and why the architects of international institutions attempt to make sure that these arrangements are viewed as fair by all potential members. He then uses the international trade regime to illustrate "fairness in action." He concludes by assessing some competing hypotheses with respect to how and why fairness might emerge as a consideration in world politics and global governance.

In chapter 5, Lloyd Gruber makes the case that major powers design international institutions not only to induce policy coordination in the present but also, just as importantly, to mobilize bias and control behavior into the future. In so doing, he calls attention to the interplay between compulsory and institutional power, on the one hand, and the determinants of institutional design, on the other. Gruber begins by noting that major powers hold sway over the design of most new institutions. As the prime movers, however, these powers are aware that their new arrangements are likely to generate both winners and losers, and that at some future date the losers – or a subset of them – could demand major changes. One might think that the original architects would therefore favor rules that explicitly prohibit such changes. Gruber, though, is skeptical. By trying to "lock in" the original terms of cooperation, the architects would be leaving disgruntled signatories little choice but to withdraw entirely from the regime, eliminating many or (in the extreme case) all of the gains it had been producing for its original sponsors. For this reason, Gruber expects most international governance structures to allow for considerable flexibility in the interpretation and application of the original rules, an expectation he suggests is exemplified by the experience of European monetary integration in the 1970s, 1980s, and 1990s.

In chapter 6, Greg Shaffer examines the relationship between compulsory and institutional power in the WTO. The United States, the European Union, and influential corporate constituencies are able to use their material resources and knowledge to design the WTO's rules and regulations that are intended to advance and protect their interests. Yet the WTO also exhibits considerable institutional power. Because WTO rules are not fixed in meaning, their application requires WTO judicial bodies to make further institutional choices. These institutional choices result in the effective allocation of decision-making authority to alternative institutional processes. To understand the operation of WTO judicial power requires an examination of how choices over the application of WTO rules differentially shape opportunities for states and their constituents in the market and in domestic and international political processes. Among the virtues of Shaffer's analysis is his illustration of how each institutional choice involves different forms of bias, affecting who gets to participate in decisions that have immediate consequences for their interests. He demonstrates the effects of institutional choice through his assessment of the WTO's controversial shrimp–turtle decision that involved conflicting trade, development, and environmental concerns.

In chapter 7, Michael Barnett and Martha Finnemore examine the international organizations that are routinely viewed as the epicenter of global governance. Yet contemporary international relations theory has a difficult time seeing international organizations as independent actors, a myopia, they argue, that is caused by the liberalism and functionalism that dominate the study of international organizations. In order to see IOs as containers of power, they offer an alternative framework for understanding the relationship between international organizations and global governance, one that highlights IOs' connections to liberalism, provides a basis for expecting autonomous action, generates a way of thinking about IOs displaying power in its many forms, and is suggestive of broader consequences of global bureaucratization.

They begin by claiming that rationalization and liberalism constitute international organizations as particular kinds of actors, ones that are able to help organize, regulate, and guide transnational interactions in ways that promote cooperation and liberal values. They subsequently argue that international organizations can be understood as bureaucracies that have a particular social form and that are constructed for a particular purpose. Consequently, IOs are conferred authority by many actors for reasons owing to their rational-legal standing, their delegated tasks, their moral position, and their expertise. This authority provides the basis of their autonomy and highlights how standing behind their technocratic appearance and their rationalized rules and routines are values and a broader social purpose. As authorities they have power. But this power has various forms. Specifically, IOs can use this authority to exercise power in ways that directly shape the behavior of state and nonstate actors (compulsory power), indirectly shape behavior at a distance in ways that are reminiscent of neoliberal institutionalist arguments (institutional power). IOs also participate in the production and the constitution of global governance (productive power). They conclude by connecting their bureaucratization argument to central issues of political theory, wondering whether and how IOs will continue to be legitimate, accountable, and able to deliver on their promise of progress.

In a contribution that blends features of compulsory, institutional, and productive power, in chapter 8 Ian Johnstone analyzes the debates in the United Nations Security Council in order to understand how legal discourse helps to constitute the actors at these moments and constrain the most powerful states at the table. International law is a critical dimension of contemporary global governance, and this is so even in the area of security politics. Johnstone begins by briefly discussing legal discourse, its relationship to international politics, and how it shapes state compliance with international law. Because states frequently defend their actions by citing legal rules, Johnstone asks who determines which interpretations of open-textured legal rules are conferred legitimacy. He argues that an interpretive community contains a particular methodology and epistemology for determining not only who is eligible to speak, but also what counts as a reasonable argument.

This international legal discourse is visible throughout international politics, dominates many international fora, and is present even at the Security Council. Johnstone observes that states want to have their actions appear legitimate in order to be persuasive, which in this forum turns on legal justifications. There are four important issues here. Although great powers can influence what is the legal discourse, there is an interpretive community that offers its own judgement. This highlights the second issue: there is an active process of debate and dialogue in and around the Security Council regarding how a particular action relates to existing legal rules as defined by the interpretive community. Third, states will use these legal norms as a way of trying to shape the behavior of others, illustrative of how legal norms can become part of compulsory power. Finally, although the legal discourse does not imprison determined great powers (or other states), it does constrain their behavior in important ways. Johnstone demonstrates this legal discourse at work in the Kosovo crisis, a hard case by any measure. In short, Johnstone's essay illuminates how legal rules are productive, are embedded in institutions that differentially constrain others, and are used by member states to directly shape the behavior of others.

In chapter 9, Mark Rupert uses the recent critique of the International Monetary Fund by Joseph Stiglitz to rethink the nature of global economic governance. Stiglitz, according to Rupert, rightly highlights the institutional and compulsory powers underlying neoliberal globalization, but a more complete analysis requires attention to structural power as identified by Marxian theory. Specifically, understanding the relations and processes of global governance entails analysis of class-based powers, the social relations of capitalism which make them possible, their historical instantiations both within and across nation-states, and the ways in which these powers have been, and continue to be, produced, reproduced, and transformed by the struggles – at once material and ideological – of concretely situated social agents. Rupert proceeds to argue that the structural power informed by Marxian theory is not sufficient to understand the dynamics of these world-order struggles, for class-based identities are crosscut by others such as gender and race, and these latter are generated through more diffuse, productive forms of power. Moreover, global expansion does not evolve effortlessly or unproblematically. Capitalism has contradictions and class tensions, and so, too, does global capitalism. Specifically, there are interstate rivalries and intraclass divisions. Moreover, there are anti-systemic movements, those which resist the neoliberal orthodoxy and refuse to pay the price of market expansion. The combination of these divisions within the capitalist classes and nascent but increasingly prominent opposition to neoliberal development could, if allowed to fester, lead to capitalism's demise. The desire to meet these political-economic challenges has led to various ideological answers, including the World Economic Forum. According to Rupert, this "entrepreneurship in the public interest" is designed to create a new global consensus regarding how to resolve the tensions within capitalism and meet the ideological challenges posed by the new transnational social movements.

In chapter 10, Ronnie Lipschutz examines how productive and institutional power are implicated in global civil society. There is a tendency to see global civil society as the antidote to a world of power as it operates in a way that is designed to counter predatory states and unregulated markets. Drawing on Michel Foucault's concept of governmentality, which is concerned not with government policies but rather with the disparate practices that are involved in the regulation and management of social life, Lipschutz argues that an increasingly diverse range of activities of global civil society is mediated through market mechanisms and thus complicit in the arrangement and ordering of social life. Said otherwise, Lipschutz highlights how a liberal discourse naturalizes the "order of things" and produces particular kinds of actors that are self-regulating and are interested in pursuing specific values and interests. Although global civil society oftentimes appears to be working against such liberal ordering, Lipschutz argues that the tendency of many transnational groups to use institutional arrangements and market mechanisms (such as consumer boycotts) only reinforces the primacy of market relations.

Because the neoliberal discourse atomizes, Lipschutz argues that any effective political resistance must be premised on more intimate group contact at the local level that incorporates global concerns.

In chapter 11, Helen Kinsella examines the relationship between productive and structural power in a critical area of international humanitarian law – the injunction to distinguish between combatants and civilians during armed conflict. Building upon the work of scholars of gender, war, and the law, Kinsella argues that, while these scholars have convincingly documented the gendered institutional and compulsory inequities in the codification and implementation of the laws of war, they have paid insufficient attention to the productive power of gender in constituting the "combatant" and the "civilian."

Her critical genealogy analyzes two crucial moments in the articulation of the principle of distinction, the production of the "combatant" and the "civilian" and the difference between them, as captured in the work of the Dutch diplomat and lawyer Hugo Grotius and in the codification of the 1949 IV Geneva Convention Relative to the Protection of Civilian Persons in Times of War. From this, she concludes that discourses of gender do not simply *denote* the difference of combatant and civilian, as is argued by various scholars, but also *produce* that difference. Therefore, it is not simply that discourses of gender govern the implementation of these categories, leading to the death of certain individuals and the protection of others, but that the very existence of these categories (and the difference between them) is dependent upon discourses of gender that naturalize sex and sex difference. Therefore, these categories are not neutral, and their very existence requires and regulates binary sex differences deemed integral to the formation of domestic (familial) and international (civilized) orders.

The final two contributions engage directly the normative foundations of global governance. In chapter 12, Himadeep Muppidi focuses on the normative dimensions of global governance. He argues that, in a world marked by diversity, any governance of the global must implicitly negotiate different imaginations or understandings of the global. A politics of global governance thus necessarily involves a politics of difference. Sharply contrasting authoritarian and democratic ways of negotiating such differences, Muppidi posits two normative models of global governance: colonial and postcolonial. He then reads critically some prominent practices in the contemporary international system to demonstrate the relationship between productive power and the reproduction of, or resistance to, colonial orders of global governance.

31

Focusing on productive power and the reproduction of colonial orders, Muppidi reveals how productive power empowers some actors as the subjects of colonial governance while relegating others to object status. The subjects of a colonial order seek to represent and institutionalize their conceptions of the global without making space for the voices or realities of those who might differ in their understandings of the global. Muppidi illustrates this point by analyzing recent Anglo-American debates over US imperialism. Turning next to the objects of global governance and their complicity or resistance to colonial orders, Muppidi argues that they carry a special burden in helping to reproduce a colonial order of global governance. But if political objects are self-reflexive, they also can resist or subvert the colonial order, a point he illustrates in various episodes.

In chapter 13, Emanuel Adler and Steven Bernstein aim to anchor a normative theory of global governance in a reworked conception of epistemes that accounts for the role of productive power and institutional power in setting the conditions of possibility for good (moral) global governance. Epistemes are tightly connected to issues of knowledge, and knowledge, in turn, is tightly connected to power as productive. Knowledge is understood by some as the normative, ideological, technical, and scientific understandings that individuals carry in their heads. Certainly knowledge can be used to help individuals control actors and outcomes, and therefore can be understood as part of compulsory power. Yet knowledge is much more encompassing, socially comprising the background knowledge that helps subjects make sense of their world and their place in it, shaping their self-understandings and their practices. In this respect, epistemes are productive. The authors then turn to examine global governance. It rests on material capabilities and knowledge, without which there is no governance, and legitimacy and fairness, without which there is no moral governance. This allows for a further distinction of the different aspects of normative foundations of global governance, specifically, a consideration of authority (who is conferred legitimacy to make decisions), epistemic validity (knowledge that is regarded as valid by a collectivity of subjects), a conception of fair practices or good governance (what sorts of activities are viewed as proper and legitimate), and practical reason (the epistemic requirements for democratic practice). In their final section they illustrate this conceptual framework with reference to international trade and the international legal system.

2   Power, institutions, and the production of inequality

Andrew Hurrell

This chapter is concerned with the ways in which power has been neglected within liberal writing on global governance and with the implications of that neglect. The first section examines the three varieties of liberal writing that dominated so much academic thinking within international relations in the 1990s and that continue to underpin much of the debate on global governance. Within this literature we find sophisticated accounts of how institutions emerge and how they function; we learn a great deal about processes of norm diffusion, socialization, and internalization; and we find illuminating accounts of the strategic choices of liberal hegemons and of how these choices may work to reinforce institutionalization. However, instead of being all-dominant, as on a neorealist reading, power recedes so far into the background that we are left with a strikingly apolitical and far too cosy a view of institutions and of global governance – especially when viewed from the perspective of weaker states (indeed perhaps from anywhere outside the United States).

In the second part of the chapter I underscore the importance of two critical aspects of how power is related to governance and globalization: the triple anchorage of states (in the international political system, in the global capitalist economy, and in transnational civil society); and the relational aspect of power and the complex ways in which power is received and understood by weaker actors.

The concluding section considers the normative implications. If power and power inequalities are so pronounced, what does this suggest for the normative ambitions of the liberal governance agenda – first in relation to the problem of legitimacy and second in terms of what one might call the political prerequisites for a meaningful moral community – either an international community of states or a global community of individuals?

Power, liberalism, and institutions
Liberal institutionalism

Much of the writing on governance and order over the past couple of decades has been rationalist in method and technocratic in character. The proliferation of international institutions is commonly associated with globalization and with increased levels of transnational exchange and communication. Institutions are needed to deal with the ever more complex dilemmas of collective action that emerge in a globalized world. Institutions are analyzed in terms of how self-interested egoists over-come the collective-action problems arising from increased interdepen-dence and interaction. It is around this basic insight that liberal insti-tutionalism is constructed and developed. Institutions are viewed as purposively generated solutions to different kinds of collective-action problems. Norms, rules, and institutions are generated because they help states deal with common problems and because they enhance wel-fare. The mainstream is heavily statist, concerned with ways in which states conceived of as rational egoists can be led to cooperate. But the same logic can be applied to governance beyond the state. On this view, states are seen as competing with international bodies, market actors, and civil society groups to provide cost-effective and efficient solutions to governance problems.

Power has certainly entered into this debate, most particularly in relation to the issue of relative gains – who gains how much from cooperative action. Here much attention has been focused on the spe-cific conditions which explain when concern for relative gains may bite, intensifying distributional conflicts and wrecking the prospects for sustained cooperation. Thus analysts have considered, for exam-ple, the impact of numbers, of alliance patterns and cooperative clus-ters, and the extent to which unequal gains can alter power rela-tionships and be plausibly turned into actual strategic advantage. It is also true that leading institutionalists have been concerned with the ways in which institutions can foster exploitation or oppression (Keohane, 2001).

Although analytically impressive, this writing rests on what one might call an optimistic Hobbesianism – an approach that acknowledges the importance of power and interest but that sees rationality and rational bargaining as offering, if not an escape from anarchy, self-help, and conflict, then at least the potential for mitigation and for a degree of cooperation. Three problems can be noted. In the first place, institutionalism is most powerful in those cases where there is both an objective common interest that can be captured by the right institutional design and a subjective sense of the value of cooperative behavior. The analyst assumes that the players view each other as legitimate and that there is a common language for bargaining; a shared perception of potential gains; and some mechanism for at least potentially securing contracting. The essential claim is that, even on Hobbesian assumptions, the state of nature can be tamed and cooperation shown to be rationally possible. And yet, as other readings of Hobbes suggest, the problems are often much more deep-rooted:

> In the absence of a sovereign authority to fix meanings, determine contested facts, and the like, the laws of nature in themselves are an inadequate foundation on which to construct and maintain social order. Similarly, Hobbes was not willing to believe that the individual urge for self-preservation could lead directly to a natural balance of violence born of rational calculation. Each of these situations would require epistemic agreement concerning the realities of the situation: the facts in the light of which individuals commonly calculated. But it was the very absence of this commonality that for Hobbes was the source of the problem in the first place: it could hardly be the solution . . . Conflict is not simply intrinsic to humanity's potential for aggression; nor can it be resolved directly through the utilitarian calculation of competing and conflicting interests. On the contrary, Hobbes believes that the answer lies in recognizing the problem: namely, the inability to resolve objectively the problem of knowing facts and morals in any straightforward manner.
>
> (Williams, 1996: 218–19)[1]

Second, and related, the dominant IR concern with power and with interests has neglected values and value conflict. Governance (whether domestic or global) has, after all, three overriding objectives: the management of power, the promotion of common interest, and the mediation of difference. Perhaps because a great deal of institutionalist writing has been concerned with the creation of institutions within the developed world, there has been a tendency to assume away the existence

---

[1] I am not taking sides here on the relative merits of these different accounts. For the best recent analysis, see Malcolm, 2003.

of fundamental differences in religion, social organization, culture, and moral outlook that may block or, at least, complicate cooperative action. These difficulties may be based on what Sen calls "the empirical fact of pervasive human diversity" (Sen, 1992: xi); or may reflect, as for Isaiah Berlin, a belief in the plurality, contradictoriness, even incommensurability of human goods. But, however conceived, diversity is a basic and common feature of humanity. The clash of moral, national, and religious loyalties is not the result of ignorance or irrationality but rather reflects the plurality of values by which all political arrangements and notions of the good life are to be judged.

Moreover, as the international legal order moves in more solidarist and transnational directions and as the "waterline of sovereignty" is lowered, so the political salience of societal difference and value conflict rises. International rules relating to human rights, to the rights of peoples and minorities, to an expanding range of economic and environmental issues, impinge very deeply on the domestic organization of society. Divergent values also become more salient as the legal order moves down from high-minded sloganizing and toward detailed and extremely intrusive operational rules in each of these fields and toward stronger means of implementation. In some areas, such as human rights, the potential importance of differing societal and cultural values has been extensively debated and analyzed. But the relevance and frequent intractability of these problems extends well beyond human rights. Thus the politics of security is driven not only by problems of trust and credible contracting, but also by deep disputes as to the values that are to be incorporated into understandings of security: whose security is to be promoted – that of states? nations? regimes? individuals? What are the legitimate means by which security should be promoted? Equally liberal governance approaches to global environmental negotiations can easily overlook the absence of a shared cultural or cognitive script that allows the largely rhetorical consensus value of "sustainability" to be translated into stable and effective operational rules. And divergent values come into sharper focus as inequalities of power grow more extreme.

Third, there is the problem of language. Language cannot be understood as a straightforward or easy facilitator of communication and collective action. Rather it is central to the immensely difficult task of imposing some minimum rationality on the chaos and contingency of political life and to understanding the perverse internal logics of power and the destructive role of rhetoric in political affairs. The problem is that all too often:

> Words carry us forward towards ideological confrontations from which there is no retreat. This is the root of the tragedy of politics. Slogans, clichés, rhetorical abstractions, false antitheses come to possess the mind . . . Political conduct is no longer spontaneous or responsive to reality. It freezes around a core of dead rhetoric. Instead of making politics dubious and provisional in the manner of Montaigne (who knew that principles are endurable only when they are tentative), language encloses politicians in the blindness of certainty or the illusion of justice. The life of the mind is narrowed or arrested by the weight of its eloquence. Instead of becoming masters of language, we become its servants.
>
> (Steiner, 1961: 56–57)

One difficulty with liberal institutionalism, then, concerns these foundational problems and their implications for understanding the relationship between power and governance; the other concerns the need to understand the wide range of ways in which power and governance intersect. Let me touch on four of them.

First, power and institutional choice. Even if institutions are about effective and efficient means of dealing with the impact of globalization and integration, we need to ask which institutions are chosen and why (Krasner, 1991). Power, not effectiveness or efficiency, is often the central determinant of that choice. For powerful states the choice is often not between institutions and no institutions, but rather which institutions offer the best tradeoff between effectiveness on the one hand and the maximization of control and self-insulation on the other. Thus the choice of institutional forum is often critical. In the western hemisphere, for example, we can note how the United States has been able to move between the United Nations and the Organization of American States to get the legitimacy that it requires (to the OAS at the time of the Cuban missile crisis, to the UN at the time of the Haitian intervention). A further example concerns Washington's ability to shift critical decisions on debt relief or financial bailouts to precisely those global financial institutions in which US power is far more securely anchored, in terms of both formal decision-making rules and informal influence.

It is also clear that interstate institutions by no means exhaust the possible routes to institutionalization and norm-regulated integration in a globalizing world. Much important work has been devoted to the study of transnational regulatory networks responsible for the development, diffusion, and implementation of an increasing range of norms, rules, and regulations. Much of this is technical and takes the form of soft law or of memoranda of understanding (on money laundering, banking and accounting standards, insurance supervision, police cooperation, etc.). But the issue of power within these networks remains vital. Such networks allow powerful states to shape and influence the process of integration without the need for formal interstate bargaining.[2] Or we can note the ways in which the United States has sought to avoid the constraints of international law and instead to rely on its own domestic law: through certification (as with drugs, human rights, religious freedom), unilateral sanctions, the use of US courts as international courts, and what Nico Krisch (2003) calls 'indirect governance' in areas that range from security regulation and aviation standards, to the development of the internet.

Activities such as these involve all four forms of power identified in the introductory chapter of this book (see table 1.1, p. 12) (a) compulsory power – think of the use of certification in US–Colombian relations and the leverage that it has provided over, for example, extradition or the legalization of the drug trade; or the role of transnational anti-drug police and intelligence networks in allowing the United States to shape the way in which the Mexican state has responded to transnational narcotics; (b) institutional power – think of the role of the 200 or so Organization for Economic Co-operation and Development (OECD) committees and the transgovernmental networks that support them in developing and promoting initiatives against corruption and money-laundering; (c) structural power – think of the role played by transnational technocratic networks of economists in diffusing neoliberal ideologies across Latin America in the late 1980s and 1990s) (Dezalay and Garth, 2002); and (d) productive power that does not simply shape the process of interaction but helps to constitute the actors who are interacting. Of course, issues of effectiveness and efficiency are involved in all of these cases. But we have to examine the political sociology of these modes of norm development and governance and the inequalities of power that are embedded within them. And, finally, one needs to

---

[2] As one of the major analysts of these developments herself notes: "In particular, government networks can be seen as a way of avoiding the universality of international organization and the cumbersome formality of their procedures that is typically designed to ensure some measure of equality of participation" (Slaughter, 2000: 199).

consider the role of power within the private authority structures that exist largely autonomous from the framework of both municipal and international law: private systems of arbitration and dispute settlement, privatized rule-production resulting from technical standardization, internal regulations within transnational firms; and private regimes governing particular sectors of the global economy.

Second, conditionality and coercion. The post-Cold War period witnessed increased calls to move beyond the traditionally soft mechanisms for securing compliance with international legal and political norms. One part (but only a part) of the debate has concentrated on the possibility that the UN might be able to function as a collective security system that can enforce the decisions of the Security Council both in cases of formal interstate aggression and in cases that stretch the traditional notion of "international peace and security." Yet such developments form only one part of a broader move toward what we can term coercive solidarism. There has also been the growth of new and multiple forms of conditionality. One category involves the institutionalized application of conditions to interstate flows of economic resources as a means of inducing domestic policy change. A further important category arises from the formalized establishment of criteria for admission to a particular economic or political grouping: the notion that membership of an alliance, economic bloc, or international institution depends on the incorporation of certain norms or rules. Thus the EU, Mercosur, the OAS, and the Commonwealth have all established explicit democratic criteria for membership; membership of the EU involves the incorporation of the entire *acquis* of immensely detailed laws and regulations; and in the Americas the "politics of the queue" mean that US-favored economic norms are adopted in order to facilitate future bargaining on an expanded Free Trade Area of the Americas (FTAA).

Conditionality is an important aspect of institutionalized power in a globalizing system, not least because it usually has a consensual element and occupies the murky space between direct economic coercion and sanctions on the one hand, and freely entered-into contractual arrangements on the other. In contrast to the drama of coercive intervention, it represents a long-term and often hidden means of shaping how other societies are organized. While studies sometimes highlight the limits of specific attempts at conditionality, it is the expansion of the agenda of conditionality and its institutionalization that is most striking. Thus the 1980s and 1990s witnessed an explosion of externally imposed conditionalities on trade, aid, and investment covering everything from the nature of economic policy (both micro- and macro-), to levels of arms spending, to the promotion of sustainable development, to the promotion of human rights and democratic governance.

These moves have important implications. Moves to coercive solidarism bring back older notions of exclusivist conceptions of international society. Control over the membership norms of international society and the capacity to delegitimize certain sorts of players through the deployment of these norms represents a very important category of power. It reminds us of the double-sided character of sovereignty within the classical state system: on the one hand, sovereignty was central to the constitutional and constitutive bargain among European states; on the other, it established a system of hierarchical authority with complex rules to determine who was, and who was not, to be accorded the status of a legitimate political community. The dominant tendency after the Cold War has not been toward the end of sovereignty but rather toward a return to an earlier world of differentiated sovereignties.

As conditionality cuts ever deeper into the ways in which societies organize themselves, so the issue of legitimate difference becomes more serious. It might be quite easy to argue that economic aid can legitimately be tied to upholding internationally agreed-upon core human rights. It is much less obvious that it should be tied, say, to some particular set of domestic economic policies deemed by an external NGO, government, or aid agency to be especially worthy. The legal and moral problems surrounding intervention focus on its coercive character. Conditionality, by contrast, is "softer" and therefore apparently less morally troubling. But, certainly in its recent forms, it is arguably more far-reaching in its attempted influence over the long-term character of how other societies develop. Moreover, conditionalities have been subject to a host of shifting objectives, economic policy ideas, and often crude political interests that have had very little to do with the interests of the poorest or most vulnerable, or with their own self-proclaimed liberal purposes.

Conditionality also raises awkward questions for how we assess claims that the international legal order has assumed an increasingly solidarist character – as, for example, in the shifting and more permissive attitudes of international society toward humanitarian intervention. Despite the doctrinal emphasis placed by international law upon state consent, there is a great deal of coercion, coercive socialization, and crude imposition that lie behind the emergence of a new norm or support for a particular UN Security Council resolution. Moreover, for weaker states, the stakes have risen substantially. The capacity to opt out of what was previously a largely consent-based legal system has declined. A state that refuses to accept either non-derogable core legal norms or those norms that are particularly prized by powerful states and embedded within institutionalized conditionalities runs the risk of being branded a "rogue" or "pariah" state. The widespread use of conditionalities therefore raises many problems concerning the legitimacy of who decides on the norms of international society and which norms are to be enforced. Such developments have magnified a fundamental tension in the character of the international legal order: between sets of rules that seek to mediate among different values and those that seek to promote and enforce a single set of universal values.

Third, power and international legal process. While it is certainly the case that the international legal order provides many power-leveling possibilities for weaker states, it is also true that power influences the character of that legal order. Thus there is a long debate on the particular role that powerful states enjoy in shaping the norms of customary international law: the power to act and to argue at a critical moment in order to crystalize a new norm (as the United States did not seek to do over humanitarian action, but has sought to do in terms of expanding customary norms of self-defense against terrorism); and the power to shape understandings of what is to count as practice (statements or actions) and whose practice is to count. Thus, too, it is important to understand the choice of legal argument as part of a strategic power-political game: in the case of terrorism, for example, the aim is to gain a degree of legitimacy and legal cover, but to avoid precedents that would constrain policy in the future.

And, fourth, the unevenness of interdependence. The institutionalist account underplays not only the capacity of the strong to choose different modes of management. It also underplays the extent to which many forms of interdependence are neither as strongly structural nor as consistently politically salient as the liberal interdependence model might suggest. Take, for example, the impact of economic and financial developments in the developing world. When in the late 1990s there was real fear of financial contagion across emerging markets, Washington became closely involved and there was much talk of the need for a new global financial architecture and for a new round of institution-building to deal with the discontents and instabilities of globalization. However, as the crisis passed for the financial system and, more importantly, for the interests of US banks, so the issue slipped off Washington's agenda.

The banks were bailed out and the Argentinas and Thailands were left to fend for themselves.

Liberal constructivism

For constructivists, institutions matter because they do more than just reflect power (as neorealists argue) or solve collective-action problems (as institutionalists suggest). They also matter because they help explain how new norms emerge and are diffused across the international system and how state interests change and evolve. Institutions may play an important role in the diffusion of norms and in the patterns of socialization and internalization by which weaker actors come to absorb those norms. Institutions may be where state officials are exposed to new norms (as on the environment); they may act as channels or conduits through which norms are transmitted (as with neoliberal economic ideas and the international financial institutions [IFIs]; or they may reinforce domestic changes that have already begun to take place (via state strategies of external "lock-in" or via pressures exerted through transnational civil society). There is much of great value in this mode of analysis. Many of the points made about power and regulatory networks can be applied to statist constructivism. The case of "liberal environmentalism" (Bernstein, 2001) provides a good example. This refers to the way in which the concept of sustainability was picked up by the OECD and the IFIs in the post-Brundtland period and transformed into a set of technical understandings that purged it of its radical elements so as to do as little harm as possible to orthodox ideas of economic development.

This section, however, concentrates on the nonstatist aspect of liberal constructivism. Nonstatist constructivists have emphasized similar processes of socialization, norm diffusion, and internalization; but have stressed transnational civil society as the most important arena for these processes and nonstate actors as the most important agents involved. Transnational civil society refers to those self-organized intermediary groups that are relatively independent of both public authorities and private economic actors; that are capable of taking collective action in pursuit of their interests or values; and that act across state borders. The roles of such groups within international society have increased very significantly: first, in the formal process of norm creation, standard-setting, and norm development; second, in the broader social process by which new norms emerge and find their way on to the international agenda; third, in the detailed functioning of many international institutions and in the processes of implementation and compliance; and finally in direct participation in many governance activities (disbursing an increasing proportion of official aid, engaging in large-scale humanitarian relief; leading efforts at promoting democracy or post-conflict social and political reconstruction). In all of these, areas, the analytical focus has been on transnational networks – for example, knowledge-based networks of economists, lawyers, or scientists; or transnational advocacy networks that act as channels for flows of money and material resources but, more critically, of information, ideas, and values (Keck and Sikkink, 1998).

Transnational advocacy groups, social movements, and transnational networks have undoubtedly played very important roles in the changing politics of global justice and in processes of norm development and institutionalization. Beyond this, very important claims have been made about the normative potentiality of global civil society as an arena of politics that is able to transcend the inside/outside character of traditional politics and to fashion and provide space for new forms of political community, solidarity, and identity (Falk, 1995, 1999; Kaldor, 1999). Sometimes the emphasis is on global civil society as a relatively autonomous self-organized public sphere in which genuine deliberation among competing positions can take place and through which some notion of international public reason can be developed. In other cases, global civil society and its linked network of "domestic" civil societies feed positively into state-based order through the provision of legitimacy and consent and into market-based order as the repository of the trust and other forms of social capital without which markets will not function. But in both views global civil society represents a pluralist and open arena for the negotiation of rules and norms based on genuine and unforced consent. It serves as a regulative ideal, but one whose potential can be gauged from the changing real practices of world politics.

And yet this image of transnational civil society and of the roles of CSOs (civil society organizations) and NGOs in global governance neglects at least four dimensions of power. First, state power. State action may by shaped by NGO lobbying but it is often state action that is crucial in fostering the emergence of civil society in the first place and in providing the institutional framework that enables it to flourish. In some cases the links with states are direct. For example, Koreniewicz and Smith have traced the crucial role of governments and international organizations in facilitating the emergence and shaping the actions of what they term "insider" networks associated with the FTAA process (Koreniewicz and Smith, forthcoming).

Most importantly, state power is increasingly determined by the ability of governments to work successfully within civil society and to exploit transnational and transgovernmental coalitions for their own purposes. Thus we need to note the very different capacity of countries to operate within these arenas. Countries accustomed to pluralist politics adapt easily to such changes. Many developing countries have found it much harder to navigate in this kind of world, perhaps due to domestic political sensitivities or to inherited traditions of very statist foreign policy-making. Even in the case of more radical grassroots movements, the issues of asymmetry and of dependence on Northern funding sources remain (Florini, 2000).

Second, power within transnational civil society. There is nothing normatively special or sacred about civil society. It is an arena of politics like any other in which the good and thoroughly awful coexist, in which the pervasive claims made by social movements and NGOs to authenticity and representativeness need to be tested and challenged, and in which outcomes may be just as subject to direct manipulation by powerful actors as in the world of interstate politics. If this is true domestically, it is, given the myriad forms of inequality in world politics, far more true globally.

Third, power within weaker societies. Transnational social action will often work to tilt the political, social, and economic playing field in weaker societies. Funding one group rather than another, and legitimizing one set of claims rather than another (say indigenous peoples in the Amazon rather than migrant workers), affects national political processes and almost certainly undermines the authenticity of democracy. Whether or not this is legitimate, it is an important aspect of the power of transnational civil society.

And finally, power and particular parts of the international system. The influence that existing NGOs and CSOs already enjoy works to favor the values and interests of Northern states and societies; and moves to expand such influence as part of attempts to democratize international institutions would amplify still further the power of the already powerful. As Woods (2003: 100) puts it, transnational NGOs "magnify Northern views – both outside of governments and through governments – in the international organizations, adding yet another channel of influence to those peoples and governments who are already powerfully represented." Of the 738 NGOs that were accredited at the WTO

Ministerial Conference in Seattle, only 97 were based in developing countries, that is, about 87 percent were based in the industrialized countries.

Liberalism, hegemony, and international institutions

A third variety of recent liberal writing focuses on the strategic choices of the United States as the dominant state in the system and on the character of the United States as a very particular kind of hegemon. This has become a popular current line of debate among those seeking to explain both the absence of overt and confrontational behavior among the major powers; and the prevalence of bandwagoning strategies whereby weaker states choose to join with the hegemonic power rather than to oppose or balance against it. One aspect concerns the notion of strategic restraint and the role of institutions in signaling that strategic restraint. If the dominant power wishes to maintain its predominant position, then it should act with strategic restraint so as to prevent the emergence of potential rivals. A rational hegemon would engage in a degree of self-restraint and institutional self-binding in order to undercut others' perceptions of threat.

John Ikenberry provides one of the clearest accounts of this logic. In all of his recent writings he has stressed the distinctive, open, and institutionalized character of United States hegemony and of the "liberal" bargain that Washington deployed for much of the post-1945 period in order to address "the uncertainties of American power" (Ikenberry, 2001a). Under the terms of this bargain:

> Asian and European states agree to accept American leadership and operate within an agreed-upon political-economic system. In return, the United States opens itself up and binds itself to its partners, in effect, building an institutionalized coalition of partners and reinforces the stability of these long-term relations by making itself more "user friendly" – that is, by playing by the rules and creating ongoing political processes with these other states that facilitate consultation and joint decision-making.
>
> (Ikenberry, 2001b: 20–21)[3]

Whether this benign, self-restrained constitutionalist order has provided an accurate image of US relations with Europe or Asia is open to some doubt. But it seems strikingly at odds with the reality of

---

[3] Mastanduno (1999: 147) gives a realist version of this idea.

Washington's relations with weaker states. It is very hard to see developing countries engaging with the United States within institutions that provide even weak degrees of consultation, let alone anything remotely approximating "joint decision-making." The degree of US power is so great that it does not need to make concessions or to self-bind in order to prevent even major developing countries from shifting to more oppositional policies. Washington has many other forms of positive and negative sanctions with which to achieve this goal.

A further aspect of this liberal argument concerns the impact of domestic pluralism on the nature of US hegemony. This is surely of great potential importance for all weaker states, but especially those in the developing world:

> A distinctive feature of the American state is its decentralized structure, which provides numerous points of access to competing groups – both domestic and foreign. When a hegemonic state is liberal, the subordinate actors in the system have a variety of channels and mechanisms for registering their interests with the hegemon. Transnational relations are the means by which subordinate actors in the system represent their interests to the hegemonic power and the vehicle through which consensus between the hegemon and lesser states is achieved. This system provides subordinate states with transparency, access, representation, and communication and consensus-building mechanisms. It supplies the means for secondary states to significantly express their concerns and satisfy their interests.
>
> (Deudney and Ikenberry, 1999b: 109–10)

There is nothing new in the idea of seeking influence by playing "Beltway politics" or by seeking to exploit the pluralism of the US domestic political system. Washington's kleptocratic and sultanistic clients in Central America and the Caribbean such as Somoza or Duvalier knew very well how to mobilize their backers in Washington. Equally, the sophistication of economic and trade lobbies has grown significantly over the past twenty years with the deployment of ever-larger sums of money on lobbying and on publicity. South Korea was an early entrant into this field, faced by the shift to aggressive unilateralism within US trade policy in the 1980s. Mexico is probably the most active developing country in this particular aspect of "intermestic politics."

But while this has become an inevitable part of weaker states' diplomatic engagement with Washington, there must surely be room for doubt as to how far secondary states can "significantly express their concerns," let alone "satisfy their interests" in this way. In part this follows from the irrelevance of many developing countries to the US domestic political agenda. In part it follows from the lack of resources and expertise. But, more importantly, this view rests on an exaggerated view of pluralism and US foreign policy. It may be true, for example, that the trade agenda is contested (over trade promotion authority, over "trade and" issues, over how protectionist the United States should be in, say, steel or agriculture). But the idea of a deeply divided polity in which a little bit of successful lobbying by foreigners can shift the agenda in their favor is illusory. Through the 1990s, there was little pluralism on many of the aspects of economic policy that most affected developing countries. Instead there was a widespread consensus in and around Washington against proposals to reform IFIs in order to manage financial crises; and in favor of using both aggressive trade diplomacy and linkage politics to force open developing country markets and to press what Washington viewed as the "logical" and "natural" path to further liberal economic reform.

Finally, there is the issue of how liberals understand the relationship between hegemony and institutions. Liberals are keen to argue that hegemony cannot adequately account for either the creation or the sustainability of institutions (Keohane, 1984). One important part of this argument stresses the role of overt efforts by the hegemon to compel or induce compliance with the rules of an institution or regime (Martin, 1992a: 27–28). If such efforts cannot be identified, liberals conclude that hegemony plays no role and that other (liberal) explanations must be sought. Yet hegemony can play crucial roles in the functioning of institutions without any overt efforts or specific policies on the part of the hegemon. The existence of hegemonic power creates a powerful logic of hegemonic deference. Weak states have such an important stake in institutions and in keeping the hegemon at least partially integrated within institutions that they are willing to accord deference to the hegemon, to tolerate displays of unilateralism, and to acquiesce in actions that place the hegemon on (or beyond) the borders of legality. The persistence of an institution in such cases flows not from the power of its rules, nor directly from the actions of the hegemon, but from the logic of hegemonic deference. The problem for weaker states is how to capture the joint gains stressed by the institutionalists, but do so in such a way as to keep the powerful both engaged and, hopefully, constrained. Managing this dilemma may well involve painful concessions to the special interests or unilateralist impulses of the strong. It might also involve acceptance of the degree to which shared purposes need to be based both on the mixed motives of the powerful and on extremely illiberal and hierarchical institutions.

Bringing power back in

The continuation of a stark divorce within academic international relations between liberalism and realism works against understanding the power/governance nexus.[4] On the one hand, liberals shy away from recognizing the full range of roles that power plays within and around institutions. On the other, neorealists are so disinterested in, or skeptical of, institutions that they do not recognize their importance for understanding power.[5] In the neorealist account, institutions are always and inevitably simple reflections of state power and of the interests of powerful states. As power shifts and as the interests of the most powerful evolve, so dominant patterns of institutionalization will automatically follow. Institutions in this view do not "matter": they have no autonomy or compliance pull of their own, either by affecting the incentives or calculations of actors or by influencing the way in which interests are understood or preferences constructed. In addition, the rhetoric of "global values" and of the "international community" will tend to reflect or to reinforce the interests of particular states at particular times.

Neorealist writers are right to stress that power matters and that powerful states will always have more options: to determine which issues get negotiated via formal interstate bodies and which are, for example, managed via market mechanisms; to influence both the rules of the bargaining game and what is allowed onto the agenda; to deploy a wide range of sticks and carrots in the bargaining process, including the threat of direct coercion; and, finally, to walk away from any institution that becomes too constraining. Institutions are not just concerned with liberal purposes of solving common problems or promoting shared values. They are also sites of power and reflect and entrench power hierarchies and the interests of powerful states. The vast majority of weaker actors

---

[4] The extreme liberal/realism divide also works against understanding the ways of power by marginalizing other theoretical perspectives, for example neo-Marxist and critical approaches.

[5] Mearsheimer (2001: 364) writes that: "Of course, states sometimes operate through institutions and benefit from doing so. However, the most powerful states in the system create and shape institutions so that they can maintain, if not increase, their own share of world power." But he says almost nothing about how this strategy of increasing power via institutions actually works.

are increasingly "rule-takers" over a whole range of issues that affect all aspects of social, economic, and political life. However, neorealists have such a reductionist view of institutions as simply reflective of state power and such a narrow and materialist view of power that they are unable to appreciate the importance of institutions to the stabilization and effectiveness of power in general and hegemonic power in particular. Power is, after all, a social attribute. To understand power in international relations we must place it side by side with other quintessentially social concepts such as prestige, authority, and legitimacy. A great deal of the struggle for political power is the quest for authoritative control that avoids costly and dangerous reliance on brute force and coercion. It is one of the great paradoxes that, because it so resolutely neglects the social dimensions of power, realism is unable to give a full or convincing account of its own proclaimed central category. There is also a great danger when international life gets harder and harsher that the realist/neorealist mantra of "see, we were right all along" will be accepted at face value. Power does matter, but that does not mean that neorealism has the intellectual tools to comprehend adequately how and why. In this section, let me pick up on two issues.

Which system?

It is a great weakness of academic international relations that "systemic theories" are often simply equated with neorealism and with the neorealist emphasis on the international political system. In addition to the international political system, states are embedded in the arenas of the global economy and of transnational civil society. The picture of the international system that dominates not just neorealism but the academic mainstream more generally misses out entirely the ways in which both competitive dynamics and the consequent definition of state interests are affected by changes in the global economic system and by the changing character of the "transnational social whole" within which states and the state system are embedded. There is a consequent tendency to distinguish too sharply between "thick" domestic norms and "thin" international norms. Many international norms (national self-determination, economic liberalism, sustainable development) are powerful precisely because of the way in which they relate to the transnational structures within which all states are embedded and to the broad social forces that have transformed the character of states and altered the dynamics of the state system.

To stress the importance of understanding power within these three arenas of international society is not to suggest that state power is unimportant, nor to take a view as to whether the state system or global capitalism "ultimately" trumps. However, as suggested in the first part of this chapter, state power very often depends on these other arenas: the existence of alternative governance options (market-based models, civil-society mechanisms); the capacity to shape social, political, and economic processes through which new international norms evolve; and the ability to navigate successfully within global civil society, including through transnational and transgovernmental coalitions.

Understanding state power is obviously more complex than the straightforward process of resource aggregation that still finds favor with many neorealists (military resources plus population plus GNP). But even adding in elements of soft power does not exhaust the range of possibilities. Thus, for example, a central element of state power relates to the differential ability of states and societies to adapt to globalization: this may be via the ability to set the ground rules of globalization (regulative norms, constitutive norms, dominant societal norms); it may be via the capacity to exploit the economic and societal opportunities provided by globalization (as with the successful exploitation of transnational civil society); or it may be via the continued capacity of governments and state elites to maintain or revive the values (sometimes ideological or religious, but most often national) that are necessary for effective social mobilization and social cohesion.

It is also crucial to highlight the ways in which developments in different arenas (interstate politics, the global economy, international institutions) and different mechanisms and channels of socialization reinforce each other in powerful and, for weaker states, constraining ways. Hence during the late 1980s and early 1990s we saw the powerful role of the IFIs in setting the economic-reform agenda, applying direct pressure for reform (often in concert with the United States), and providing the institutional validation necessary to gain credibility in capital markets. The WTO Uruguay Round provides further examples of enforced adaptation to a world in which the norms of economic liberalization were being set by the strong, in which political coalitions able to challenge or modify those norms were weakening, and in which those norms were in turn increasingly shaping market pressures, especially the investment strategies of transnational capital. For example, the acceptance of intellectual property reform by countries such as India and Brazil followed from the overall bargain that was emerging within the General Agreement on Tariffs and Trade; from very direct coercion on the part of the United States; and from an awareness that a failure to change would affect the willingness of transnational corporations to invest.

Understanding these constraining systemic pressures was central to dependency theory – however much dependency theory was subject to a wide range of conceptual and empirical weaknesses. Indeed, it is another of the paradoxes of academic international relations that dependency theory flourished at a time when the South was less externally dependent than at any time since 1900. Dependency theory faded intellectually just as real and renewed dependence set in with the debt crisis of the 1980s, the triumph of market liberalism, and the reassertion of US hegemony.

Power relations and the reception of power

All too often, power is seen only from the top down. Neorealists understand hegemony simply as domination that is achieved on the basis of coercive military power in the hands of powerful states. As both liberals and Gramscian theorists have long recognized, such an approach ignores the obvious point that power is relational and that the stability of hegemonic power depends on consensus as well as coercion and on the capacity to engender collaboration.[6] And yet even the most sophisticated of such writers have tended to concentrate either on the logic of imposition and on the structural power of global capitalism, or on the actions and policies of the dominant power in securing consensus (Ikenberry and Kupchan, 1990). The reception of power and the ways in which power is understood from the bottom up have been downplayed.

Pericentric theorists of imperialism taught us a long time ago that even formal empire depended on varieties of indirect rule and that, in a very important sense, the end of empire came when the imperialists ran out of willing collaborators.[7] If this was true of formal empire, it is still more true of informal empires and hegemonic systems. Thus US hegemony in the western hemisphere has involved coercion, military intervention, and protracted occupation. But it has depended far more

[6] For a liberal view, see Keohane, 1984: chap. 2. Gramscians such as Cox (1994: 49) and Stephen Gill (1993) focus on the "transnational process of consensus formation among the caretakers of the global economy."
[7] For the classic statement, see Ronald Robinson, 1972. As he wrote (originally in 1953): "Any new theory must recognise that imperialism was as much a function of its victims' collaboration or non-collaboration – of their indigenous politics – as it was of European expansion" (1972: 118).

commonly on the mutual construction of collaborative liaisons in which weaker states and state elites came to see themselves as having a stake in the hegemonic project, and on the diffusion of dominant economic and political ideas. Sometimes hegemony takes on a "strong" character: active cooperation with the hegemon either out of genuine conviction or rational calculation. Sometimes it flows from resignation and the belief that there is no alternative.

If we think about how weaker states have adapted to the changing constraints and opportunities of both globalization and the end of the Cold War, we can think in terms of three images or models. At the liberal end, we can identify a process of *progressive enmeshment*. This develops the Kantian notion of a gradual but progressive diffusion of liberal values. Successful diffusion follows, partly from increased economic interdependence and the spread of liberal economic ideas; partly from the degree to which a liberal legal order comes to sustain the autonomy of a global civil society; and partly as a result of the successful example set by the multifaceted liberal capitalist system of states. The dynamics here are provided by notions of emulation, learning, normative persuasion, and technical knowledge. As indicated in the first part of this chapter, this image glosses over the roles played by coercion and conditionality and skirts far too delicately around the importance of power hierarchies and asymmetries. Notions of rational learning and normative persuasion represent only a partial and rather apolitical view of how dominant ideas and practices are absorbed and internalized by subordinate states and state elites.

At the other extreme, we can think of a crude but straightforward process of *hegemonic imposition*. Proponents of this view might be political neorealists for whom particular sets of dominant liberal ideas will naturally reflect the interests of powerful states and for whom "socialization" derives either from great power imposition or from the competitive dynamics of the state system.[8] Or they might be neodependency writers, particularly those with strongly Gramscian inclinations who lay greater emphasis on the changing dynamics of global capitalism and on the role of transnational social forces and the formation of new transnational class alliances.[9] Yet, while coercion is indeed important, there are serious problems with the idea of imposition. As with old-style dependency theory, it fails to give sufficient weight to domestic

---

[8] For this thin view of socialization, see Waltz, 1979.
[9] For the straightforward imposition thesis, see Petras and Morley, 1990.

dynamics and to particular historically contingent political developments and path-dependent processes. It tells us far too little about the
actual mechanisms of influence, how the big Gramscian or neorealist
picture plays out in particular cases and about the important degrees of
variation across cases. So "imposition" provides just as unhelpful (and
in many cases empirically inaccurate) a guide to the specific ways in
which external pressures are received, interpreted, and acted upon in
the weaker state as "learning" does.

Coercive socialization provides an alternative to these extreme positions, one that captures many aspects of the adaptation of weaker and
developing countries to the end of the Cold War and to globalization
processes. Coercive socialization describes the ways in which interaction within a highly unequal international system leads to the adoption
and incorporation of external ideas, norms, and practices. As part of the
process of internalization, historically embedded conceptions of interest
shift, actors reevaluate their political options, organizational structures
are revised, and a changing institutional context provides the framework for an evolving set of bargains between state and society. Socialization certainly involves material forces, incentives, and constraints
that result from interstate political competition and from market competition within the global economy. But it is also heavily influenced by
the ideas, norms, and shared understandings that define and give meaning to both of these material structures, and by the institutions in which
they are embodied.

Normative implications

This chapter has sought to illustrate how the many forms of power
described in the introductory chapter play out in contemporary practices of global governance. However, the links between power and governance are hardly new. Indeed, inequality was fundamental to classical
understanding of order within the European state system. In the first
place, it was precisely the inequality of states that, for the classical theorists of the state system, differentiated international life from the state of
nature among individuals and that opened up the possibility of international society as a distinct form of political association. Second, institutionalized forms of hierarchy were central to pluralist understandings
of how international order might be nurtured and sustained and to
the political norms through which those understandings were institutionalized. Although the logic of the balance of power might indeed

operate automatically, its dangers and inevitable frictions could be minimized by the recognized managerial role of the great powers. Great
powers could promote order by managing relations between themselves
(through diplomacy, conferences, missions, joint interventions), but also
by exploiting their own unequal power over subordinate states within
their spheres of influence and alliance systems. More important still,
the classical state system was an imperial order. International relations
theorists of many persuasions tell stories based around balanced or balancing power and around the hegemonic struggles of the core powers.
All too often they neglect the second face of the European state system:
its imperialism and the extent to which colonialism was one of the principal institutions of international society. Order or "governance" was
therefore a function of both balanced power *and* unequal or hierarchical
power.

Now it is true that much changed during the challenge to the Western dominance of the international system that characterized the period
1900 to 1990 – especially in relation to decolonization but also in terms
of the struggle for equal sovereignty and the struggle for racial equality. It is also the case that equality has entered into many aspects of the
normative structure of international society (Hurrell and Woods, 1999:
chaps. 1, 3, 4, and 9). And yet, although disguised by the rhetoric of
sovereign equality, this older hierarchical conception of order remained
extraordinarily powerful and influential throughout the twentieth century. Thus, for example, the Cold War "order" and the long peace of
1945–89 were constructed in very traditional fashion around attempts to
regulate the balance of power between the superpowers (through arms
control agreements, summits, and mechanisms of crisis management)
and through the exploitation of hierarchy (through the mutual, if tacit,
recognition of spheres of influence and the creation of an oligarchical
non-proliferation system designed to limit access to the nuclear club).
Moreover, even as the idea of sovereign equality gained ground and as
international institutions expanded so dramatically in both number and
scope, hierarchy and inequality have remained central. Sometimes the
"ordering" role of hierarchy is formalized, as in the special rights and
duties of the permanent members of the UN Security Council, or the
weighted voting structures of the IMF or World Bank. More often it can
be seen in powerful political norms: as in the practice of *ad hoc* group-
ings and contact groups to deal with particular security crises; or the
role of the G7 (now G8) in attempts to manage not just global economic
issues but a great deal more besides; or the way in which international

financial management is dominated by closed groups of the powerful (as in the Bank of International Settlements or the Financial Stability Forum).

Many normative problems flow from this picture. But two merit particular attention. The first has to do with legitimacy; the second with what one might call the political prerequisites for a meaningful global moral community.

For individual hegemonic states or groups of powerful states, hierarchical modes of governance have obvious attractions. But this option comes at a cost. The cost might derive from forgoing more effective and efficient modes of institutionalized governance (as institutionalists would emphasize). But it might also derive from the absence of sufficient legitimacy to ensure the acceptance by weaker states of unequal power and a willingness to cooperate in shared institutions. This old need for major powers and hegemonic states to seek legitimacy has been altered by two sets of developments. First, understandings of legitimacy have been profoundly affected by the emergence of a more solidarist and normatively far more ambitious legal and normative order (in terms, for example, of the use of force, human rights and self-determination, the management of the environment). In particular the use of force and more general moves toward the coercive enforcement of international norms (involving both the use of force as well economic sanctions and conditionalities) make it very difficult to exclude arguments about legitimacy.

And, second, the legitimacy problem has been transformed by the conditions of globalization. The management of globalization necessarily involves the creation of deeply intrusive rules and institutions and debate on how different societies are to be organized domestically. This is a structural change. If states are to develop effective policies on economic development, environmental protection, human rights, the resolution of refugee crises, the fight against drugs, or the struggle against terrorism, then they need to engage with a wide range of international and transnational actors and to interact not just with central governments but with a much wider range of domestic political, economic, and social players. If you want to solve problems in a globalized world, you cannot simply persuade or bully governments into signing treaties, and are therefore inevitably drawn to become involved with how other people organize their own societies.

Of course powerful states have the capacity to intervene unilaterally and directly. But such actions are expensive (in terms of material costs, domestic political costs, and international opposition). So institutions play a crucial role both in legitimizing this ever-deeper intrusion and in acting as a buffer between powerful states and the implementation of agreed-upon international rules and norms. Here the tradeoff for the powerful is between the attractions (and often real benefits) of managing international problems on the basis of hierarchical modes of governance, on the one hand, and the structural need for deeper involvement and broader participation, on the other.

In current debates on global governance, the legitimacy problematic has two distinct sources, which are often insufficiently disentangled. In the first place, the problem results from a general tendency of governance to seep beyond the confines of the state and of the political community represented by that state. Such accounts lay great stress on generalized, even systemic, processes of institutional enmeshment and on the thickening of an ever-expanding regulatory layer of governance both above states and across societies. As a result, many have highlighted the democratic deficits of international bodies from the EU to the WTO and the absence of adequate systems of accountability and representation. In the second view, however, the problem of legitimacy does not rest on any such general tendency, but rather on the degree to which the structures of global governance are contaminated by the preferences and special interests of the powerful. The *density* of international and world society has undoubtedly increased along both solidarist and transnational dimensions, reflecting changes that are unlikely to be easily reversed. And yet the elements of *deformity* are equally evident. We are not dealing with a vanished or vanishing world, as transformationists are wont to argue, but rather with a world in which solidarist and cosmopolitan models of governance coexist, usually rather unhappily, with many aspects of the old Westphalian order.

In the first place, there is deformity in terms of the distribution of advantages and disadvantages: in the way, for example, security is defined and the choices are taken by institutions and states as to whose security is to be protected; or, very obviously, in the massive inequalities of the global economic order; or in the past and present consumption of ecological capital. Second, there is deformity in terms of who sets the rules of international society. Institutions are not, as some liberals would have us believe, neutral arenas for the solution of common problems but rather sites of power, even of dominance. The vast majority of weaker actors are increasingly "rule-takers" over a whole range of issues that affect all aspects of social, economic, and political life. Third, there is deformity in terms of the very different capacity of states and societies to adapt to the demands of a global economy, combined with the extent to which the economic choices of developing counties are if not dictated, then certainly shaped by the institutions dominated by the strong and often backed by coercion in the form of an expanding range of conditionalities. And, finally, deformity is evident in the limited capacity of international law and institutions to constrain effectively the unilateral and often illegal acts of the strong. In this sense we are moving not beyond sovereignty but rather returning to an earlier world of differentiated and more conditional sovereignties.

The links between power and governance explored earlier in this chapter clearly complicate the search for solutions to the problem of legitimacy. If, as I have argued, unequal power is such a pronounced feature of transnational civil society, then looking to NGOs as the representatives of excluded transnational stakeholders and cultural constituencies will not work. Indeed, such representation may exacerbate global inequality as well as undermining the autonomy of the democratic process within existing states. Equally, concentrating on the reform of existing institutions will achieve little if a central part of the problem is the capacity of powerful states to influence whether such institutions exist in the first place. The response of some liberals is to expand the scope of formal institutions and to politicize many aspects of global market transactions. But doing this not only runs up against the strongly anti-multilateral impulses of the currently dominant hegemonic power; but it also has to confront the more principled reasons why democracy and constitutionalism cannot be unproblematically transferred to the suprastate level.

The second implication that flows from the relationship between unequal power and global governance is more troubling still for liberalism. What is the international or global community that can legitimately define and promote applicable principles of global justice? For some, the answer can be found in a simple appeal to some universal notion of rationality. And yet it is unclear why such appeals should be accepted. What meaning can be attached to even the purest and most serene universalist voice – whether of the Kantian liberal or the religious believer – if those to whom it is addressed do not believe themselves to be part of even the thinnest and most fragile shared community? What do we mean by universal reason? Whose reason? As MacIntyre (1985: 6) points out, "the legacy of the Enlightenment has been the problem of an ideal of rational justification which it has proved impossible to attain." Others seek to ground the notion of an international or global community on the increased density of either international society and of transnational civil society. The strengthening and thickening of the institutions of global governance become central to the meaning of that much appealed-to "international community."[10] But before accepting such an appeal, we have to inquire into the social and political conditions that might make for a meaningful global moral community and the degree to which they correspond to what actually exists or is likely to exist. At a general level these might include: some acceptance of equality of status, of respect, and of consideration; some commitment to reciprocity and to the public justification of one's actions; some capacity for autonomous decision-making on the basis of reasonable information; a degree of uncoerced willingness to participate; a situation in which the most disadvantaged perceive themselves as having some stake in the system; and some institutional processes by which the weak and disadvantaged are able to make their voices heard and to express claims to unjust treatment. The analysis of the links between power and global governance in the first part of the chapter is no doubt incomplete. And yet insofar as it captures important elements of contemporary practice, it should underscore just how far we are from attaining even these minimal conditions. Little wonder, then, that the rhetoric of an international community engenders such skepticism and cynicism among so many people in so many parts of the world.

[10] For an excellent analysis of this concept, see Paulus, 2001.

3 Policing and global governance

Mark Laffey and Jutta Weldes

In a brilliant discussion of power in world politics, Cynthia Enloe has argued that, while much of international relations scholarship has been obsessed with power, the discipline has in fact dramatically "*under*estimat[ed] the amounts and varieties of power it takes to form and sustain any given set of relationships between states" (1996: 186). She criticizes in particular the tendency of IR scholars to study only the powerful on the assumption that such a focus will provide insights into and explanations of world politics. Instead, she argues, if we focus on the "margins, silences and bottom rungs" (ibid.: 188), we can see the myriad forms and the astonishing amounts of power that are required for the system to exist at all. In this chapter we take up Enloe's challenge. Specifically, we explore power in global governance by examining the increase in and transformation of policing that accompanies, and indeed helps to produce, the globalization of a neoliberal form of capitalist restructuring. Examining mundane practices of policing long ignored within a discipline more attentive to the upper reaches of state power enables us to demonstrate the massive amounts and the intricate relations of power that underpin what Peck and Tickell term the "neoliberalization" of social spaces and relations (2002). These policing practices, we argue, are integral to contemporary global governance and implicate power in all its forms. Beginning with coercion or compulsory power, we trace out the workings of global governance through institutional, structural, and productive forms of power as well.

Neoliberal discourses of world politics, with their characteristic emphases on free trade and free markets, flexible labor and competitiveness, privatization and commodification, are organized around and explicitly aspire to "the achievement of a market utopia on the world scale" (Cox, 1996a: 191). We understand neoliberalism as a form of

productive power, one intimately linked to ongoing processes of capitalist restructuring. Through the policies it promotes and the forms of political, social, and economic restructuring it entails, neoliberal discourse
contributes directly to contemporary efforts both to intensify capitalist
logics and to extend them to ever more social domains. The use of the
term "utopia" to characterize this project of capitalist restructuring is apt
(e.g., Weeks, 2001). As numerous scholars have pointed out, there is a
"rather blatant disjuncture" between the claims made for neoliberalism
and "its everyday political operations and societal effects" (Neil Brenner
and Theodore, 2002: 5). In this chapter, we show how practices of policing are being reworked, marshaled, and deployed to, as it were, bridge
the gap. It takes a lot of power to produce and maintain a neoliberal
world. Out of the contested processes through which neoliberalization
takes place, in particular practices of privatization and commodification, there emerges a new structure of global governance, a structure
nowhere more apparent than in contemporary practices of policing.

Processes of capitalist restructuring made possible through discourses
of neoliberalism take different forms in different places, shaped by local
social struggles and the particular context of social relations within
which they occur. They also implicate power of diverse kinds. We highlight, first and foremost, the impressive levels of physical coercion, a
form of compulsory power, and in particular the routine and mundane
policing practices underpinning the ongoing process of neoliberalization. The production of neoliberal order, we show, is physically enforced
by specific actors through policing practices that are irreducibly and
simultaneously local, national, regional, and transnational. The centrality of coercion to contemporary world order and some of the connections between neoliberalism, global governance, and coercion are evident in the aftermath of the events of September 11, not least in the
forcible imposition of privatization on Iraq. But coercion is also glar-
ingly apparent in practices and institutional innovations that long pre-
date the attacks on the Pentagon and the World Trade Center. We examine two cases: the worldwide policing of social unrest brought about
by policies of privatization; and the policing of "anti-globalization"
protests, an increasingly common international phenomenon in the last
two decades of the twentieth century. The common thread that binds
together these publicly sanctioned moments of coercion, we argue, is
the role of policing in the reproduction of capital and its internationalization. Neoliberalism entails extensive and intensive policing in order
to transform existing social structures and relations in the service of the

internationalization of capital, and also because it thereby sets in motion social processes that challenge or threaten the reproduction of capitalist structures. In our analysis, then, policing emerges as a key mechanism through which a neoliberalizing global capitalist order is both effected and defended in the face of these challenges and threats.

The chapter is organized as follows. First, we identify the integral relations between global governance and policing when viewed through the prism of neoliberalism. Second, we show where and how different forms of power – institutional, structural, and productive as well as coercive (compulsory) – are manifested in the policing practices that both enable and reinforce the practices of commodification and privatization at the heart of neoliberalism. Third, we illustrate our argument in two case studies: the policing of privatization and of "anti-globalization" protests.

Policing and global governance through the prism of neoliberalism

On its face, the connections between policing, in particular everyday practices of policing in specific locales, and global governance are not obvious. Global governance is most commonly understood to imply not local but intergovernmental or supranational arrangements. The notion of "global governance" emerged in the early 1990s as a central problematic of liberal understandings of globalization and its implications.[1] In particular, the growth of transborder relations was producing a growing set of global problems that needed global solutions in the form of global governance. As the Commission on Global Governance argued rather triumphally in 1992, "international developments [i.e., the end of the Cold War] had created a unique opportunity for strengthening global co-operation to meet the challenge of securing peace, achieving sustainable development, and universalizing democracy" (Commission on Global Governance, 1995: 359). For the commission, as for most others, global governance meant "global institutional arrangements" (ibid.: 368). Although it defined *governance* per se quite broadly as "the sum of the many ways individuals and institutions, public and private, manage their common affairs," it defined *global* governance as "primarily"

---

[1] Representations of world politics in terms of global governance express a form of productive power, elements of the reworking of the situated subjectivities of diverse social subjects.

about "intergovernmental relationships," always recognizing that it involved as well nongovernmental organizations (NGOs), citizens' movements, multi- and transnational corporations, global markets, and the global mass media (ibid.: 2). This concentrated focus on international or transnational institutions as the locus of global governance has, of course, been reproduced in many academic analyses, whether by the founders of the journal *Global Governance* (Knight, MacFarlane, and Weiss, 2001), by analysts of regimes (e.g., Keohane, 2002b), by democratic theorists (e.g., Held, 1995), or by liberal theorists of "governance without government" (e.g., Rosenau and Czempiel, 1992).

Conventional conceptions of global governance also tend to stress its fundamentally pacific character, focusing attention onto issues of cooperation and policy coordination. Global governance, in this view, is not about violence or coercion but rather about the cooperative establishment, promotion, or restoration of order, usually under conditions of consensus among the leading members of the international community (chap. 2, this volume). Of course, the pacific and cooperative character of global governance does not mean that the world is a peaceful place or that there is no longer a need to be concerned about security. The contemporary world order, as George Bush the Elder said just after the end of the Cold War, "remains a dangerous place" (1990: 1333). It has been saddled with a seemingly endless proliferation of threats – a veritable "dysplasia" of the global body politic (Manning, 2000: 195) – many of which are linked to increased interdependence produced by ongoing processes of global change. As the Commission on Global Governance (1995: 366–68) explained, with the opportunities of globalization come "challenges" and "problems," while "new sources of instability and conflict – economic, ecological, social, humanitarian – call for rapid collective responses and new approaches to security." Policing, in a variety of forms, is the standard response to many of these "problems," translating principles of global governance into practices of governing on the ground. Even so, in most accounts of global governance, violence and coercion are seen as temporary and exceptional practices directed primarily to regions outside the central zones of liberal international order, as in practices of peacekeeping for example (Paris, 2002).

In this chapter, we understand policing as "a governmental activity" or a mechanism of governance, and indeed a crucial one (Sheptycki, 2000: 201). So understood, policing encompasses diverse forms of power. Of course, defining policing as "acts of governance directed toward producing security" (Johnston, 2000: 10) does not assume that security is realized; it says nothing about whose security is promoted; and it does not assume that it is carried out only by state apparatuses or within their own territory. Thus, policing can be and often is unsuccessful, it can be and always is discriminatory, and it can be and increasingly is "undertaken by a wide range of agents, including state police, but also including private citizens and commercial companies" (ibid.), and across borders.

Over the past three decades, policing – understood even in the most conventional sense – has undergone a series of transformations. Examples include the growth of private policing as well as the increasing prominence of "transnational" policing (e.g., Jones and Newburn, 2002). The changes in policing since the 1970s have been attributed to bureaucratic and professional logics, that is, to factors internal to the institutions of policing itself (e.g., Andreas, 2000; Deflem, 2000). Such explanations are unconvincing, however: they miss the significance of the wider social context within which claims for increased resources and the expansion of bureaucratic missions make sense. The character of contemporary policing is indelibly shaped by the rise to dominance of what analysts variously refer to as "market society" (Ian Taylor, 1999: esp. chap. 2) or "late modernity" (Garland, 2001: chap. 4). "Post-Keynesian policing" (O'Malley and Palmer, 1996) emerges out of and reflects the strategies adopted by capital in the 1960s as it sought to restore profitability and growth in a world dramatically transformed from what it had been only a quarter of a century before (Arrighi, 1994). Out of these reactions emerged a new international division of labor, a new global financial architecture, and a new post-Fordist (or at least an after-Fordist) developmental model (Lipietz, 1989; Peck and Tickell, 1994). Across the globe these changes are driven by and intimately linked to processes of neoliberal globalization. The changing character of policing participates in and is an indicator of these shifts in the structure of global governance. As a mechanism of governance, policing reflects the social relations in the context of which it takes place and which it helps to secure, including those of class (e.g., Hall, et al., 1978; Chevigny, 1995).

There is, of course, no single globalization (see chap. 12, this volume). In this chapter, we discuss the neoliberal discourse of globalization – a form of productive power – that dominates both political and economic discussions of the contemporary world order (e.g., Agnew and Corbridge, 1995: chap. 7). It is this conception of globalization that is celebrated by international business and promoted by states. Globalization and the neoliberalism with which it is often elided are the common sense of our time. But globalization is not just "a thing out there": it is a self-fulfilling prophecy. "The very discourse and rhetoric of globalization," as Hay and Marsh argue, serve "to summon precisely the effects that such a discourse attributes to globalization itself" (2000: 9). Practices said to be necessary responses to globalization – such as the deregulation of capital and labor markets, the autonomy of central banks, the dismantling of the welfare state, the privatization of public services, and the celebration of competitiveness – in fact produce it. Globalization in this sense – as a discursively constructed *fait accompli* – is fantasy (Paul Smith, 1997). As such, a central question for analysis is not what globalization is, but what, as discourse, it does. At the heart of the myriad processes glossed as "globalization," we argue, is the contemporary accelerated expansion of capital, both the intensification of capital's logics where already established and the extension of these logics to new spaces. From this angle, globalization in its neoliberal form emerges as a world-order project (McMichael, 1997), and a harbinger of the new order in the making. In the twenty-first century, despite the resurgent interest in problematics of security and force prompted by the so-called war on terrorism, globalization remains one of the most important and powerful keywords. *The National Security Strategy of the United States of America* (*NSS*; White House, 2002) released by the White House in September 2002 states unequivocally that the twentieth century issued in "a single sustainable model of sustainable success: freedom, democracy and free enterprise" (ibid.: "Introduction"). According to the *NSS*, a central aim of US security policy is to unleash a new era of global economic growth through the genius of free trade and free markets, in the service of producing a richer and freer world. As demonstrated in Iraq, the "single sustainable model of sustainable success" – neoliberal globalization, in other words – will be selectively exported by force if necessary, in the interests of producing greater global security.

In contrast to its boosters' claims, however, neoliberal globalization – like its predecessor, modernization – undermines the life chances and living conditions of much of the world's population, in the global South and in the North (e.g., Gowan, 1999; Caroline Thomas, 1999; Sutcliffe, 2001). As Brenner and Theodore (2002: 5) observe,

> On the one hand, while neoliberalism aspires to create a "utopia" of free markets liberated from all forms of state interference, it has in practice entailed a dramatic intensification of coercive, disciplinary forms of state intervention in order to impose market rule on all aspects of social

life . . . [W]hereas neoliberal ideology implies that self-regulating markets will generate an optimal allocation of investments and resources, neoliberal political practice has generated pervasive market failures, new forms of social polarization, and a dramatic intensification of uneven development at all spatial scales.

Neoliberalism, increased social and economic insecurity for millions of the world's people, and the continuing centrality of state power to world order are thus bound tightly together. The impoverishment and dislocation that result from neoliberalism lead to social unrest of various kinds, including protest, criminal entrepreneurship, and migration. Many of the everyday "threats" associated with the "downside" of globalization – such as corruption, violations of human rights, and violations of intellectual property rights – are constructed around phenomena associated with the implications of the intensification and extension of capital logics to diverse new social domains. Each of these social "ills," directly linked to the consequences of globalization for the state and state/society relations, elicits policing, i.e., acts of governance or rule directed toward the promotion of security, defined in neoliberal terms. Corruption, for instance, is a problem because it undermines the transparency and confidence necessary to business and trade. Human rights violations concern political rights, not economic and social ones. Violations of intellectual property rights are about investors' profits, not the dissemination of knowledge in the public interest or the economic inefficiencies produced by enforcement efforts. All of these and other forms of insecurity entail policing.

Globalization is often defined in opposition to the state: globalization is about the state's loss of control over processes of modernization and subject formation, over flows of capital and culture, people and goods (e.g., Appadurai, 1996; Ohmae, 1990). But as analysis of the changing character of policing demonstrates, such a view is mistaken. The persistence of state power is particularly evident in relation to policing in the North Atlantic region (e.g., Herbert, 1999), for example, but also elsewhere. Moreover, it is state action – including coercion – that makes neoliberal globalization possible: states are "agencies of the globalizing trend" (Cox, 1996b: 155; Panitch, 1996). At the same time, the state – and policing – is also transformed by neoliberal globalization (Neil Brenner, 1997: 156). At stake is the remaking of the state in ways that favor the interests of transnational capital – and in particular finance capital – over local or industrial capital, labor, and democratic publics. Lesley

Gill (2000: 181–82) articulates this very well in relation to the Bolivian state, for example:

> As the state increasingly shuns "the nation" and nation-building projects to attend to the claims of global creditors, it fails to deal with the demands of ordinary people for decent jobs, health care, education, and a range of other services. The ensuing crisis has threatened the domestic legitimacy of the state and prompted neoliberal policy makers to adopt a number of strategies to fortify the state's authority . . . As the state's policies push more people into poverty, the state increasingly calls upon the army and militarized police forces to repress the so-called dangerous classes and to control the wide-spread alienation from the retreating state.

These transformations in the character and focus of policing are not restricted to particular states but extend across the international system as a whole, taking in local, national, regional, and international institutions and practices, including coercion and policing. Policing, as we demonstrate below, is integral to world-order maintenance in the context of capital's continuing efforts to extend the logic of privatization and commodification to ever more social relations and domains.

Global policing and the different forms of power

Central to the burgeoning coercive apparatus constitutive of the liberal world order is the extension and enforcement of property rights. This entails not only the physical enforcement of existing property rights – protecting privatized industries, for instance – but also the creation of new property rights – such as the privatization of water or the commodification of genetic and biological materials. This coercive apparatus also contributes to the criminalization of diverse activities – making it illegal for farmers to save licensed seeds from one year to the next, for example, or for citizens to assemble to protest privatization and neoliberal policies more generally – and the expansion and deepening of institutions and practices designed to cope with them. It is widely accepted that the sovereign territorial state of Westphalian mythology is undergoing rapid transformation in the context of globalization. But, at the same time, it is also being reinforced as a major locus of policing practices. Significantly, the coercive capacities of the state are nowhere more clearly manifest than at precisely the moments of "global governance" – the meetings and summits of the international financial institutions

(IFIs), the G8, and the like – applauded by neoliberalism's proponents as a sign of a more cooperative world and protested by supporters of a different, more democratic, globalization.

Our analysis points to the inextricable interconnection between and among different forms of power. Take the case of the policing of "seed piracy." The Monsanto Corporation, a major producer of genetically engineered seeds, has "successfully brought to US court farmers who had saved soybean seeds bought from Monsanto, replanted them and shared them with their neighbors" (Verzola, 1998). The company sends Pinkerton operatives into farmers' fields; it "sponsors a toll-free 'tip line' to help farmers blow the whistle on their neighbors"; and it "has placed radio ads broadcasting the names of noncompliant growers caught planting the company's genes" (Weiss, 1999). In 1998, Monsanto had over 475 "seed piracy" cases in the United States, and was actively investigating over 250 of them. One case involved Kentucky farmer David Chaney. In September 1998, Chaney was caught by Monsanto investigators and prosecuted for "seed piracy." He pleaded guilty to the "heinous crime" of saving and replanting seeds, specifically Roundup Ready soya beans (UK House of Commons, 1999). He was required to pay a fine, or "royalties," to Monsanto of $35,000 and to destroy the entire crop because he had received the beans "under new product licenses, driven by patent protection, whereby there is an everlasting obligation to pay to biotech companies royalties on their seeds" (ibid.). In addition, as in other cases, he was required to give Monsanto access to all of his production records for the subsequent five years, and to grant Monsanto complete access to any property he owned or leased, allowing Monsanto employees to inspect, collect, and test his soybean plants and seeds for the next five years (Verzola, 1998).

This case, which finds echoes in similar struggles in India and elsewhere, illustrates some of the ways in which different forms of power operate together. Most obviously, we see multiple instances of the deployment of compulsory power. Monsanto uses its resources, mainly financial and legal, to compel others in situations of conflict. It does so by hiring private detectives to snoop around farms, by hiring lawyers to prosecute farmers, by physically monitoring the farms of those convicted of "seed piracy." The state enters the picture in the form of the courts through which Monsanto sues the farmers, and which enforce the fines and the other penalties. Both Monsanto and the state police the activities of farmers, using power to coerce reluctant and even resistant populations to accept the privatization of nature.

At the same time, this exercise of compulsory power, whether by Monsanto or the state, operates only in the context of, and indeed is partly made possible by, the other three forms of power. The second type of power enters in the form of institutional constraints and institutional rules. In this case, bias is mobilized on behalf of corporate actors, who benefit from rules of the game – the legal institutions – that allow for the prosecution of "seed pirates," and specify or allow for particular remedies, such as enforced royalty payments, continued surveillance, and the like. The third type, structural power, is pervasively at play as well. This type of power, as the constitution of differential social capacities of actors in structured relation to each other, appears most obviously in the structures of property rights of corporate capitalism. The expansionary logics of capitalism, and their attendant dynamics of privatization and commodification, for instance, are evident in the creation of property rights in genetically modified seeds, such that corporations are owners of the property and farmers are empowered only to lease it from them. These property rights – the commodification and privatization of nature – provide the grounds on which the institutional, legal rules regarding "seed piracy" are developed. And finally, these moments of compulsory power, and the institutional and social relational structures of power in which they are embedded, are themselves constituted by, while they help to (re)produce, productive power. In particular, a focus on this fourth form of power highlights the production of meaningful practices, and thus of the very subjects assumed by the other notions of power, because discourse constitutes the subjectivity of social beings with their respective practices, responsibilities, and identities. In this case, the neoliberal discourse constitutes privatization and commodification as "efficient" – and therefore desirable – ways to organize social and economic life. On this basis, the multinational corporation, Monsanto, is constituted as the innovator and hence the rightful "owner" of "genetically enhanced" seeds, and the Kentucky farmer, David Chaney, as a "criminal" engaging in "seed piracy."

Interestingly, this case highlights as well the mutual constitution of power and resistance. We might characterize resistance as being orthogonal to power: it encompasses all four forms we have discussed, but their social orientation is shifted. A counterhegemonic discourse has emerged that at least attempts to reverse these constructions, charging Monsanto with deploying a "gene police" (e.g., Weiss, 1999) to enforce its appropriation of nature through "terminator technology" that engineers "dead" seeds that cannot reproduce themselves (e.g., Hayes, 1999).

Farmers construct Monsanto's campaign as a "reign of terror" (Weiss, 1999). One critic noted that, as a result, "Our rural communities are being turned into corporate police states and farmers are being turned into criminals" (cited ibid.). The other forms of power are present as well. For instance, some farmers, like Percy Schmeiser, exercise direct decision-making power (compulsory power) by refusing to allow Monsanto to inspect their fields. They do this on the basis of institutional power, like the right to private property enshrined in US law, which, as noted above, is expressive of the structures of capitalist social relations (structural power), which allocate interests, such as both the farmers' and the corporations' drive to make a profit.

As this brief example dramatically demonstrates, there is no single, central logic to power and resistance. Instead, power and resistance are mutually constituted in diverse locations and through various practices. The exercise of power that establishes seeds as private property generates resistance. The exercise of power as resistance generates particular forms of corporate and state policing. In the end, the dominant neoliberal discourse is, unsurprisingly, more successful in constituting privatization as a self-evidently necessary objective while producing "globalization" itself as inevitable and the contemporary order as benign and desirable. But the fact remains that these seemingly opposed forms of power are in important ways mutually constitutive. They collaborate in the constitution of diverse and pervasive forms of global governance.

Global governance on the ground: policing in practice

In this section, we examine two cases of policing. Both are related to – a response to as well as the cause of – threats to different aspects of globalization. Both involve all four forms of power. Both are central to contemporary global governance and also expose its fundamentally coercive nature. We examine, first, the global policing of the social unrest brought about by the privatization essential to post-1970s globalization. These protests have literally been global, extending across Latin America, Asia, and Europe, and their policing has been thorough, although sometimes ineffective. We then turn to the policing of anti-capitalist/anti-globalization protests launched at the main supranational institutions of "global governance," such as the IFIs and the WTO, and highlight their increasingly violent nature.

Policing privatization

Since the 1970s, privatization policies have been pursued in the core, and enforced on the periphery, by the major institutions of global governance, notably the IMF, the World Bank, and more recently the WTO. The IMF's Structural Adjustment Programs, for example, have mandated privatization since the 1970s, and its "Poverty Reduction and Growth Facility," inaugurated in 1999, generally requires privatization as well. The main defense of privatization – an umbrella term encompassing a range of policies, from attracting private investment into state-owned enterprises to their outright sale – is that it brings efficiency and cost-effectiveness (state-owned enterprises, in contrast, being "inefficient, politicized, non-commercial, and costly to the economy" [Ashley Brown, 2001: 116]). This neoliberal economic principle, moreover, is firmly rooted in a deep-seated ideological commitment to privatization: "the drive to privatize," says one analyst, has become "an article of faith" (ibid.). Not surprisingly: after all, capitalism *is* social relations of production constituted in private property rights, and globalization is their expansion across the remaining nonprivate bits of the globe, or of human activity.

The accelerating rush toward privatization encompasses many sectors of the economy. State-owned enterprises, infrastructure, and utilities have been targets of the IFIs' privatization drive, ably assisted and promoted by local capitalist agencies and state managers, since the 1970s. More recently, attention has turned to the privatization of services. The WTO's General Agreement on Trade in Services (GATS) has contributed to this extension. As one critic described it, the GATS "unleashes transnational corporations to roam the planet and buy up any public services they fancy. Everything from hospitals, post offices and libraries to water and education" (Newman, 2000). The drive toward privatization presupposes commodification. Through the WTO's Trade-Related Intellectual Property Rights, for example, plant varieties – genetically engineered ones like Monsanto's Roundup Ready soybeans (Dawkins, Thom, and Carr, n.d.) – and indigenous biogenetic materials – like Thai jasmine rice (IMC Global, 2001) – are becoming commodities available for privatization by multinational corporations (see, e.g., Mittal and Rosset, 2001).

Disputes over these privatization measures have erupted since the IMF riots of the 1970s. Privatization has led to increased concentration of wealth, income inequality, poverty, and alienation, generating significant social unrest. Anti-privatization protests, in turn, have spanned the globe. In the past few years, significant demonstrations took place in Puerto Rico over the privatization of the telephone company (1990–98), in South Korea over the privatization of basic telecommunications (1995) and social services (2001), in Panama City over the privatization of the Water Institute (1998), in Istanbul during May Day celebrations over Turkey's privatization policy (1998), in Rio de Janeiro over the privatization of Telebras, Latin America's biggest telecommunications firm (1998), in London against the privatization of the railway system (1999), in Haiti over the privatization of the national telephone company (1999), in Romania over the privatization of industry (1999), in Hong Kong by civil servants opposing the privatization of public services (1999), in Costa Rica against the privatization of utilities (2000), in El Salvador over the privatization of health services (2000), in Paraguay over the privatization of telephone, water, and railroad companies (2000), in Johannesburg against privatization of basic services (2001), in Thailand over the privatization of Thai jasmine rice (2001), in Italy over the proposed privatization of schools in Rome (2001), in Argentina over the privatization of an oil refinery (2001), and in Colombia over the privatization of public services (2001) – to cite only a few of many examples. Almost all of these protests elicited major policing responses; many resulted in substantial injuries, and some in fatalities.

Social unrest and the attendant protests are expected by the IFIs. As Palast (2001) notes, the World Bank's Interim Country Assistance Strategy for Ecuador, for instance, stated several times "with cold accuracy – that they expected their plans to spark 'social unrest.'" The plan calls for "facing down civil strife and suffering with 'political resolve.'" Resolve is generated and manifests itself in a variety of ways, including efforts to insulate political elites from popular forces, to lock states into these policies through international institutions such as the WTO, and of course policing, much of it violent. The policing of anti-privatization protests highlights explicitly the connection between coercion and property. After all, property rights are, by definition, exclusionary: that is their purpose. Policing enforces the exclusion.

The Bolivian *guerra del agua* – the Water War – provides an illustration.[2] In April 2000, massive protests – including general strikes and transportation blockages – erupted across Bolivia in response to the

---

[2] Water privatization in particular has produced protests, and policing, around the world, from Peru to Indonesia, South Africa to Poland (Finnegan, 2002).

privatization of water and subsequent price increases. President Hugo Banzer declared martial law, called out the army, suspended most civil rights, and closed local radio stations (Kruse, 2001). In the city of Cochabamba, the publicly owned water system had been sold to Aguas del Tunari, which was operated in part by International Waters Limited, a British subsidiary of San Francisco-based Bechtel Enterprises (Zoll, 2000). The sale was in response to the IMF's, World Bank's, and Inter-American Development Bank's structural adjustment program for Bolivia, which required that water provision be privatized (Third World Traveler, 2000). The new company raised prices dramatically, sometimes by as much as 60 percent.[3] The resulting mass protests, which were brutally policed by the military and riot police, lasted for four days. In the end, six people were killed, including a seventeen-year-old, Victor Hugo Daza, who was shot in the face (Finnegan, 2002), and at least 175 people were injured, including two children blinded by tear gas (Third World Traveler, 2000).

Despite state repression, the protests were successful, at least at first, forcing the government to retreat from privatization. But the story does not end there, and the victory may be more symbolic than real. Under provisions of the GATS, Bechtel is suing Bolivia for $25 million in lost potential profits resulting from the abrogation of the water privatization agreement (Shultz, 2001). The case has been brought to the International Centre for the Settlement of Investment Disputes. "The next battle in the 'Water War'" (Kruse, 2002) is being fought in "an international tribunal housed at the World Bank that holds all of its meetings in secret," without public participation, scrutiny, or accountability (Earthjustice, 2002).

Despite widespread protests, privatization measures are accelerating. The World Bank Group's new Private Sector Development (PSD) Strategy has stepped up the privatization of infrastructure and basic services by attaching privatization conditions to adjustment loans (Globalization Challenge Initiative 2002).[4] The privatization drive has regional manifestations as well. The Free Trade Area of the Americas (FTAA) amounts, in one analyst's view, to the "privatization of a hemisphere,

---

[3] Water bills showing 60 percent increases are posted on the Center for Democracy's website, e.g., www.democracyctr.org/bechtel.waterbills/morales.htm.
[4] While the IFIs "encourage" states to privatize through coercive policies, the World Bank also helps investors find public assets to buy. To this end, the Multilateral Investment Guarantee Agency (www.miga.org/), established as part of the World Bank Group in 1988, has a website called "Private Link" with the task of "linking investors to privatization opportunities in emerging markets" (privatizationlink.com/).

under US control" (Chossudovsky, 2001: 3). The FTAA, like the GATS, will allow for the privatization of whole municipalities: "water, sewer systems, roads and municipal services would be owned and operated by private companies (rather than citizens)" (ibid.). And, under FTAA rules, governments have no recourse: the FTAA grants "a 'charter of rights' to corporations, which would not only override national laws but also enable private companies to sue national governments, demand the annulment of national laws and receive compensation for potential lost profits which result from government regulation" (ibid.: 4). Further policing will undoubtedly be necessary.

As the prevalence and extent of anti-privatization protest indicate, these policies are decidedly unpopular: aggressively promoted by external agencies as well as local capital and state managers, they are also often opposed by the majority of the population. This means that we are witnessing elected governments – e.g., in South Africa, South Korea, Bolivia, the UK – implementing policies that the majority of their citizens oppose. But the governments are generally unresponsive to these popular constituencies, even in the face of massive protests, because they are more influenced by, or even beholden to, other constituencies, internal and external. Even where governments are ultimately responsive to popular demands, as in the Bolivian case, the mechanisms of global governance – e.g., the GATS or the FTAA – override local democratic preferences. This, it seems, is global governance.

The policing of privatization, and the case of water privatization in Bolivia in particular, illustrate both the pervasiveness of power as global governance and the inextricable interconnections between and among different forms of power. The discourse of neoliberalism underlies the entire process: it has successfully come to define privatization as a good – as productive of profits, efficiency, and cost-effectiveness – and state ownership as bad – as necessarily inefficient and costly. It thus defines private actors like Bechtel as responsible and accountable corporate citizens and efficient providers of public services, while publics, for example, are unruly and politicized. This discourse – a form of productive power – is of course made manifest in the organizations of corporate capitalism – the massive and convoluted corporate entities like Bechtel and its subsidiaries – and the private property relations – a form of structural power – on which they rest. These institutions of corporate capitalism, in turn, are maintained through institutional power such as the rules of the unaccountable International Center for the Settlement of Investment Disputes. Compulsory power is also rampant in this example: it is exercised not only by the state in its repressive policing, but by Bechtel in its litigation, and by the protesters, whose resistance (again based on multiple forms of power) is central to the development of these coercive practices of global governance.

Policing governance

Images of anti-capitalist and anti-globalization protesters confronting rank upon rank of heavily armed riot police in mass demonstrations have become commonplace in the past few years. Dramatic protests have occurred at many recent "ritual celebrations of economic global-ization" (Ericson and Doyle, 1999: 589) – including, for example, the Asia-Pacific Economic Cooperation (APEC) summit in Vancouver (1997), the WTO meeting in Geneva (1998), the WTO meeting in Seattle (1999), the IMF/World Bank meetings in Washington and Prague (2000), and the World Economic Forum in Davos, the FTAA "Summit of the Americas" in Quebec, the EU summit in Gothenburg, and the G8 sum-mit in Genoa (all in 2001).[5] At the last of these, reflecting the increasing violence with which such protests have been prosecuted and policed, 23-year-old Carlo Giuliani was killed by Italian police, shot twice in the head, and then run over by his killer's jeep (Butterfield, 2001).

While it has been argued that anti-globalization protests are important to host nations because, by allowing them to display their democratic qualities, they contribute to the state's legitimation strategy (Ericson and Doyle, 1999: 591–92),[6] the symbolic summitry of "global gover-nance" is increasingly heavily policed. Policing of the APEC meeting in Vancouver (1997), an early example, was highly politicized and involved the extensive deployment of police forces, including snipers. These police forces "made illegal preventive arrests, censored peaceful expres-sion, and assaulted protesters who were already dispersing" (ibid.: 602). The "Battle of Seattle" in 1999 also involved massive – if incompetent and misdirected (ACLU, 2000: 3–4) – policing. Once it became clear that the police were unprepared for the scale of the protests, Seattle's

---

[5] A more extensive and global list can be found in Bircham and Charlton (2001: 340–41).

[6] Leaders are also choosing more remote meeting sites. The WTO meeting in 2001, held in Doha, Qatar, made protest difficult, as did the 2002 G8 meeting in the remote Canadian resort of Kananakis, in the Rocky Mountains. Both were heavily cordoned off, in spite of their general inaccessibility. Nonetheless, protests, and policing, have continued, notably at the World Bank–IMF meeting in Washington in 2002, and the Evian G8 summit in 2003.

mayor declared a state of emergency and established a 25-square-block "no-protest zone" in the downtown area. Police barred people from expressing views critical of the WTO, ordered others to remove buttons and stickers from their clothing, and confiscated signs and leaflets. The police were armed with tear gas, pepper spray, clubs, and rubber bullets, and deployed them against mainly peaceful protesters and bystanders, including local residents and shoppers. Individual acts of police brutality and "excessive force" were widespread, hundreds of people were improperly arrested, and many of those detained were abused and mistreated in jail (ibid.: 4–6). Between Vancouver and Seattle, the violence of policing had escalated notably. After Seattle it continued to escalate. In Quebec, police used plastic bullets, tear gas, and water cannons (Rights and Democracy, 2001). And worse was to come: live ammunition was used in Gothenburg, where three protesters were shot ("Three Protesters Shot," 2001); it had fatal consequences at Genoa.

Although Foreign Minister Hubert Vedrine of France said before the 2001 Genoa summit that "We cannot continue to organize large-scale international meetings under the protection of the police; we must build a system of dialogue" with protest groups ("EU: Anti-Globalization Movement Prepares for Genoa Summit," 2001), at Genoa the policing was even more obtrusive and menacing. In "the greatest display of police violence in Italy in decades" (Catalinotto, n.d.), the "leaders of seven major industrialized countries, plus Russia, met behind steel barricades that sealed off a large area of the old center around the port. The unprecedented security reinforced the image of powerful politicians cut off from their own people and the world" ("Genoa G8 and the Aftermath," n.d.). Local police and the *carabinieri* – the Italian national police – armed with live ammunition and some in armored personnel carriers and on horseback, patrolled the restricted areas, using tear gas and water cannon to disperse protesters. The city was patrolled by helicopters, reporters were detained and searched, and many suspects brutally beaten (FAIR, 2001). The day before the meeting NBC Nightly News reported that "over 20,000 Italian police are on high alert, the port's shipping lanes closed, surface-to-air missiles deployed at the airport. The site of tomorrow's economic summit is now a two-square-mile no-go zone, shops closed, every resident's ID checked" (ibid.). The aircraft carrier USS *Enterprise* sat in the harbor (Butterfield, 2001).

Although such massive policing can be argued to produce rather than prevent violence (e.g., ACLU, 2000), states have responded to protests against "the democratic deficits" (Scholte, 1997: 26) of global governance with ever-expanding policing.[7] European reactions are noteworthy in this regard.

- In 1990, the Schengen Implementing Convention established extensive police cooperation not only for prosecuting crimes but also for the conduct and coordination of expansive surveillance. It includes "intelligence gathering and comprehensive automated data exchange on persons not suspected of any offense under criminal law" ("Secretive 'Sirenes,'" 1996/97) and grants wide freedoms to the "police authorities" notably to "prevent" as well as detect criminal offenses (Article 46 SIC, ibid.).
- In 2001 the German government, supported by Italy, proposed to the EU "Heads of central bodies for public order and security" the creation of a "Special Unit" – an EU riot police – that would "cooperate internationally to de-escalate situations where possible and combat violence with appropriate firmness where necessary" (in Statewatch, 2001c).
- In 2001, Belgium and the Netherlands proposed that the EU draw up "further detailed common EU public order criteria" as the grounds for "refusing entry to EU citizens and expelling EU citizens from EU member states." This would be used to contain not only "football hooligans" but also anti-globalization and other demonstrators. The major objective: "preventing 'known troublemakers'" – what UK prime minister Tony Blair called an "anarchists' traveling circus" – "from leaving their own country to join a protest in another" (in Statewatch, 2001a).
- In 2001, in the aftermath of the shootings at Gothenburg, proposals were developed that criminalized protest in the EU by allowing for "the ongoing surveillance of any group whose concerns might lead them to take part in an EU-wide protest" (Statewatch, 2001b).

It is commonplace to treat Schengen membership as abolishing border controls and promoting free movement of people around in Europe. In fact, however, much of the cooperation entailed in Schengen is concerned with "increased policing and control of people" ("Secretive

---

[7] Mike Moore, then director-general of the WTO, for example, defended the democratic accountability of WTO agreements by arguing that they are "negotiated by Ambassadors and Ministers who represent their governments. We operate by consensus and every member government, therefore has veto power." Moreover, "governments are in turn accountable to parliaments" and "elected parliamentarians are the measurable and accountable representatives of civil society" (2001: 2).

'Sirenes,'" 1996/97). The consequences are apparent. As Tony Bunyan, editor of *Statewatch*, has said:

> We are living in very dangerous times in many senses. The use of armed and specially trained paramilitary police units to counter protests in the EU will tend to escalate violence not diminish it. But, more importantly, it is part of a strategy to treat protesters as the same kind of "threat" as terrorists. This can only lead to the curtailment of the right to free movements and the democratic right to demonstrate.
>
> (in Statewatch, 2001c)

Contrary to myths of progressive enlightenment in liberal democracies, the savage policing of political protest, particularly by labor but also by other marginalized groups, has long been a defining feature of public life in the North Atlantic region. Prominent examples include the policing of the civil rights movements in the United States and Northern Ireland, as well as the willingness of the British state under Margaret Thatcher to use extreme levels of force against the miners' strike in 1984. In this sense, the evident willingness of liberal democratic states coercively to police anti-globalization protests is nothing new. It is through policing as a mechanism of structural reproduction that the rule of capital is defended and cemented in place. But as the array of social subjects rendered insecure by the ongoing processes of globalization continues to expand, so it becomes increasingly difficult not only for the state to present itself as the representative of all its citizens, but also to claim that the protests are the actions of a radical, marginal few. Perhaps this helps to explain growing limitations on free speech, civil liberties, and popular protest itself, and also answers the question: "Why must every meeting of the world's financial managers be accompanied by police tactics to stifle free speech and disrupt the opposition?" (Guma, 2001).

Again, the policing of anti-capitalist and alternative globalization protests illustrates several important points regarding power and global governance. First, the exercise of power through policing – coercive global governance – develops through its engagement with resistance. Power and resistance are mutually constituted, if not equally effective. Second, different forms of power are again intertwined: the neoliberal discourse does not recognize the "democratic deficits" of global governance, instead treating sites of global governance like the G8 and WTO as institutions of democracy. Democratic protest, in contrast, becomes "criminal" activity; "known troublemakers" become international outlaws. These discursive constructions manifest themselves in the central institutions of regional and global governance, most notably the EU, IFIs, WTO, and G8. These institutions, in turn, are protected through legal structures and practices – like public order policing – that concretize the compulsory power of the state and elicit the compulsory power of protesters. Third, the policing of protest begins to indicate the irretrievably heterarchic character of such policing practices, and thus of global governance. While we typically associate global governance with precisely those global-level institutions against which protesters demonstrate, the policing of these demonstrations – through surveillance, information exchange, "no-protest zones," preventive arrests, military deployments, and ultimately lethal force – indicate that coercive global governance actually takes place at all levels, through an increasingly coordinated system of local, national, regional, international, and transnational institutions and practices, including, fundamentally, in the North Atlantic.

Conclusion

"Hierarchies are multiple," Enloe reminds us, "because forms of political power are diverse" (1996: 193). In this chapter, analysis of the policing of globalization has enabled us to show the relations between global governance and class power (see also chap. 9, this volume). Examination of the seemingly mundane practices of policing highlights the quite staggering amounts of coercion integral to the allegedly benign and pacific liberal order, and also points to the numerous ways in which particular forms of power do not operate in isolation. On the contrary, coercive power always operates within a larger context that implicates other forms of power as well. As we have demonstrated, these diverse forms of power reflect and reinforce a particular set of hierarchies, most notably but not exclusively between those who own capital and those who do not.

Social analysis, like the operation of power, is never neutral (Max Weber, 1949). Whether we like it or not, our efforts to comprehend the world inevitably express a politics: a set of commitments to how the world should be. Claims to value-neutrality are just so much special pleading: better to be honest about what we think is important. With that in mind, a more thorough and extended analysis of global policing – of the coercive practices underpinning global governance – would focus attention not only on the different analytical types of power – compulsory, institutional, structural, and productive – but also on the intertwined hierarchies of power as they are viewed from the "bottom rungs": hierarchies organized around gender, race, bureaucracy, and other relations. Such an analysis is necessary because different hierarchies "do not sit on the social landscape like tuna, egg, and cheese sandwiches on an icy cafeteria counter, diversely multiple but unconnected. They relate to each other, sometimes in ways that subvert one another, sometimes in ways that provide each with their respective resiliency" (Enloe, 1996: 193). Locating the relations between power and global governance might, for example, lead to examination of the ways in which gender is policed to facilitate, and indeed enable, national-level economic restructuring and the efficient and profitable internationalization of capital, while muting class-based protest (e.g., True, 1999; Wichterich, 2000). After all, "The bedroom's hierarchy is not unconnected to the hierarchies of the international coffee exchange or of the foreign ministry" (Enloe, 1996: 193). Attention to race or postcolonial categories would open up similar types of questions. Global governance is made real in everyday practices of regulation and rule such as policing that shape and determine people's lives. Power is always in some sense local. A central task for analysts of power in global governance, then, is to trace out where and how the global is implicated in the local, and vice versa.

4   Power, fairness, and the global economy

Ethan B. Kapstein

The process of economic globalization has come under widespread attack in recent years. These attacks are not simply economic or material in nature, coming from workers or industrialists whose jobs and incomes are directly threatened by the consequences of greater openness. Beyond these interest-based grievances, a host of activists, policymakers, and scholars have come to see the policies of openness, and the associated outcomes, as being fundamentally "unfair" or "unjust" to many peoples, especially the poor, and to many countries, particularly those in the developing world. These critics question the very morality and legitimacy of existing global economic arrangements. There is no shortage of pronouncements to that effect.

Thus, a Washington-based policy analyst has called the trade policies of the United States and European Union an "ethical scandal" (Gresser, 2002: 14), while the US trade representative has branded European protection of its agriculture "immoral" (Becker, 2003). The Belgian foreign minister has proclaimed the need for an "ethical globalization" (Verhofstadt, 2002), and the former United Nations High Commissioner for Human Rights, Mary Robinson, has even launched an "Ethical Globalization Initiative." The president of the World Bank, James Wolfensohn, laments that "something is wrong" with the global economy, while his former chief economist, Nobel prize winner Joseph Stiglitz, has glibly remarked, "Of course, no one expected that the world market would be fair . . ." (2002a: 24).

What all these remarks suggest is that power and material self-interest have trumped fairness and justice in the design of international economic institutions and policies. Most students of world politics would not find that assessment particularly surprising, given that the international system is an anarchic realm in which insecurity is rife and morality

80

is scarce if not absent. If powerful actors exploit those who are weak, it is because nobody can prevent them from doing so. From this "realist" perspective, it is considerations of fairness that are puzzling and need to be explained.

The existence of widespread poverty and misery in the midst of plenty makes one wonder whether concerns with justice and fairness have played any role whatsoever in shaping the design of the global economy. To be sure, it would be too much to defend present-day international economic arrangements as representing a fair deal for all agents, for clearly that is not the case. But it may also be too much to assert that fairness considerations have been irrelevant to the design of our institutions for trade, finance, and development, and that only compulsory power and material interests matter. As with many things in social science, greater illumination may be found between the glaring extremes.

What, then, is the relationship between power and fairness in the basic structure of the global economy? To date, scholars of global governance have devoted relatively little attention to the "fairness factor" in international economic relations.[1] Rational-choice theorists tend to overlook fairness as an essential characteristic of institutional design because of their foundational assumption that self-interested actors are always trying to maximize some objective welfare function. The game-theoretic model most often used to illustrate that behavior is the Prisoner's Dilemma Game (PDG), which yields cooperative outcomes only in its iterated form. As I will show, however, evidence from experimental economics using the Ultimatum Game (UG) among other settings casts doubt on this behavioral assumption. For their part, power-oriented theorists overlook the role that fairness might play in the design and maintenance of institutions because, in their worldview, seemingly normative concerns can hardly be expected to play a decisive role in the international system. The constant threat of war leaves little or no room for ethical considerations. But that is a theoretically impoverished view of fairness.

What neither the rational-actor nor the power-oriented schools has recognized is the extent to which "fairness matters" to institutional design (see Keohane, 1989). Briefly, I argue that fairness matters to those who wield compulsory power because of its instrumental value in contributing to the robustness and stability of social arrangements. In this

---

[1] For important exceptions, see Keohane, 1989; and Albin, 2001.

rendering, fairness may be conceptualized as part of the software that is used to program institutional power. In the absence of fairness considerations, the fundamental legitimacy of international institutions is more likely to be questioned by the participants, and especially by those participants who come to believe that the status quo set of policies and institutions – what I call the "basic structure" of the global economy – is failing to promote their interests. As Andrew Hurrell writes in his contribution to this volume, "A great deal of the struggle for political power is the quest for authoritative control that avoids costly and dangerous reliance on brute force and coercion" (chap. 2, this volume: 49). Fairness considerations are inserted into institutional arrangements to provide a hedge against future threats to these basic structures. In other words, there is power *in* fairness.[2]

Once established, institutions, in turn, serve to "lock in" a given fairness discourse, using their institutional power to define the boundaries of appropriate behavior by member states. Fairness considerations thus also serve to constrain the actions of those who are capable of exercising compulsory power. When powerful states act in ways that others view as being unfair – a charge frequently leveled at the administration of President George W. Bush, for example – the "moral authority" or "soft power" of the dominant actor is diminished, potentially undermining its systemic influence or ability to cajole even friends and allies into providing it with assistance, whether it be help in securing and rebuilding Iraq, or in negotiating a multilateral trade deal (Nye, 2004). Great powers thus disregard the institutional norms that they have promulgated at their peril.

To draw an example from the trading system, "protectionism" has in recent years become something of a dirty word in international economic discourse, a policy that is beyond the pale of acceptable state behavior. A huge academic and public policy literature bolsters the case for free trade, in support of institutional power. States that promote "unfair" trade practices are not eligible for membership in the World Trade Organization (WTO), and remain marginalized from the global economy. While protectionism, of course, still remains the rule rather than the exception in trade policy the world over – again one thinks of the Bush administration's steel tariffs as a prominent example – it now carries with it a lurid tint of illegitimacy. Thus, the quotes that appear at the opening of this chapter suggest that protectionism by the industrial

---

[2] I thank Michael Barnett for emphasizing this point.

countries is "immoral" and "unfair." Indeed, even the Bush administration sought to defend its steel tariffs in instrumental terms, as the politically expedient price to be paid for winning greater trade promotion authority for the president. Nevertheless, the failure of the United States and European Union to open their markets to free trade, and the effects of that protectionism on developing countries, has increasingly been the subject not just of economic but of moral condemnation as well.

As already emphasized, the insertion of normative considerations such as fairness into institutional structures is hardly in opposition to the exercise of state (or class, or interest-group) power. To the contrary, ideas of what constitutes fairness are institutionalized by those who control material and ideological resources as a way of insuring their stock of assets and future stream of rents. Again to cite Hurrell, "Institutions are not just concerned with liberal purposes of solving common problems or promoting shared values. They are also sites of power and reflect and entrench power hierarchies and the interests of powerful states" (chap. 2, this volume: 48).

But I will argue that Hurrell's view on the role of norms, like fairness, in shaping institutional structures and policies is perhaps too pessimistic. While I agree that norms are used to legitimate and codify the interests of those who are powerful, the distributive outcomes that are at least partly generated by these norms also matter to political stability. A system that proclaims "all men are created equal," but then acts to enslave or discriminate against particular groups of persons, will not forever be able to maintain the manifest contradiction between principles and deeds. A certain fairness discourse therefore implies a certain distribution of the gains from political cooperation.

To provide an example, current disputes between "North" and "South" within the context of the international trade regime are essentially about the fairness of the present-day order. But if my analysis is accurate, we should expect to see – despite the "setback" at the WTO's summit in Cancun, Mexico, in September 2003 – continuing movement on the part of the industrial countries in the direction of greater openness towards imports from the developing world, including agricultural and textile imports, which have been at the heart of recent trade disputes. To be sure, the bargains struck between rich and poor states will undoubtedly leave the former with most of their asset base. But the bargain of greater openness must create some space for the possibility of upward mobility as well, as exemplified by the economic success of several East Asian "tigers" during the postwar era and more recently of China and

India. In essence, by institutionalizing norms of fairness, the powerful seek to maintain status quo *structures* at the price of some relative loss of their wealth and power.

I will examine this relationship between compulsory power, institutional power, and norms of fairness by focusing on the particular case of the international trading system, which, at least in theory, provides states with the world's neatest vehicle for upward economic mobility. The chapter proceeds as follows. In the next section, I define more precisely the concept of fairness and discuss some of the evidence from experimental economics that highlights its importance. In the following section, I provide a case study of "fairness in action," by examining the international trade regime. I conclude by assessing some competing hypotheses with respect to how and why fairness might emerge as a consideration in world politics, and with thoughts for future research.

Defining fairness

The study of international institutions has been largely shaped in recent years by two contrasting theoretical traditions. First, the rational-choice approach begins with the supposition that states face "market failures" of various kinds, and that they seek to engage in cooperative ventures in order to promote more efficient political and/or economic outcomes. In the absence of collective action to curb arms races or trade wars, states will build more weapons and impose higher tariffs than is optimal from a social welfare perspective. The fundamental normative question this raises for rational-choice theorists is: what actions *should* self-interested governments take in order to achieve and maintain international cooperation?

In seeking to understand international interactions and the demand by governments for institutions and regimes, rational-choice theorists have relied heavily over the years on insights drawn from observation of the PDG, since that model seems to address several issues that are prevalent in world politics. Among those issues, the lack of credible commitment and, as a consequence, the temptation to "cheat" on agreements that have been reached are particularly harmful to the prospects for cooperative undertakings. From a normative perspective, therefore, the PDG suggests that improved information flows and iterated transactions among players are necessary to the achievement of mutually beneficial cooperation, and rational-choice theorists conceive of institutions as being critical to the provision of these services. In his contribution to this volume (chap. 5), Lloyd Gruber points to some of the serious limitations associated with this approach to the study of institutional design and maintenance.

Those who emphasize power politics, in contrast, focus instead on the distributive consequences of international cooperative schemes. Far from viewing international agreements as necessarily efficiency-enhancing, they view them instead as reflections of the distribution of compulsory power in a given issue area. Powerful states determine the rules of the game, who gets to play, "and, ultimately, who wins and who loses" (Krasner, 1991: 366). The primary function of international institutions, from this perspective, is to legitimate and codify the preferences and interests of those actors who possess compulsory power.

From a modeling perspective, power-oriented theorists rely heavily on the Battle of the Sexes Game as a framework for understanding world politics. In the Battle of the Sexes, multiple equilibria are possible and therefore the main problem to be addressed, according to Stephen Krasner, is the one of "which point" along the Pareto "frontier will be chosen" (ibid.: 340). The exercise of compulsory power is central to that decision and to the distributive outcomes that follow in its wake. In short, the governments of powerful states choose the point that advances their particular interests, whether defined in economic or security terms.

To date, students of international institutions, no matter their theoretical orientation, have made surprisingly little use of the UG, which has also been extensively tested by experimental economists. Under the one-shot UG, a Proposer (P) and a Respondent (R) have the opportunity to divide a sum of money. P makes an offer to R, who can either accept it or reject it. If R accepts the offer, P and R divide the money according to P's proposal. If R rejects the offer, however, both P and R must walk away from the table empty-handed, so that neither of them wins any money at all.

The rational-actor model of world politics would lead us to predict that P would make R a distributive offer of, say, 99/1; that is, P would offer R 1 unit, while keeping 99 units for herself. For the rational actor in this one-shot game, 1 > 0 so both P and R are made better off even by this "egoistic" division.

But experimental economists, repeating the UG in a variety of countries and under a variety of conditions, have observed a puzzling result. Time and again they find that Rs reject such one-sided offers when they are made, and that, in fact, Ps rarely make such offers to begin with. When the one-shot UG is played, it is more likely than not that P will offer R something like a 60/40 split; indeed, Rs will rarely accept proposals that are below 60/40, suggesting that they prefer nothing at all to a division they consider to be "unfair."[3]

Why do fairness considerations often trump material ones in game-theoretic settings? In players' minds, fairness is usually linked to three central or core concepts: *reciprocity*, *equity*, and *legitimacy*. At bottom, to act "fairly" towards someone is to behave in a way that you hope would be reciprocated were circumstances reversed. The puzzle is why a player would "reciprocate" even in a one-shot interaction, as do most players of the UG, who tend to offer 60/40 splits even when, as we have seen, the "rational" split would be 99/1. The answer seems to be that reciprocity reflects a social norm that is widespread in the human and many other animal species.[4] One reason might be because it represents a form of insurance or risk-sharing. That is to say, if I behave kindly to you when you are hungry, and share some of my food with you, perhaps you will do the same for me should the situation reverse.

At the same time, empirical studies in game settings have demonstrated that some individual subjects – both human and animal – are more "reciprocally minded" than others. An interesting research question at the present time is how and why the traits of these reciprocally minded individuals become dominant within a species. An analogous question might be raised of international cooperation as well; viz., are some states more "reciprocally minded" than others (e.g., democracies, which domestically rely heavily on the reciprocity principle)? This question suggests that institutions may be viewed as mechanisms for linking "reciprocity-minded" agents, and perhaps as instruments for ensuring that cooperation within the group will continue to obtain should a reciprocity-minded individual be replaced or deposed by one who is more "egoistic." Again, this idea finds resonance in Lloyd Gruber's chapter (chap. 5, this volume), in which he discusses the design of the European Monetary System.

[3] For a useful review of the literature, see Fehr and Gachter, 2000.
[4] An alternative approach emphasizes reputational concerns. Thus, if I am "soft" in negotiations with you and accept an "unfair" share, then my negotiating stance will become widely known and I will always receive a small payoff. It may be better to act tough, even at the cost of forgoing an agreement today, so that my reputation precedes me in future.

Fairness and equity are similarly linked in players' minds. Indeed, according to economist Robert Frank, "A fair transaction as one in which the surplus is divided (approximately) equally" (1988: 165). Agents begin their bargaining over how to divide a pie with the premise of equal shares; it is deviations from equality that must be explained and justified.

In thinking about this relationship between fairness and equity, consider an example drawn from the financing of international institutions. In most cases, national contributions to these organizations are based on the share of the total gross product represented by each member state. If the United States' economy, for example, represents 25 percent of the gross product of, say, that of the membership of the United Nations, then it is commonly held that Washington should contribute one-quarter of the UN's operating budget. Note that the financing decision is *not* based on the expected utility that a state may be expected to gain from institutional membership. Since the United States, for example, arguably gets less utility from its UN membership than, say, Syria does, perhaps Syria should pay more for its membership. But, for some reason, expected utility is not considered an equitable method for assessing contributory support.

Finally, there is a link between fairness and the legitimacy of social arrangements and institutions.[5] An electoral system, for example, can claim that it is fair only when it accurately reflects and records the preferences of each voter: thus the battle between Al Gore and George W. Bush over Florida's voting results following the 2000 presidential election. The very legitimacy of that election was questioned due to the confusing nature of the Florida ballot and its mishandling by several thousand voters, which led to their ballots not being counted at all. An electoral system which effectively denies the vote to a particular group, or which is corrupted by the counting of false ballots, will likely come into question, and eventually pressures for reform will accumulate.

This type of legitimacy is really procedural in its orientation. But issues of distributive or substantive legitimacy also arise in the context of procedural fairness. To take an electoral example again, one of the most devilish problems that confronted the founders of the American republic was how to give each state in the newly created union a fair voice in the Congress. If the constitution was viewed by the smaller states as being unfair to their interests, then it would have had no chance of

---

[5] I thank Michael Barnett for highlighting this point.

approval by them. The founders responded to this challenge, of course, by devising a bicameral legislature with different numbers of representatives assigned to each state in the House as a function of their population, but with identical representation in the Senate. The great powers, Massachusetts and Virginia, had to accept this political compromise if the union they both desired was to come into being at all.

This distinction between procedural and distributive legitimacy is relevant to international organizations as well. Returning to the United Nations, there are well-established procedures for calling a Security Council meeting to discuss and debate responses to particular international crises. It is rare, however, for the council to reach a consensus on the use of force to meet a crisis, thus forcing individual members to determine whether they will act unilaterally or as part of a coalition of the willing. These unilateral actions, in turn, undermine the Security Council's very mandate of safeguarding world peace through collective security. Thus, even though the council's procedures may have been followed to the letter, those procedures often leave unresolved the issue of how the international community should meet the particular crisis at hand – especially of who should bear the military burden, and under what conditions. Clearly, there is often a mismatch between the UN's procedures and the outcomes that it seeks to achieve, between its procedural and its substantive or distributive justice.

As I will show in this chapter, there are sound, rational reasons for states to incorporate considerations of fairness into the design of international institutions – considerations which respond to state demands for reciprocity, equitable treatment, and procedural and distributive legitimacy. From a game-theoretic perspective, I will argue that the concern with fairness arises from the stochastic nature of world politics: that is, from the uncertainties that world politics engenders. That is certainly true with respect to, say, the terms of trade. Stochastic shocks make predictions about the future terms of trade near-impossible, and this uncertainty may well play a role in shaping multilateral agreements that all members view as being more or less fair.

But considerations of fairness also reflect the exercise of compulsory and institutional power. Power and fairness need not be in opposition; to the contrary, they are best viewed as mutually reinforcing. Thus, powerful actors will advance particular definitions of fairness as a way of protecting from attack their own conception of what constitutes an equitable and legitimate social arrangement, with "free-trade" policies providing a prime example from the global economic realm. In that way, fairness contributes directly to the maintenance of the status quo regime.

Yet power and fairness may also subvert one another.[6] As already suggested, great powers may often act in ways that weaker actors view as being "unfair," and this disjunction between norms and deeds can slowly work to erode institutional structures. At the same time, by respecting norms of fairness, those who wield compulsory power may find themselves losing some ground to new actors. It is in this murky space between power and fairness that institutions must struggle to survive.

Fairness, uncertainty, and institutional design

The international environment poses risks and uncertainties to states in both the economic and security realms.[7] Governments cope with that uncertainty through self-help mechanisms of various kinds, and by joining together in international institutions which can act as insurance agencies. The multilateral trading system, for example, provides each state with insurance against the unraveling of any single bilateral arrangement; thus, if a state loses, for whatever reason, one of its trading partners, it has many others it can turn to without having to negotiate new agreements each and every time a crisis hits. Uncertainty and risk therefore cast a shadow over institutional design.

The international relations literature asserts that risk and uncertainty may be mitigated by improved information flows, and therefore that a key role of international institutions is to provide states with information about what others are doing. When trade agreements are bilateral, State A must always worry about the potentially more favorable deals that State B has struck with States X, Y, and Z. In a multilateral setting, whereby states agree to common trade policies and share information about their imports, exports, tariffs, and quotas, the likelihood of "beggar-thy-neighbor" trade wars is decreased.

Institutions also contribute to risk mitigation by lengthening the shadow of the future, providing the foundation on which one-shot transactions are transformed into long-term relationships on the basis of reciprocity.[8] Traditionally, international agreements have relied heavily

---

[6] I thank Raymond Duvall for highlighting this point.
[7] The distinction I make in using these terms is that we can assign a probability to risk, but not to uncertainty.
[8] For a more elaborate rationalist theory of institutional design, see the special issue of *International Organization* 55, 4 (Autumn 2001), on "The Rational Design of International Institutions."

upon what Robert Keohane has called "specific reciprocity," referring to "situations in which specified partners exchange items of equivalent value in a strictly delimited sequence" (1986: 4). In trade negotiations, for example, countries offer up tariff concessions of equal value in the quest for a deal. The game-theoretic strategy of "tit-for-tat" provides an example of specific reciprocity, and its power in promoting cooperative outcomes should not be underestimated.

As Robert Axelrod demonstrated in *The Evolution of Cooperation* (1984), tit-for-tat maximizes payoffs to the players in an iterated as opposed to one-shot Prisoner's Dilemma Game. Since trading relations are likely to be iterated, specific reciprocity would appear to be a sound strategy for the players to adopt. In practice, it figures prominently in the international trade regime that is institutionalized within the World Trade Organization (WTO).

But cooperation based solely on the norm of specific reciprocity should not be confused with an international arrangement that all players will consider to be just or fair or of mutual advantage. As Keohane has written, "Because reciprocity implies returning ill for ill as well as good for good, its moral status is ambiguous" (1986: 10). An equivalent nuclear exchange may provide a good example of specific reciprocity, but it could hardly be considered an arrangement of mutual advantage.

Further, and of greater consequence from my perspective, equivalent exchange may simply be unfair in a world of unequal state actors. Imagine a trade regime based only on specific reciprocity. Country A will offer up, say, $100 million of tariff reductions to its trading partners in the WTO if Countries B, C, and D do the same. But if Country A is, for example, the United States of America, and Country B is Bangladesh, specific reciprocity will either fail as a formula or provide fewer benefits to each party than would be the case under an alternative arrangement.

Instead, fairness will dictate that each party make trade concessions on the basis of its economic capability, so that A makes $100 million of trade concessions while it accepts at the same time B's offer of $25 million in tariff reductions. Following Keohane, I call that alternative approach to negotiation "diffuse reciprocity." In the multilateral trade rounds, it is generally known as "relaxed reciprocity," or the provision of unequal benefits to, say, developing countries. As Keohane writes, under "diffuse reciprocity . . . the definition of equivalence is less precise, one's partners may be viewed as a group rather than as particular actors, and the sequence of events is less narrowly bounded. Obligations are important. *Diffuse reciprocity involves conforming to generally accepted standards of behavior"* (ibid.: 4; emphasis added).

Why would great powers adopt a policy of diffuse or relaxed reciprocity in which they provide a level of benefits to smaller, weaker states that may not be returned in full? From a rationalist perspective, the answer is because the resulting international structure is likely to be more robust as a result.[9] As Donald Puchala and Raymond Hopkins have written, "The degree of bias may make a considerable difference in a regime's durability... 'Fairer' regimes are likely to last longer, as are those that call for side payments to disadvantaged participants.... Furthermore, it can make a difference whether the norms of a regime permit movement between the ranks of the advantaged and disadvantaged" (1981: 66).

Legal theorists Francesco Parisi and Nita Ghei provide, from a game-theoretic perspective, some important reasons why a norm of diffuse reciprocity is likely to provide a more stable basis for cooperation. They examine a game setting in which players "undertake repeated transactions in a stochastic game" (n.d.: 23). What this means is that there is an element of randomness attached to possible outcomes, or "role reversal" in which, say, State A might be a winner in one round of play but a loser in a subsequent round. They label the strategic relationship between the actors under this condition of randomness one of "stochastic reciprocity," though they define this term in the same way as I have treated diffuse reciprocity.

Under the condition of diffuse reciprocity, we must imagine a number of states that have multiple interactions over time, and across a wide range of issues. States will be strong in some issue areas and weak in others; certain about the distributive consequences of some agreements, uncertain about others; confident that the terms of trade will be to their benefit in certain periods, but will go against them in others. *It is notable that international trade exhibits these very characteristics;* the terms of trade may very well shift from one period to the next, favoring Country A at one point in time and Country B at another. As a consequence, the gains from trade are uncertain. Economic growth rates are also suggestive of role reversal, or the possibility that one country's growth will exceed

---

[9] To be sure, one could also fashion an argument based on altruism, by trying to demonstrate that decision-makers adopt a policy of diffuse reciprocity because they believe it is the "right" thing to do.

another's in different periods. In short, over time and across issue areas, the economic system is characterized by a fair degree of randomness as to which states will emerge as winners and which as losers.

Under these stochastic or random conditions, "A high probability of future interaction is more likely to increase the expected payoff from cooperation" (ibid.). This is a critical finding, for imagine a state that breaks off its commercial relations with its trading partners every time the terms of trade turn against it. That sort of "rational," short-term maximization behavior would quickly lead to the collapse of trading arrangements. By designing a system that helps stabilize trade expectations in the presence of stochastic shocks, commercial relations can be maintained to the *long-run* benefit of both parties.[10]

This point is worth emphasizing as it has received little attention in the trade policy literature. In theory, a state could maximize its welfare by renegotiating trade deals whenever the terms of trade were in its favor; in short, it could act to extract rents from the system. But trade agreements tend to be longstanding and based on such sticky normative concepts as "most-favored-nation" status, and the question is: why is that the case? The hypothesis I am advancing here is that uncertainty about the terms of trade encourages negotiators to strike a bargain that each of them views as being fair over the long run.

If the threat of role reversal seems farfetched as a causal driver in international relations, perhaps another way to think of stochastic reciprocity is in terms of insurance or risk-sharing. Just as individuals seek insurance or risk-sharing mechanisms to tide them over when a crisis strikes, so states seek such devices in the forms of military alliances, customs unions, and trade agreements. And by institutionalizing such arrangements and making it costly to escape from them, the insurance or risk-sharing qualities are greatly enhanced.

Iteration and diffuse reciprocity are thus likely to yield more benefits to each player than the noncooperative alternatives. Stochastic reciprocity suggests that "an agent cooperates, not in expectation of a specific reciprocal reward, but some general reciprocal return in the future" (ibid. 24). Keohane recognized a similar possibility when he asserted: "States in reciprocal relationships with one another often do not have identical obligations" (1986: 8).

---

[10] I again emphasize that the long-term nature of these arrangements would seem to challenge some of the assumptions that inform modern political economy theory, which features rent-seeking (or vote-maximizing) politicians.

Now an environment in which stochastic shocks may cause role reversal reminds us of John Rawls's "original position," or model of decision-making with respect to the social contract. It will be recalled that Rawls's original position imagines a group of representative individuals who meet from behind a veil of ignorance, knowing only that they are expected to create enduring principles for their social interactions and institutions. These representative individuals may be expected to reach agreements in the collective interest because they imagine the changing life circumstances that could confront them or their children; in short, they must imagine the possibility of role reversal, whereby a healthy person becomes ill, a rich person becomes poor. Keohane does not cite Rawls but makes a similar point when he writes of cooperation under diffuse reciprocity, "In such international regimes, actors recognize that a 'veil of ignorance' separates them from the future but nevertheless offer benefits to others on the assumption that they will redound to their own advantage in the end." (ibid.: 23).

The concept of diffuse reciprocity, of unequal exchange, is also consistent with Rawls's "difference principle," or the notion that just societies should maximize the life chances of those who are least advantaged. As Rawls says of this principle, it "expresses a conception of reciprocity. It is a principle of mutual benefit . . . The social order can be justified to everyone, and in particular to those who are least favored; and in this sense it is egalitarian" (1971: 102–03). Similarly, the concept of reciprocity in the global economy must be one that takes into account the resources and capabilities of each and every state, including those that are least advantaged.

Keohane stresses that unbalanced economic relations need not provide "an unsatisfactory basis for long-term relationships." In support of this view he cites the work of anthropologist Marshall Sahlins, who has shown that among "primitive" tribes "a measure of imbalance sustains the trade partnership, compelling as it does another meeting" (cited in 1984: 129). Keohane suggests "In the world political economy, international regimes make temporary imbalances feasible, since they create incentives (in the form partly of obligations) to repay debts" (ibid.). Again, it is *both* the *iterated* and *reciprocal* nature of the social arrangement that helps promote rules and outcomes that are viewed as just by the trade regime's participants.

Nations that interact on the basis of diffuse reciprocity, and that view their transactions as being repeated or iterated, will enjoy a much wider scope for mutually beneficial international cooperation (Axelrod, 1984). But, as already noted, great powers can often do well in the absence of fairness considerations, by simply extracting rents or tribute from the international system. In trade policy, for example, a large country can make "a take it or leave it offer to the other (small) country, taking all the gains from trade" for itself (Eaton, 2003: 1). The United States, for example, was certainly in that position after World War II, but it did not adopt an optimal-tariff or a take-it-or-leave-it trade policy. Instead, it sought to create a multilateral, rule-based trade regime. Why did it do so? It is to this puzzling relationship between power and fairness that we now turn.

Power, fairness, and the international trade regime

Traditionally, the discourse of power and the discourse of fairness have rarely been joined in the international relations literature; instead, they are usually seen as being in opposition. Thus, states that possess compulsory power exploit weaker states, while monopolistic firms abuse their customers. The strong do what they will; the weak suffer what they must. In such renderings, there is no evident role for fairness.

But considerations of fairness can contribute to the maintenance of given systems of compulsory and institutional power. This assertion is borne out by empirical evidence from recent international trade negotiations. Surprisingly, neither the United States nor the European Union have exploited their compulsory power in trade to extract *all* the rents that they can from the international system, and more particularly from developing countries. To the contrary, it appears that the concept of diffuse or relaxed reciprocity *has* played a role in shaping the international trade regime, if less completely than one would wish if that arrangement were to be accepted as being fair or just to all states. Again, I do not wish to argue that the international economy is fair or just, but more modestly that considerations of fairness have influenced many of the institutional arrangements that now govern international transactions.

For example, in a path-breaking paper, Kenneth Chan (1985) sought to explain the results of the Tokyo Round of trade negotiations that took place between 1973 and 1979. He hypothesized that a trade round could reflect *efficiency* concerns, in which the objective of the negotiators is to maximize global output, or what he called *egalitarian* or *equity* concerns, in which the countries sought an agreement which each of them considers to be fair. He contrasted several different proposals to the multilateral forum, from the US proposal, which was most "efficient" in terms of tariff reductions, to the Swiss proposal, which was most "fair," as defined in terms of concessions that each member state would have to give. Based upon his empirical analysis of the completed trade round, he concluded that "the major determinant" of the agreement that was reached – the Swiss proposal – was "the *egalitarian* nature of the solution" (ibid.: 463; emphasis in original).

"Why," Chan asked, "are *egalitarian* considerations so important in international negotiation? A plausible explanation is that each player has (roughly) equal destructive power. Each player could easily develop an opposing 'Force,' by joining forces with some dissatisfied developing countries (or small developed countries) who were left on the 'periphery' of the negotiation" (ibid.).

Chan's argument brings power and fairness together in the context of the trade agreement. The trading system is designed in such a way as to give each state some influence over the proceedings. That provides it with at least procedural legitimacy, and in so doing helps ensure the robustness of the regime which, after all, is hugely beneficial to the most powerful states. The "price" the powerful states pay – that of giving each participant a "vote" – is small compared to having a relatively open global economy at work. At the same time, those voting rights ensure an agreement that is neither efficient nor purely mercantilist, but reflects the interests of each and every negotiating party, at least to some small degree.

This finding must pose a puzzle to theorists like Andrew Hurrell, who reject the notion that great powers, like the United States, might restrain their own capacity to gather monopoly rents in the interest of long-term stability – though admittedly this poses an interesting question from the political economy perspective, in which politicians are modeled as short-term maximizers. Hurrell writes that "The degree of US power is so great that it does not need to make concessions or to self-bind in order to prevent even major developing countries from shifting to more oppositional policies" (chap. 2, this volume: 46). But this overlooks the possibility that great powers might sometimes wish to "buy options" that help provide insurance against system instability, if the price of that option is relatively low. By giving up some power over the trading system, the United States helps to maintain a structure that operates in its interest. The central point is that fairness considerations help to strengthen institutional power.[11]

Chan also notes that the "egalitarian spirit" was reflected in the Tokyo Round declaration which states, "To this end, co-ordinated efforts shall be made to solve in an equitable way the trade problems of all participating countries . . . The negotiations shall be conducted on the basis of the principles of mutual advantage, mutual commitment and overall reciprocity" (cited in Chan, 1985: 464). It is notable that the phrase "overall" reciprocity was used rather than "specific" reciprocity, to reflect the notion that the trade round's definition of reciprocity could be understood only in terms of the varying capacities of states to offer up meaningful concessions (that is, liberalization measures) over market access.

In a similar exercise, J. Michael Finger and his World Bank colleagues sought to understand the outcomes of bargaining in the Uruguay Round. They hypothesized that states would adopt a negotiating posture shaped by the exigencies of domestic political economy, or what they call a mercantilist bargaining model, in which each state seeks to maximize *its* own economic benefit. They then evaluated this hypothesis against the actual pattern of tariff reductions that occurred. Again, like Chan, they found that the negotiation was powerfully shaped by "a sense of fairness, of appropriate contribution" (Finger, Reincke, and Castro, 1999: 7). In their interviews with trade negotiations, the concept of fairness that emerged was one of "sacrifice for the common good," in which industrial countries cut their tariffs by significantly more than the amount demanded of developing countries.

To be sure, in neither the Tokyo nor the Uruguay Rounds did the negotiating parties, including the advanced industrial countries, adopt a principle of free trade, nor can the final agreements be viewed as "fair" from the perspective of most abstract theories of distributive justice. To the contrary, commentators have argued that the Final Act of the Uruguay Round was "unfairly asymmetrical, especially in the leniency with which it treated agricultural and textile and clothing protection by developed countries" (McCulloch, Winters, and Cirera, 2001: 168). Industrial countries continue to maintain high tariff walls, quotas, and non-tariff barriers against the exports of the less developed economies, mainly in agriculture and textiles, and this can hardly be considered as an arrangement of mutual advantage.

---

[11] I thank Raymond Duvall for highlighting this point.

Further, to the extent that specific reciprocity based on equivalent exchange still forms the hard core of the trade liberalization process between the United States and the European Union, developing countries must continue to remain marginalized. As a result, studies of the Uruguay Round found that "developed countries will receive the lion's share of the welfare gains generated by the trade barrier reductions" (Harrison, Rutherford, and Tarr, 1995: 242). The Uruguay Round also included an Agreement on Trade-Related Aspects of Intellectual Property Rights (TRIPS) which many observers have condemned as being unfair to developing countries.

Overall, therefore, it would be difficult to defend the "rules-based" international trade regime as one that is just to all participating states; compulsory power and mercantile interests continue to drive the multilateral negotiations. But *ideas* of fairness, in the specific form of diffuse reciprocity, have animated and even influenced trade talks in surprising ways, and continue to do so. The idea that developed countries should give up more in the way of trade concessions to developing countries than they receive from them has remarkable durability, and despite the collapse of the trade talks at Cancun it still shapes the current "Doha Development Round." To the extent that the United States and European Union continue to protect and subsidize their agriculture, such actions are now widely seen as being "unfair" to poor countries that need market access in that area in order to grow. In the following section, I speculate on why it is these fairness considerations have come to play the role they do in contemporary international life.

Economic fairness and hegemonic power

If only to a minor degree, ideas of fairness have shaped and are shaping cooperative arrangements among nation-states. This is largely for instrumental reasons, in that considerations of fairness are necessary to the realization of a more durable and robust world order. An economic system that is patently unfair and unjust will be one that encourages rebellion. Knowing this, powerful states will engage in economic relations with weaker ones based on the norm of diffuse reciprocity.

Ideas of fairness therefore cast a shadow over international economic arrangements, however modest, however fleeting. These ideas have left a "residual" on the global economy that is not readily explained by reference to the distribution of compulsory power, efficiency concerns, or the influence of special-interest groups. But what are the sources of those ideas? Why is fairness discourse so prevalent in international economic relations today, when it was much less prominent in decades past?

An obvious place to begin the search for an answer is in the ideas and policies of the dominant power that led in creating many of the international institutions that now characterize the global economic and security environment, the United States. While realist theory can help illuminate the background conditions that prompted Washington to play a leadership role after World War II, it does less well in explaining the specific content of the policies it adopted. In recent years, however, a growing number of scholars have sought to explain the *ideas* that informed American policymakers as they sought to shape the postwar world. The fact that Washington devoted so much time and energy to the building of international institutions during the 1940s is one of the reasons why the ideational sources of policy have risen to the fore as a topic of research.

As G. John Ikenberry and Charles Kupchan have written of the American hegemonic project, "During World War II and its immediate aftermath, the United States articulated a remarkably elaborate set of norms and principles to guide the construction of a postwar international order . . . these norms represented a vision of political and economic order organized around a vision of liberal multilateralism. In the political realm, great power cooperation . . . would replace balance-of-power politics. In the economic realm, a system of liberal, nondiscriminatory trade and finance . . . would be established . . . *the exercise of US hegemonic power involved the projection of a set of norms and their embrace by elites in other nations*" (1990: 300; emphasis added).

But what were the specific sources of those norms? Following such scholars as Louis Hartz (1948) and Robert Packenham (1973), one might argue that they were drawn from America's own mythical past – its own narration of how the United States managed the process of political and economic development without the sort of social disruption that characterized European polities. In this version of history, the United States did so in part by creating a level playing field which enabled every citizen to realize his or her talents and ambitions, no matter their starting position.

From this perspective, the issue that policymakers therefore faced following the end of World War II was how to inject this domestic system of cooperation into the international system if a peaceful and prosperous order was to be established. One instrument that seemed most useful from that perspective was free trade. In terms of economic theory at least, free trade enables every country to exercise its comparative advantage and, in so doing, to join the world's long-run average growth rate. And from the standpoint of political philosophy, it had been argued ever since Montesquieu and Kant that free trade promoted peaceful relations among nations. In an important sense, free trade abroad was Washington's answer to the philosophy (if not practice) of equal opportunity at home: a policy that enabled every state to advance its own economic and security objectives.

To be sure, in promoting this "free-trade" policy, the United States has underplayed the fact that the existing rules that actually structure these arrangements often act to the detriment of developing countries, for example by maintaining tariff barriers against their exports of agriculture and textiles, or by making it costly for them to take advantage of the dispute settlement procedures that have been established. Washington has provided the discourse of international liberalism but not necessarily the substance, as its own markets remain protected across many product lines.

Furthermore, an explanation for the presence of fairness considerations in trade agreements that is grounded on American "values" confronts another, historical, difficulty, and that is the relative absence of these concerns – at least toward the developing countries – in the original, postwar design of the free-trade regime, embodied in the General Agreement on Tariffs and Trade (GATT). As already noted, the GATT was grounded on the mercantilist principle of strict reciprocity, in which concessions delivered by Country A had to be matched by Country B if a bargain was to be reached between them. That method tended to marginalize small countries in the multilateral trade rounds, particularly those from the developing world that lacked a customs union like the European Community to negotiate on their collective behalf. It is only recently, particularly since the Uruguay Round of trade talks in the 1980s, that developing country concerns have risen high on the trade agenda. This suggests the intriguing possibility of a normative change, a change in the very meaning of the objectives that the trade regime is supposed to serve. If that is the case, further research on the causes of that normative change are clearly needed.[12] Is it a reflection of growing developing world power? Do the industrial countries fear that the structure they have created may be threatened by the rise of these new

---

[12] A useful model is provided by Finnemore, 1996.

actors? Or is the world becoming more "cosmopolitan" in its normative orientation, perhaps due to the spread of democracy since the end of the Cold War?

Whatever the ultimate sources, it is certainly tempting to argue that the concepts of fairness that we observe today at work in the international economy – for example, the concept of a rules-based, free-trade regime grounded on the liberalization principle of diffuse reciprocity – are, at bottom, manifestations of the power, interests, and values of the world's dominant power. But does that necessarily mean that Washington's approach to fairness in the global economy is necessarily illegitimate from the perspective of other capitals? To put this in other words, could it be that the United States has identified an approach to institutional design that each member state accepts has involved considerations of fairness from *its* own national perspective? Is there something like an overlapping consensus in international society, no matter how thin that might be, with respect to what a fair economic order might look like?

In fact, the brilliance of the United States' international order might be found, as John Ikenberry (2001a) has so eloquently argued, in its quasi-constitutional structure. Unlike systems built on raw compulsory power, the United States has generally shielded its material interests behind an ideological cloak of justice and fairness. It has created institutions in which all member states have at least some political voice. It has listened to and considered their views, so long as those views expressed support for the basic structures of economic life. And it should not be forgotten that, versus at least some of the alternatives – say a Soviet- or Nazi-led world order – that system has been a generous one in important respects.

But I opened this chapter by asserting that fairness was crucial to the robustness of the basic structures that constitute international relations. Institutions that are deemed to be unfair to their member states will not stand. In a bipolar era, when the United States faced an immediate military threat to its survival, the incentives for the United States to promote fairness in institutional design may have been greater than they are today. Can the United States be powerful and fair at the same time? Is the postwar order threatened by the existence of a unipolar power?

That question is at the heart of many of the contemporary disputes between Washington and its friends and allies, whether the controversies be over trade policy, the environment, or the pursuit of national security. The United States, which played the leading role in the creation of a "rules-based" international system after World War II, now seems all too quick to abandon it when unilateral solutions appear at hand. That approach to world politics is fraught with unnecessary risk.

If fairness demands anything at the present time, it is that Washington negotiate with its partners in the context of the regimes it once helped to establish. That policy would not be driven by altruistic motives. Without fairness considerations firmly in place to harness and restrain the constant exercise of compulsory power, there can be no durable global governance. Self-styled realists, both in government and the academy alike, need to acknowledge that there *is* power in the pursuit of fairness.

5 Power politics and the institutionalization of international relations

Lloyd Gruber

This chapter lays out the core elements of a new "power-politics" theory of institutional design. The theory shares the neoliberal premise that (some) international institutions really do matter, in the sense of playing a more-than-trivial role in sustaining long-term cooperation among self-interested states. It also recognizes the importance of grounding the study of institutions, even epiphenomenal ones, in rational-choice foundations. Yet whereas many of our existing institutionalist models view the institution-building process as a collective endeavor, the reality – and the starting point for the broader power-politics model sketched out here – is that some participants in this process wield disproportionate influence over the final outcome. While everyone in the collectivity may be taken into account to some degree, there is no reason to suppose everyone will be taken into account to the *same* degree. The preferences expressed by those participants who are the least unhappy with the non-institutionalized status quo – or who, like the architects of the European monetary regime that forms the centerpiece of this chapter's empirical discussion, have the capacity to remove that status quo from the set of feasible alternatives – will almost certainly carry greater weight. That being the case, institutionalist scholars would do well to focus their analytical attention on the distinctive problems and dilemmas confronting these pivotal actors.

And, indeed, logic suggests that the kinds of problems and dilemmas confronting these more powerful actors *would* be distinctive. Of

For their helpful comments and suggestions on earlier drafts of this chapter, I would like to thank Delia Boylan, James Caporaso, Andrew Cortell, Jeffry Frieden, Geoffrey Garrett, Charles Glaser, Peter Hall, Miles Kahler, Richard Locke, Lisa Martin, Terry Moe, Thomas Oatley, Kenneth Oye, Beth Simmons, Duncan Snidal, and especially Michael Barnett and Bud Duvall.

particular concern to this pivotal subgroup – the members of the enacting coalition – would be the emergence of new actors who dislike their new cooperative arrangement (at least in its present configuration) and who might even want to destroy it. Though one can assume the enactors would benefit from the institutions they established, those same institutions might not look so beneficial to the governing officials who assume office after the prime movers have left the political stage.

The fact that an institution need not be conducive to the interests of all of its members presents the original coalition of beneficiaries with a particularly challenging institutional design task. For now, rather than merely deterring opportunists or establishing focal points, the institutional structures devised by the "winners" must reduce the natural inclination of regime opponents to sabotage these structures (or redirect them toward very different purposes) should they, the "losers," ever find themselves in a position to do so.

Which kinds of cooperative arrangements and institutions would meet these criteria? The answer offered here is straightforward: the kinds of structures most likely to survive a loser's coming to power are those that explicitly allow for subsequent revisions in the initial rules of the game – albeit with the proviso that these be determined not *unilaterally*, with each member government deciding for itself how to interpret the relevant articles or provisions, but *supranationally*, through negotiations that take place in accordance with a well-defined set of collective decision-making principles and procedures. Insofar as supranational regimes of this kind are becoming more prevalent, it is because they are attractive to the winners who engineer them. And the reason they are attractive – an important, if not the sole, appeal of these regimes' relatively flexible institutional structures – is that they help mitigate the regime losers' destructive ambitions. The losers still lose, but they are not as disgruntled as they would have been in a less accommodating, more rigid institutional system. As for the winners, the short-term gains they enjoy are lower – they are appeasing their opponents, after all – but the durability of their new arrangements more than compensates for this reduction, ensuring that the institution-building enterprise continues to produce what is, for the prime movers at least, a positive net payoff.

Of direct relevance here are arguments dating back to the 1950s and 1960s about the exercise of influence through agenda control. As was noted in the introduction to this volume, an important contribution to that earlier debate was the simple – in retrospect, too simple – definition of power put forward by Robert Dahl in his famous 1957 article, "The Concept of Power." Actor A exercises power over Actor B, explained Dahl, to the extent that A succeeds in getting B to do something that B would not otherwise do. Attention immediately turned to the question of *means*: how, exactly, does A pull this off?

On one side of the debate were early proponents of pluralist theory, including Dahl himself. At the risk of oversimplification, pluralists held that the key to A's getting B to alter its behavior was A's greater ability to mobilize a coalition in support of its preferred policy alternatives and, in so doing, obtain their passage into law. Other scholars criticized pluralists like Dahl for concentrating exclusively upon A's ability to defeat B in head-to-head contests between each other's preferred alternatives. The best-known argument for broadening Dahl's conception of power remains that of Peter Bachrach and Morton Baratz (1962). According to Bachrach and Baratz, a less visible, but no less pervasive, way of exercising influence is for A to deny B the opportunity to vote for alternatives that would undermine A's interests were they to be adopted:

> Of course power is exercised when A participates in the making of decisions that affect B. But power is also exercised when A devotes his energies to creating or reinforcing social and political values and institutional practices that limit the scope of the political process to public consideration of only those issues which are comparatively innocuous to A. To the extent that A succeeds in doing this, B is prevented, for all practical purposes, from bringing to the fore any issues that might in their resolution be seriously detrimental to A's set of preferences.
>
> (1962: 948)

In raising the possibility that certain political actors may be able to exert their will indirectly, without resort to legislative victories or coercive threats, the model of power set forth in this chapter bears a strong resemblance to the notion of agenda control elaborated by Bachrach and Baratz. Here, the As are the governments that make up a new institution's enacting coalition and the Bs – the actors for whom these governments set the agenda – are the regime's other founding members (at the beginning of the process) as well as these members' and the enactors' domestic successors (as the action moves into the future). In both the initial and later stages of the institution's life cycle, the enactors' power is "diffuse," placing it squarely in the second column of

Barnett and Duvall's power matrix (table 1.1, p. 12). This diffuseness is most apparent in the ex-post stage, where the initial prime movers' agenda powers constrain the behavior of everyone's political heirs. The As cannot exert direct pressure against these future Bs – as much as they would like to – because the As are not around to do the pressuring. Yet even in the initial stages of the institution-building process (when the As *are* around), the prime movers' powers are still more likely to be diffuse than direct. Efforts to exercise direct leverage in the Barnett–Duvall sense of "compulsory power" typically impose high costs on the compeller and compellee alike and are thus riddled with credibility problems. Rather than applying direct pressure and dealing with these problems, an A who wants to alter the behavior of a B is far more likely to engage in indirect methods, chiefly, as I elaborate below, those involving the manipulation of B's choice set. Being indirect, these methods leave it to B to decide how to respond, and so B's decision, though limited to a circumscribed set of options, remains strictly voluntary. Governments excluded from the original enacting coalition might wish that the coalition had proposed a less biased set of institutions, but these governments – the Bs – still *choose* to participate in these arrangements. Power is exercised, but no one's hands are tied.

Nor is anyone subjected to brainwashing or indoctrination. Those in positions of power would certainly like to influence the underlying preferences of their opponents. This sort of activity – "creating or reinforcing social and political values," as Bachrach and Baratz put it in the passage quoted above (see also Baumgartner and Burns 1975; Gaventa 1980; Lukes 1974) – is never easy, though, and is unlikely to prove necessary in any case. When it comes to institution-building, the enactors can typically get what they want – a highly insulated governance arrangement – without transforming anyone's core preferences or identities. If the price of destroying a new governance structure is set high enough (and the cost of participating in it brought down low enough), a new institutional equilibrium can survive the coming to power of even the staunchest, most vociferously self-identifying regime opponent.

The fact that this opponent remains in the regime does not imply that it has been converted from a "loser" into a "winner." It may simply, and quite rationally, be choosing the least costly course of action available to it. The deeper question, of course, is why there are not more alternatives (e.g., the status quo) in the loser's choice set. And here again the answer suggested by my argument is perfectly compatible with Bachrach and

Baratz's larger claims about the strategic manipulation of the agenda.[1] Just as Bachrach and Baratz's voter is forced to choose between X and Y when it really prefers Z, here the enacting coalition's successors must choose between joining or opting out of an institution they never much liked and would never have created themselves had they been standing in the shoes of their predecessors. In both cases the loser's ultimate choice is rightly viewed as a function of actions taken by the winners: the losers see themselves as victims of a "power play." But the winners do not achieve their objectives through compulsory power. They neither outvote their opponents à la Dahl nor engage in the blatant acts of coercion and intimidation that so animate traditional realists. As the agenda-control literature reminds us, there are other, less transparent (but potentially no less effective) means of exerting power.

What do we call this kind of power? The right-hand column of table 1.1 (p. 12) suggests two possibilities. Diffuse (i.e., indirect) power relations can be "institutional" or they can be "productive." In what follows I emphasize the institutional dynamic, though this just pushes the argument back a step: what is institutional power? How does it work? How *well* does it work? Though pertaining to but one cell in the matrix, these are not easy questions. There are, it turns out, different types of institutional power. Bargaining power should be distinguished from what I have elsewhere termed "go-it-alone power," for example, and each in turn must be distinguished from the longer-lived power that accrues to the prime movers by virtue of the free hand they enjoy in designing (rigging?) new institutions. Distinctions of this sort should become clear as I proceed.[2] Suffice it to say that, even by itself, the upper right-hand cell of table 1.1 is a lot to tackle.

The remainder of this chapter is organized as follows. Section 2 takes a brief look at what other international relations scholars have had to say about recent institutional developments, and about the politics of institutional choice more generally. I then put forward my own perspective, one that flows directly out of the theoretical logic I have begun

---

[1] A similar argument underlies Marxist theories of exploitation (see, e.g., G. A. Cohen, 1979, and Elster, 1983). When workers submit to capitalist institutions, it is not because anyone holds a gun to their heads. It is because their employers exercise exclusive control over the resources necessary for human survival, a privilege they enjoy as a result of having earlier, and in some cases quite fortuitously, accumulated sufficient quantities of capital. For Marxists, workers are indeed better off selling their labor power, but that is only because the alternatives with which they are presented – unemployment, impoverishment, starvation – would be even worse.

[2] See Gruber, 2000 and 2001, for a more complete discussion.

fleshing out in this introductory discussion. Section 3 thus asks how the knowledge that a regional or multilateral regime may one day include a preponderance of members who do not believe they are benefiting from it[3] should be expected to influence the decision-making of the initial prime movers, the coalition of actors who, by virtue of their more powerful ex-ante positions, can dictate what form the regime initially takes. Might the threat posed by these (future) losers incline the original enactors toward more flexible, and hence more elaborate, institutional structures than they might otherwise want or prefer? And, if so, just how flexible must these structures be? In short, how might the choices of the prime movers be altered by the realization that the cooperative arrangements they are about to inaugurate will engender strong opposition, if not immediately, then at some point after they, the primary beneficiaries, have lost power domestically?

Section 4 uses my answers to these questions to shed new light on the origins and structures of the euro's institutional precursor, the European Monetary System (EMS). This brief case study singles out the French left as the EMS enemy most likely to bring about the regime's demise. It was not, in other words, an *external* enemy – Britain's anti-EMS Tories, for example – that most concerned the regime's Franco-German enacting coalition. It was an *internal* enemy – France's newly resurgent Socialist Party. Having identified the Socialists as the EMS loser whose potential to wreak havoc was of greatest concern to the regime's French and German enactors, I then show how these concerns can help us make sense of the latter's otherwise perplexing institutional choices. Had it not been for the growing threat posed by the Socialists, France's conservative president and his German counterpart would never have created the open-ended and inclusive monetary structure with which, in 1978, they endowed "their" EMS. Moving from the empirics back to the broader theoretical story, section 5 concludes.

Rationalist perspectives on supranational governance

Like other proponents of the new institutionalism, neoliberal theorists of international relations see the process of institutional choice as being

---

[3] Or who, while not necessarily favoring a return to the non-institutionalized status quo, would nonetheless prefer that the terms of institutional membership be revised in a direction more conducive to their own interests.

guided primarily by efficiency considerations, with groups of actors (for neoliberals, states or governments) struggling to choose whichever institutional forms will enable them most effectively to respond to market failures, mitigate collective-action problems, and generally further their common interests.[4] This line of analysis begins with the observation that certain policy objectives – even seemingly "domestic" ones like generating economic prosperity – are difficult for nations to achieve on their own. From this it is but a short step to the conclusion that, by acting in concert, national governments can significantly improve their collective welfare; if all make the necessary behavioral adjustments, all benefit. While these behavioral adjustments might not look so beneficial to outsiders, for those on the inside – for the cooperators themselves – the move to a coordinated outcome is assumed to afford Pareto-improving gains, leaving each participant at least as well off as it was under the previous, noncooperative status quo.

So far, so good. The problems come when cooperation fails to emerge spontaneously. Just as the fear of being exploited prevents the two prisoners in the Prisoners' Dilemma Game (PDG) from cooperating to lighten their sentences, so too, neoliberals argue, the fear of exploitation can prevent groups of nations from coordinating their policies in ways that could leave each of them unambiguously better off. To be sure, any nation that anticipated being "suckered" could threaten to retaliate against its partners should the envisaged cooperative gains fail to materialize. In principle, then, the expectation of future reprisals and loss of reputation could itself be sufficient to keep everyone in line (Axelrod, 1984; see also Michael Taylor, 1987). That's the good news. The bad news is that this Axelrodian path to cooperation can work only if each partner is able to distinguish the opportunistic behavior it seeks to deter from the cooperative behavior it wishes to encourage. This is where formal institutions enter the story.

The information argument

Of all those institutional functions that neoliberal theorists have identified as having a salutary effect on the prospects for cooperation, those involving the collection and distribution of information are usually considered the most important.[5] Why? Because it is only when actors are

---

[4] Representative works here include Abbott and Snidal, 1998, Keohane, 1984, and Moravcsik, 1998. For a realist critique, see Mearsheimer, 1994/95.
[5] See particularly Chayes and Chayes, 1993, Keohane, 1984, and Mitchell, 1994.

able to distinguish cheaters from cooperators that they can be expected to dole out punishments (to opportunists) and rewards (to fellow cooperators) appropriately.

It is fair to say that Axelrod initially underestimated the importance of these informational requirements. After conceding that "recognition and recall" are both critical to the success of collective action, his book *The Evolution of Cooperation* quickly dismisses their practical significance, noting that the informational demands of strategies like tit-for-tat, which "respond only to the recent behavior of the other player," are so limited that even bacteria can fulfill them. "And if bacteria can play games," writes Axelrod (1984: 174), "so can people and nations." But while its informational requirements may be lower than those of other strategies, even tit-for-tat requires that the players who deploy it able to determine whether their partners have cooperated or defected in their most recent move of the game. This might not be difficult for bacteria, but for people and nations it can be quite a complicated matter. In fact, virtually all transactions between human agents entail some degree of privately held information.

That said, imperfect (or asymmetric) information is likely to pose a greater impediment in some situations than in others. In multiplayer games, for example, there is always a chance that one player will misinterpret defection by a second player as cheating when in fact the second player is merely retaliating against a third player for committing an unwarranted defection in a previous round (Bendor, 1987; cf. Oye, 1986: 18–20). And similar difficulties could arise in a strictly bilateral interaction. Suppose, for example, that effective control over the policy realm in question were to change hands within one of the parties to a bilateral agreement at some point after the game had commenced. In that event, the other party might find itself lacking vital information about how its new transaction partner had behaved in its prior dealings, and thus whether that new partner was likely to prove as reliable a cooperator as its domestic predecessors had been before their ouster.[6]

Enter institutions. In "noisy" environments like these, neoliberals suggest that international institutions can play a useful role in formalizing

---

[6] Downs and Rocke (1995) discuss some of the strategies that mutual-gains-seeking cooperators might use to surmount this particular source of uncertainty. Section 3 below offers further analysis of the relationship between domestic politics and the formation of international institutions, a topic which, as Downs and Rocke correctly note, does not fit comfortably within the unitary-actor framework of most international relations theory.

the initial terms of cooperation, monitoring subsequent behavior, and efficiently transmitting information about each party's past and present records of compliance. The upshot is that where international institutions exist and operate as intended – keeping each member state apprised of how its partners are behaving and, should there be an unwarranted defection, clearing up any ambiguity about the identity of the true culprits – international cooperation may not in fact be so difficult to achieve (or to sustain) after all.[7]

At first blush, this perspective would seem sufficient to account for the remarkable institutional developments of recent years. Delve beneath the surface, however, and the standard account quickly runs into problems, for even if one accepts the basic thrust of neoliberal institutionalist theory – that institutions facilitate collective gains by helping states overcome obstacles to cooperation – the responsibilities delegated to today's international institutions often go beyond, sometimes well beyond, what many of the theory's original proponents had in mind.[8]

The incomplete contracting argument

Recognition of the yawning gap between (neoliberal) theory and reality has led in recent years to an exciting new round of theoretical innovations and refinements.[9] Often using the European Union as a reference point, contributors to this body of work draw extensively upon economic theories of hierarchy, organization, and firm structure, none of which take the institutional requirements for cooperation to be as easily satisfied as earlier IR scholars had envisaged. True, institutional agents may well be necessary to perform the tasks of monitoring compliance and identifying defectors. But as long as each cooperation partner is

---

[7] Along these lines, Milgrom, North, and Weingast (1990) suggest that purely informational mechanisms may be able to sustain cooperation even in the extreme case in which none of the players has ever encountered its current partner before or expects to do so again in the future.

[8] Very few of today's international institutions operate merely as collectors and transmitters of information. In addition to serving as watchdogs, passively monitoring compliance with whatever rules their member states have agreed to uphold, most of these institutions also empower supranational entities of one kind or another to modify these rules – or to clarify their "true" meaning – once they have taken effect. Inasmuch as a trend toward supranational governance may be said to exist, it has thus far been primarily a regional phenomenon; see, e.g., Haggard, 1997, and Kahler, 1995. A number of global regimes would also fit this characterization, however, the most visible examples being multilateral economic and financial institutions (e.g., the WTO and IMF) as well as security arrangements like the UN.

[9] See, e.g., Dixit, 1996; Garrett and Weingast, 1993; Lake, 1999a; Moravcsik, 1998; Pollack, 1997; and Yarbrough and Yarbrough, 1992.

clear about what is permitted and forbidden, these tasks can be carried out fairly easily. To proponents of the new economics of organization, the real challenge lies in ensuring that the partners really *are* clear about what is permitted and forbidden – and at all times, not just at the beginning of the process.[10]

In international relations, questions about what it means to cooperate or defect are endemic. In part, this is because the individuals who negotiate international agreements are often guided by time-sensitive domestic political concerns, and so rush into deals without taking the time to set forth their terms as carefully as might be the case in less political environments. But some degree of imprecision or incompleteness is inherent in all agreements, at least all those intended to endure for more than a very short length of time. In a world of rapid political, economic, and technological change, it's simply not possible to determine ahead of time which types of conflicts and questions will arise over the lifetime of a long-term contractual relationship between two states. And even if it were, the contracting parties (i.e., the individuals who preside over the governments of these states) would not necessarily have the information, let alone the time, to specify appropriate responses for each one. Before deciding on an appropriate response, these parties would first have to consider whether the particular rule violation in question was the product of deliberate malfeasance rather than an inadvertent, and thus innocent, misreading of their agreement, for only in the former case, and perhaps not even then, would retaliation against the defector be warranted. Lacking any independent authority, neoliberalism's watchdog agencies would be unable to render such distinctions, leaving the door open for each party to the agreement to read its (ambiguous) provisions as it pleased.

Alternatively, the parties to an international pact or treaty could agree ahead of time that a particular set of collective decision-making procedures would be followed whenever a dispute over a particular clause or provision in the agreement needed adjudicating. Otherwise, an unstructured and open-ended – hence time-consuming – bargaining process would be necessary each time there arose a new set of circumstances not explicitly covered by the unavoidably indeterminate language of the agreement. In the course of trying to resolve these contractual ambiguities to everyone's satisfaction, international cooperation could quickly devolve into chaos.

---

[10] Cf. Kreps, 1990; Milgrom and Roberts, 1992; and especially Oliver Williamson, 1985.

The multiple-equilibria argument

Although the analytics and implications of the Prisoners' Dilemma Game continue to fascinate theoretically oriented students of international cooperation, the last several years have seen the theoretical spotlight shift toward the related but analytically distinct *coordination* dilemma.[11] Historically, much of the controversy between neoliberals and realists has centered around the issue of enforcement, with neoliberals proposing – and realists disputing – various solutions to the problem. That the problem of enforcement emerged as a hot topic of debate was perfectly natural, since international cooperation is possible only insofar as the parties involved trust each other to keep their promises. Strictly speaking, however, the types of difficulties that arise in trying to ensure that all parties do in fact follow through are second-order problems. The initial problem is getting a group of would-be cooperators to make these promises in the first place. Why, in practice, might this prove to be a major hurdle?

Perhaps some parties to the negotiations believe their future cooperation partners would reap a disproportionate share of any ensuing joint gains (Grieco, 1990). The world envisioned by many realists is one in which these kinds of relative-gains concerns are both serious and pervasive, and in which (as a result) security-conscious states encounter few opportunities for mutually beneficial deal-making. Yet careful analysis of the coordination dilemmas highlighted in work by Stephen Krasner (1991) and others raises a different possibility: perhaps reaching agreement is difficult because states encounter too many, not too few, opportunities for collective gain.

Having belatedly come to appreciate the potential seriousness of this multiple-equilibria impediment to cooperation, scholars of international relations are now moving energetically to explore its implications for supranational governance. Might supranational arrangements foster collectively desirable outcomes by limiting the number of potential equilibria? According to some analysts, institutions provide focal points along the lines previously suggested by Thomas Schelling (1960: esp. chap. 4; cf. Young, 1994: 110–11). Common sense suggests that this

---

[11] Opportunistic incentives (à la PDG) and coordination dilemmas are not, of course, the only impediments to successful contracting. To date, however, the new institutionalist literature – particularly as it has been applied by students of international relations – has given these problems the lion's share of attention (as opposed, say, to the problem of variable tastes or preferences). For more nuanced treatments, see Furubotn and Richter, 1997, and the contributions to Koremenos, Lipson, and Snidal, 2001.

focusing role would be of greatest importance in situations similar to the Battle of the Sexes-type scenario discussed in Krasner's study, in which the underlying preferences of each would-be cooperator differ (1991: 339–42).[12] Yet even if what these actors confronted were a "pure" coordination dilemma, it is still possible that they would be better off ceding agenda-setting powers – here, the right to designate the initial terms of agreement – to a third party.[13]

Broadening the debate: the "power politics" of institutional design

The interweaving of neoliberal theory and the new economics of organization is a relatively recent phenomenon and, as with all research endeavors in their early stages of development, a good deal of work remains to be done. Yet while most contributors to the literature see their task as one of deepening the paradigm and refining its core logic, the task of broadening the argument is, I would argue, at least as important. To that end, this section asks what would happen if the powerful actors who set the institution-building process in motion had the capacity to impose their own institutional choices on other actors in the system. This scenario puts the members of the enacting coalition in the driver's seat, and everyone else suffers what they must.[14]

The importance (to the enactors) of insulating the new equilibrium

For the sake of argument, let's assume that there is in fact a coalition of governments able to present their neighbors with a *fait accompli* – a set of institutional arrangements the latter will have to accept lest, in holding out for the old status quo, they end up being shut out of the (new) game altogether. Now the theoretical task becomes one of explaining why the actors who make up this powerful coalition would ever want to do their bidding through governance structures that afforded non-coalition members some role, however institutionally delimited or

---

[12] See also Martin, 1992b; Garrett and Weingast, 1993; Morrow, 1994; Fearon, 1998; and Koremenos, Lipson, and Snidal, 2001.

[13] The point is sometimes illustrated with reference to the agenda-setting powers exercised by the European Commission, most transparently during negotiations over the landmark Single European Act of 1986 (see, e.g., Cameron, 1992; Garrett, 1992; and Pollack, 1997).

[14] "The strong do what they can; the weak suffer what they must" (Thucydides, 400 BC).

circumscribed, in determining how unforeseen circumstances and conflicts are to be dealt with. By doing this – granting their institution's relatively disadvantaged signatories some scope to mitigate their losses – the members of the dominant coalition would seem to be diminishing rather than increasing their own gains from cooperation.

Imagine, however, that one of enacting coalition's relatively disadvantaged partners were to be suddenly turned out of office by a political party whose leaders were much less approving of the institutional arrangement they had inherited. Or, to take it one step further, imagine that one of the enactors *themselves* were to be ousted from office and succeeded by an anti-institution party or coalition. In either of these cases – but especially, one suspects, in the latter – the original group of enactors would have a serious problem on their hands. What if these (new) regime losers felt their continuing participation in the arrangement would leave them absolutely, not just relatively, worse off? Their best course of action under these circumstances might be to withdraw altogether – or to use the threat of doing so as a means of forcing the regime's other members to dramatically restructure the regime's internal design and operation.

Could the enactors really be pushed around in this fashion? Not as long as they retained their earlier positions of dominance. But, as noted earlier, the power initially enjoyed by the members of the enacting coalition would always be somewhat tenuous; the enactors are merely governments, after all, and governments do not last forever. Nor would any of the original enactors be able to appeal to a higher international body (a world court, for instance) in the event that their regime was to be taken from them and reengineered to serve a set of objectives that they themselves did not fully support.

To be sure, tampering with the enactors' regime would not be an entirely costless activity and, indeed, logic suggests the enactors would do whatever they could to make these costs – the price their opponents would pay were they to exercise their exit options – as high as possible. Below I suggest a few ways the enactors might go about this. For now, though, I want to emphasize the flip-side of the enactors' problem, which, from an institutional-design standpoint, is the more important: for, just as the prime movers would have a stake in raising the penalty for opting *out* of their regime, so, too, would they have an interest in reducing their successors' costs of staying *in* the regime.

This suggests a quite different explanation for the "incompleteness" we observe in so many cooperative interstate arrangements. Why don't the creators of these arrangements fully specify their terms of cooperation ex ante? The standard explanation is that the creators, being boundedly rational, are simply unable to devise a complete contract. But this is not the only possibility. From a political standpoint, an incomplete regime may actually be preferable. By fleshing out the terms of cooperation ahead of time, the creators would be denying future opponents of the regime, who might one day include the initial prime movers' own domestic successors, any opportunity to moderate its terms, reformulating or simply reinterpreting them in ways intended to make their continued participation in the arrangement somewhat less burdensome than it would otherwise be. It's for this reason, I would submit, and not (at least not exclusively) out of the more narrowly construed efficiency considerations emphasized by previous scholars, that the contractual terms embodied in many of today's regional and multilateral institutions take the more flexible forms they do.[15]

Extending the logic

That's not the end of the story, though, since the *most* flexible arrangements would be ones in which each party could interpret the rules however it wished. Dropping the costs of compliance to zero – making it possible for signatories to renegotiate the terms of a treaty from the ground up (Koremenos, 2001) – would provide the enacting coalition with the greatest protection against its regime's would-be destroyers. At the same time, however, this would come at the price of completely eliminating the benefits that accrue to members of the enacting coalition itself.

In fact, the enacting coalition would almost never need to pay this price; in most cases, simply moderating the costs of participation would suffice. Why? Because institutions – all institutions – have a way of generating their own societal constituencies.[16] Some of this is automatic: expectations adjust to the new reality, costs are sunk, nature takes its course. In the absence of major interventions, however, constituency-building typically proceeds slowly, occurring over decades rather than

[15] Although government turnover is the internal threat upon which I have been focusing thus far, *within*-government preference shifts are certainly also possible (see, e.g., Stokes, 2001). Like the threat of government turnover, then, the possibility of radical policy U-turns is something a new regime's creators would presumably want to take into account. See Rosendorff and Milner, 2001, for a related perspective.

[16] As, for example, the GATT/WTO has generated a constituency among export producers. See, e.g., Destler and Odell, 1987.

years or months. This, of course, poses something of a problem for the prime movers, who would like their new institutional creation to be surrounded as quickly as possible with a broad-based, ever-expanding coalition of friends and supporters. Given the immediacy of their concerns, the prime movers would want to pursue every available means of expediting this "natural" constituency-building process.

What *are* the available means? One is simply to delay the new arrangement's full implementation. This keeps the bulk of its costs from kicking in until after the dust has settled and societal expectations have already begun to adjust. Trade negotiators often employ this strategy, granting allowances for step-by-step implementation and phased-in concessions to especially sensitive sectors or even whole countries. The prime movers could also make use of the bully pulpit, launching an aggressive publicity campaign directly linking their new set of institutions to values and principles embraced by large segments of their societies and the larger global community. Here, too, the purpose would be to enlarge the pool of potential stakeholders and thereby temper the destructive zeal of regime opponents who might one day be in a position to subvert the new institutional status quo.[17]

Last but not least, members of an enacting coalition could make a special effort to hasten passage of their new organization's enabling legislation. There would be costs to hasty legislative action, as indeed there would be costs to all the insulation devices discussed here. Setting an early date for ratification of a new treaty would mean limiting the amount of time available for scrutinizing alternative proposals and hence for allowing the enactors to determine exactly which scheme would stand the best chance of advancing their interests. These costs, however, would need to be set against the benefit to the prime movers of getting something "out there" as quickly as possible, even if that something did not accord quite as closely with their underlying preferences as another institutional arrangement that might have been chosen. The sooner their new structure was up and running, the sooner would citizens, interest groups, and other elements of civil society begin developing a vested interest in its perpetuation, and the greater its prospects of withstanding a future decline in the enacting coalition's initial influence.

---

[17] Because it is aimed at transforming the underlying preferences of certain actors – specifically, the losers – this last strategy comes closest to the concept of productive power depicted in the lower right-hand cell of table 1.1 (p. 12).

Power politics and institutional variation

If my analysis to this point is correct, we should not be surprised to find regional and multilateral institutions being designed and engineered by a small subset of their founding members – the ones who were initially, if only temporarily, the most powerful. Might these actors' interests in congealing their distinctive preferences influence the types of governance arrangements they engineered, predisposing them toward more elaborate – and more flexible – supranational structures than they would otherwise prefer?[18] This, I have argued, is exactly what one ought to expect.

Not that considerations of this kind would always be germane, of course. Nor, even when power-entrenching motivations were germane, would they necessarily dominate the different motivations and incentives that institutionalist scholars are accustomed to discussing. Even if the fragility of an enactor's new institution – the prospect that it might one day lose control of its own creation – did weigh heavily in its mind, the opportunism and coordination problems emphasized by previous scholars could weigh even more heavily. There is certainly no reason to assume that because power-politics considerations are salient in a particular case, other considerations must therefore be irrelevant. My point is simply that the new institutionalism's theoretical equation may be missing a very important set of explanatory variables. But these omitted variables – whether the enacting governments' cooperative agenda is well or poorly received by their domestic opponents "back home," whether the political parties representing these opponents stand a realistic chance of assuming office in the near future, and so on – are variables, not constants. As such, the model allows for considerable variation in institutional outcomes: the "threat" of domestic political turnover could be less threatening in some historical periods or geographic regions and more threatening in others.

Take the case of Asia, a region where, for the moment at least, the supranationalization phenomenon discussed in this chapter would seem to be occurring at a decidedly slower pace than it is in other parts of the globe, with what little cooperation there is in the area taking place, as Joseph Grieco and others have noted, through "strictly intergovernmental accords with little aspiration to significant forms of supranational authority" (Grieco 1997b: 169; see also Aggarwal 1995; Crone 1993; and Haggard 1995). Why is this? The explanation given by Grieco

---

[18] The term "congealing" is borrowed from Riker, 1980: 445.

is that Asian countries are uniquely sensitive to relative gains. Drawing on the logic of institutional design presented here, I would offer a different explanation. Insofar as Asian regimes have historically lacked the "governance" features that one finds in a North American Free Trade Agreement or an EU, it is, I would suggest, because the political protection provided by these more flexible governance arrangements was simply not required. After all, these regimes were initiated by political elites who enjoyed comparatively high levels of political stability and encountered little or no significant (i.e., politically salient) domestic opposition. The lesson here is that the insulation incentives discussed in this essay may be stronger in some parts of the world than in others, in which case one would expect to find corresponding differences in each region's preference for supranational delegation.

In addition to varying by region, certain institutional features can also be expected to vary by issue or policy area. It is often assumed, for example, that left- and right-wing parties diverge on matters of security policy less than they diverge on questions of economic, social, or environmental policy. If this is true – and I think it is – it suggests a parsimonious explanation for the greater completeness of most security arrangements. While other preferences display considerable partisan-induced variation, security preferences remain fairly constant as one moves across the ideological spectrum. As a result, the potential for significant government-to-government variation in how the "national interest" is perceived tends to be lower in the security realm than in other areas of policy. And because domestic political uncertainty is lower, the attractions of institutional flexibility and delegated (hence indirect) authority are correspondingly weaker.[19]

Institutional engineering and the cooptation of the French Socialists: the system worked

Is there a power politics of institutional design and, if so, how might its internal logic differ from that of other institutionalist arguments more familiar to students of international relations? Having provided some of the analytical groundwork necessary for answering these questions, I want now to supplement this theoretical discussion with a more concrete analysis of a well-known case: the 1979 inauguration of the

---

[19] This line of analysis suggests one of many interesting avenues for future research. On the institutional politics of NATO, see McCalla, 1996.

European Monetary System (EMS) and the historic shift toward collective decision-making and adjudication it embodied.

A first cut

If the analyses offered by Ludlow (1982) and others are correct, sometime around 1977 the two prime movers behind the EMS – President Valéry Giscard d'Estaing in France and Chancellor Helmut Schmidt in Germany – developed a mutual interest in stabilizing the franc–mark exchange rate.[20] The fact that both leaders stood to benefit from a Franco-German exchange rate agreement did not mean that such an agreement would be signed, however, or, if signed, that it would necessarily be adhered to. Looking at the situation from the standpoint of France, some analysts have suggested that Giscard's *optimal* strategy would have been to uphold such an agreement until – but only until – the inflationary expectations of French workers had begun to adjust to what they perceived as the new "franc fort" reality (see, e.g., Melitz, 1988). Under standard assumptions, a franc devaluation at that point would have permitted Giscard's supporters to enjoy the benefits associated with an undervalued currency – increased demand for French exports, faster output growth, and the like – without at the same time having to endure the higher rates of wage inflation normally produced by a depreciating currency.

There would also be a downside, however. By breaking his promise with Schmidt, Giscard would have signaled to the French public that his future pronouncements, whether on economic policy or any other matter, were not to be trusted. Making matters worse, a surprise devaluation in France would have exacerbated inflationary pressures in Germany, no doubt prompting a retaliatory response from authorities at Germany's central bank (with whom Giscard and Schmidt were both involved in a repeated game). By provoking a Bundesbank-engineered economic slowdown in Germany, Giscard's defection might well have ended up dampening, not stimulating, foreign demand for French exports.

Following this line of reasoning, one could conclude that exchange rate coordination among sufficiently farsighted European governments was not really so difficult to achieve after all. Given that beggar-thy-neighbor exchange rate policies offered no lasting advantage to the

---

[20] On the politics surrounding the creation and early years of the EMS, Ludlow's book remains the definitive work. See also De Cecco, 1989; Frieden, 1994; Gruber, 2000; Heisenberg, 1999; McNamara, 1998; Moravcsik, 1998; and Oatley, 1997.

would-be defector (France) – and they certainly did not benefit the exploited party (Germany) – a Franco-German exchange rate agreement would have been self-enforcing. By this logic, however, a simple treaty should have sufficed. Why, then, did the French and German architects of the EMS go to the trouble of establishing a quasi-legislative suprana-tional governance structure?

Recall that for cooperation to emerge within the context of an iterated Prisoners' Dilemma Game, each player has to believe that a defection in the current round of the game will be met with retaliation in some future round.[21] In practice, however, this condition is likely to hold only insofar as the players are familiar with the histories of their current part-ners. Thus one could argue that all of the European governments that participated in the EMS negotiations had an interest in pre-specifying, as clearly and precisely as possible, the standards by which their future behavior would be judged.

Drafting the EMS treaty was itself, in this view, a kind of "cooperative device" (Fratianni and von Hagen, 1992: 129). Though necessary, how-ever, it was not sufficient, for the EMS charter was sure to be incomplete. Without a well-developed body of rules for dealing with unforeseen contingencies and special circumstances not specifically covered by the treaty – the onset of a recession in one member country but not in any of the others, for example – there would be nothing to stop each EMS signatory from interpreting the treaty differently, creating a crisis that could lead to a breakdown of the entire system.

To address this problem, the founders of the EMS could have stipu-lated that all disputes concerning matters of treaty interpretation be set-tled through open-ended intergovernmental negotiations. This is not, however, what the founders did. Instead, they specifically required that all such disputes be adjudicated by "a common procedure" (Article 3.2). The effect of this provision was to take these disagreements out of the hands of individual member governments and transfer them to a higher collective decision-making structure. Which structure? The one the founders had in mind was the European Monetary Commit-tee, a permanent body made up of the deputy governors from the cen-tral banks of each EMS signatory, senior representatives from member countries' finance ministries, and two representatives of the European Commission. Once the EMS charter came into force, this body assumed

---

[21] For applications of the theory of repeated games to issues concerning monetary and exchange rate policy, see Kydland and Prescott, 1977 and Barro and Gordon, 1983.

responsibility for determining whether prevailing economic conditions warranted a readjustment of exchange rates and, if so, which EMS signatories would be permitted to devalue and by how much.[22]

The fact that EMS signatories were willing to adhere to a predesignated set of collective decision-making procedures has been described as "a revolutionary development [touching] at the very heart of monetary sovereignty" (Tsoukalis, 1989: 63). What inspired this dramatic departure from past practice? The answer just given – a straightforward application of new institutionalist reasoning – may seem incontrovertible. Surely the actors who designed the EMS could anticipate that a simple exchange rate agreement would not be fine-grained enough to cover all possible contingencies and that, in all likelihood, signatories of the regime would use the resulting ambiguities (particularly during periods of crisis and instability) as a pretext for driving down the value of their currencies. Indeed, it was precisely to prevent this sort of thing from happening – or so, as suggested above, one might plausibly argue – that the "principals" who drafted the treaty decided to empower a higher-level "agent." Had it not been for the expectations-clarifying role of the European Monetary Committee, many of the regime's signatories would have taken every opportunity to free-ride (knowing they could do so without patently violating the letter of the original treaty), and the EMS, wracked by compliance problems, would have met an early death.

A closer look

As superficially compelling as it is, this line of analysis suffers from at least two serious weaknesses. The first is that it views the designing of the EMS as a collective endeavor when, as Ludlow's account makes clear, it was largely dictated by just two individuals: the president of France and the chancellor of Germany. That Giscard and Schmidt did not go out of their way to consult their European counterparts would not have mattered if their European partners had held similar preferences. But in Italy and the United Kingdom, at least, these partners did *not* hold

---

[22] Technically, of course, an EMS member state whose request for a devaluation was denied by the European Monetary Committee could go ahead and devalue anyway; the committee's decisions were authoritative only insofar as national governments chose to honor them. Refusing to comply, however, would have meant exiting the system and thus forgoing any benefits of participation or (of greater salience to governing officials in Italy and the UK) incurring the costs of exclusion. Either way, it was an extremely risky move, and one that for well over a decade EMS member governments were loath to undertake.

similar preferences. In fact, governing elites in Italy and the UK were decidedly unenthusiastic about the EMS, a regime whose creation they did not initially support and to which they consented only after France and Germany's go-it-alone capabilities had rendered it a *fait accompli*.[23]

Granting that Giscard's and Schmidt's institutional preferences counted for a lot more than those of their counterparts in Italy or Britain, how well does the previous analysis do in explaining those preferences? Were the two EMS enactors as intent on lowering the ambiguity and information barriers to successful collective action as the above account implies? Perhaps, though this requires us to believe that the regime's French and German sponsors were just waiting for the right opportunity to defect from their initial agreement. In fact – and this is the second big problem with the "first-cut" new institutionalist account I have just been elaborating – there was little for either leader to gain by double-crossing the other.

Take the German chancellor. With the Bundesbank maintaining its tight-fisted control over Germany's money supply, it would have been pointless for Schmidt even to try to deviate from the path of low inflation. If provoked, the Bundesbank would have been only too quick to raise German interest rates, which is exactly what it had done in 1973, the last time a German government had tried to enact a large fiscal stimulus. As for Giscard, his free-rider incentives were only slightly stronger; he was, after all, a conservative. It's true that in 1976 his administration had been moved to withdraw the franc from the Snake, the forerunner to the EMS in which France had been intermittently participating since 1972. By the end of 1976, however, Giscard had come to appreciate the limitations of franc depreciation as a strategy for stimulating economic growth (see, e.g., de Boissie and Pisani-Ferry, 1998). As long as French workers remained unwilling to moderate their wage demands – a safe bet given the militancy of France's labor movement and anti-labor orientation of the government – a continuously depreciating franc would have exacerbated the very inflation problem that Giscard and his newly appointed prime minister, Raymond Barre, had been working so urgently to redress.

But this raises an interesting question. Given how averse both of them were to inflation, why didn't the regime's French and German

---

[23] As it was, Britain did not enter the regime until 1990, and even then its government did so with considerable ambivalence. For the Italian perspective, see De Cecco, 1989; Frieden, 1994; Gruber, 2000; and Spaventa, 1980.

prime movers draft a more complete, Snake-like agreement explicitly prohibiting the signatories of their regime from devaluing their currencies? Had they done so – had they endowed the EMS with a tighter, less flexible set of rules – they could have avoided many of the "realignment-uncertainty" problems that were to surface later on, fueling unwarranted speculation and instability within the financial markets (Fratianni and von Hagen, 1992: 146–53).[24] These potential gains notwithstanding, however, the architects of the EMS opted for a more open-ended institutional arrangement. The question is why.

A power-politics perspective

Drawing on my earlier theoretical discussion, I would argue that one important impetus for their decision was the expectation, shared by Giscard and Schmidt alike, that one day soon their own power would wane and a new political actor – including, quite possibly, an EMS loser – would emerge to take their place. To be sure, Germany's involvement in the EMS was at little risk of being terminated by a future German government.[25] In France, however, Giscard's low-inflation, tight-money orientation was anything but secure. Even before the outbreak of the second oil crisis in 1978–79, many observers were skeptical that the conservative president would be able to fend off his Socialist challenger, François Mitterrand, in the next presidential election.[26]

Were Mitterrand to succeed in capturing the presidency, his natural inclination would be to end France's participation in the EMS. In so doing, he would of course be forgoing any credibility bonus he might have enjoyed by virtue of continuing to link the (weak) franc to the (strong) D-mark. On the other hand, Mitterrand shared the view of most other Socialist leaders at that time that the costs of obtaining this bonus far exceeded its potential benefits. Nor was this view entirely without

---

[24] This last point was often cited as an argument for EMU; see, e.g., Padoa-Schioppa, 1986.

[25] Even if the chancellor's own Social Democratic Party were to be turned out of office, its coalition partners, the neoliberal Free Democrats, were likely to remain a vital part of any new governing coalition, as were the conservative Christian Democrats. Both parties were supportive of the EMS.

[26] Public support for the French left, and particularly for the Socialists, had increased dramatically over the course of the 1970s. Given the personal popularity of their leader (whom Giscard had defeated in 1974 by only the slimmest of margins) and the steady rise in France's rate of unemployment, the possibility of a Socialist victory in the next presidential election, which was scheduled for 1981, had to be taken seriously indeed.

foundation. Given the left's well-known aversion to austerity, it was safe to assume that the transitional phase during which inflationary expectations in France converged to those in Germany would extend over several years, if not decades, during which thousands of French workers would be forced out of their jobs. It is hardly surprising, then, that France's two left-wing parties failed to support the EMS initiative when it was first proposed in 1977. Had these parties captured a majority of seats in the parliamentary elections held the following year (as pre-election polls predicted they would), it is quite likely that that Giscard's proposal would have been rejected – perhaps resoundingly so – in which case the European Monetary System might never have seen the light of day (Ludlow, 1982: 85).

It is true that critics of the EMS could also be found in other countries – most notably, again, in Italy and the UK (Gruber, 2000: chap. 8). Yet only in France did opponents of the regime have the potential to single-handedly bring about its demise. Had President Mitterrand decided to pull the franc from the system, as he very nearly did in the early 1980s (Cameron, 1989), the Italian lira and British pound would have been certain to follow, and the regime would have effectively ceased to exist. Nor was this scenario worrisome only to the regime's supporters in France; the possibility of a French pullout was also a source of acute concern to the regime's sponsors in Germany, many of whom feared that a future return to a system of freely floating exchange rates would cause the Deutschmark to appreciate rapidly against the franc, forcing up the price of German-produced goods and services in some of Germany's leading export markets.[27]

As they set about designing their new cooperative framework, Giscard and Schmidt thus had to take particular care not to load it down with rigid Snake-like rules and structures that France's left-wing opposition parties would be only too quick to abandon if, as seemed increasingly likely, they were one day to gain control of the French presidency, the National Assembly, or both. Although there would be some loss in terms of disciplining inflation, a looser institutional structure would have the virtue of extending their new arrangement's lease on life. Hence the view shared by governing officials in both France and Germany and embraced (not surprisingly) by their counterparts from Italy and the UK that "however strict the system might eventually become, flexibility, and more particularly provisions for changes in

---

[27] These concerns are discussed in De Cecco, 1989; Gruber, 2000; and Heisenberg, 1999.

exchange rates, would have to be written into the arrangement from the beginning" (Ludlow, 1982: 159; see also Padoa-Schioppa, 1986).[28]

But while the EMS afforded its member states a degree of flexibility not enjoyed by signatories of the Snake, its institutional structure was not – because it did not need to be – so malleable as to permit a newly empowered French Socialist administration to escape the need for austerity altogether. Rather than permit each member state to decide for itself whether it was deserving of special dispensation, Giscard and Schmidt transferred authority over all EMS realignment requests to a collective decision-making body, the aforementioned European Monetary Committee, whose decisions were meant to be arrived at by consensus. There was thus no *guarantee* that a member state's devaluation request would be granted. As it turned out, the EMS opponents of greatest concern to the regime's two architects did not fare as poorly under the arrangement as they might have under a newly reconstituted Snake. Still, in the end – though the French Socialists did (wisely) refrain from withdrawing the franc from the system – the deck remained firmly stacked against them.

From anarchy to organization: the hidden face of power

For several years now, rational choice theorists of international relations have been moving aggressively to incorporate the kinds of power-driven distributional considerations that earlier IR scholars, for all of their talk about hegemony and leadership, had tended to ignore or relegate to secondary status. The result has been an outpouring of new work aimed at demonstrating a simple (though previously neglected) theoretical point: international institutions can have profound distributional consequences, benefiting powerful states far more than – even, potentially, at the expense of – weaker states (see, for example, Grieco, 1993; Garnett and Weingast, 1993; Gruber, 2000; Krasner, 1991; Martin, 1992a; and Oatley and Nabors, 1998).

This is reasonable enough, as far as it goes. Yet if what we want to know is why some of these institutions are formal and others informal, some supranational and others intergovernmental, some accommodating and inclusive and others inflexible and hierarchical, the recognition that

[28] Had it not been for their fear of provoking West Germany's central bank (whose president was initially inclined toward the status quo), the evidence suggests that President Giscard and Chancellor Schmidt would have introduced even greater flexibility into the regime than they did. See Kaltenthaler, 1998: chap. 3.

"powerful states do better" does not take us very far. As a result, scholars interested in these sorts of questions do not generally look to power-oriented theories for inspiration. Most draw instead upon the earlier transaction-cost tradition of institutionalist research (cf. Koremenos, Lipson, and Snidal, 2001). Although contributors to that earlier body of work may not have paid enough attention to distributional issues, they did at least tell us something useful and important about institutional structure – as to date, by and large, exponents of the new power-politics models have not.

But to say that these models have not been put to use in helping us understand the nitty-gritty of institutional design is not to say they are *incapable* of doing so. Quite the contrary: power-oriented perspectives have a great deal to contribute to institutionalist theory. It's just that the work of clarifying that contribution, of explaining precisely how power considerations enter into the institutional design calculus, has not yet been done. My goal has been to fill that gap – or to begin filling it, since there is more than enough room for different (and competing) perspectives. The theoretical territory here is largely uncharted, the empirical terrain vast.

At the same time, it strikes me that any serious analysis will have to begin, as I have begun here, with the "enactors." These are the pivotal players in the institution-design process, the ones who, at the outset of that process, command the greatest power. Why are they powerful? Earlier in my discussion I delineated two possibilities (see also Gruber, 2000: chap. 3). One is that the enactors' interest in moving to a new form of regional or multilateral organization is just not as urgent as it is for other participants in the process and so, having less to lose, they are able to hold out longer for their first-choice institutional structures. Alternatively, the powerful actors, though no less dissatisfied with the anarchic status quo than anyone else, may have the capacity to alter that status quo unilaterally. It isn't hard to see how this go-it-alone capacity – the ability to opt out of collective negotiations, proceed on one's own, and still derive positive gains with respect to the baseline (anarchic) status quo – would afford an enormous advantage to whichever subset of the larger collectivity was lucky enough to possess it.[29] For the purposes of this analysis, however, the precise source of the enactors'

[29] To be clear, the powerful actors in this second scenario only indirectly control the actions of the weak, a consequence of the former's having removed the status quo from the choice sets of the latter. As noted earlier, this places the relationship within the upper right-hand cell of table 1.1 (p. 12): institutional power subsumes go-it-alone power, just as

power advantage was of less importance than the fact that they had one – they could get the other participants to accede to their demands – for this implied that their institutional preferences would carry considerably greater weight than those of the other institution-builders sitting around the table. If our goal is to understand why the institutions of global governance take the forms they do, I proposed that we inquire into the strategic calculations and incentives of these more powerful participants, the ones who wield the greatest bargaining and/or go-it-alone power at the outset. What kinds of problems are these actors likely to be worried about, and to try as best they can to preempt or mitigate, as they go about the task of designing "their" institutions?

If previous institutionalist scholars are right (see especially Oliver Williamson, 1985), two such problems should loom particularly large. One is the risk of ex-post opportunism, referred to above as the incomplete-contracting problem. Another is the risk of ex-ante coordination failure, or what I termed the multiple-equilibria problem. There is, however, a third institutional-design problem which, though less familiar to students of global governance, may loom even larger in the minds of the pivotal players. This third problem, the nature and implications of which I have focused on in this chapter, stems precisely from the "power-politics" fact that (most) international agreements afford some signatories substantially greater gains than they afford others. The same could be said of domestic agreements, of course, or indeed of any agreement or contract whose signatories wish it to endure for more than a very short period of time. Rarely do long-term transactional relationships benefit each party by exactly the same amount. Yet the fact that such asymmetries exist in most long-term *international* relationships holds a special significance, for the beneficiaries of these relationships (including the prime movers whose idea it was to establish them in the first place) do not have the luxury of appealing to a higher body in the event that their transaction partners – some of whom may not benefit nearly as much – decide one day to radically overhaul the terms of their ongoing relationships.

These things can happen. A government presiding over one of the institution's relatively disadvantaged member states could be turned out of office, for instance, bringing to power a new government whose leaders see the terms embodied in the enactors' regime as producing

---

it also subsumes what might be called bargaining or hold-out power (cf. Hirschman, 1945; Raiffa, 1982; Rubinstein, 1982).

not just relative losses but also *absolute* losses. Even if it decided not to withdraw from the arrangement, this new actor would be in a position to wreak havoc, demanding full-scale changes in the rules of the game that its predecessors, along with all of the arrangement's other founding members, had previously agreed to uphold. The original enactors would not be required to adopt those changes, of course. But by the time the threat surfaced, the members of the once-powerful enacting coalition might no longer have the capacity to fend it off. Indeed, they might not be around at all, having themselves fallen prey to the vicissitudes of their own domestic politics. Should something like this ever occur – if even one of the enacting governments were to be succeeded in office at some point in the future by an anti-cooperation party or coalition – the institution in question would be rendered particularly vulnerable, as would the future benefit streams anticipated by the signatories who had been profiting from it.

It is not farfetched to think these kinds of scenarios would weigh heavily on the minds of the enactors during the initial period, as they considered the relative pros and cons of different institutional configurations. Would they weigh even heavier than the opportunism and coordination problems emphasized by previous institutionalist scholars? I think they could, though the answer would surely depend on the particulars of the case. Suffice it to say that the power-politics side of the institutional-design story deserves closer scrutiny than it has received thus far in the international relations literature.

Substantively, the payoff here could be enormous. My own view is that power politics, though frequently hidden from view, has been fueling much of the international cooperation and institution-building we have recently been seeing across Europe, North America, and the developing world – a possibility that further underscores the need for new ways of thinking about the relationship between state power and global governance. And yet, while the world around them may be undergoing extraordinary change, most scholars remain quite content with the theoretical status quo. In their view, what is needed is not a full-scale theoretical reorientation; it is a synthesis of the institutionalist theories we already have. As a well-known review of the monetary-integration literature concludes, "The efficiency considerations that are the economist's bread and butter, the self-interested political behavior whose analysis comes naturally to the political scientist, and the institutional approach that has gained increasing favor under the banner of 'the new institutionalism' need to be blended to provide a balanced picture of the integration process" (Eichengreen, Frieden, and von Hagen, 1995: 6).

This blending is already well underway. Indeed, for all the acrimony between neoliberals and realists, members of the two dominant schools of international relations theory have spent the last several years laying the foundations for an elegant, higher-order synthesis, one that takes the diverse strands of a larger rational-choice literature on cooperation and institutions and fashions them into the unified analytical framework outlined in section 2 of this chapter. But are we really any closer to providing the "balanced picture" everyone claims to want?

As Europe's recent experience with monetary integration suggests, the problem with current research is not that our theories are too disparate. The real stumbling block is that these theories have been put to use in understanding only one side of the globalization and political integration story – the side having to do with collective action, efficiency, and mutual gains. If we want to understand the other side – the one concerning winners and losers, zero-sum conflict, and the struggle to achieve and maintain power – we must first discard the analytical biases that have led international relations theorists to overlook it.

6 Power, governance, and the WTO: a comparative institutional approach

Gregory Shaffer

The World Trade Organization (WTO) is a central site for global governance. The WTO, founded in 1995, and its predecessor, the General Agreement on Tariffs and Trade (GATT), founded in 1947, are in large part products of US entrepreneurship, persuasion, and pressure, made possible by the United States' hegemonic position in world politics. The WTO institutionally constrains domestic political choices over trade and intellectual property matters, and implicitly over any regulatory policy that is trade-related, including environmental and labor policies. WTO institutional processes help spur changes in civil society and business–government relations. The WTO's detailed rules, backed by a relatively binding dispute-settlement system, implicate not only states' economic and security interests, but also state constituents' profits and norms. As a result, states and state constituents actively try to shape the WTO's agenda, its rules, their application, and their effects.

This chapter makes three central points. First, the chapter charts the myriad ways in which the United States, the European Union (EU),[1] and influential constituents within them advance their interests through the WTO. They predominate because they wield considerable material and ideational resources that provide them with advantages in economic relations in any institutional context. Section 1 examines the various means through which these actors directly and indirectly shape and

Thanks go to Michael Barnett, Bruce Cronin, Bud Duvall, Neil Komesar, Duncan Snidal, and the participants in the PIPES workshop for their comments on earlier drafts, and Zrinka Rukavina and Jeannine Haas for their research assistance.
[1] The technical name for the entity representing European Union interests before the WTO is the European Communities of EC. Article XI of the 1994 Agreement Establishing the WTO refers to "the European Communities" as an original member of the WTO. The term EU or European Union often is used by commentators, even though it is the EC that, technically, is a member of the WTO.

deploy WTO law and, in the process, may be constrained by it. It thus illustrates compulsory and institutional power.

Second, the chapter shows how WTO judicial bodies, as any court, exercise institutional power when they decide legal cases. Section 2 demonstrates how the WTO's supreme judicial body, the WTO Appellate Body, faces decision-making options that, in turn, shape participation in the market and in multiple domestic and international political settings. Because WTO rules are not fixed in meaning, their application requires WTO judicial bodies to make further institutional choices. These institutional choices result in the effective allocation of decision-making authority to alternative institutional processes. To understand the operation of WTO judicial power, we thus need to examine how the application of WTO rules differentially shapes opportunities for states and their constituents in other institutional contexts.

In this way, the chapter shows how global governance consists of multilevel, interacting, nested layers of institutional rules and processes in which decisions made in one institution affect participation in other institutional settings (Tsebelis, 1990).[2] In a world of large numbers and complexity, influence is often (if not always) mediated through institutions. Institutional rules and decision-making processes create opportunities for skewed participation, permitting some actors to indirectly constrain the options, actions, and understandings of others. To adapt from Schattschneider, institutional power consists of the mobilization of bias (1960: 71). This mobilization of bias, however, is not fully controlled by any particular actor. Actors that help define institutional rules and procedures may also be restricted by them. The term *institution*, as used in this chapter, is conceived broadly and interchangeably with the term governance mechanism. By institution, the chapter refers to any social decision-making process, including political, judicial, and market processes.[3]

In short, the paper adopts an institutional perspective for assessing law's power, differing from (and complementing) perspectives that focus on legal discourse and legitimization processes. While constructivists focus on law as a discursive process which affects outcomes

---

[2] This chapter's analysis of nested institutions differs from that of Tsebelis, for example, in that the chapter focuses on institutional choices made by courts, and not political actors instrumentally advancing their goals. Like Tsebelis, however, the chapter addresses how decisions in one arena have consequences in others (1990: 9).

[3] See also Komesar, 1995: 9; and Wendt, 1992: 395 ("self help and power politics are institutions").

because actions must be justified and legitimized in legal terms (see Johnstone, chap. 8 in this volume), this chapter addresses judicial power as a form of second-order (or meta-) institutional power, through the judicial process's ability to shape participation in other institutional contexts. It shows how a WTO judicial decision, as that of any court, affects who participates and how they participate in other institutional settings in the determination of a policy outcome.

Third, the chapter illustrates the normative implications of institutional choice. In particular, it shows why, from a normative perspective, institutional analysis should be comparative. Comparative institutional analysis is a conceptual framework for assessing governance mechanisms in terms of the relative participation, direct and indirect, of affected parties in alternative institutional settings (Komesar, 1995, 2002). Section 3 contends that, since all institutional processes are characterized by biased participation, the key question is how parties participate, or otherwise are represented, in an institutional context in comparison with non-idealized alternatives. Whether from a positive, strategic, or normative perspective, a central global governance question is: *what are the relative effects of alternative institutional mechanisms on participation in the resolution of transborder governance issues that pit the interests of powerful states and powerful constituents within them against those of weaker states and their constituents or of weaker constituencies in powerful states?* The response to this question requires a comparative-institutional-analytic approach. As the chapter shows, because of the open-ended nature of WTO rules, the WTO Appellate Body itself can engage in comparative institutional analysis and assess institutional alternatives in terms of their relative biases. The issue is not whether biases exist (they exist in all institutional contexts) but, rather, what are the effects of an institutional process on participation in the weighing of competing concerns compared to its non-idealized alternatives.[4]

---

[4] Although the chapter focuses on the editors' first two conceptions of power – *compulsory* and *institutional* – comparative institutional analysis can also be applied to the other two – *structural* and *productive*. To recall, structural power (borrowing significantly from Marx) denotes the structural constitution of subjects' capacities, and productive power (borrowing from Foucault) consists of the discursive production of a subject's identity. When analysts of structural and productive forms of power recognize that there are variations in "false consciousness" and "constructed identity" along a continuum, then comparative institutional analysis again is relevant from a policy perspective, since some governance arrangements will facilitate a comparatively "truer," less constrained representation of interests and identities than others (see, e.g., Hayward, 2000: 7).

This chapter demonstrates the effects of institutional choice through its analysis of one of the WTO Appellate Body's most controversial decisions, one which has been referred to as a constitutional-like case for the WTO and global governance – the United States shrimp–turtle case. The case involved the interaction of domestic and international trade, environmental, and development concerns.

Compulsory and institutional power in the WTO context: the shaping, application, and effects of WTO rules

Governance mechanisms, while they may be designed to channel and constrain power, are also shaped and exploited by powerful actors through diverse and complementary means. This section examines how the advanced industrial powers and corporate interests within them shape and deploy the WTO's rules to advance their interests over others. These actors' influence operates both directly and diffusely, illustrating the exercise of both compulsory and institutional power.

Compulsory power: asymmetric material resources and the setting of WTO rules

The WTO's two largest trading members, the United States and the European Union, clearly exercise more clout than any other WTO members to define WTO rules and procedures. Even though all WTO members have one vote in the WTO, the United States and EU wield more control in shaping WTO rules because of the importance of their vast markets to other countries. As Hirschman (1945) noted, the essence of market power is the capacity to obstruct commercial exchange. Economic coercion and constraints play a greater role than military coercion in the trade and regulatory realms. The mere threat of sanctions, more than their actual imposition, is typically the most effective tool (Bayard and Elliott, 1994; Drezner, 2003).

The United States and EU enhance their leverage in WTO multilateral negotiations through forum-shifting. They play countries off each other through engaging in simultaneous bilateral and regional negotiations, thereby threatening to deny benefits to some countries that they offer to others (Gruber, 2000; Braithwaite and Drahos, 2000). Weaker states may agree to US and EU demands under a bilateral agreement so as to gain or retain access to US and EU markets, and, in the process, obtain an advantage over developing country competitors. Once a developing country agrees to such demands, it will more likely favor their multilateral application, such as over intellectual property protection, so that it is not disadvantaged against developing country competitors in that particular domain. In large part, this explains developing countries' eventual agreement to the WTO Agreement on Trade-Related Aspects of Intellectual Property Rights (TRIPS Agreement).

The United States and EU are able to combine market power and their ability to forum-shift with vast material and informational resources that they deploy to their advantage in the drafting and application of WTO rules (Braithwaite and Drahos, 2000: 196). Most developing countries are able to post only one or a few representatives in Geneva to follow WTO matters before the WTO's numerous councils, committees, and working groups. Yet as a former divisional director in the WTO's secretariat notes, it is "estimated that there were 2,847 meetings in the WTO in 1997, or an average of 10 meetings per working day."[5] WTO members with greater resources, such as the United States and EU, thus drive WTO agendas. As a result, the United States and EU have fashioned rules whereby they can continue to protect and subsidize their domestic producers in the agricultural and textile sectors, while developing countries agreed to more costly commitments (Ostry, 2002; Sanger, 2001). It is estimated that developed countries provide about US $1 billion per day in agricultural subsidies, with about half coming from Europe (UNDP, 2003: 123).[6] The United States still applies an average tariff rate of 14 percent to goods from Bangladesh (primarily textile products), but only 1 percent to imports from France ("Cancun Challenge," 2003). In contrast, developing country implementation of the TRIPS Agreement is estimated to result in wealth transfers from developing countries to the United States of around $5.8 billion per year (Maskus, 2000: 142).

Power is also exercised in terms of the issues that weaker states do not even consider raising in WTO negotiations (Bachrach and Baratz, 1963). At times, the United States and EU do not even need to voice their interests because smaller countries do so for them, anticipating US and EU responses. For example, the chair of a WTO negotiating group, who was an ambassador to the WTO from a smaller developed

---

[5] See Sampson, 2000, citing Communication from Egypt, High Level Symposium on Trade and Development, mimeo, WTO, March 17, 1997. As of November 1999, twenty-eight WTO members did not even maintain permanent offices in Geneva (WTO Focus, 1999).

[6] Annual figures are broken down in the OECD's database, at www.oecd.org/document/23/0,2340,en_2825_293564_4348119_1_1_1_1,00.html [January 15, 2004].

country, outspokenly defended US interests against challengers so as "to keep the US and EU in the tent." In the ambassador's words, "They have options that smaller countries don't have . . . My god, look what the US did in Iraq."[7] Although Brazil, India, and other leading developing countries attempted to set WTO negotiating agendas at the Doha and Cancun ministerial meetings in 2001 and 2003, they also tried to do so in the past. Over time, however, the United States and EU can deploy market power and forum-shifting strategies to isolate them until they eventually succumb (Steinberg, 2002).[8]

Powerful constituencies in the United States and Europe advance their interests through harnessing US and EU leverage. They use states as agents, just as they, in turn, act as agents for states (Shaffer, 2003a). The most successful constituencies are large multinationals and trade associations, such as those in the services and pharmaceutical sectors that lobbied for, and now benefit from, the General Agreement on Trade in Services (GATS) and the TRIPS Agreement (Sell, 2003). Although noncommercial groups wield much less clout, they too can use the US threat of withholding market access to cause smaller countries to change their regulatory policies, as over trawling techniques for shrimp, as examined below. Businesses and nongovernmental groups in smaller countries, however, are unable to harness state power to advance their international priorities. Although such businesses and nongovernmental groups may exercise considerable influence in their domestic political contexts, their governmental representatives exercise little influence internationally.

Compulsory power: asymmetric deployment of ideational resources

Much of the politics over global governance involves not direct coercion, but rather contests over principles, such as reciprocity, the free flow of products and information, national treatment, harmonization, deregulation, and national sovereignty. As Braithwaite and Drahos state: "Both economic and military coercion are cost-intensive," whereas "principles, with their attendant rule complexity, bring about a

---

[7] Private conference at which the ambassador spoke, followed by a private discussion, July 2003.
[8] Immediately following Cancun, the United States was already able to press six Latin American countries to leave the so-called G21 negotiating block that was led by Brazil. The United States did so by offering to negotiate preferential bilateral trade deals with these countries (i.e., through forum-shifting). See Pruzin, 2003.

long-term convergence of expectations among actors" (2000: 530). Converged expectations can spur the internalization of norms and habits of compliance (ibid.: 563).

Principles and norms are forms of power informed by strategic interest and position that are more diffuse in their effects. Those with material and informational resources and elite status are adept at deploying discursive tools, whether in negotiation or litigation, or through the provision of "technical assistance." The United States and US corporate constituents promote ideas about the benefits of intellectual property protection for investment (Sell and Prakash, 2004). Developing countries without the desired property regimes are labeled "pirates." Representatives of pharmaceutical trade associations work with US and EU officials to draft "model" laws and to teach as "faculty" in workshops organized by the World International Property Organization regarding intellectual property law and its enforcement (Shaffer, 2003a). Drake and Nicolaidis (1992) likewise reveal how an epistemic network of academics, other "experts," US trade representatives, and US industry reshaped perceptions of services as "traded" goods, gradually breaking down developing country resistance to the incorporation of financial, telecommunications, and other services into the new WTO regime.

Institutional power: deploying WTO rules through litigation and negotiation in its shadow

The United States and European Union can also exercise power through the WTO. Even though WTO rules may be neutral on their face, they are not used equally by all parties. Just as in domestic litigation (Galanter, 1974), the "haves" come out ahead in litigation at the international level where legal expertise is highly specialized and expensive. The WTO's most powerful members and their constituents have the resources and incentives to apply trade law to their advantage through WTO judicial procedures and bilateral negotiations in the shadow of a potential WTO claim. Multinational firms are the world's largest traders and consequently the most directly affected by the details and interpretive nuances of WTO rules. They have the resources to engage in complex, prolonged litigation in a remote forum, which they are willing to dedicate to these issues because of their stakes. Large and well-organized interests hire lawyers and economists and form public–private partnerships with US and EU public authorities to prevail in WTO litigation and in settlement negotiations conducted in the shadow of WTO law (Shaffer, 2003a).

The United States and EU remain by far the predominant users of the system, and thereby have been most likely to advance their larger systemic interests through the judicial process. Their participation rates as parties or third parties in fully litigated WTO cases are around 97 percent (US) and 82 percent (EU) respectively (Shaffer 2003a). Although developing countries have high per capita stakes in trade disputes (often higher than the United States or Europe relative to their economies), their aggregate stakes are smaller. Because of their smaller stakes in the trading system they are less likely to be repeat players who benefit from economies of scale. The uncertain benefits from litigation are less likely to surpass the costs of developing or hiring expertise for litigation, especialsly after discounting for the risks of losing a case or of noncompliance (Shaffer, 2003b).

The United States and EC are also better situated to bargain in the shadow of a potential WTO claim. Where the United States and EU can absorb high litigation costs by dragging out a WTO case, while imposing them on developing country complainants, they can seriously constrain developing countries' incentives to initiate a claim, and correspondingly enhance developing countries' incentives to settle a dispute unfavorably. WTO law casts a weaker shadow over settlement negotiations for countries that lack lawyers conversant in WTO law. When developing countries are unable to mobilize legal resources cost-effectively, their threats to invoke WTO legal procedures lack credibility. They thus wield less bargaining leverage in WTO law's shadow.[9]

In addition, settlement negotiations over trade disputes have a reciprocal impact on WTO judicial decision-making. Judicial decision-making occurs in the shadow of bargaining, a phenomenon that is particularly pronounced in the international trade context. It is a common error of trade law academics to view WTO judicial opinions as the end of the process. Rather, WTO cases are ultimately resolved through diplomatic negotiations that take place in the context of the judicial decisions. WTO judicial panels may shape their decisions to induce either compliance or amicable settlement, and thereby uphold the system. The WTO Appellate Body has used ambiguous holdings so as to facilitate powerful WTO members' ability to comply (Shaffer, 2003b), as will be shown in Section 2.

---

[9] Bush and Reinhart (2003) provide statistical evidence regarding developed country advantages in both litigation and settlements.

Institutional power: ideational resources in institutional context

Institutions privilege different norms and the participation of different actors. Trade officials and trade norms shape bargaining within the WTO to a greater extent than in environmental fora. Trade officials attempt to use trade–environment negotiations in the WTO to frame negotiations in other institutions (Shaffer, 2001: 77). Similarly, by concentrating rule-making in the WTO as opposed to in an organization focused on development, such as the United Nations Conference on Trade and Development (UNCTAD), the United States has structured negotiations largely in terms of "reciprocal" trade concessions, as opposed to development "rights," wealth distribution, or the meeting of basic human needs. The United States and EU have similarly used the World Bank and International Monetary Fund to induce developing countries to liberalize their markets. The Bretton Woods institutions have used both coercive material tools (liberalization as a condition of financing) and normative ideational ones (liberalization as "good governance") (Stiglitz, 2002b). Developing countries are advised to liberalize unilaterally in their "self-interest," even though the United States and EU themselves require "reciprocity" to open their markets (Lawrence, 2003), which could harm their terms of trade.

U.S. public and private actors attempt to shape WTO judicial decision-makers' perceptions of principles, alternatives, and the desirability of outcomes in WTO litigation. US commercial and nongovernmental groups demand that WTO panels accept amicus curiae briefs, knowing that they are well positioned to file legal submissions. They harness challenges to the WTO's legitimacy in demanding greater deference to WTO panels' review of US anti-dumping measures or US import bans imposed on (allegedly) environmental grounds. Southern nongovernmental groups are particularly wary of how Northern groups rhetorically shape "trade–environment" discourse in order to elide issues of "development" and thereby privilege their interpretations of legal texts (Chimni, 2000; Shaffer, 2001).

Asymmetric avoidance of institutional constraints: use of "legal" protection and extra-legal coercion

The United States and EU have deployed extra-legal tools to induce changes in developing country regulations and regulatory practices that actually comply with WTO rules. Intellectual property firms, in particular, have used US domestic legal procedures (under Section 301 of the 1974 Trade Act) to press US authorities to remove special tariff preferences granted to developing countries if they do not provide "adequate and effective" protection of US intellectual property rights. In this way, private actors attempt to use US market power to compel developing countries to grant greater intellectual property protection than required under the TRIPS Agreement. Weaker states and their constituents are less able to deploy these extra-legal tools because they do not hold the requisite carrots and sticks. They do not wield sufficient market power to constitute a meaningful threat (sticks), and they hold fewer inducements, such as the grant of special tariff preferences (carrots), that they can withhold.

Powerful WTO members, such as the United States and EU, and powerful constituents within them also retain greater flexibility to avoid the constraints of WTO rules. The United States and EC have ensured that WTO rules provide numerous legal exceptions to market access that they are experts at manipulating, in particular anti-dumping and anti-subsidy provisions. Under these provisions, the United States, EU, and their corporate and labor constituencies can trigger procedures before domestic administrative bodies on the grounds that imported foreign products are sold in an "unfair" manner, thereby justifying compensatory tariff protection. US and EU bureaucratic agencies, working with domestic producer interests, can manipulate price differentials to ensure high dumping and subsidization margins, thereby triggering prohibitive tariffs that eliminate foreign competition. The mere threat of an anti-dumping lawsuit can coerce foreign producers to raise prices, reduce their imports, or simply cease importation. Similar to the tax lawyer's advice to high-net-worth clients, why cheat and risk being caught for cheating when you can pay a "good" lawyer to get you the same "legitimate" result (Weidlich, 2002). Statistical evidence reveal that lower-income developing countries fare far worse in US anti-dumping proceedings. They "are more likely to be targeted, less likely to settle cases, more likely to confront high dumping duties and less likely to bring cases to the WTO" (Bown, Hoekman, and Ozder, 2003). Again, it is more difficult for weaker states and their constituents to play these legal games successfully.

Nested governance: the impact of WTO decisions on participation in other institutions

Institutional choice does not end with the referral of a matter to the WTO. Rather, the WTO judicial process itself must make second-order institutional choices when faced with a legal claim. In applying WTO "law," the WTO Appellate Body can effectively allocate decision-making authority to market mechanisms, to political or administrative processes at the national or international levels, or to itself. Each institutional choice provides different direct and indirect opportunities for affected parties to participate in the weighing of competing interests and concerns. By shaping a party's relative participation in the conflict's resolution, this institutional choice affects the ultimate outcome.

In global governance, institutions are nested vertically and horizontally. The vertical allocation of authority involves the level of social organization that decides regulatory policy, from the local to the global. The horizontal allocation of authority involves choices between market processes, political and administrative processes, judicial processes, and other governance mechanisms. When the WTO Appellate Body decides a legal claim, it necessarily confronts issues of vertical and horizontal allocation of authority. The Appellate Body, for example, must determine the amount of deference to show to national and local regulations that affect foreigners. In doing so, it shapes the operation of these second-order governance mechanisms.

Biased participation characterizes each of the decision-making processes to which a WTO judicial body can allocate authority. Although the biases may be parallel, they are never uniform. This section compares the resulting biases for affected states and constituents under five institutional choices. In order to ground analysis in a specific context, this section uses a particularly controversial international trade dispute as a vehicle – the WTO shrimp–turtle case. The WTO case involved conflicts over the appropriate balancing of trade, environmental, and development priorities of constituents and states at vastly different levels of development.

Background

The story of the WTO shrimp–turtle dispute starts with US legislation that, in part, was enacted to protect the environment and, in part, to protect a domestic industry. The U.S. legislation took the form of a ban on the importation of shrimp from countries that do not impose shrimp-trawling regulations to protect endangered sea turtles in a manner comparable to US domestic regulation.[10] The supporters of the US regulation included environmentalists concerned about endangered marine species and the US shrimping industry concerned about competition from Thai and other imports. These two groups clashed in the domestic US struggle over whether shrimping boats must use "turtle excluder devices" (named TEDs)[11] in their shrimp nets to protect sea turtles from drowning. They clashed before an administrative body (the National Marine Fisheries Service) and before US federal courts. The US shrimping industry called TEDs "trawler elimination devices" because of the loss of shrimp catch and the costs of using them. The environmentalists contended that TEDs are cheap and that the loss of shrimp is minimized if TEDs are properly used. When the environmentalists prevailed domestically, the two groups joined forces to press Congress, and then the US Department of State and the federal courts, to ban imports of wild shrimp from any country that does not mandate comparable shrimp-trawling methods (i.e. the use of TEDs) in waters where the sea turtles might be present. The resulting import restrictions spurred South and Southeast Asian nations to initiate a trade claim in January 1997 against the United States before the WTO's dispute settlement system (Shaffer, 1999).[12]

Alternative institutional choices

In deciding the case, the WTO Appellate Body implicitly faced a choice among at least five institutional alternatives. Each institution would

[10] The US law, Section 609 of US Public Law 101-169 of Nov. 21, 1989, mandated that shrimp cannot be imported into the United States unless "the President shall certify to Congress" that either (i) the "fishing environment of the harvesting nation does not pose a threat [to] . . . such sea turtles," or (ii) the foreign government has adopted "a regulatory program governing the incidental taking of such sea turtles . . . that is comparable to that of the United States," and "the average rate of that incidental taking by the vessels of the harvesting nation is comparable" to that of US vessels. The president delegated to the State Department the authority to make the required certifications.
[11] The "turtle excluder device" is a mechanism which permits turtles to escape from trawling nets to avoid drowning. TEDs are relatively inexpensive, costing between $75 and $400 in the United States, and less in developing countries (Shaffer, 1999).
[12] The four complainants, India, Malaysia, Pakistan, and Thailand, maintained, among other matters, that the US import ban on shrimp and shrimp products (i) violated the prohibition of quantitative restrictions in GATT Article XI, and (ii) were not permitted under the exceptions set forth in GATT Article XX. The United States maintained that the restrictions were permitted under exceptions for the conservation of natural resources and the protection of animal life and health.

favor some parties over others on account of the dynamics of participation in its decision-making process. The five institutional alternatives
were:

(1) to show deference toward the domestic political authority impos-
    ing the trade restrictions, thereby allocating decision-making to US
    national political and judicial processes; this allocation, in turn,
    would favor US constituents participating in those processes, which
    largely consisted of US producer groups and environmental groups;
(2) to issue an injunction against the trade restriction, thereby allocat-
    ing decision-making to the marketplace, likely favoring producer
    interests in developing countries;
(3) to refer the matter to another international political body formed
    pursuant to an international treaty, thereby allocating decision-
    making to an international political process; here the effects on par-
    ticipation are unclear, in part on account of the uncertain and frag-
    mented status of international institutions;
(4) to balance the substantive interests at stake pursuant to a vague stan-
    dard on a case-by-case basis, thereby allocating substantive decision-
    making over the conflict to itself; the Appellate Body, of course, is
    itself subject to political pressures and constraints;
(5) to review the process, as opposed to the substance, of the national
    decision, thereby sharing decision-making authority between a
    national body that determines substantive policy, and an interna-
    tional judicial body that reviews the national procedure for due pro-
    cess, transparency, and "good-faith" multilateral efforts, again favor-
    ing US constituents, although to a lesser extent than in (1) above.

(1) A policy of deference: allocation of authority to national political and judicial processes

First, the WTO judicial body could show deference to the country implementing the trade restriction, thereby effectively assigning decision-
making authority to a national political process, subject to judicial
review before national courts under national law. For example, a WTO
judicial panel could find that the US national legislation and implementing regulations are in compliance with WTO rules so long as they have an
environmental aim (Howse and Regan, 2000). Environmental activists
and many legal scholars maintain that WTO rules should be interpreted
to permit trade restrictions imposed unilaterally on account of foreign production processes that are environmentally harmful (Bodansky,

2000). Some contend that WTO rules should be interpreted in deference to the "local values" of the country imposing the trade restriction (Nichols, 1996). Others propose that WTO judicial panels should decline jurisdiction or apply a political-exception doctrine in politically charged cases that implicate trade and environment policies, in which case the national import restriction would remain unchallenged (Dunoff, 1999). Proponents of WTO deference to such local decision-making maintain that the WTO's predecessor organization (the GATT) was trade-biased because its judicial panels focused on protecting trade of physically "like" products, and not on protecting social values reflected in the production process.

International deference toward national regulatory decisions has certain merits from the perspective of participation. Participation in democratic decision-making at the national level is of a higher quality because of the closer relation between the citizen and the state, the consequent reduced costs of organization and participation, and the existence of a sense of a common identity and of communal cohesiveness – that is, of a *demos*. Moreover, given the lack of an international political process to adopt regulatory controls to suit changing contexts, there are strong policy grounds for deferring to domestic political choices for regulating market transactions.

National decision-making processes, nonetheless, can also be highly problematic from the perspective of participation. Producer interests are generally better represented than those of consumers on account of their higher per capita stakes in regulatory outcomes. Producer interests' predominance arguably explains a great deal of protectionist legislation (Olson, 1965; McGinnis and Movsiean, 2000). Moreover, even where national procedures are relatively pluralistic – involving broad participation before administrative and political processes that are subjected to judicial review – they do not take account of adverse impacts on unrepresented foreigners. Neither environmental groups nor US shrimp-lobbying associations, nor their political representatives, took the interests of Asian shrimpers into account, even though the US ban affected around $1 billion of Thai imports, glutting the Thai market with low-priced shrimp, wiping out Thai investments, and allegedly spurring a number of suicides of Thai shrimp farmers.

A policy of deference to national import bans that are imposed because of foreign environmental practices also has asymmetric effects. This institutional choice permits powerful countries with large markets, such as the United States, to use their market leverage to compel foreign regulatory change, while developing countries, holding most of the world's population, wield no such clout. Developing countries are not in the position of imposing unilateral trade bans on US products because of the United States' profligate energy consumption, nor are US environmental groups calling for these measures, even though the stakes are much higher. If global warming causes the Indian Ocean to rise, much of Bangladesh will be submerged – perhaps good for sea turtles, but not for millions of Bangladeshis.

In short, were the WTO Appellate Body to defer to the US legislation and its administrative application, then it would effectively allocate decision-making over the appropriate balance of the trade, environmental, and development concerns at stake to a US political and administrative process. Such a decision-making process, however, would be particularly biased against affected foreigners. Moreover, a general policy of showing such deference would have asymmetric effects. The United States' and EU's market power facilitates their ability to compel developing countries to modify regulatory policy, while developing countries wield no such clout.

(2) WTO injunction: allocation to the market

Second, the WTO Appellate Body alternatively could apply a stricter standard of review of national import restrictions. The Appellate Body could apply a rule that all import bans are in violation of international trade law if they do not protect health or life *within* the jurisdiction imposing the restriction. The Appellate Body would not look to the purpose behind the legislation, but rather to its effects.

The Appellate Body could, in particular, review the trade restriction in relation to alternative measures that are less restrictive of trade. Import bans would be particularly scrutinized because of the more market-friendly means available to inform consumers of foreign environmental impacts. Product labeling, in particular, could inform consumption decisions (and, indirectly, foreign production decisions) in a less draconian manner. Such an approach would effectively shift decision-making over the appropriate balance among trade, environmental, and development goals from a national political process to the market.

The initial WTO judicial panel in the shrimp–turtle case, the WTO's version of a trial court, took this route. The WTO panel showed little deference to the US national regulation, and did not seriously address the regulation's alleged environmental merits. Although the US regulation was not discriminatory on its face, the panel held that the very nature of the US measure, a trade ban based on foreign production methods that did not threaten health or life in the United States, was in violation of WTO rules and threatened the trading system.[13] The panel's broad ruling – based on the type of the measure, and not on its alleged purpose or the details of its implementation – could foster greater commercial certainty, thereby facilitating crossborder trade, promoting development, and protecting a liberal international trading system.

This market-based model has many benefits from the perspective of participation in the decision-making process over the concerns at stake. A market-based decision-making mechanism can permit more individualized participation in determining the proper balance between trade and environmental goals. In this manner, markets can enhance democratic voice. Marketers of shrimp caught with TEDs could label their products "sea-turtle-safe." Consumers, informed through advertising campaigns, could choose which shrimp to buy on the basis of how the shrimp were caught. In choosing between shrimp, US consumers would implicitly choose among alternative regulatory regimes for the trawling of shrimp. Such a WTO approach could stimulate not only product competition, but also regulatory competition (McCahery, et al., 1996; Esty and Geradin, 2000). Thai and US regulatory requirements for the trawling of shrimp would be in competition when consumers select which shrimp to buy.

The market decision-making mechanism, however, is also subject to bias, resulting in skewed participation in the determination of the appropriate balance of the policy concerns. Markets are subject to information asymmetries, externalities, and collective-action problems. Information costs would be high. The labels could be misleading. Even if the labels were accurate, many consumers would not take the time to adequately review them. Some consumers, even if informed, might decide to buy the cheaper shrimp and free-ride on more environmentally concerned purchasers. Other purchasers might refrain from buying "sea-turtle-safe" shrimp because they doubt that their purchasing decisions would be effective in light of other consumers' actions. The views of environmentally concerned citizens who do not eat shrimp would not

---

[13] There are two levels of judicial review in the WTO dispute-settlement system: the panel stage and, if the panel's decision is appealed, the Appellate Body stage. In its decision, the WTO panel held that, by "conditioning access to the US market" on a change in a foreign government's environmental regulatory policy, the US measure "threatens the multilateral trading system." It repeated this assertion of a threat to the system nine times. See e.g. paras. 7.44, 7.45, 7.51, 7.55, 7.60, and 7.61, WTO, 1998b.

be represented in the market process. US environmentalists thus fear that competition between environmentally protective US shrimping rules and nonexistent foreign shrimping rules would result in a "race to the bottom" toward less protective regulations. US environmental groups are wary that US shrimpers would join other producer groups in demanding that the US Congress overhaul or create exceptions to the US Endangered Species Act in order to "level the playing field" of competition against foreign competitors. In this case, producer groups might pressure Congress to relax US requirements on the use of TEDs.

Yet a WTO injunction against the US trade measures, resulting in regulatory competition between shrimp-trawling rules, could also facilitate a third order of decision-making in addition to the WTO judicial process and the market. As with all injunctions, to the extent that transaction costs are low, the parties could negotiate a bilateral or multilateral solution that would attain the United States' trade and environmental goals. In the shrimp–turtle case, the United States and Asian countries could agree by treaty that all shrimp trawlers be required to use turtle-protecting devices, in exchange for the United States paying some form of compensation to the Asian countries. The payment could take the form of cash, technical assistance, or increased access to the US market in other commercial sectors. In other words, regulatory competition can spur regulatory convergence, especially where US regulators fear that firms engaging in regulatory arbitrage can undermine US regulators' authority (Macey, 2003).

A negotiated political solution to the trade–environment–development linkage, spurred by a WTO injunction of US unilateral measures, could be more efficient and more equitable. The side payment could represent an exchange of preferences, balancing developed and developing country concerns. Wealthier countries would pay compensation to developing countries which, in exchange, would enact and enforce regulations to protect endangered sea turtles in line with wealthier country priorities. Richer and poorer countries would simply bargain over the amount that balances their respective priorities for environmental protection and economic development. From the perspective of equity, the developing countries would receive something in return for imposing regulatory measures desired by a US Congress responding to US constituent demands. There would be no more taxation of developing countries (in the form of US-required regulatory requirements and bureaucratic and enforcement costs) without representation. The cost of South and Southeast Asian sea-turtle-protection programs in line with

US preferences would not be borne solely by South and Southeast Asian constituencies. Developing countries and their constituents would be better protected from great power coercion.

The negotiation of the requisite side payments, nonetheless, could be complicated, since shrimp and sea turtles are found in multiple jurisdictions. The negotiations could create perverse incentives, with one country intentionally harming the environment in order to hold out for more compensation (Chang, 1995). Negotiators likewise would face collective-action problems, since countries might fear that a free-rider that did not enforce the regulations could gain a competitive advantage over them. They therefore might refuse an agreement that would be to their mutual benefit.

In short, were the WTO Appellate Body to make the institutional choice of allocating decision-making to the market through issuing an injunction, it would shape how affected parties participate in a market-based institutional process. This institutional process would provide different opportunities for participation from under the first alternative of deference. Both choices would entail tradeoffs involving the mobilization of different biases. On the one hand, allocation of decision-making authority to a market process would be subject to collective-action problems and externalities, potentially resulting in fewer undertakings to address the plight of endangered sea turtles. On the other hand, were a court to show total deference to US regulatory demands, the United States would have little incentive to engage in multilateral bargaining, so that we would never know the impact of collective-action problems in international political negotiations spurred by a WTO injunction. Overall, a WTO injunction could enhance developing countries' leverage in international bargaining over the appropriate balance among the trade, environmental, and development issues at stake.

(3) The international regulatory alternative: allocation of authority to an international political body

Third, a WTO judicial body could refer the matter to another international decision-making body, a positive rule-making body, to balance the competing trade, development, and environmental claims of constituencies around the world. This alternative institutional allocation would involve greater centralization of rule-making at the international level, often referred to as "positive integration," in contrast to "negative integration" promoted through the regulatory-competition model

(Tinbergen, 1965). WTO members have already harmonized substantive law over intellectual property protection under the TRIPS Agreement. On environmental matters, harmonized rules currently are enacted on an *ad hoc* basis in numerous fora, usually under the auspices of UN organizations (such as the United Nations Environmental Programme, UNEP) working in conjunction with interested states and (sometimes) nongovernmental organizations. Former WTO director General Renato Ruggiero supported the formation of a World Environment Organization to act as a counterpart to the WTO on trade and environment matters. Some commentators have promoted the incorporation of environmental agreements into the WTO itself so that the WTO would become a global regulatory organization, and not just a trade organization with regulatory implications (Guzman, 2004).[14]

The primary problem with centralized international rule-making is that nations distrust international political processes for regulatory policy, and wish to maximize their national autonomy. They thus require international rule-making to be made by treaty, which binds only signatory states that ratify the treaty. Secondary rule-making, if contemplated at all, often requires consensus, whether by the treaty's terms or by nations' practice, so that each nation effectively retains a veto right. If the treaty provides for simple or qualified majority voting, the resulting resolutions may be nonbinding, the body's jurisdiction may be severely restricted, or the bodies' members may ignore the formal voting rules and operate by consensus.[15] Although the Agreement Establishing the WTO formally provides for majority or supramajority voting, including for interpretations and amendments, WTO decisions are made infrequently and always by consensus.[16] The WTO political/legislative system, in contrast to its judicial system, is thus relatively weak.

---

[14] Alternatively, a standing committee operated under joint WTO–UNEP or WTO–UNEP–UNCTAD auspices could serve as an *ad hoc* forum to engage experts to assess local environmental, developmental, and social contexts, to negotiate compromise solutions, and to raise funds to implement them (Shaffer, 2001).

[15] See, e.g., Sands and Klein, 2000: 266 (noting "a trend toward a search for 'consensus' as opposed to reliance on the results of formal voting").

[16] As Posner and Rief state, "At least one thing is clear about WTO interpretations and amendments: they are not designed to be taken regularly or readily. In fact, there has not been a single interpretation or amendment adopted since the WTO came into effect in 1995, and there were only six amendments (the last in 1965) in the previous forty-eight years of GATT. Moreover, the interpretation or amendment process – particularly, achieving a consensus – is only likely to become more difficult as the number of WTO members grows" (2000: 504). See WTO Agreement Arts. IX and X. See generally Bhala and Kennedy, 1998: § 4(f)(3).

The current structure of international trade, environmental, and development organizations, moreover, is fragmented. Different institutions have overlapping and uncertain jurisdiction, reflecting the *ad hoc* nature of their creation. For example, there currently is no multilateral treaty that directly addresses most fact-specific trade–environment–development conflicts, as was the case in the shrimp–turtle dispute. The Convention on International Trade in Endangered Species covers only the trade of endangered species, not their preservation through domestic regulatory requirements. The United Nations Convention on Biological Diversity, although it addresses the need to create new mechanisms at the national level to conserve biodiversity, imposes no specific standards and creates no global standard-setting body. Even were the United Nations Convention on the Law of the Sea to provide clearer guidance, neither the United States nor Thailand have ratified it.[17] Similarly, the United States, Thailand, and Malaysia are not parties to the Bonn Convention on the Conservation of Migrating Species of Wild Animals, which has sponsored initiatives for the conservation of marine turtles.[18] The WTO itself has a Committee on Trade and Environment that continues to debate how WTO rules should handle import bans imposed on account of foreign environmental practices, but it has been unable to reach a consensus (Shaffer, 2001).

Each alternative centralized political institution could favor different actors on account of that institution's rules, norms, and procedures. Environmental NGOs tend to favor an environmental forum that brings together environmental ministries, as well as the NGOs themselves, because the institutional context and normative frames can better promote an environmental agenda. Locating decision-making in UNCTAD, in contrast, could facilitate more of a development orientation to policy-making.

The designation of the forum as an environmental, trade, or development body, however, might not matter were international environmental rule-making to affect states' economic interests and to be enforceable before a court empowered to authorize sanctions. One reason that

---

[17] UNCLOS was concluded on December 10, 1982, and entered into force on November 16, 1994. The United States and Thailand have signed the convention, but have yet to ratify it. India, Malaysia, and Pakistan have signed and ratified it. See Multilateral Treaties Deposited with the Secretary General, status at November 18, 1997 (www.un.org/Depts/Treaty/final/t2). Articles 61, 62, 192, and 193, in particular, cover conservation issues.

[18] The Bonn Convention was concluded in 1979 and came into force on November 3, 1983.

NGOs have greater access to decision-making in UNEP is because it is a relatively weak organization that relies largely on the development of norms through "soft-law" mechanisms (Chayes and Chayes, 1995; Haas, Keohane, and Levy, 1993). Were UNEP or another environmental organization to assume greater rule-making and enforcement power, it might be less effective because states would be more vigilant in protecting their economic interests within it. For example, harmonized international food safety standards have been adopted through the Codex-Alimentarius Commission, a joint venture of the UN Food and Agriculture Organization and the World Health Organization. However, the incorporation of Codex standards into the WTO's Agreement on Sanitary and Phytosanitary Standards has transformed decision-making in Codex. In reaction to a series of WTO disputes over food standards, nations began to send trade representatives to Codex meetings instead of food safety experts.

The United States is likewise wary of UNCTAD, seeing it as an organization dominated by developing countries that called for the creation of a "new international economic order" throughout the 1970s (Krasner, 1985) and that still promotes large capital and technology transfers. The United States has thus effectively relegated UNCTAD to being a research body for developing countries. Were developing countries to attempt to make UNCTAD a negotiating forum for rule-making over the interface of trade, environmental, and development policies, the United States would likely refuse to participate and would use its diverse material and ideational resources to undermine UNCTAD initiatives.

Allocation of decision-making authority to a centralized international political process is – as is each alternative – subject to tradeoffs in terms of participation over the appropriate weighing of trade, environmental, and development concerns. Even were international political processes made more robust, they would be subject to serious biases on account of resource imbalances, collective-action problems, and general citizen disinterest in a distant forum. First, the bureaucracies of Northern countries have greater resources, and larger, more experienced staffs. Second, Northern-based interest groups, whether commercial or environmental, have the funds to better represent their views at the international level than do NGO and commercial interests in developing countries. Third, voting mechanisms would be extremely difficult to design (Kahler, 1993). Voting designated by country would be undemocratic, and voting designated by population would favor a few countries, such as China, over others. Moreover, even were centralized international governance mechanisms to facilitate relatively greater voice of a broader array of stakeholders, these mechanisms may be unsuited to respond to local norms, needs, and conditions in rapidly changing environments, and they could confront considerable challenges to their legitimacy.

Nonetheless, since powerful states exercise market and political-military power in the absence of international political structures, the development of new international governance mechanisms could be more important for constituents in less-powerful states to the extent that these states participate in the institution's design, operation, and oversight. Centralized bargaining that addresses sustainable development concerns could provide a focal point for political negotiations that could make the conflicting norms, priorities, and interests at stake in trade–environment–development conflicts more transparent (Shaffer, 2001). Through bringing developing country perspectives to the fore that might otherwise be squelched in a polarized "trade–environment" litigation context, centralized bargaining could potentially facilitate targeted financial transfers that would be more equitable and efficient in addressing environmental and development goals.

In short, participation in an international political secondary rule-making process would also be skewed. In light of the current decentralized and fragmented nature of international institutions, it is not clear where international regulatory decision-making would occur. The WTO Appellate Body's direct use of this institutional alternative was thus severely restricted. Were the WTO Appellate Body to attempt to facilitate international political negotiation over the appropriate weighing of competing concerns in the shrimp–turtle dispute, it would need to take a different path, as examined below.

(4) The judicial alternative: an international court's balancing of substantive norms and interests

Under a fourth approach, the WTO judicial bodies themselves could "balance" competing preferences for trade, development, and environmental protection in their review of the facts of specific cases under open-ended standards (Esty, 1994: 156). The WTO Appellate Body took this direction, in part, when it reversed much of the initial panel's decision in the shrimp–turtle case. Rather than apply a generic analysis to all import bans based on foreign production and process methods, and thereby delegate second-order decision-making to the market, the Appellate Body turned to the "facts making up" the "specific case," and sought to maintain "a balance . . . between the right of a Member to invoke an exception under Article XX and the duty of that same Member to respect the treaty rights of the other Members."[19]

Judicial bodies are better situated to weigh expert evidence and disputed facts in a specific case that is brought before them in order to balance competing concerns. WTO panels increasingly call on experts to testify about environmental and health-related issues relevant to trade disputes in order for the panels to weigh the factual evidence. The panel in the shrimp–turtle case asked the parties for a list of individuals having expertise on matters of sea-turtle conservation, and then designated five marine biologists from this list to report to it as an "expert review group." The panel asked the expert group detailed questions concerning the status of sea turtles in the complainants' waters, their migratory patterns, the relative effectiveness of the complainants' sea-turtle-conservation measures, the relation of shrimp trawling to sea-turtle conservation, and the socioeconomic conditions of the shrimping industry. In this way, WTO judicial bodies can try to take account of the trade, environmental, and development interests and concerns at stake.

Participation within the judicial process, however, is far from neutral. First, as discussed in Section 1, the United States and the EU, as repeat players in WTO litigation, are able to mobilize legal resources more cost-effectively than developing country governments. The dynamics of litigation thus favor them, and, indirectly, their constituents. WTO insiders, for example, found that Malaysia failed to develop available factual and legal arguments in its WTO challenge of the United States' implementation of the Appellate Body's shrimp–turtle decision.[20] Second, constituents are dependent on their national representatives to put forward their concerns, and they do not have equal access to these officials. Their access is a function of domestic political processes that favor discrete producer groups with high per capita stakes in a given claim. Third, where a WTO judicial body accepts an amicus curiae brief from a private party, whether that brief is attached to the government's brief or submitted independently, developed countries and developed country environmental NGOs are more likely to have the resources and legal expertise to submit persuasive arguments and frame debates before WTO judicial panels. Many developing countries fear that the arguments presented

---

[19] WTO, 1998a, paras. 155–59 at www.wto.org.
[20] Interviews with delegates, private lawyers, and members of the WTO secretariat, July 2003, Geneva.

to WTO judicial panels could, as a result, be further skewed in favor of actors from developed countries. Developed country NGOs are also located closer to Geneva to organize parallel demonstrations outside the WTO's Geneva-based premises and complement legal arguments with more direct pressure on the judges.

The WTO Appellate Body was reluctant to allocate substantive decision-making authority to itself in the shrimp–turtle case. It realized that it lacked the legitimacy to engage in a delicate balancing of the priorities of constituencies from countries of widely disparate levels of development under open-ended standards. Although, as any court, WTO judicial bodies are not elected, they are even more subject to legitimacy challenges than domestic courts because of the more fragile social acceptance of their decisions. The WTO Appellate Body thus took a proceduralist turn.

(5) The proceduralist turn: international judicial review of the process of national decision-making

Under a fifth institutional alternative, instead of engaging in a balancing of substantive concerns, the WTO Appellate Body can review the national decision-making process to ensure that it takes into account the views of affected foreign parties. The WTO Appellate Body applied this process-based approach in the shrimp–turtle case. The Appellate Body returned the substantive issue to a lower vertical level of decision-making – that is, back to the U.S. Department of State which was responsible for implementing the US legislation – subject to certain procedural conditions. By reviewing the due process and transparency of the State Department's implementing procedures, the Appellate Body attempted to enhance the representation of affected foreign parties and thereby counter the national biases of domestic legislative and administrative bodies.

To facilitate the participation of foreign stakeholders, the Appellate Body took two primary tacks. First, the Appellate Body faulted the implementing regulations of the U.S. Department of State for a *lack of multilateralism.* The Appellate Body's report noted that the United States had successfully negotiated the signature of an Inter-American Convention for the Protection and Conservation of Sea Turtles, which demonstrates that "multilateral procedures are available and feasible" (paras. 166–70). The report found that the United States never seriously attempted to negotiate a similar agreement with the four Asian complainants. In this way, the Appellate Body tried to foster a more centralized (albeit *ad hoc*) political approach by requiring the United States to attempt first to negotiate harmonized substantive rules before implementing a ban that could trigger a dispute before the WTO judicial process.

Second, the Appellate Body faulted the United States for the *national biases* in its procedures for determining the import restrictions. The Appellate Body effectively required the United States to create an administrative procedure pursuant to which foreign governments or traders would have an opportunity to comment on US regulatory decisions that affect them. The Appellate Body held that the application of the US measure was "arbitrary" in that the certification process was not "transparent" or "predictable," and did not provide any "formal opportunity for an applicant country to be heard or to respond to any arguments that may be made against it" (para. 180). It admonished the United States for failing to take "into consideration the different conditions which may occur in the territories of .... other Members" (para. 164). It required the United States to assure that its policies were appropriate for the local "conditions prevailing" in the developing countries.

Process-based review may seem ideal, since it is relatively less intrusive than substantive review and it directly focuses on the issue of participation of domestic and foreign parties. However, process-based review also raises serious concerns, in particular, because processes can be manipulated to give the appearance of consideration of affected foreigners without in any way modifying a predetermined outcome. Even if international case-by-case review were possible (which it is not), it will be difficult, if not impossible, for an international body to determine the extent to which a national agency actually takes account of foreign interests. Powerful actors can thus go through the formal steps of due process without meaningfully considering the views of the affected parties. In the shrimp–turtle case, the U.S. Department of State simply revised its procedural rules to comply with the Appellate Body's criteria, while still requiring developing country shrimpers to use US-mandated "turtle excluder devices" if they wish to sell their shrimp in the US market.

By focusing on process, the Appellate Body also created legal uncertainty for future disputes where bargaining takes place in the shadow of WTO law. Countries with market power, such as the United States, can exploit this uncertainty by harnessing their market leverage to coerce weaker countries. Weaker countries may not bring a legal challenge because it may be simpler and cheaper to simply succumb to the stronger country's demands in light of the uncertainty of the substantive law and the costs of the legal procedures (Hudec, 2000). Nonetheless, by creating uncertainty, the Appellate Body ruling may also have opened some space for multilateral political negotiations. Through its in-depth examination of the legitimacy of the environmental claims and the need for adaptation to developing country contexts, the Appellate Body decision may have helped frame subsequent bilateral negotiations between the disputing parties, as discussed in Section 3.

Normative choices: the need for comparative institutional analysis

As shown in Section 2, the WTO Appellate Body, as any court, exercises second-order institutional power. In rendering a decision, the WTO Appellate Body can shape decision-making in different institutional processes in which different parties are favored. Participation is biased under each of the five institutional choices examined, as under any governance mechanism. From a normative perspective, however, the ultimate policy question is which institutional mechanism results in relatively less-biased participation compared to the non-idealized alternatives.

The WTO Appellate Body ultimately had to hold the US import ban either legal or illegal, or to decline jurisdiction, in which case the ban would have remained in effect. The WTO Appellate Body's decision thereby set a default rule around which the concerned parties could negotiate. This default rule plays an important role in structuring any political negotiation, both for the dispute in question and for future disputes. If the default rule is that the United States can restrict developing country imports on environmental grounds, developing countries will more likely be forced to accept US requirements without any compensation because of the United States' greater bargaining leverage. If the default rule is that the United States cannot ban imports on these grounds, but rather can only resort to market-oriented labeling devices, developing countries are in a stronger negotiating position to demand compensation in exchange for modifying their domestic regulations.

Since the United States is central to the WTO's existence, and since the shrimp–turtle case was followed closely by US environmental and producer groups, the Appellate Body was somewhat constrained from holding that all US trade restrictions based on foreign production methods are WTO-illegal. The United States likely would not have complied with such a ruling, impairing the efficacy of the WTO's legalized dispute-settlement system. Moreover, the United States may have refused to negotiate around the injunction so as to provide financial assistance to South and Southeast Asian nations in return for their enactment of sea-turtle-protection policies. The explanation lies in the manner in which the US political process accounts for the respective costs and benefits to the United States of an import ban, on the one hand, and financial assistance for conservation efforts abroad, on the other. An import ban results in higher prices for consumers, but that cost does not appear on sales receipts and is difficult to calculate. A line-item budget allocation for Asian sea-turtle conservation, in contrast, is easily reported in the media. Moreover, an import ban directly benefits US producer interests, and these producers have little interest in the financing of environmental conservation efforts in developing nations (Shaffer, 2000: 630). The US Congress was thus less likely to authorize such environmental expenditures.

The result of US noncompliance and refusal to finance environmental adaptation in developing countries would have been a worst-case scenario for the WTO institutionally. There would be no improvement in sea-turtle conservation, no protection of developing countries from US market coercion, disregard for a WTO ruling, and the potential unleashing of further mass protests against the institution. The WTO once more would have been an easy target for Northern environmental groups to condemn it as a pro-business, anti-environment, anti-democratic organization responsible for environmental destruction. Environmentalists, trade protectionists, and sovereign nationalists in the United States could join ranks to call into question the continued existence of the WTO. Such a ruling could have threatened to undermine the very system that the initial WTO shrimp–turtle panel allegedly was attempting to protect. The WTO Appellate Body operates not as an ideal neutral judge, but one that takes into account its own interests and thus shapes decisions to encourage compliance and negotiated settlement (Jay Smith, 2003).[21] It is not free from political pressure, even if it does not expressly take that pressure into account in the language of its decisions.

---

[21] As McDougal and Lasswell wrote, "Since the legal process is among the basic patterns of a community, the public order includes the protection of the legal order itself, with authority being used as a base of power to protect authority" (1959, 10).

As regards the WTO itself, should we thus conclude that the WTO is rigged against developing country interests so that they should never have joined the institution and it should be disbanded or radically curtailed? In the shrimp–turtle case, had there been no WTO, the US legislation and implementing regulations would have been enacted pursuant to a political process in which developing country constituents were unrepresented. Developing countries would have been compelled to change their shrimp-trawling methods to meet US requirements if they were to retain access to the US market for their products.

The Appellate Body decision in the shrimp–turtle case, in contrast, actually induced a US administrative agency to revise its rules so as to work more closely with affected foreign interests before it restricted their imports. Most importantly, the United States confined its trade restrictions to apply on a shipment-by-shipment basis. That is, the United States no longer bans *all* imports of wild shrimp from a country that fails to enact legislation imposing US regulatory requirements. Rather, the United States implemented a certification system that restricts shrimp imports only if they are actually caught by trawlers not using turtle excluder devices. Following the WTO Appellate Body ruling, a US court of appeals overruled a lower court's finding that the US statute required a country-wide ban, taking note of the WTO decision.[22] In short, both US administrative and judicial officials responded to the Appellate Body's decision. The revised U.S. policy on shrimp imports was significantly less coercive, since it did not force developing countries to change domestic regulations for all shrimp trawling (whatever the shrimp's destination), but only for the trawling of shrimp that are sold in the US market.

In addition, the United States increased its efforts to negotiate a regional treaty to address the plight of endangered sea turtles in the Indian Ocean and South Pacific, leading to a memorandum of understanding and action plan signed in 2001.[23] If US environmental groups continue to desire that developing countries change their regulations

[22] See *Turtle Island Restoration Network v. Donald Evans*, 284 F.3d 1282, 1289–1290 (2002) (majority). When an environmental group challenged the revised US State Department regulations, the US government argued that the WTO ruling constituted "the law of nations," and that "an act of Congress ought never to be construed to violate the law of nations, if any other possible construction remains." See *Turtle Island Restoration Network v. Donald Evans*, 284 F.3d 1282, 1303 (2002) (dissent).
[23] Memorandum of Understanding on the Conservation and Management of Marine Turtles and Their Habitats of the Indian Ocean and South-East Asia, 2001, www.wcmc.org.uk/cms/.

to cover all shrimp-trawler operations, regardless of the shrimp's destination, and if the United States continues to negotiate a treaty with these countries, both sides retain some bargaining leverage to potentially reach an end result where priorities over trade, environmental protection, and development promotion are relatively better balanced. The key term here is *relatively* better balanced, compared to the institutional alternatives of eliminating the WTO or curtailing its dispute-settlement system's jurisdiction. The WTO Appellate Body, within the institutional constraints that it faced, attempted to foster second-order institutional processes of less-biased participation that involve reduced coercion and increased inclusion of affected parties.

Conclusion

In a world of large numbers and complexity, no governance mechanism provides for completely unbiased participation or representation of affected interests. All institutions are imperfect. Power asymmetries are always present. As a result, this chapter suggests that the assessment of power's role in the WTO or any other global governance mechanism should be a multilevel, comparative institutional one, or the assessment will be of limited use from a policy perspective.

Scholars of different ideological orientations tend to identify their ideological goals with particular institutions and thus tend to idealize these institutions. Power tends to disappear within their preferred institutions. Neoliberals, taking from neoclassical economics, tend to idealize the operation of "free" markets that operate frictionlessly toward an "equilibrium" of supply and demand. Marxists tend to idealize the alternative of state control of resources through political processes, sometimes following a revolutionary change that results in a "classless" society of absolute equality. Communitarians tend to idealize decision-making by local communities in which "deliberation," and not strategic bargaining, prevails. Civil society advocates tend to idealize models of global democracy through self-organizing transnational nongovernmental networks. Promoters of the "rule of law" tend to idealize the role of omniscient courts that neutrally apply even-handed law.

Yet these institutional predilections are mistaken. Powerful actors can manipulate markets, as markets are beset by problems of externalities, information asymmetries, and strategic oligopolistic behavior. Local deliberative communities can inflict severe costs on outsiders, as demonstrated by zoning decisions that exclude minorities and the poor.

Courts have limited resources to address the range of social conflicts, and the use of judicial processes is enormously expensive, favoring parties with financial resources and high per capita stakes. Self-serving elites can capture centralized administrative processes that are beset by collective-action problems. Collective-action problems likewise undermine the representativeness of self-organizing "civil society" networks. In short, meaningful policy analysis cannot focus on the defects of a single institution while failing to apply the same rigor to its alternatives.

Institutional choice is often deployed strategically. The United States, working in conjunction with business constituents, engages in forum-shifting to achieve its objectives sequentially. The United States ultimately brought intellectual property protection and telecommunications liberalization to the WTO through forum-shifting among bilateral negotiations, regional agreements, and alternative multilateral institutions. Nonbusiness actors also use alternative fora to advance their goals. Environmental activists were able to press a powerful state (the United States) to adopt domestic sea-turtle-protection regulations and then induce that state to use its market power to effectively multilateralize these regulatory requirements.

Strategic actors, however, do not control institutional choice. They operate in a world of uncertainty in which they cannot accurately predict the results of alternative institutional processes. When an issue comes before a multilateral institution, they do not fully control either the process or the outcome. Multilateral agencies, including courts, thus have some discretion to render decisions involving institutional choices that shape participation in the balancing of competing priorities, as shown in the shrimp–turtle case.

Analysis of the operation of power in global governance is necessary because it permits us to better understand how global governance mechanisms are structured, how participation and decisions within them are shaped, and how they affect distributional outcomes and, potentially, social structures. Section 1 assessed how the United States, EU, and their constituents have played a central role in setting WTO rules, in shaping trade principles and norms, in using the WTO judicial process, and in advancing their interests in the dispute-settlement system's shadow. Section 2 showed how the WTO Appellate Body, as any court, can exercise second-order institutional power. The WTO Appellate Body can effectively allocate decision-making over policy matters brought before it to alternative decision-making processes, each of which favors different actors to varying extents.

Section 3, however, shows why an assessment of power's operation within a single institution is insufficient, since policy analysis requires an understanding of the *relative* biases in available institutional alternatives. Eliminating the WTO will not eliminate the exercise of power. Rather, power will simply be manifested in other ways. In some cases, attempting to reduce bias in the WTO may reduce opportunities for weaker parties because the power of the United States, EU, and their constituents will manifest itself outside the WTO institutional context in more biased ways. In social contexts involving high numbers and complexity, institutional alternatives often suffer from similar biases (Komesar, 1995: 23). Yet even where there are parallel biases, they will not be uniform. In criticizing how power operates in any institution, policy analysts need to view it counterfactually in relation to nonidealized institutional alternatives.

7 The power of liberal international organizations

Michael Barnett and Martha Finnemore

International organizations are at the hub of most theoretical and historical discussions of global governance. Politicians, publics, and theorists alike believe that a globalizing world requires mechanisms to manage the growing complexity of crossnational interactions, and international organizations are the mechanism of choice. As a result of this vision, states have established more and more international organizations (IOs) to perform an increasingly varied array of tasks. IOs now manage conflicts, both international and civil. They promote economic growth and free trade, they work to avert environmental disasters, and they are actively involved in protecting human rights around the globe.

The reasons states turn to IOs and delegate critical tasks to them are not mysterious or controversial in most of the scholarly literature. The conventional wisdom is that states create and delegate to IOs because they provide essential functions. They provide public goods, collect information, establish credible commitments, monitor agreements, and generally help states overcome problems associated with collective action and enhance individual and collective welfare. This perspective generates important insights, but the statism and functionalism of this view also obscures important features of IOs, making it difficult to see the power they exercise in global governance. First, the functionalist treatment of IOs reduces them to technical accomplishments, slighting their political character and the political work they do. It also presumes that the only interesting or important functions that IOs might perform are those that facilitate cooperation and resolve problems of interdependent

The authors would like to thank the participants at the conference on "Who Governs in Global Governance?" at the University of Wisconsin-Madison in April 2003, Tom Biersteker, and especially Bud Duvall for comments on the essay.

161

choice. However, IOs do much more. IOs also construct the social world in which cooperation and choice take place. They help define the interests that states and other actors come to hold and, we will argue here, do so in ways compatible with liberalism and a liberal global order. These are important exercises of power that the functionalist view neglects.

Second, the statism of many contemporary treatments of IOs treats them as mere tools of states and has difficulty seeing them as autonomous actors who might exercise power. Despite all their attention to international institutions, there is a tendency among many to treat IOs the way pluralists treat the state. IOs are mechanisms or arenas through which others (usually states) act. The regimes literature is particularly clear on this point. Regimes are "principles, norms, rules, and decision-making procedures." They are not purposive actors. IOs are thus passive structures; states are the agents that exercise power in this view. Yet IOs can, indeed, be autonomous actors with power to influence world events. IOs have autonomy because they have authority. When scholars using neoliberal institutionalism and principal–agent models think about authority, they imagine delegated authority. In this view, authority is a commodity over which states have property rights; it can be transferred to (or withdrawn from) an IO. This is a highly limited view of authority, both conceptually and substantively. Authority is not a commodity but an attribute generated from social relations. An actor cannot have authority in a vacuum; actors have authority because of the particular relations they have with others. The reason IOs have authority, we argue, is that the rationalization processes of modernity and spreading global liberalism constitute them in particular kinds of relations to others. IOs are bureaucracies, and Weber recognized that bureaucracy is a uniquely authoritative (and powerful) social form in modern societies because of its rational-legal (i.e., impersonal, technocratic) character. But IOs are also conferred authority because they pursue liberal social goals that are widely viewed as desirable and legitimate. IOs are thus powerful both because of their form (as rational-legal bureaucracies) and because of their (liberal) goals. This authority gives them a sphere of autonomy and a resource they can use to shape the behavior of others in both direct and indirect ways.

In this essay we offer an alternative framework for understanding the role of international organizations in global governance, one that provides a theoretical basis for expecting autonomous action by IOs, suggests new ways of understanding the various forms of IO power, and highlights the connections of IOs to global liberalism.[1] Section 1 briefly develops the argument that rationalization and liberalism constitute IOs as particular kinds of actors, ones that are able to help organize, regulate, and guide transnational interactions in ways that promote cooperation and liberal values. Section 2 argues that IOs can be usefully characterized as bureaucracies and are conferred authority for reasons owing to their rational-legal standing, their delegated tasks, their moral position, and their expertise. A focus on the authority of IOs generates three important insights: (1) it shows how authority provides the basis of IO autonomy; (2) it highlights how (often liberal) values and social purpose stand behind IOs' technocratic appearance, rules and routines; and (3) it shows how authority provides a resource that IOs use to exercise power in ways that directly shape behavior (compulsory power), indirectly shape behavior at a distance (institutional power), and contribute to the constitution of global governance (productive power). We conclude by considering several normative issues raised by our argument regarding IOs and global governance.

Liberal international organizations

Our contemporary architecture of IOs can be understood as an expression of two central components of global culture – rationalization and liberalism. Max Weber introduced the concept of rationalization in order to describe the process whereby modes of action structured in terms of means and ends, often using impersonal rules and procedures, increasingly dominate the world. Weber clearly saw rationalization as a historical process that was increasingly defining all spheres of life, including the economy, culture, and the state. Liberal ideas have seen a similar, perhaps related, expansion across the globe. Liberal political ideas about the sanctity and autonomy of the individual and about democracy as the most desirable and "just" form of government have spread widely, as have liberal economic notions about the virtues of markets and capitalism as the best (and perhaps the only) means to "progress." These two cultural strands have constituted IOs in particular ways. Rationalization has given IOs their basic form (as bureaucracies) and liberalism has provided the social goals which IOs all now pursue (democracy, human rights, and material progress via free markets). We take up each of these in turn.

---

[1] This essay draw heavily from Barnett and Finnemore, 2004.

IOs are bureaucracies and the modern bureaucracy is, in many ways, exemplary of the rationalization process. It is defined by four central features (Beetham, 1996: 9–12). Modern bureaucracies exhibit *hierarchy*, for each official has a clearly defined sphere of competence within a division of labor and is answerable to superiors; *continuity*, where the office constitutes a full-time salary structure that offers the prospect of regular advancement; *impersonality*, where the work is conducted according to prescribed rules and operating procedures that eliminate arbitrary and politicized influences; and *expertise*, where officials are selected according to merit, are trained for their function, and control access to knowledge stored in files. The modern bureaucratic form is distinguished by the breaking down of problems into manageable and repetitive tasks that are the domain of a particular office, and then co-ordinated under a hierarchical command.

These are the very qualities and traits that led Max Weber (1978a) to characterize modern bureaucracies as more efficient than other systems of administration or organization and reflective of the rationalization processes that were unfolding:

> Bureaucracy exemplified "rationality" ... because it involved control on the basis of knowledge; because it clearly defined spheres of competence; because it operated according to intellectually analyz-able rules; because of the calculability of its operation; finally, because technically it was capable of the highest level of achievement.
>
> (Beetham, 1985: 69)

Bureaucracies, in Weber's view, are a grand achievement in that they depoliticize and depersonalize decision-making, and subject decisions to well-established rules. Decisions, therefore, are made on the basis of technical knowledge and the possession of information. Decision-making procedures informed by these qualities define a rationalized organization, one that can deliver precision, stability, discipline, and reliability.

Yet rationalization is not the only source of legitimacy for bureaucra-cies. We do not defer to bureaucracy and empower it simply because it is a bureaucracy. We defer because bureaucracies serve valued social goals. These rationalization processes are always linked to a broader collective purpose – to notions of "progress," development, justice, security, and the autonomy to develop self-fulfillment (Boli and Thomas, 1999: 38). Historically, bureaucracy has been linked to a variety of social visions. Communism was particularly adept at calling bureaucracy into service.

Nationalist, theocratic, and authoritarian regimes of various kinds have all made use of bureaucracy and provided it with purposes of different kinds (James Scott, 1998). But, internationally, liberalism has colored our attitudes toward the role of international organizations in global governance.

Liberalism has dominated thinking about IOs, both theoretically and in policy circles. Enthusiasm for international organizations as policy prescriptions flows directly from some of the most fundamental theoretical tenets of classical liberalism: a belief in progress and in the capacity of technological change and markets to transform the character of global politics in positive ways by creating ever-expanding material resources that can ameliorate social conflicts. IOs, in the liberal view, are both promoters and managers of these changes. They bring the benefits of progress to those in need and at the same time manage conflicts that may accompany these changes in a nonviolent, impartial, and rational way (see Keohane, 1990; Zacher and Matthews, 1995; Doyle, 1995). They also are valued because of the view that they help to bring about progress, nurturing development, security, justice, and individual autonomy (Boli and Thomas, 1999). Given these virtues, it is hardly surprising that liberals have been the most ardent and longstanding champions of IOs in policy circles (and the most attentive to IOs in the scholarship).[2]

---

[2] For instance, Harold Jacobson's opening sentence of his *Networks of Interdependence* (1979: 1) is: "This is an optimistic book, though I hope not an unrealistic one." He then proceeds to offer a succinct statement that captures most of the classic liberal themes linking progress, change, the prospect of harmony of interests, and the central role of IOs to that end. This positive view of international organizations has been reinforced in recent years by the emergence of an "analytic liberalism" which draws on microeconomics (economic "liberalism") to understand international politics. This view suggests that international organizations provide coordination that enables states to overcome collective problems, produce Pareto-improving outcomes, and perform various functions that enable states to overcome obstacles to cooperation. Implicit in this view are a number of assumptions about IOs, that they are welfare-improving for their members, as well as rational and impartial servants of their members. Given these assumptions, it is hardly surprising that contemporary liberal scholars draw heavily on economistic and rationalist approaches to the study of organizations. These approaches come out of economics departments and business schools and are rooted in assumptions of instrumental rationality and utility maximization. The fundamental theoretical problem for this group, laid out first by Coase and more recently by Williamson, is why we have business firms. Within standard microeconomic logic, it should be much more efficient to conduct all transactions through markets rather than "hierarchies." Consequently, the fact that economic life is dominated by huge organizations (business firms) is, itself, an anomaly. The body of theory developed to explain this focuses on organizations as efficient solutions to contracting problems, incomplete information, and other market imperfections.

As a historical matter, the creation of most international organizations has been part of a larger liberal project emanating from the West. In this view, international organizations are purveyors of progress, modernity, and peace. The first public international unions were created in the middle of the nineteenth century with an eye to spurring greater commercial ties and interdependence. The desire to introduce standardized weights and measures and to coordinate various communication and transportation lines were justified on the grounds that they would promote greater commerce and interdependence between states (Murphy, 1994). These functional associations would not only provide the technical and bureaucratic means to further economic liberalism; the growing interactions were also hypothesized to lead to more pacific relations between states (Russett and O'Neal, 2001; Mitrany, 1966). But IOs were evaluated not only on the grounds that they would promote greater and more profitable and peaceful interactions between states. There was also a liberal assumption that IOs would champion basic liberal values such as freedom, autonomy, and liberty against the lingering absolutism of the day (Iriye, 2002: 13). In other words, these "technical" activities were hardly apolitical and value-neutral and instead were serving cultural ends (Murphy, 1994; Boli and Thomas, 1999).

The next big push of IO-building came after World War I and is most closely associated with the liberal internationalism of Woodrow Wilson. He and other advocates of IOs saw them as able to sustain and promote basic liberal values such as national self-determination, group and minority rights, free trade, and democracy. These general ideas were clothed in notions of progress and order. As Martti Koskenniemi (2002) brilliantly chronicles, those who gathered at Versailles believed that the League of Nations and other international associations not only might help avoid a return to war but also could help civilize nations and bring about progress. In their view, the creation of more liberal states would help to produce a more stable international order. Liberalism, in essence, operated at two connected levels: a liberal domestic order would favor a liberal international order, and a liberal international order would favor a liberal domestic order (Iriye, 2002: chap. 2). This transnational liberal order would produce stability and progress. International organizations such as the League of Nations were designed not only to more rationally steer the world but also to produce a more liberal world that would be self-regulating in more desirable ways.

Despite Cold War tensions, the period after World War II saw an explosion of international organizations, most avowedly liberal in their character and missions. Many of those who were involved in the creation of these IOs were self-identified liberals, but realists, too, valued these international organizations as valuable tools for projecting US power and constructing a liberal international order (Murphy, 1994; Burley, 1993). The half-century of international organization activity between 1945 and 1989 reflects this conscious effort and was largely successful at achieving its goals. The economic institutions set up at Bretton Woods were heavily involved in promoting and sustaining an "embedded liberalism," attempting to guide the international economy away from the mercantilistic practices of the interwar period and toward a regulated but increasingly open international trade regime (Ruggie, 1982). The UN was pivotal to the epochal change from the era of empires to the era of sovereign states, helping to engineer a relatively peaceful decolonization process. The UN also assisted the birth of the human rights regime in this period, laying the groundwork for its extraordinary expansion since the end of the Cold War. IOs thus regulated the postwar world and helped to constitute a largely liberal world order.

With the end of the Cold War, major constraints on expanding liberalism disappeared and the relationship between IOs and construction of a liberal global order became unmistakable. In both their discourse and their activities, IOs revealed a liberal self-understanding and a liberal vision of the role they could and should play in the world. As they have for a century, advocates and staff of IOs hold that the world is being transformed by modernization processes, and that IOs are essential to manage the worst and guide the best of these processes. They also forward human rights and democracy as important principles for shaping and defining not only international but also domestic politics. While the state remains the cornerstone of international politics, many IOs attempt to promote the sanctity of the individual and give greater voice to various identity-based associations and collectivities. The liberal template is particularly noticeable when IOs attempt to "save failed states." Drawing from liberal models of the state, the architects and administrators of these rebuilding tasks nurture liberal practices. Good states have the rule of law and elections that result in changing governments and market economies, and international organizations of all kinds work hard to promote this model (Barnett, 1997). Through their activities and programs, many IOs articulate a notion of progress that is defined largely by liberal principles.

Yet liberalism is not of a piece and, as IOs have attempted to spread and stabilize liberal values, they have confronted contradictions in liberalism and counterattacks from opponents. Contradictions and problems in the liberal vision are well known. Market economies tend not to produce equal distributions of wealth, thereby undermining equality and possibly human rights. Public bureaucracies, often called in by liberal polities to ameliorate the worst effects of markets, are not noted for their efficiency or accountability (Finnemore, 1996: 131–35). Democracy, understood as majority rule and competitive elections, might very well clash with liberal tenets of the rule of law and individual rights when they fail to elect upholders of either liberalism or democracy, producing "illiberal democracies" (Zakaria, 2003). Possible contradictions such as these within liberalism produce much of the politics we see within Western states, and as it spreads around the globe, exported in significant part by IOs, they have created similar tensions both within and among non-Western states as well.

One of the most consequential tensions in the Western (now global) liberal model that is currently fueling conflict around international organizations is the tension between free-market capitalism (liberal economics) and state autonomy (liberal self-determination norms). In the postwar "embedded liberal" compromise, as described by Ruggie (1982), states were understood to have a legitimate role in protecting societies from the harshest features of free-wheeling capitalism, and were accorded substantial autonomy in devising social policies to protect their people from unwelcome features of global markets. International institutions as they operated in the postwar period respected, even celebrated, this buffering role of states as part of the rightful role political communities should play in the global order. Over time, and particularly since the 1980s, however, this buffering role for states has come under attack by pro-market forces of globalization, and international organizations have often been on the front lines of this dismantling of the embedded liberal compromise. The International Monetary Fund, World Bank, and the World Trade Organization have all consistently pushed for greater integration into world markets, even at the cost of domestic social compacts, as the only road to economic growth and prosperity (Stiglitz, 2002b). Although international organizations are not alone in pushing the agenda from regulation to deregulation (nor are they even the most consequential actors), they are clearly among the most visible proponents. They have been central in legitimating this move and, as a consequence, have become lightning rods for political opponents of it, as events in Seattle, Prague, and Washington show.

Rationalization and liberalism have helped to constitute IOs. Certainly states are responsible for establishing them and delegating to them certain functions and tasks. States do this because they expect IOs to be a more effective governance mechanism, enabling them to get the best and avoid the worst of globalizing processes. But states create IOs in a specific historical and cultural context, one in which rationalization and liberalism figure prominently, and these two features have constituted IOs as particular kinds of subjects. IOs take the modern bureaucratic form because of modernity's belief that its organizing principles provide a more rationalized, precise, and efficient way to govern the world. And IOs are valued because of the liberal vision of "progress" they help realize for states and their citizens. As we will see in the next section, this combination has been particularly powerful. As bureaucracies pursuing valued goals, IO become authorities in modern life and are able to help create a liberal world that they are then particularly well suited to regulate.

The authority of IOs

Dominant approaches to international organizations all produce an image of IOs as lacking agency and autonomy, even though they arrive at this conclusion through different theoretical channels. Utilitarian, economistic, and regime approaches deny agency or autonomy by treating IOs only as arenas for action by others, while more structural approaches like that of the institutionalists in sociology treat IOs as mere accretions of global culture, dutifully enacting their scripts. In neither case are IOs autonomous agents. The understanding we offer, of IOs as constituted by both rationalization processes and global liberalism, provides a different view. In this section we show how IOs have been constituted in very particular ways such that they are endowed with authority, ergo autonomy, precisely because they are rationalized, liberal actors.

By authority we mean the ability of one actor to deploy discursive and institutional resources in order to get other actors to defer judgement to them (Lincoln, 1994). Authority has several important characteristics that concern us here. First, authority is a social construction and is part of social relations. It cannot be understood and, indeed, does not exist apart from the social relations that constitute and legitimate it. Second, one of authority's most prominent features is the character of the social relations it entails: authority requires some level of consent from other actors. An actor may be powerful regardless of what others think, but she is only authoritative if others recognize her as such. Other levers of power may be seized or taken, but authority must be conferred. Third, when actors confer authority and defer to the authority's judgement, they grant a right to speak and to have those statements conferred credibility. There is always a range of opinions about any contentious political problem, but not all views receive equal weight or equal hearing. Authority helps an actor's voice be heard, recognized, and believed.

Fourth, this right to speak credibly is central to the way authority produces effects. Because individuals defer judgement to those who are conferred authority, they are likely to alter their behavior in ways that are consistent with the directions laid out by that authority. Authority involves more than the ability to get people to do what they otherwise would not; authority often consists of telling people what is the right thing to do. There is a persuasive and normative element in authority that is tightly linked to its legitimacy. The exercise of authority in reasonable and normatively acceptable ways bolsters its legitimacy. Conversely, it is because we believe in the legitimacy of authorities that we often follow their directives and think those directives are right and necessary, even when we do not like them. This does not imply that compliance is automatic, however. Actors might recognize an authority's judgement as legitimate but still follow an alternative course of actions for some other set of reasons. Indeed, sometimes there are alternative voices, each viewed as an authority, that are giving different judgements and instructions to actors.

IOs are conferred authority because they embody rational-legal principles that modernity values and are identified with liberal values that are viewed as legitimate and progressive. Bureaucracies, international and otherwise, contain authority that derives from their rational-legal character. This argument is most closely associated with Weber's claim that modern bureaucracies are conferred authority because they are organized along rational-legal principles that modernity highly values. In contrast to earlier forms of authority that were invested in a leader, legitimate modern authority is invested in legalities, procedures, and rules and thus rendered impersonal. This authority is "rational" in that it deploys socially recognized relevant knowledge to create rules that determine how goals will be pursued. The very fact that they embody rationality is what makes bureaucracies powerful and makes people willing to submit to this kind of authority. According to Weber (1978b: 299),

> in legal authority, submission does not rest upon the belief and devotion to charismatically gifted persons . . . or upon piety toward a personal lord and master who is defined by an ordered tradition . . . Rather submission under legal authority is based upon an *impersonal* bond to the generally defined and functional "duty of office." The official duty – like the corresponding right to exercise authority: the "jurisdictional competency" – is fixed by *rationally established* norms, by enactments, decrees, and regulations in such a matter that the legitimacy of the authority becomes the legality of the general rule, which is purposely thought out, enacted, and announced with formal correctness.

It is because national and IO staff are perceived as performing "duties of office" and as implementing "rationally established norms" that they are viewed as possessing authority.

Yet this instrumental character of bureaucracy – their need to serve others – means that rational-legal authority, alone, is not sufficient to constitute it. Rational-legal authority gives international organizations their basic form (bureaucracy) and behavioral vocabulary (general, impersonal rule-making), but the form requires some substantive content. Bureaucracy must serve some social purpose (as Weber and others have noted). It is the values and people it serves that make bureaucracy, including international organizations, respected and authoritative. We identify three broad categories of such substantive authority that undergird international organizations and make them authoritative actors – delegation, morality, and expertise. Central to our analysis is that IOs are viewed as pursuing goods and ends that are culturally valued – and doing so through means that are viewed as technical, apolitical, and rational. Thus, international bureaucracies are hardly the value-neutral, technical instruments that they often present themselves as being, and instead are authorities that are invested with cultural content. In the case of IOs, that content has a strong liberal character. Delegation to IOs tends to happen within a distinctly liberal framework of participation, accountability, and transparency; and the moral purposes IOs draw on for legitimacy (for example, promoting human rights and democracy) are decidedly liberal.

At a rudimentary level the authority of international organizations is *delegated authority* from states (Sarooshi, 1999; Keohane and Nye, 2001; Abbott and Snidal, 1998). International organizations are authorities

171

because states have put them in charge of certain tasks. The UN's authority to do peacekeeping comes from the mandate given to it by member
states through the Security Council. The authority of the Office of the
UN High Commissioner for Refugees derives from its statute created by
member states. The European Commission's authority derives from the
powers delegated to it by the European states. Member states delegate
to the IMF the authority to act in certain domains regarding international financial matters. International organizations are thus authoritative because they represent the collective will of their members who
are, themselves, legitimate authorities.

At first glace, this type of authority would not appear to provide
any autonomy for international organizations at all and is fairly consistent with the functionalist view of international organizations. However, the delegation process is not so simple, nor is the kind of authority
delegation confers. States often delegate to international organizations
tasks which they cannot perform themselves and about which they
have limited knowledge. Mandates to international organizations are
often vague or broad, or contain conflicting directives. Consequently,
mandates need to be interpreted and, even with oversight, the agenda,
interests, experience, values, and expertise of IO staff heavily color any
organization's response to delegated tasks. Thus, international organizations *must* be autonomous actors in some ways simply to fulfill their
delegated tasks (Abbott and Snidal, 1998).

As in the case of rational-legal authority, though, delegation authorizes international organizations to act autonomously only to the extent
that they appear to be serving others, in this case the delegators. Delegated authority is always authority on loan. To use it, international
organizations must maintain the perception that they are faithful servants to their mandates and masters. However, serving their mandates may often conflict with serving particular desires of particular
(often powerful) state masters, and sorting out these tensions can be a
major activity for many international organizations. Whatever solution
is worked out, though, international organizations must be presented
as *not* autonomous, but instead as dutiful agents.

International organizations also can embody *moral authority*. IOs are
often created to embody, serve, or protect some widely shared set of
principles and use this status as a basis of authoritative action. The
UN secretary-general, for example, often uses the organization's status
as protector of world peace and human rights to induce deference from
governments and citizens. The Office of the UN High Commissioner for

Refugees similarly uses its moral duty to protect refugees as a basis for autonomous action on their behalf. In addition to such straightforward mandated moral authority, however, international organizations often traffic in another kind of moral appeal. IOs of all kinds often emphasize their neutrality, impartiality, and objectivity in ways that make essentially moral claims against particularistic self-serving states. Thus, we see the heads of international organizations expending considerable energy attempting to demonstrate that they are not doing the bidding of the great powers but instead are the representative of "the international community." The moral valence here is clear: international organizations are supposed to be more moral (ergo more authoritative) in battles with governments because they represent the community against self-seekers.

This aspect of moral authority also allows international organizations to present themselves as depoliticized and impartial. Obviously, defending moral claims is political and in some sense partisan, but to the extent that international organizations present themselves as champions of the shared values of the community against particularistic interests, they draw support for their actions. IOs defending peace and human rights, for example, can claim their actions are neutral and impartial because these are motherhood-and-apple-pie values that we all profess to love.

Finally, international organizations also contain *expert authority*. One important reason why states create bureaucracies is that states want important social tasks to be done by individuals with detailed, specialized knowledge about those tasks. Nuclear proliferation should be monitored by physicists and engineers who know about nuclear weapons; the HIV/AIDS epidemic should be handled by doctors and public health specialists who know about disease prevention. Specialized knowledge derived from training or experience persuades us to confer on experts, and the bureaucracies that house them, the power to make judgements and solve problems. Deployment of specialized knowledge is central to the very rational-legal authority which constitutes bureaucracy in the first place since what makes such authority rational is, at least in part, the use of socially recognized relevant knowledge to carry out tasks (Brint, 1994: 7).

Expertise thus makes international organizations authoritative, but it also shapes how these organizations will behave in important ways. Just as international organizations authorized by a moral principle must serve that principle and make their actions consistent with it to remain legitimate and authoritative, so too, when international organizations are authorized by expertise, they must serve that specialized knowledge and make their actions consistent with it. The IMF cannot propose any policies it chooses. It can only offer policies that are supported by the economic knowledge it deploys. In fact, the organization will not readily entertain policy options not supported by its expertise. Professional training, norms, and occupational cultures strongly shape the way experts view the world. They influence what problems are visible to staff and what range of solutions are entertained (Brint, 1994; Schein, 1996).

Like delegated and moral authority, expert authority also creates the appearance of depoliticization. By emphasizing the "objective" nature of their knowledge, international organizations are able to present themselves as technocrats whose advice is unaffected by partisan squabbles. Some kinds of expertise make this presentation easier than others. For instance, quantification vastly enhances the power of these claims of political neutrality and impartiality. Ironically, the more successful experts are at making numbers "speak for themselves" and yield clear policy prescriptions without interpretation from bureaucrats, the more powerful those policy prescriptions are. The greater the appearance of depoliticization, the greater the power of the expertise.

These four types of authority – rational-legal, delegated, moral, and expert – each contribute in different ways to making international organizations autonomous actors. However, in exercising each type, IOs must manage an important paradox. On the one hand, bureaucracies are always created to defend or promote values, and their promotion of (or embodiment of) widely held social values is what gives them authority and legitimacy. Bureaucracy is inevitably linked to a broader normative order that gives purpose and meaning to all social action, including that of bureaucrats (Zabusky, 1995; Herzfeld, 1993). On the other hand, bureaucracies often justify their power on the basis of their supposedly objective and rational character. In fact, however, such objectivity does not and probably cannot exist, but the myth of such objectivity is central to their legitimacy.

To reconcile contradictory demands of rational objectivity and service to social values, bureaucracies rely on self-effacement. They present themselves as embodying the values of the collectivity and as serving the interests of others – and not as powerful and commanding deference in their own right. To be authoritative, international organizations must be seen to serve some valued and legitimate social purpose and, further, they must be seen to serve that purpose in an impartial and technocratic way. The power of international organizations, and bureaucracies generally, thus lies with their ability to present themselves as impersonal and neutral – as *not* exercising power but instead serving others (Fisher, 1997; Shore and Wright, 1997). The presentation and acceptance of these claims is critical to their legitimacy and authority. IOs work hard to preserve this appearance of neutrality and service to others. The need to appear as impartial servants is central to understanding IO behavior, particularly since in many situations there is no neutral or apolitical ground for international organizations to occupy.

IOs are constituted by both rationalization processes and liberalism, and, accordingly, their practices are reflections of these relations of social constitution. On the one hand, they try to act in impartial, technocratic ways as required by the rational-legal authority that constitutes them. On the other hand, their missions for which they were created require them to pursue and promote social goods that may be deeply politicized. It is this paradoxical blending of their technical form with deeply held values that generates authority and autonomy for IOs, but also creates contradictions and tensions to be managed. In the next section, we examine the way IOs use their authority and show how IOs are able not only to regulate directly and at a distance, but also to help constitute the world that needs to be regulated.

IOs, authority, and power

By recognizing that IOs have authority (i.e., that others defer to their judgement), we gain a new perspective on how IOs can exercise power. In this section we show how IOs are able to use their authority to regulate what already exists and thus exhibit compulsory and institutional power. We also show how IOs contribute to the social constitution of the world and thus play an important role in shaping subjectivities, fixing meaning, and weaving the liberal international order; in this way, they exhibit productive power.

Compulsory power: authority as a normative resource to direct behavior

Typically international relations scholars discount the ability of IOs to exercise power because they assume that the most meaningful and significant resources are material. Certainly there are times when IOs have this kind of power. Sometimes IOs do have material resources. They often have money, even guns, and can use these to influence the behavior of others. The World Bank can use its money to get small farmers to do what it wants. The UNHCR can use food and other resources to shape behavior of refugees. UN peacekeepers sometimes have guns (or can call upon those who do have guns) to coerce parties in conflicts. Such power over nonstate actors is often overlooked by our state-centric discipline, but IOs also, on occasion, shape state behavior. For example, the IMF can coerce states into adopting policies they would not otherwise adopt because of its ability to deny funds or to categorize a country as not on the "right track." While IOs never have the material might to coerce the strongest states into actions they actively oppose, IOs do have material means to shape the behavior of many states on many occasions – a fact often overlooked by IR scholars.

IOs also can use normative resources to shape the behavior of state and nonstate actors. In this instance of compulsory power, IOs use their normative (and sometimes material) resources to try and get other actors to alter their behavior. IOs are quite candid in their beliefs that one of their principal functions is to try to alter the behavior of states and nonstate actors in order to make sure that they comply with existing normative and legal standards. Officials in international organizations often insist that part of their mission is to spread, inculcate, and enforce global values and norms. Although IOs often use techniques of teaching and persuasion that fall outside power, they also use various sorts of shaming techniques or material sanctions to get states and nonstate actors to comply with existing or emergent international practices (Katzenstein, 1996; Finnemore, 1996; Legro, 1997). Armed with a notion of progress, an idea of how to create the better life, and some understanding of the conversion process, many high-ranking staff of IOs claim that their goal is to shape state action by establishing "best practices," by articulating and transmitting norms that define what constitutes acceptable and legitimate state behavior. The European Union, for example, is hard at work persuading members to reconfigure domestic institutions and practices in ways that harmonize with European and international standards. The Organization for Security and Co-operation in Europe is similarly engaged. The greater the material sanctions used to alter behavior, the more this activity looks like what Andrew Hurrell, in chapter 2, calls coercive socialization.

IOs, like all other actors using rhetoric to shape the behavior of others, can and do use a variety of techniques for this purpose. They may frame issues in particular ways, so that desired choices seem particularly compelling or manipulate incentives so that the sanctions and penalties associated with particular policies are excessively high. They may exploit emotions of decision-makers and publics, creating empathy for landmine victims, refugees, and genocide survivors. They may use information strategically, gathering some kinds of information but not others. They may manipulate audiences strategically, inviting or including only some kinds of participants in their bureaucratic process (for example, the economists and bankers "doing" development) but not others (peasants and informal laborers who are the objects of development).[3]

Normative resources are certainly not the only forces shaping the policies of the state and nonstate actors with which IOs deal. Rhetoric and authority are frequently supported by material resources, sometimes (but not always) held by resource-rich states. But to overlook how states and organizational missionaries work in tandem is to overlook a fundamental way in which they are able to directly change behavior.

Institutional power: guiding behavior at a distance

IOs can also guide behavior in ways that are both indirect and unintended. IOs can structure situations and social understandings in ways that channel behavior toward some outcomes rather than others. There may be no overt conflict in this exercise of power. Indeed, part of the power exercised here is the creation of nondecisions when situations are structured such that actors perceive no choice to be made. Furthermore, power can operate indirectly. Power need not be a local phenomenon, and IOs often change behavior in ways that are that are historically and spatially distant. This is most obvious in instances when international organizations' rules and norms have lingering effects, when policies and rules established at one time have echoes long into the future. It is also apparent when behavior is not directly caused by the institution but when it is an "intervening variable" or operating in conjunction with other causes.

One example of this is the way international organizations can exercise power through their agenda-setting activities (Cox and Jacobson, 1971; Pollack, 2003). IO staff frequently have the formal and informal capacity to determine the agenda at fora, meetings, and conferences. This capacity gives them the a substantial role in determining what

---

[3] For a taxonomy of tools of persuasion, see Finnemore, 2003: chap. 5.

is – and is not – discussed. Therefore, agenda-setting capacity gives IO staff considerable influence over what policies are passed and motions are carried. This sort of agenda-setting power is not hard to find. The UN secretary-general frequently structures the options for particular peacekeeping operations and, therefore, establishes the parameters and the directions of the debate in the Security Council. The UN secretary-general's decision to make humanitarian intervention a defining theme of his 1999 address to the General Assembly shaped subsequent discussions. EU officials are renowned for possessing this sort of influence. UNHCR staff shape the discussions at Executive Committee meetings. World Bank officials are directly involved in drawing up the agenda for meetings. In this significant way, IO staff can help to orient discussions and actions in some directions and away from others.

Another way in which IOs have institutional and indirect power over behavior is through classificatory practices. An elementary feature of bureaucracies is that they classify and organize information and knowledge. This classification process is a form of power because it "moves persons among social categories or . . . invent[s] and appl[ies] such categories" and, therefore, constitutes a way of "making, ordering, and knowing social worlds" (Handelman, 1995: 280; see also Starr, 1992). The ability to classify objects, to shift their very definition and identity, is one of bureaucracy's greatest sources of power. This power is frequently treated by the objects of that power as accomplished through caprice and without regard to their circumstances, but is legitimated and justified by bureaucrats with reference to the rules and regulations of the bureaucracy. The IMF has a particular way of categorizing economies and determining whether they are on the "right track," defined in terms of their capital accounts, balance of payments, budget deficits, and reserves. To be categorized as not "on track" can have important consequences for the ability of a state to get external financing at reasonable rates, to get access to IMF funds, or to escape the IMF's conditionality demands. The world is filled with individuals who have either been forced or chosen to flee their homes, and the UNHCR operates with a classification scheme that distinguishes between refugees, migrants, internally displaced peoples, and other sorts of displaced peoples or those who cannot return home. The UNHCR's unwillingness to extend refugee status to groups or individuals can leave them on the margin or physically vulnerable (Hurrell-Bond, 2002). Similarly, classification of a conflict as a "civil war" or "genocide" triggers one set of responses by international actors rather than another.

Productive power: constitution

Authorities not only regulate but also help to constitute the world. IOs are an important part of a broader process that is helping to constitute a liberal global order that is productive of particular kinds of actors and associated practices. This is consistent with the argument we made in section 1. To recall, we suggested that IOs are constituted by rationalization and liberalism and that they, in turn, are central to the diffusion and deepening of this rationalized and global liberal order. IOs, in this crucial respect, are involved not only in helping to regulate the social world (as neoliberal institutionalists claim), but also in constituting that world that needs to be regulated. IOs do constitutive work, helping to shape the underlying social relations that create categories of action, fix meanings, shape subjectivities, and define the good life. IOs are not alone in this process. International NGOs have played a crucial role. So, too, have resource-laden great powers. But IOs, because of their number and, crucially, because of their authority are central actors in this process.

One important aspect of this power is that IOs are often the actors who help to constitute the problems that need to be solved. Problems do not simply exist out there as objective facts; they are defined as problems by some actor (often an IO) through a process of social construction (Edelman, 1988). Thus, coordination and cooperation problems are not part of some objective reality that stands outside experience but are subjectively defined and constituted within social experience – and authorities help create that subjective reality (Raz, 1990). Authorities are often the ones who help to determine whether a problem exists to be solved; they define the problem for others, offering judgements about what kind of problem it is. As authorities, IOs do much of this work in global governance. Development agencies, for instance, were very much involved in determining that "development" was an omnibus solution to a set of problems associated with the inability of countries to apply resources in efficient ways to further economic growth (Escobar, 1995). In this respect, authorities help to define problems in relationship to a category of actions and goals that they view as good and legitimate.

Not only do authorities, such as IOs, help identify problems, they also help solve problems by crafting particular solutions to them and persuading others to accept them. Often there are a great many ways in which a problem might be addressed. Identifying the particular solution to be pursued is extremely consequential and an important exercise of power. Once such a problem is identified and a solution is proposed, the next logical step is to identify a set of actors that should take responsibility for implementing the solution. Authorities such as IOs once again step into the breach. They are often viewed as qualified to manage these solutions to already identified problems and to coordinate the activities of others.

IOs thus use their rules to define problems, craft solutions, and assign responsibilities for action. Their rules may be contested at times. They may also conflict with other rules. But because authorities are frequently defined in terms of their expertise and knowledge, they are viewed as eminently qualified to render a judgement on these matters. They are oftentimes perceived as doing good and, because their intentions are honorable and they are experts in their field, they are given the legitimate right to intervene (Fisher, 1997).

A good example of this process in action is offered by James Ferguson's (1994) analysis of development organizations in Lesotho. Development agencies have as their very *raison d'être* the production of (economic) development. Third World countries are in particular need of their assistance because they are lacking in both development and the expertise and resources to accelerate development. But development agencies have a readymade solution to the problem of development – more market mechanisms. If development is not occurring, then it is because the economy and polity are not organized properly. So, the development agencies propose various policies that are designed to institutionalize market mechanisms but also to teach producers how to respond efficiently and properly to market signals. In this way, they view their goals as transforming self-sufficient "peasants" into market-dependent "farmers." Although development officials see the introduction of the market as a technical solution to the problem of development, the consequence of this technical solution is deeply political because it completely upends social relations in the family, between producers and consumers, and between the village and the state apparatus. In this way, as development agencies attempt to bring about progress and development, they introduce particular solutions to particular problems that not only regulate what currently exists but also help to constitute new social relations that require regulation.

Another example comes from peacekeeping and peacebuilding activities. The second-generation peacekeeping operations that emerged after the end of the Cold War were designed to help states move from civil war to civil society. As the UN intervened in order to save failed states, it attempted to redeem the fallen by producing states modeled on the image of the Western state. Accordingly, peace operations were designed to create a particular kind of state, one that had working markets, was a working democracy, had the rule of law, and the like. In short, these were intended to be liberal, democratic states (Paris, 1997; Barnett, 1997). Many parts of the UN system were involved in this constitutive work (as were NGOs and INGOs, other IOs, and states), and the expectation was that liberal states would be self-regulating and would not require repeated intervention by the international community.

IOs thus help to make a more liberal and rationalized world. They help determine what is progress and what constitutes the good life, both for their own work and for the rest of us. Their notions of progress and the good life, though, are inextricably tied to liberal categories and ideas. They emphasize individual autonomy, democracy, and market economics as the preferred progressive forms of social organization, and remake social institutions which do not conform to these notions. In this important sense, IOs are constituting the world in ways that reflect the same global values that constitute them as social actors.

Conclusion

For much of the past half-century, international organizations have been praised and have benefited from the presumption that globalization requires IOs at the hub of any system of global governance. The reasons for this enthusiasm were many. Historically, traditional liberal sentiments favored international organizations as champions of community interests over self-seeking states, and as clearly preferable to the alternative mode of conflict resolution, war, which was so painfully evident in the early twentieth century. Theoretically, neorealists and neoliberals might have disagreed about the conditions under which international organizations might be effective, but they agreed that they could do important work in furthering state interests where they were allowed to work. For both policymakers and scholars, international organizations provided solutions to an array of policy problems, and challenges to their essential goodness were few and far between.[4]

---

[4] As several observers have noted, there was automatic approval for almost any sort of "international project" to the extent that "anything international is good, as long as it is international." See Kennedy 1994, cited in Klabbers (2001: 225). The first quote is from Kennedy, the second from Klabbers.

This general enthusiasm has waned over the last decade. There is growing concern that the "progress" IOs bring comes at a steep price as individuals, peoples, and states all find it increasingly difficult to control their own fate. Consequently, there are subtle signs of a growing interest in reining in the reach of international organizations. Whereas once international law operated on the implied-power doctrine – international organizations can move into new areas of competence unless it is specifically denied by member states – over the past decade international courts have been increasingly likely to rely on the specialty (or attribution) doctrine – international organizations are limited to the powers specifically delegated to them (Klabbers, 2001: 231). Similarly, IOs are increasingly interested not in regulating but rather in deregulating – a development that mimics what has taken place at the state level (ibid.: 238). Subsidiarity and the possibility of opting out, once a concern only in the EU, have become important principles for many areas of governance. Further, there is also a growing sense that formal, bureaucratic international organizations are too ossified and slow to respond efficiently in a globalizing world. Informal networks and similar decentralized, less bureaucratic forms of governance have become all the rage in many policy circles as an antidote to perceived bureaucratic sclerosis. Thus, there is a growing interest in protecting the local over the universal, an implicit recognition that bureaucracy's presumption that "one-size-fits-all" mentality can be highly inefficient. There is also a growing interest in using policy networks that use different architectures to address specific issues (Keohane and Nye, 2001; United Nations, 2000: chap. 2). There is a growing concern about whether IOs are truly promoting social justice, and whose vision of social justice they are promoting (Steve Weber, 2000). There is a growing interest in IO accountability, transparency, and the democratic deficit. The more international organizations are pushed to the forefront of global governance, the more frequent are the catcalls and criticisms – and the more interested are social movements and states keen to question their actions, to limit their powers, and to search for alternatives.

These developments speak directly to the question of the authority and legitimacy of international organizations. They challenge whether states are likely to continue to delegate to international organizations at the same rate or with the same reflexiveness, whether international organizations will be able to claim the same degree of expert authority in relationship to other expert claims, and whether international organizations will be able to maintain the same level of moral authority. What this portends is a challenge to IO legitimacy on at least three dimensions. First, these developments threaten procedural legitimacy, which considers actions legitimate to the extent that they follow a decision process that is viewed as proper and right, which in this context means conforming to democratic principles. Increasingly, legitimate procedures involve transparency, democratic deliberation, and local participation. On all three counts, IO procedures have been found wanting. Second, they threaten substantive legitimacy, which involves not process but decision output and whether that output is consistent with the values of the broader political community. Refugee policies that violate refugee rights, development policies that impoverish people, and peacekeeping missions that fuel, rather than end, conflicts have all undermined the legitimacy of various international organizations. This legitimation problem is exacerbated by the simple fact that, increasingly, international organizations are involved in multifaceted governance projects that leave them accountable to different political constituencies at different moments, and those constituencies do not all agree on what constitutes substantive success. Finally, the legitimacy of international organizations is very much bound up with ongoing debates over who, exactly, are "the governed" in global governance. Are international organizations governing a community of states or are they governing a community of peoples? Much of the current dissatisfaction with global governance generally and international organizations specifically stems from champions of "the people" who believe their interests are being forgotten. This is certainly true in the protests against the international financial institutions, but the issue is also central in the discussions within the EU, where opinion polls consistently show that publics believe the union is an elite project and are deeply skeptical about its virtues.

Neither international organizations nor the tensions that are inherent in their liberal mission are likely to disappear any time soon. This rather fatalistic observation we owe to Max Weber. One hundred years ago he observed that his Prussia was becoming bureaucratic. He welcomed this development, recognizing that it would enable an increasingly complex society to coordinate its activities in a more rational, objective, and peaceful manner. He was further heartened by the realization that the bureaucracy was helping to inculcate in his fellow citizens the very liberal, rational values that he prized. But his joy was quickly moderated by his concern that a bureaucratic world had its own perils, producing increasingly powerful and autonomous bureaucrats who can be "spiritless" and driven by rules, and who can apply those rules in ways that harm the very people whom they are expected to serve. For the remainder of his life, Weber feared that the very bureaucracy that was needed to keep a society democratic, prosperous, and healthy might also undermine society's well-being.

What Weber observed at the beginning of the past century at the domestic level, we observe at the beginning of the new century at the global level. States have built a metropolis of international and regional organizations that are intended to help them facilitate interdependence and manage its excesses. Without international organizations, states would be less likely and able to reap the fruits of commercial exchange, find nonviolent dispute mechanisms, or solve their environmental problems. But international organizations are not only helping states coordinate their activities, they also are shaping which activities the international community values and holds in high esteem. Beginning in the nineteenth century and continuing into the twenty-first century, international organizations have been disseminating the liberal values that are the foundations for a global liberal culture. But the very source of their power to do good might also be the source of their power to do harm, to run roughshod over the interests of states and citizens that they are supposed to further. We live in an age when international bureaucracies are necessary to manage globalization, and desirable because they can nurture a global liberal culture. But that will come at a cost.

8   The power of interpretive communities

Ian Johnstone

Analyses of the role of law in international politics tend to revolve around a central question: is law a reflection of power or a constraint on power? Answers to that question are unsatisfying (and inconclusive) when reduced to an inquiry into the power of law to directly affect behavior. In this chapter, I seek to broaden that inquiry by considering the impact of law in terms of the different forms of power elaborated in this volume. I do so by examining the relevance of legal norms and discourse in the Security Council of the United Nations. My argument is that the legal discourse demonstrates three forms of power: it shapes the conditions or terms of interaction among all those associated with Council practice (productive power); it indirectly steers action in a certain direction (institutional power); and, when wielded effectively by individual actors, it can directly affect the positions of states (compulsory power).

One might imagine that compulsory power alone is determinative in Security Council deliberations. Clearly, states with the greatest material resources and the veto dominate the terms of debate in the Council and hold disproportionate *power over* others. By offering rewards and wielding threats, they can secure votes to impose binding obligations and enforce those obligations through economic sanctions and military action. They may also wield "soft power," inducing compliance

This chapter draws heavily on Ian Johnstone, 2003, "Security Council Deliberations: The Power of the Better Argument," *European Journal of International Law* 14(3): 437–80. The first draft of this paper was written for a conference organized by Michael Barnett and Bud Duvall, at which I received thoughtful comments from many participants. I am especially grateful to the co-organizers as well as Duncan Snidal and Bruce Cronin, who served as discussants of the paper. Due to the thorough and very perceptive comments of all four, the chapter is greatly improved. Any errors, of course, are my own.

through persuasion and the force of ideas, as well as material incentives and disincentives (Nye, 2002). But compulsory power does not tell the whole story; institutional power and productive power are also exhibited in Council debates and decisions. The Security Council is not totally dominated by the United States, or even the five permanent members (the P5). Moreover, their influence is derived in part from the normative and institutional framework embodied in the UN Charter. The authority conferred by the Charter extends the reach of the P5 beyond their power to directly control the behavior of other international actors. Yet they are also constrained by that framework, because if they ignore it or act in a manner that flagrantly undermines it, their ability to draw on institutional power in the future is diminished.

The fact that legal argumentation is common in the Security Council adds another dimension to the complex relations that exist in and around the institution. Law is, fundamentally, a discursive practice. Legal discourse, as I have argued elsewhere, occurs within interpretive communities composed of participants in a particular field or enterprise (Johnstone, 2003). These communities emerge from discursive interaction in the international legal system, and they help to define the rules and norms that become embedded in institutions. The rules and norms in turn affect the dynamics of interaction within the institution. Interpretive communities set the parameters of acceptable argumentation – the terms in which positions are explained, defended, and justified to others in what is fundamentally an intersubjective enterprise. In this way, legal discourse is itself a form of productive power.

The chapter is divided into two sections. I begin by outlining a conception of law as a process of justificatory discourse, and explain the role of interpretive communities in that process. In the second section, I examine the Security Council as a deliberative setting that deals with some of the most divisive issues in world politics, and yet where legal norms are often invoked to explain, defend, justify, and persuade. I analyze the debates surrounding NATO's intervention in Kosovo in 1999 to show that legal discourse does count, even in the Council, a conclusion that is reinforced by the even more acrimonious deliberations over Iraq in 2003. Legal considerations did not prevent either intervention, but the discourse shaped the context in which decisions were made, and may shape how debates are waged and decisions made in the future.

186

The role of interpretive communities

A distinctive feature of the international legal system is its decentralized character: there is no global legislative body, no central tribunal with compulsory jurisdiction over all disputes, and no administrative body with overarching executive powers. The decentralized and *ad hoc* nature of the system has led respected commentators to suggest that law is of little relevance to international peace and security, that such law as exists merely reflects the distribution of material resources among states. Law is a tool of state power.

An alternative perspective, more widely held among legal scholars and increasingly by international relations theorists, is that law operates largely through a particular form of discourse – a process of verbal interchange or "diplomatic conversation" in which the role of legal norms figures prominently (Chayes and Chayes, 1995: 118–19; Franck, 1995; Abbott and Snidal, 2000). In this conception, international law is interpreted and applied through the discursive interaction of relevant actors, usually in response to specific disputes or international incidents and often in international organizations. It is driven by a felt need to justify: "an effort to gain assent to value judgements on reasoned rather than idiosyncratic grounds" (Kratochwil, 1989: 214). Whatever a state's motivations for action, to be persuasive it cannot base its legal case purely on grounds of self-interest (Schachter, 1989: 59).

Thus there is a substantial tradition of legal writing that presents a conception of law as fundamentally a discursive process. The invocation of legal norms imposes limits on the style of argument or mode of deliberating (Kratochwil, 1989: 210; 2000: 51; Sunstein, 1996: 13). This helps account for law's distinctive character, as it is situated in the broader context of international politics, state power, and state interest. Even if law is a tool of power, it must be wielded in a distinctive manner if it is to have the desired effect.

Why states feel compelled to engage in legal discourse, to justify actions on the basis of law, is a complex question. Both instrumentalist and constructivist reasons can be posited. From an instrumentalist perspective, states care about collective judgement of their conduct because they have an interest in reciprocal compliance by and future cooperation with others, as well as a more long-term interest in the predictability and stability of a law-based international system. From a constructivist perspective, membership and participation in that system can generate a sense of obligation to comply with its rules, regardless of the instrumental benefits such compliance may bring. Indeed, the *practice* of law serves to blur the distinction between calculations of interest and a sense of feeling bound. Once states see themselves as having an interest in participating in the international legal system, "then the idea of obligation and the normativity of the rules . . . acquire a degree of distance from the immediate interests or preferences of states" (Hurrell, 1993: 60).

Both sets of reasons, moreover, are tied up with reputation. As Louis Henkin concluded years ago, "every nation's foreign policy depends substantially on . . . maintaining the expectation that it will live up to international mores and obligations. Nations generally desire a reputation for principled behavior, for propriety and respectability" (Henkin, 1979: 52). Reputational concerns often weigh in favor of observing law or, what may be the same thing, refraining from putting forward implausible legal interpretations that are likely to be recognized and branded as such. The more tightly bound states are in international regimes, the more valuable is a reputation for reliability. As Chayes and Chayes (1995: 27) put it:

> for all but a few self-isolated nations, sovereignty no longer exists in the freedom of states to act independently, in their perceived self-interest, but in membership in reasonably good standing in the regimes that make up the substance of international life . . . The need to be an accepted member in this complex web of international arrangements is itself the critical factor in ensuring acceptable compliance with regulatory agreements.

The need to remain a member in good standing is felt more acutely by states with the least compulsory power, but even the materially strong feel pulled to justify their conduct in principled terms, because they benefit from the stability that the international legal system provides (Hurrell, 1993; Schachter, 1989). A reputation for law-abidingness is not the only kind that matters in world politics, but to the extent that a state sees benefits from participating in a regime or institution, it has an incentive to convince others that it plays by the rules of that institution (Keohane, 1997).

From a constructivist perspective, concerns about reputation and status relate to a sense of being part of a community and becoming socialized to its norms. As governmental and nongovernmental actors interact, they generate and interpret international norms, which can become internalized domestically. It is through this "repeated cycle of interaction, interpretation, and internalization that international law acquires its 'stickiness,' nation-states acquire their identity and that nations come to 'obey' international law" (Koh, 1997: 2655; Finnemore and Sikkink, 1998: 896–905). More concretely, compliance becomes a matter of habit as the rules of the system become embedded in bureaucratic routine and legal structures. The creation, interpretation, and implementation of law generate a predisposition towards compliance, not shared by everyone, but sufficiently widespread to influence the climate of opinion. And because the internalization occurs in all participating states, a transnational network coalesces whose members share at least some expectations, beliefs, and understandings about the nature of the legal regime in which they participate. Embedded in their respective systems, they operate in relative harmony.

The concept of an interpretive community

If states feel compelled to justify their actions on the basis of law, who decides which justifications will do? Legal practice is fundamentally an exercise in interpretation (Dworkin, 1982: 527; Sunstein, 1996: 167). To claim that law is a distinctive form of reasoning implies that good arguments can be distinguished from bad. In the decentralized international legal system, courts and other third-party arbiters are sometimes asked to make that distinction, but often the only interpreters of the law are domestic officials who are institutionally and politically predisposed to positions that favor their government or state. Does that mean any argument will do? No, because in any interpretive dispute, the range of possible legal arguments that can acceptably be deployed is not infinite (Alvarez, 2001: 136; Koskienniemi, 1989: 48). Good arguments *can be* distinguished from bad. The concept of an interpretive community explains why.

The originator of the concept, Stanley Fish, never defines interpretive community precisely, but rather explains it in terms of its function in interpretive practice. Designed to avoid the pitfalls of both pure objectivity (meaning resides in the text) and pure subjectivity (meaning resides in the reader), it is best understood as a way of speaking about the power of institutional settings, within which assumptions and beliefs become matters of common sense (Fish, 1980; Abraham, 1988: 122–24). The interpretive community constrains interpretation by providing the assumptions, categories of understanding, and "stipulations of relevance and irrelevance" that are embedded in a particular practice or enterprise (Fish, 1989: 142). All professional interpreters, Fish argues, are situated

189

within an institutional context, and interpretive activity makes sense only in terms of the purposes of the enterprise in which the interpreter is participating. Furthermore, a given text is always encountered in a situation or field of practice and therefore can only be understood in light of the position it occupies in that enterprise. Texts do not have properties before they are encountered in situations; the meanings they have are always a function of the circumstances in which they are encountered. Thus, interpretation is constrained not by the language of the text, or its context, but by the "cultural assumptions within which both texts and contexts take shape for situated agents" (ibid.: 300). Meaning is produced neither by the text nor by the reader but by the interpretive community in which both are situated.

The idea of interpretive communities helps explain why discourse about competing interpretations within a field of practice or enterprise is possible as long as there is an understanding, largely tacit, of the enterprise's general purpose. Disputes over meaning are resolvable through the "conventions of description, argument, judgment and persuasion as they operate in this or that profession or discipline or community" (ibid.: 116; 1982: 562). The professional interpreter is a participant in a particular field of practice and is engaged in an activity that must be persuasive to others. In that capacity, he or she acts as an extension of an institutional community; failure to act in that way would be stigmatized as inconsistent with the community's conventions. In other words, if the interpreter proffers an interpretation that reaches beyond the range of responses dictated by the conventions of the enterprise, he or she ceases to act as a member of the relevant community.

The notion of an interpretive community is meant to describe the nature of interpretation, not a collection of people, but it is useful to consider who might actually belong to this community to appreciate that the concept is not a mere abstraction. In the international legal field, it is easiest to imagine two concentric circles: an inner circle composed of all individuals directly or indirectly responsible for the formulation, negotiation, and implementation of a particular legal norm; and an outer circle of lawyers and others engaged in professional activities associated with the practice or issue area regulated by the norm. The inner circle consists primarily of a network of government and intergovernmental officials who, through the process of creating and living by rules, come to share assumptions and expectations, and develop a body of consensual knowledge. This consensual knowledge yields understandings and stipulations of relevance that lead them to interpret a text in common. The outer circle is an amorphous group of all those regarded as possessing expertise in international law and/or special knowledge in the relevant field. It includes political leaders, diplomats, judges, government officials, international civil servants, lawyers, scholars, and nongovernmental actors who participate directly or indirectly in the international legal process. Analogous to what Schachter (1977: 217) has called "the invisible college of international lawyers," the concept is similar to an epistemic community (Haas, 1992a). The interpretive community's principal function is to offer legal opinions and to pass judgement. Its job, so to speak, is to decide which interpretation of a treaty or other law is best.

The competency or expertise of those in the outer circle comes from training and immersion in international law or the substantive field in which an interpretive dispute arises. As participants in a field of practice, they have learned its purpose and conventions not as a set of abstract rules but through the acquisition of "know-how," a mastering of discipline or technique (Postema, 1987: 304). Their values may vary with the political and cultural community from which they hail, but the members of the legal interpretive community share a perspective and way of understanding the world acquired through their immersion in the law and interaction with one another. The influence of members of the outer circle derives from the concerns states have about anticipated judgements of their actions and claims of justification. The credibility of their judgements turns on the extent to which they are seen to speak as true masters. Their perceived expertise is a source of authority (Barnett and Finnemore, chap. 7 in this volume). The collective wisdom of international lawyers in the field of peace and security may not carry the cachet of, say, scientists in the environment field but, legal advisers do play a distinctive role because they are specialists in the law. A creative government lawyer can invoke arguments that suit her client's ends but, to do this successfully, she must formulate positions that meet the test of legal credibility (Schachter, 1989: 50). Who administers that test? The interpretive community does. The opinion of a government legal adviser is a gauge of what the judgement of the interpretive community is likely to be; the opinion of a legal adviser to an intergovernmental organization is that plus an element of community judgement itself.

Legal discourse as an intersubjective enterprise

Legal discourse within an interpretive community is necessarily an intersubjective enterprise. As Ruggie and Kratochwil (1986: 764) have argued about international regimes generally, we know them "by their principled and *shared* understanding of desirable and acceptable forms of social behavior." To participate in a regime is to engage in a collectively meaningful activity, an activity collectively understood. Gerald Postema's (1987: 309–10) description of friendship as a social practice helps illustrate the point:

> The history of the friendship is a common history and the complex meaning of the relationship is collectively constructed [by the friends] over the course of the history . . . [T]he shared life of friends engenders common perception, a common perspective, and common discourse. Friendship is characterized, ultimately, not by sympathy or consensus, but by common deliberation and thought . . . A friend's understanding of the relationship could only be achieved through interaction with the other.

Similarly, international law is an intersubjective enterprise. Interpretation is the search for an intersubjective understanding of the legal norm at issue: the interpretive task is to ascertain what the law means to the parties to a treaty or subjects of the law collectively rather than to any one of them individually. International legal interpretation is not "a conversation with [one]self, as joint author and critic" – Ronald Dworkin's (1986: 58) metaphor – but rather an interactive process, the parameters of which are set by an interpretive community. While there are likely to be disagreements about the proper interpretation of a rule, "purely idiosyncratic uses are excluded even if the use of the concepts remains contestable and contested" (Kratochwil, 2000: 52). Discursive interaction both constrains interpretation and helps shape the intersubjective understandings and beliefs that make "authoritative" interpretation possible. It helps mold the process of decision-making by establishing what counts as legally relevant and who counts in the debate (Toope, 2000: 98). In other words, international law is at once the language of international society and an important determinant of who has a voice.

To summarize, an interpretive community loosely composed of two concentric circles of professionals associated with a field of legal practice sets the parameters of discourse for that practice and affects how the law is interpreted. It is in effect the arbiter of what constitutes a good legal claim – the institutional mechanism closest to an impartial judge that most international disputes provide. Its influence is exercised by passing judgement, wielded directly by evaluating particular interpretations and applications of the law, and indirectly in the way states measure their own interpretations against anticipated judgement of the community. The interpretive community, as a result, is the locus of various types of power. By setting the parameters of legal debate, it evinces productive power, and, by steering action in a direction that can only be justified in terms of accepted legal norms, it wields institutional power. The interpretive community is not free of compulsory power, however. There are dominant actors who do wield disproportionate influence because they have greater access to the venues of authoritative discourse, and the resources to advance certain points of view and suppress others. But their influence is not in direct proportion to material power because the understandings the strong as well as the weak have about international life – and about their own interests and identities as international actors – are determined partly by the legal discourse the interpretive community makes possible.

The Security Council as a forum for justificatory discourse

International legal discourse takes place in various settings, but tends to be especially intense in international organizations where there is an expectation that positions will be backed by arguments based on collective interests and justified in terms of principles that apply equally to all who are similarly situated. When the relevant law is the UN Charter, the Security Council is the central arena. Legal arguments are often used in Council deliberations, even by its dominant members. In this section, I look first at the Council as a deliberative setting, where the different forms of power are exhibited. I then offer an analysis of the debates over NATO's intervention in Kosovo to demonstrate the impact of legal norms and discourse. These norms did not directly affect the behavior of the intervening states, but did shape the context in which decisions were made and presented to relevant publics, and ultimately affected the aftermath of the intervention and altered the terms of debate on humanitarian intervention.

The Security Council as a deliberative setting

The Council is an unlikely place for legal discourse. It deals with some of the most divisive issues in world politics, where one would expect legal arguments to be dwarfed by political considerations. Indeed, the notion that deliberation of any sort matters in the Security Council may seem rather farfetched. As Thomas Risse (2000) notes, pluralistic security communities based on a collective identity and shared values and norms might constitute a "common lifeworld" in Habermas's terms, as might certain heavily regulated issue areas such as human rights, the environment, and trade. But the Security Council is different. It was designed to be as heterogeneous as possible, dominated by five permanent members with little more in common than victory in World War II (and, later, the possession of nuclear weapons), joined by ten other countries elected by the UN General Assembly every two years on the basis of geographical diversity. Is discourse on the basis of law possible in that setting? My argument is neither that a "common lifeworld" exists in the Council, nor that it must exist for legal discourse to occur (Lose, 2001: 186–87; Toope, 2000: 98). All that is necessary is that the members believe that they are in an ongoing relationship, and that they share a general understanding of the purpose of the enterprise in which they are collectively engaged. In terms of the UN Charter, the enterprise is the maintenance of international peace and security. The contours of what that means have emerged and evolved through practice. The Council has not yet gone the way of the Council of the League of Nations because its members continue to believe it serves a useful purpose; accordingly, they think twice before making arguments that will undermine the credibility and value of the institution.

Debates in and around the Security Council do occur within a minimal framework of shared meanings and understanding about the norms of international life. The normative framework is embodied in the UN Charter, supplemented by treaty law, decisions, and opinions of the International Court of Justice, and declarations from bodies such as the General Assembly and Human Rights Commission. Most important, Security Council practice has shaped – and been shaped by – the normative framework. There are standard forms of argument used to appraise and ultimately accept or reject competing claims, a discourse that is fundamentally about the limitations imposed by the Charter and the relative weight to be assigned to the overarching purposes of the UN at any given time. The ability to engage in that discourse effectively is important. Although there is no formal requirement that votes in the Council be backed by good arguments, influence depends to an extent on competence in the discourse, the "rules" of which are not written but followed as a matter of practice by participants in the enterprise.

This normative framework, moreover, has evolved since the UN was founded. The evolution is most striking in the field of human rights and the related concept of human security. The emergence of a dense web of international and regional human rights instruments in the first forty-five years of the UN's existence has been followed by a series of so-called humanitarian interventions authorized by the Security Council since 1991. The five permanent members have been dealing with each other on an almost daily basis for the past thirteen years, debating "the new world order" in a variety of contexts, on immediate crises and thematic issues such as the protection of civilians in armed conflict. From northern Iraq, through Bosnia, Somalia, and Sierra Leone, to East Timor, collectively they have found a way of authorizing – or endorsing after the fact – operations that would have been unthinkable during the Cold War. The immediate response to events of September 11 supports this image of convergence among the P5. They all but endorsed US "self-defense" action against Al-Qaeda and the Taliban; they authorized the substantial peacekeeping and reconstruction effort underway in Afghanistan today; and they unanimously adopted SC Resolution 1373, an unprecedented act of law-making which requires every country in the world take steps to suppress the financing and harboring of terrorist organizations. The diplomatic debacle surrounding Iraq demonstrates the fragility of P5 harmony but, as I will argue below, it actually reinforces rather than undermines the argument that legal norms and discourse are a constraint.

The P5 can be seen as an exclusive club with a shared history and set of experiences. They have learned about each other and have acquired some shared understandings, including about how each views their rights and responsibilities under the UN Charter. Paraphrasing Rawls and Habermas, practice within the Council has contributed to "overlapping lifeworlds" among its members, at least to the point where it is not nonsensical to talk about a discourse on the basis of the relevant norms. The normative framework is not sufficient to yield a single "right answer" in Dworkin's (1986) sense, but it is enough to distinguish good arguments from bad. The language of law is the glue that holds the "overlapping lifeworlds" together.

Is this minimal normative framework enough to channel or constrain compulsory power? Is the distribution of material and voting power in the Council so unbalanced that the dominant states can simply ignore the expectation that they back up positions with "good arguments"? Five members have the veto and other sources of leverage that give them substantial control over the Council's agenda. And, since 1991, most deliberations have taken place in informal consultations, out of the public eye, with no official records kept, and little opportunity for the broader interpretive community to directly affect the terms of debate. It is clear that the Council is far from an ideal deliberative setting.

A closer look, however, suggests that the deliberations are not inconsequential, that productive and institutional power do count. To begin with, the fifteen members of the Council are formally equal in the sense that debates among them are nonhierarchical, at least in principle, and the arguments of each are entitled to equal consideration. This formal equality is reinforced by Article 24 of the Charter, which stipulates that the Security Council acts on behalf of the entire UN membership. Thus even the smallest members count equally as representatives of the international community and are at least notionally expected to speak for all in the collective interest. Moreover, nonmembers are allowed to speak in open meetings and – a recent innovation – "private" meetings. The civilian and military heads of peacekeeping missions, as well as the heads of relevant UN agencies, are often invited to the Council. Even nonstate parties to conflicts and NGOs have spoken in so-called Arria formula gatherings. And the relative ease of access to the Secretariat and diplomats (of some countries) stationed at UN headquarters means that the more active and credible NGOs have little trouble making their voices heard.[1] In sum, the Security Council is not a sealed chamber, deaf to voices and immune to pressure from beyond its walls.

Moreover, despite the increase in informal consultations, the glare of publicity does affect Council decision-making. The outcomes of many Security Council debates – the resolutions and statements adopted or defeated – are very public and are usually accompanied by explanations of votes. More open meetings are now held before voting, which puts pressure on Council members to explain their positions publicly. Because arguments based on self-interest are less capable of withstanding public scrutiny, at a minimum, "the civilizing force of hypocrisy" comes into play (Elster, 1998), compelling governments to match deeds with words, at least enough to dodge charges of blatant hypocrisy (Risse, 2000: 32). Most of the effort at persuasion takes place in private, where one would suppose legal arguments count for less, but this effort is influenced by the subsequent need to justify. If a Council majority threatens to push a matter to a vote, those contemplating a veto may hesitate if

---

[1] On recent innovations in Security Council practice, see UN Document S/RES/1353, 13 June 2001, and UN Document S/1999/1291, 30 December 1999. For influential analyses of the powerful new role NGOs play in international affairs, see Keck and Sikkink, 1998; Finnemore and Sikkink, 1998.

they have doubts about whether their explanation will pass muster with the outside world. In other words, debates in private are animated by arguments that will be used later to justify positions in public, where the outer circle of the interpretive community sits ready to pass judgement. Indeed the informal consultations of the Security Council are not treated by the members as completely private. With fifteen representatives, plus aides and Secretariat staff present, rarely is a word uttered that the speaker would not want to be known publicly. Since there are no official records of the meeting, the utterances can always be denied, a not insignificant point, but the glare of publicity does find its way into even informal consultations of the Security Council, if only through the cracks in the windows.

The Kosovo case

Kosovo is a hard case. Debates in and around the Council were about the propriety of humanitarian intervention without explicit authorization, and it is clear that legal considerations were not determinative. Various legal justifications for the action can be (and were) posited, ranging from a customary law right of humanitarian intervention, combined with a narrow reading of the UN Charter Article 2(4) prohibition against the use of force, to broad readings of the Chapter VII resolutions adopted months before the NATO campaign (Resolutions 1160, 1199, and 1203), combined with tacit endorsement after the fact (Resolution 1244). Strong counterarguments to each claim can be (and were) made; indeed, the weight of scholarly opinion is that none of the justifications passed muster and thus the intervention did violate international law.[2] Yet there is much in the debates to suggest that legal discourse was not irrelevant, and that the aftermath of the intervention can be explained only in terms of the interplay of compulsory, institutional, and productive power. I have analyzed the debates at length elsewhere, particularly those of March 24, 1999, when the NATO airstrikes began, and March 26, the day Russia's draft resolution condemning the intervention lost by a vote of 12 to 3 (Johnstone, 2003).[3] My purpose here is to highlight four features of the discourse to illustrate the power of interpretive communities.

---

[2] See for example, Roberts, 1999; Chesterman, 2001: 206–19; Simma, 1999; Cassese, 1999. For editorial comments, see: Henkin, et al., 1999; White, 2000; Kritsiotis, 2000; Glennon, 2001.

[3] For records of the debates, see 3988th meeting of the Security Council, 24 March 1999, S/PV.3988; 3989th meeting of the Security Council, 26 March 1999, S/PV.3989.

First, the variegated nature of the legal argumentation is revealing. All direct participants in the debates on both sides invoked legal norms and principles, but pressed them with varying degrees of vigor. Because Council members were not unified on the norm of humanitarian intervention, arguments ranged from clear assertions of legality or illegality (e.g., Russia, China, the UK, and the Netherlands) to more tentative statements about the legal context in which the intervention took place (e.g., the United States, Canada, Brazil, Argentina, and Slovenia). But the mere fact that legal arguments were advanced by all members of the Security Council, including the P5, suggests that the normative framework provided by the Charter and other instruments must be robust enough to warrant an effort to justify positions on legal grounds. And because there is an interpretive community to "guard" that normative framework, the law is not infinitely manipulable. If it were, either legal arguments would not have been made or they would all have been more straightforward claims of (il)legality since there would be no need to worry about the test of credibility (who would administer that test?). It is in anticipation of judgement by the interpretive community that legal arguments are advanced. The variegated nature of the arguments itself is circumstantial evidence of meaningful (not epiphenomenal) legal discourse.

Second, concerns about precedent affected the legal positions taken by supporters of the intervention, and those concerns are only intelligible if something like an interpretive community is at work. The United States consistently asserted the legality of intervention, but ultimately relied on a "laundry list" of factors and a general claim of legitimacy, rather than a single legal justification,[4] in part because it was concerned about the precedent that could be set by acceptance of a doctrine of humanitarian intervention. Some NATO allies, including Germany, Portugal, and Belgium, shared that concern.[5] Others, such as the UK and the Netherlands, showed more confidence in the legal case, but the net

[4] In addition to the statements of Ambassador Peter Burleigh, S/PV.3988 (at 5) and S/PV.3989 (at 4–5), see President Clinton's Address to the Nation on NATO Airstrikes on March 24, which lists the earlier resolutions, humanitarian concerns, the need for regional stabilization, the impact of refugee flows, and NATO's reputations as factors justifying the intervention (Weller, 1999: 498). On that same day, the US Mission to the UN circulated a list of ten factors supporting NATO action in Kosovo without specifying the precise legal justification ("Factors Supporting NATO Action in Kosovo"; document on file with author).

[5] See for example, statement of Foreign Minister Kinkel of Germany, October 16, 1998, quoted in Simma, 1999: 13. For more on the positions of NATO allies, see Duke, Ehrhart, and Karadi, 2000; and Haglund and Sens, 2000: 187, 190.

result of these different views among NATO countries was a collective decision (or nondecision) to emphasize the legitimacy of the action, without denying its legality, while putting forward a range of factors to justify it.

Russia and China were also concerned about the precedent, not so much because they feared "humanitarian intervention" against themselves (a highly unlikely prospect), but because they were disturbed by the notion of a value-driven intervention (Baranovsky, 2001: 17–18; Zhang, 2000: 121). The Islamic world was not unambiguously supportive of NATO. Not even Bosnia or Albania were explicit about the legality of the intervention in their statements in the Security Council (as nonmembers). Among countries in the Middle East, there was sympathy for the suffering of fellow Muslims, but they also feared that NATO interference if unchecked would extend to their part of the world, to combat terrorism, for example (Karawan, 2000: 218). This ambivalence is telling. If the legal discourse were meaningless, Islamic leaders would have had fewer qualms about giving in to natural (and politically beneficial) sympathy for the Kosovar Albanians by offering their wholehearted support to the intervention. The Kosovo "precedent" does not make intervention anywhere else more likely unless one assumes some mechanism for issuing credible judgements that it really is a precedent – some way of evaluating whether like cases are being treated alike. In a decentralized legal system, that mechanism can only be the interpretive community – it is what gives the whole notion of precedent its bite.

Third, a broad circle of actors other than government representatives weighed in, passing judgement on the plausibility of legal claims. On the day the NATO bombing started, the UN secretary-general issued a carefully worded statement observing that "there are times when the use of force may be legitimate in the pursuit of peace," while adding that "under the Charter the Security Council has primary responsibility for maintaining international peace and security . . . and therefore the Council should be involved in any decision to resort to force" (Annan, 1999a). Opinions among international legal scholars were varied, but leaned in the direction of illegality. Jose Alvarez (2001: 136) notes that even commentators who supported the objectives of the intervention found NATO's action to be inconsistent with the Charter, and points to a significant degree of uniformity among them about the range of tools they used in interpreting the Charter. NATO countries almost certainly sought the advice of their legal advisers and, since the advice they received would have been based on the same raw legal material available to the scholars, they would have been conscious of the difficulty in making a case that differed substantially from the conclusions drawn by legal scholars after the fact. Concerns about plausibility – and the reputational costs associated with advancing implausible arguments – are evidence of a functioning interpretive community. The interpretive community in effect says about farfetched claims: "your position is not only patently self-serving – it is legally untenable" – a judgement governments seek to avoid.

Fourth, the legal discourse affected developments after the intervention. It had an impact on the enunciation of NATO's new strategic concept. For some time prior to the Washington Summit of April 1999, the United States and the UK had been pushing for a revision of NATO policy to allow the alliance to intervene out-of-area (and not in self-defense) without a Security Council authorization, a position that was resisted by France and Germany in particular (Nicole Butler, 2000: 276). While all NATO countries supported the Kosovo action in the end, the experience was sufficiently disturbing to many that, contrary to expectations, the new strategic concept reinforced the role of the UN and implicitly treated the Kosovo case as an exception.[6]

Similarly, the felt need to return to the Security Council for a long-term solution illustrates that legal boundaries may be pushed but, for a new legal interpretation to be generally accepted, those pushing must work to some extent within what are regarded as the legitimate venues for discourse. There was a palpable sense of relief when Resolution 1244 – establishing the UN-led civilian mission in Kosovo (UNMIK) and authorizing the NATO-led security presence (KFOR) – was adopted by a vote of 14–0, with China abstaining. The return to the Charter framework was welcomed by virtually every country involved in the debate, albeit in very different terms. Russia and Brazil, for example, were grateful that the Security Council had resumed its "rightful role," while Canada and the Netherlands saw in Resolution 1244 a step in the direction of redefining sovereignty and security to include conceptions of human rights.[7] The United States conspicuously did not express relief about the return to the Security Council, but recognized that, in order to bring the air campaign to an end in a satisfactory manner, a follow-on ground presence would be required, and the only politically realistic way of

[6] See paragraph 31 of the Alliance's Strategic Concept, 1999. NATO Press Release NAC-S(99)65 – 24 April 1999. See also Nicole Butler, 2000: 282.
[7] For statements of members of the Council on the adoption of Resolution 1422, see 4011th meeting of the Security Council, 10 June 1999, S/PV.4011.

achieving that was by returning to the Security Council. The acting legal adviser at the time, Michael Matheson (2000), was particularly frank: "As soon as NATO's military objectives were attained, the Alliance quickly moved back under the authority of the Security Council. This process was not entirely satisfying to all legal scholars, but I believe it did bring the Alliance to a position that met our common policy objectives without courting unnecessary trouble for the future." In short, the return to uncontroverted legality was the device that provided both a face-saving compromise for those that opposed the intervention and a vehicle for keeping the NATO consensus intact when it was beginning to fray. It alleviated the morning-after regrets by diluting the threat to international legal order the NATO intervention was seen as presenting, and reinforced the sense that institutions are an important check on the unilateral exercise of power in the name of collective values.

Ironically, in an *ad hoc*, reactive way, the Kosovo experience may have vindicated the role of the UN as the principal forum for seeking consensus on bitterly contested norms. The event – and the debate provoked by the secretary-general's later statement that "the core challenge to the Security Council and the UN as a whole in the next century is to forge unity behind the principle that massive and systematic violations of human rights ... cannot be allowed to stand" (Annan, 1999b) – reinforced an emerging consensus that such intervention is lawful with Security Council authorization, while reaffirming the principle that it is unlawful without it, though there may be rare cases in which a "blind eye" will be turned to violations of the law in situations of extreme humanitarian necessity. Legal discourse did not prevent NATO's action in Kosovo, but it profoundly shaped domestic and international debates about its propriety, affected the aftermath, and ultimately changed the normative climate in which future decisions about humanitarian intervention will be taken.

Conclusion

International organizations are central arenas for legal discourse. Discourse in the Security Council is bounded by a set of values whose origins reside in the UN Charter. Those values are in need of interpretation and, as argued above, the normative framework within which the discourse occurs can evolve. Precisely how this normative evolution occurs raises complex questions about the relationships between different types of power. Clearly the dominant actors in the Security

Council (especially the United States) have the greatest ability to control the terms of debate as well as win votes (or veto resolutions they oppose). Moreover, there is evidence of a conscious effort by these actors to shift the terms of debate in recent years, in respect of not only humanitarian intervention, but also the newly minted doctrine of preemption. But to assume that compulsory power is the only kind at work in the Security Council misses something important. Even the United States is constrained by the terms of the discourse it sets. "Hoist on the petard" of a professed commitment to human rights (Rieff, 1999), the United States and other Western governments cannot lightly ignore demands to act on those professed commitments, as they did in East Timor. In other words, the dominant actors have disproportionate influence in writing the rules of the game, but they cannot alter those rules (shift the terms of debate) instantaneously and at will. This suggests an interesting connection between the various types of power considered in this volume. The institutional power of the dominant actors – the ability to steer debate and action in a particular direction – is not simply a less direct form of control. It is bound up with discursive or productive power, which, as Barnett and Duvall argue (chap. 1 in this volume), acts on the socially advantaged and disadvantaged alike. The dominant voices in Security Council debates are products of the discourse, as are weaker voices. To an extent, they are all members of the same interpretive community constituted by the very terms of the discourse.

The more recent deliberations over intervention in Iraq reinforce the point. History is likely to judge that intervention less kindly than the one in Kosovo, in part because of the differing normative contexts. NATO's action in Kosovo, though widely viewed as unlawful, built on an evolving legal framework and may have contributed to an emerging consensus on humanitarian intervention. The Iraq intervention, on the other hand, was perceived as a sharp break from the existing normative and institutional framework, for which the United States has paid a price, economically, politically, and in other ways. There is ample evidence that legal norms and discourse mattered. Most of the six "swing-vote" countries in the Council could not bring themselves to sign on to the war, despite the incentives offered and threats made, because the style and content of the deliberations meant they could not justify doing so to their own constituents. Instead of hammering away at the one issue on which the Council had already agreed – namely the need to rid Iraq of WMD programs – Bush administration officials spoke at diplomatically inopportune moments about tenuous linkages to acts of terrorism, a doctrine of preemption that was hard to square with existing international law, and about the desire to transform the entire Middle East. Moreover, they often spoke in a manner that suggested the goal was not to adapt existing norms and institutions to new threats, but rather to tear down those norms and institutions and start again from scratch. This made it very difficult for leaders of the six countries to vote with the United States, even if calculations of short-term interests might have weighed in favor of doing so.

One may argue that, by going ahead anyway, the United States proved that legal norms and institutions are no constraint. But even the United States seems to have been influenced by the "force of the better argument." Its legal case shifted from counterterrorism to enforcement of Security Council resolutions when it became obvious that the former claim was not persuasive to international audiences.[8] Urged on by Spain (a supporter) and France (an opponent), the United States withdrew the famous second resolution when it became obvious the draft would not win even a bare majority of votes in the Council. Doing so helped salvage some credibility for the Security Council and a shred of legality for the action. The decision to go to war having been made, it was better to do so on the basis of existing resolutions rather than push the doomed draft to a vote, rendering it all but impossible to claim that the military action was being taken to enforce Security Council demands. Moreover, the mounting difficulties of rebuilding Iraq without much international support provide evidence of the costs associated with defying the existing normative and institutional framework. The American people sense that they are paying a higher price than they would have had their government acted multilaterally. In the end, it may turn out that the price was worth paying, but that only proves law and institutions are not an absolute constraint; it does not prove they are no constraint at all.

States with the greatest military and economic power are less constrained in their behavior and better able to affect the behavior of others than the less materially well-endowed. But even in the field of peace and security, institutions can enhance the exercise of compulsory power. For that reason, they are valued and, because they are valued, they constrain even the dominant actors – blatant disregard for the conventions of an

---

[8] There is no better evidence of this than the letter of March 20, 2003, from the United States to the president of the Security Council, setting out the legal justification for the war. The letter does not say a word about self-defense against terrorism; the legal case is based entirely on the enforcement of existing Security Council resolutions relating to Iraq's weapons of mass destruction (S/2003/351, 21 March 2003).

institution will destroy it. The jury may still be out on whether the United States continues to value the Security Council, but even hard cases like Kosovo and Iraq demonstrate the impact of institutional power. Moreover, uses of force in international affairs do not occur in a normative vacuum. Norms affect how states define and defend their interests in discursive interaction with other states and relevant actors. As I have argued in this chapter, legal discourse is a form of productive power, which is connected to the power of interpretive communities. In a global environment lacking any normative or institutional framework, interpretive communities would wield no influence; even in the aftermath of Kosovo and Iraq, it is clear we do not yet live in such a world.

9   Class powers and the politics of global governance

Mark Rupert

Criticism of the vastly unequal powers entailed in neoliberal globalization is no longer the exclusive province of those stigmatized as
economic ignoramuses, extremists, and malcontents – "flat-earth advocates," "dupes," and "knaves" as Thomas Friedman notoriously characterized them (1999). Indeed, the former chairman of the US president's
Council of Economic Advisers, former chief economist at the World
Bank, and Nobel laureate Joseph Stiglitz has penned one of the most
widely noted critiques of the neoliberal "Washington Consensus" and
the institutional powers which have enacted it on a global scale (Stiglitz,
2002b). Taking Stiglitz's intervention as a jumping-off point, I will argue
in this essay that his critique of the interactional (institutional and compulsory) powers underlying neoliberal globalization is valuable, but
radically incomplete. More specifically, I claim that the interactional
powers identified by Stiglitz presuppose constitutive, structural forms
of power such as those identified by Marxian theory. Understanding the
relations and processes of global governance entails analysis of class-
based powers, the social relations of capitalism which make them possible, their historical instantiations both within and across nation-states,
and the ways in which these powers have been, and continue to be produced, reproduced, and transformed by the struggles – at once material
and ideological – of concretely situated social agents. But I will further
suggest that classical Marxian categories are not by themselves sufficient to understand the dynamics of these world-order struggles, for
class-based relations and identities are crosscut by others such as gender

I am grateful to Jim Glassman, Bill Robinson, Hazel Smith, and Scott Solomon for their
generous and thoughtful comments on a draft of this paper. Michael Barnett and Bud
Duvall provided exemplary editorial guidance and constructive critique in the process of
revision.

and race, and these latter are generated through more diffuse, productive forms of power. In short, I argue that a dialectical understanding of class-based powers is necessary, if not sufficient, for understanding social powers more generally, and issues of governance which implicate those powers.

Stiglitz and globalization's discontents

A distinguished academic economist drawn into important policy roles, Stiglitz has had first-hand experience inside the governing institutions of neoliberal globalization. He shares with the mainstream of his profession a general presumption in favor of markets as the institutional form which – barring "market failures" and "externalities" – will tend to maximize choice, efficiency, prosperity, and freedom (2002b: 53–54). However, Stiglitz rejects the "market fundamentalism" (ibid.: xii, 16, 36, 73–74, 196) which for decades has been the governing ideology of the International Monetary Fund (IMF), authorizing the imposition of austerity, privatization, and market liberalization on scores of developing countries facing chronic indebtedness and recurrent balance-of-payments crises. Contrary to neoliberalism's dogmatic insistence on the prioritization of markets, Stiglitz leans toward a view of the economy as embedded within larger sets of social institutions (ibid.: 55, 76–77, 209, 247). If those institutions are not deliberately arranged so as to support more sustainable, equitable economic growth, liberalization of trade or finance will not by themselves produce these outcomes (ibid.: 74, 78, 91–92, 218–19). Insofar as the IMF's exercise of institutional and compulsory power over indebted developing countries has proscribed state action to secure these preconditions – even as it imposed austerity, privatization, and liberalization – the results have been unnecessary economic contraction and social dislocation, compound opportunity costs of lost economic growth, impoverishment, and deepening inequality, economic instability, and political backlash. Stiglitz fears that these perverse outcomes may imperil the broader economic and social gains which he believes globalization could bring, if properly managed. While the original, Keynesian orientation of the Bretton Woods institutions might have been open to securing the social preconditions for "globalization with a human face" (ibid.: 252), Stiglitz believes that the Washington Consensus which has been entrenched most firmly at the IMF since the Reagan–Thatcher era is ultimately self-defeating (ibid.: 12–15).

To account for this perverse system and its governing ideology, Stiglitz begins to look toward the political relations and social powers at work in the global economy: "The [global economic] institutions are dominated not just by the wealthiest industrial countries but by commercial and financial interests in those countries, and the policies of the institutions naturally reflect this" (ibid.: 18).

The problem appears to be rooted in a contradiction – institutionalized disavowal of the implicitly public, political character of these institutions and their activities, and a concomitant lack of public accountability or participation:

> There was a certain irony in the stance of the IMF. It tried to pretend that it was above politics, yet it was clear that its lending program was, in part, driven by politics.
>
> (ibid.: 47)
>
> The IMF is a public institution, established with money provided by taxpayers around the world. This is important to remember because it does not report directly to either the citizens who finance it or those whose lives it affects. Rather, it reports to the ministries of finance and the central banks of the governments of the world.
>
> (ibid.: 12; also 102, 206–07, 225)

These latter institutions, in turn, "are closely tied to the financial community," their officials often drawn from banks or financial firms to which they will return upon completing their term of public service. By virtue of these ties, "the IMF was . . . reflecting the interests and ideology of the western financial community," upholding the sanctity of private property and contract, and striking preemptively at perceived inflationary tendencies which might erode the real value of creditors' assets. Instead of approaching development as a broad-based "transformation of society," IMF policies became focused upon "protecting investors" (ibid.: 19, 109, 130, 172). Despite the political character and public consequences of what they are and what they do, the institutions of global economic governance are not directly accountable to the public, but are politically and ideologically predisposed toward bankers and investors from the major capitalist countries. While at times using epistemically cautious language to argue that the IMF behaved *"as if"* it was dominated by financial interests (ibid.: 207, 216; emphasis in original), at other times Stiglitz is bold and direct, concluding that the institutions of global governance are "antidemocratic," "a disenfranchisement" of people worldwide, in effect a "new dictatorship of international finance" (ibid.: xiv, 247, 248).

The prescription which Stiglitz offers for these ills includes institutional reform and policy reorientation in order to encourage sustainable, equitable development:

> There need to be changes in institutions and in mind-sets. The free market ideology should be replaced with analyses based on economic science, with a more balanced view of the role of government drawn from an understanding of both market and government failures.
>
> (ibid.: 250, also 252)

Along these lines, there are concrete proposals for regulating short-term capital flows, for increasing transparency within the IMF, for reinstating its original, more limited mandate of addressing balance-of-payments crises, developing less restrictive and destructive responses to crises, and other such issues. But Stiglitz seems aware that just below the surface of his diagnosis and prescriptions there are larger political issues, involving the construction of new forms of global political participation:

> *The most fundamental change that is required to make globalization work in the way that it should is a change in governance.* This entails, at the IMF and the World Bank, a change in voting rights, and in all of the international economic institutions changes to ensure that it is not just the voices of trade ministers that are heard in the WTO or the voices of the finance ministries and treasuries that are heard at the IMF and World Bank.
>
> (ibid.: 226; emphasis in original)

In passages such as these, Stiglitz is calling for "broad participation that goes well beyond experts and politicians" (ibid.: 252) – a global economy the governance of which entails new forms of democratic participation by those whose lives it affects. He is, in effect, calling for restructuring the world economy in ways which recognize its interpenetration by the political, and the creation of new kinds of publicly conscious, democratic actors in that new economy. In so doing, he implies that the problems of global governance cannot ultimately be resolved at the level of interactional power (compulsory or institutional), but implicate generative structures and the social agents whose social identities and capacities for action are shaped by those structures. A brief theoretical digression will help to clarify the bases of this claim.

Structural power

My thinking has been strongly influenced by Jeffrey Isaac's understanding of power grounded in critical realist ontological claims regarding the internal relation of structure and agency within the process of (re)producing social reality. He situates the analysis of power within an open-ended materialist dialectic of real, effective social structures (understood in a generative sense as internal relations) and active, interpretive social agents. In his view, power is "socially structured capacity" for action, "implicated in the enduring structural relations that characterize a society and . . . exercised by intentional human agents who participate in these relations" (Isaac, 1987: 7, 9). The ability of some agents to influence the behaviors of others (i.e., power over) presupposes that those agents are enabled to engage in socially meaningful action (power to), and this in turn depends upon their situation in enduring sets of social relations in terms of which identities and powers are differentially distributed to agents (the structural and productive aspects of power). In this sense, social power (of the structural and productive kinds) is a condition of possibility for social action (ibid.: 72, 76). Where such powers to act are distributed asymmetrically, Isaac speaks of structured domination (ibid.: 84). The implication of this distinction is that we may understand social power as an omnipresent condition for social agency without presupposing that domination is a necessary or universal condition of human life. It is possible, then, to imagine social relations that would empower social agents in ways that might facilitate greater social self-determination and equity rather than simply reproduce forms of domination and exploitation.

Crucially, structures – including structures of domination – have histories; they are (re)produced or transformed only through the mediation of historically concrete agency. In this view, structures cannot (re)produce themselves in abstraction from agency; nor is agency reducible to structural determination. Even though agents may be assigned particular powers to act in certain ways by virtue of their structural position, the actualization of these powers is contingent upon the complex interactions and (ideologically mediated) interpretations of concretely situated historical agents. Dominance relations, "like all social relationships, [are] chronically negotiated and renegotiated on the basis of reciprocal [if not necessarily symmetrical] possession of powers" (ibid.: 91). The reproduction of social powers, dominance relations, and the practices that sustain them is therefore always problematic, contestable. How, indeed whether, structures are (re)produced is determined by routine interactions and (more or less explicitly political) struggles among historically situated social agents whose actions are enabled and constrained by their social self-understandings. Viewed in terms of processes of structural (re)production, the dialectical interdependence of structural and ideological-discursive or productive forms of power, as well as their enactment in institutional contexts and exercises of compulsory power among concretely situated agents, become crucial. Accordingly, I will attempt to follow Isaac's methodological injunction:

> The analysis of power must examine those structural relationships that distribute the capacity to act. But it must also examine the concrete history whereby those relationships are maintained and changed, and the forms of organization of those groups whose activity makes these things happen.
>
> (ibid.: 94)

I will sketch below structures of class-based power generally characteristic of capitalism in its various forms, some of the ways in which these structures have been historically instantiated on a transnational scale – including institutional forms – and some ways in which the contemporary reproduction of these structures and their institutional forms is problematic. Finally, I will examine one concrete form of organization through which the agents of global capitalist power have attempted to (re)produce their identities, forge a common political project, and overcome or assimilate resistances – the fabulous World Economic Forum. Insofar as the forum, and the non-governmental organizations and social movements which support or challenge its legitimacy within an emerging transnational civil society,[1] may be seen as contesting the shape of global structures of social power or domination – struggling, in effect, over future possible worlds and the kinds of persons who may live in them – I would claim that these political dynamics merit treatment as integral aspects of global governance processes. Institutional analyses such as that offered by Stiglitz are important but, unless they are connected to processes of structure and agency which generate and animate the contradictions Stiglitz identifies within global institutions, they will not illuminate the ways in which global governance issues reflect the tensions and possibilities of capitalism.

Power and class relations

As Ellen Wood (1995) has argued with great force, the critical leverage of a Marxian critique of capitalism is generated by its explicit focus on

---

[1] For a defense of this notion of transnational civil society, see Rupert, 1998; 2003.

the social power relations which inhere in, and yet are obscured by, the structures and practices of capitalist production and exchange:

> The fundamental secret of capitalist production disclosed by Marx . . . concerns the social relation and the disposition of power that obtains between workers and the capitalist to whom they sell their labor power. This secret has a corollary: that the disposition of power between the individual capitalist and the worker has as its condition the political configuration of society as a whole – the balance of class forces and the powers of the state which permit the expropriation of the direct producer, the maintenance of absolute private property for the capitalist, and his control over production and appropriation . . . for Marx, the ultimate secret of capitalist production is a political one.
>
> (ibid.: 20–21)[2]

Capitalist social relations generate the possibility of asymmetrical social powers distributed according to class. Socially necessary means of production are constituted as private property, exclusively owned by one class of people. The other class, whose exclusion from ownership of social means of production is integral to the latter's constitution as private property, are then compelled to sell that which they do own – labor-power, that is, their capacity for productive activity – in order to gain access to those means of production and hence – through the wage – their own means of survival. As a consumer of labor-power, the capitalist may control the actual activity of labor – the labor process – and appropriate its product, which is then subsumed into capital itself. In Isaac's apt summary, "The capitalist class thus possesses two basic powers: the power of control over investment, or appropriation; and the power to direct and supervise the labor process" (1987: 126; the locus classicus is Marx, 1977: 291–92; see also Bowles and Gintis, 1986: 64–91; Wood, 1995: 28–31, 40–44).

As employers, capitalists and their managerial agents attempt to assert control over the transformation of labor-power – the abstract, commodified capacity for labor – into actual labor. They seek to maximize the output of workers in relation to wages paid for labor-power, and may lengthen the workday or transform the labor process itself in order to do so (Marx, 1977: 948–1084; on the latter tendency as it was

---

[2] It is possible, I would argue, to mount a political critique of capitalism without committing oneself to Wood's more fundamentalist claims about the universal and overriding significance of class relative to other social relations of domination (see Wood, 1995: 256–63, 266–70, 282–83).

expressed in Fordist workplace regimes, see Rupert, 1995). In the social position of investors, their decisions directly determine the social allocation of labor and resources – the pace of aggregate economic activity and the shape of the social division of labor – and indirectly limit the scope of public policy through the constraint of "business confidence" and the implicit threat of "capital strike" (F. Block, 1977: 16; Bowles and Gintis, 1986: 88–90). Insofar as these social powers are effectively privatized – associated with private ownership and exchange of property among juridically equal individuals in an apparently depoliticized economic sphere – they are ideologically mystified and democratically unaccountable (Paul Thomas, 1994; Wood, 1995).

Anti-democratic and disabling as they might be, these class-based powers are neither uncontestable in principle nor uncontested in fact. The social powers of capitalist relations are reciprocal, constituting a "dialectic of power," subject to ongoing contestation, renegotiation, and restructuring. They represent forms of social power which are historically particular, which share identifiable structural characteristics but are concretely (re)produced in particular forms which vary across space and time.

As such, class powers must be actualized in various concrete sites of social production where class is articulated with other socially meaningful identities resident and effective in those historical circumstances. Capitalist power over waged labor has been historically articulated with gendered and raced forms of power: separation of workplace from residence and the construction of ideologies of feminized domesticity rationalizing unpaid labor; ideologies of white supremacy rationalizing racial segregation and inequality; gendered and raced divisions of labor; and so forth. These relations of race and gender have had important effects on class formation (Barrett, 1988; Johanna Brenner, 1993; Goldfield, 1997). This implies that in concrete contexts class has no actual existence in pure form, that it cannot be effectively determining without itself being determined. However, this is not to say, in some pluralist sense, that class is only one of a number of possible social identities all of which are equally contingent. Insofar as productive interaction with the natural world remains a necessary condition of all human social life (Marx, 1977: 290), I would maintain that any account of social power relations that abstracts from the social organization of production must be radically incomplete.

Understanding the instantiation of the structural powers of capital thus entails engagement with the other aspects of power. In the particular sites where they are (re)produced, the (contradictory) structural powers of capital, and the potential for resistance which these embody, are played out through interaction with discursively constructed, materially embodied, and institutionalized identities of gender and race.

Class power as global power

While I would agree with the claim that capitalist class powers have never been more effectively global, I am equally persuaded that these powers have never been contained within the confines of particular states. Recent Marxian scholarship has argued persuasively that capitalism may be fruitfully understood as a transnational social system which has encompassed the system of sovereign states as well as the seemingly discrete sphere of the capitalist economy: "The separation of the political and the economic indicates precisely the central institutional linkage between the capitalist economy and the nation state: that is, the legal structure of property rights which removes market relationships from directly political control or contestation and allows the flow of investment capital across national boundaries" (Rosenberg, 1994: 14; but compare Lacher, 2002). It is through these latter processes of transnational economic activity that the privatized powers of capital have been projected on an increasingly global scale, "[f]or under this new [i.e., modern] arrangement, while relations of citizenship and jurisdiction define state borders, any aspects of social life which are mediated by relations of exchange in principle no longer receive a political definition (though they are still overseen by the state in various ways) and hence may extend across these borders" (Rosenberg, 1994: 129).

Scholars sharing a broadly historical materialist perspective have identified historical processes through which internationally active segments of the capitalist class have organized to frame common interests, project a universalizing worldview which effectively depoliticizes the economic sphere, and coordinate their own political action to realize their interests and visions (van der Pijl, 1984; 1998; Stephen Gill, 1990; 1995; Rupert, 2000; Sklair, 2001; Steger, 2002).[3] Capitalism's

---

[3] The significance of globalization within a historical materialist frame is, however, very much a matter of debate. Some important positions are staked out by contributors to Rupert and Smith, 2002.

longstanding globalizing tendencies have been substantially realized in a particular historical context, and this has been the political project of a tendentially transnational – if also US-led – historic bloc comprising particular fractions of the capitalist class, state managers and international bureaucrats, journalists, and mainstream labor leaders. Through this project, the globalizing capitalist bloc has (re)produced its structural powers on a transnational scale. It has embedded these powers in particular ideological and institutional forms promoting market-based relations among fictively individuated consumers and producers, and facilitating thereby the unimpeded transnational flow of capital, goods, and services. And it has deployed compulsory power to contain rival political projects of nationalist (as opposed to global) orientation as well as to dismember those institutional forms which afford working people some modest ability to defend themselves against the variously instantiated powers of capital.

Constructing the institutional infrastructure of international trade and finance, this historic bloc fostered the growth of international trade and investment through the postwar decades, especially within and between the so-called triad regions. Moreover, with the founding of the World Trade Organization in 1995, the institutional infrastructure of liberalization has been substantially strengthened and extended. The WTO wields institutional powers of surveillance and enforcement unprecedented at the international level, and has extended its ambit to include trade in services as well as trade-related investment and intellectual property issues (WTO, 1998; Wallach and Sforza, 1999). This reflects a broadening of the agenda of liberalization beyond tariff reduction to encompass "harmonization" of (formerly "domestic") rules and regulations governing business insofar as these appear, from the liberal perspective, as potential non-tariff barriers to trade.

A second aspect of postwar processes of globalization has been the emergence of multinational firms and the transnational organization of production (Dicken, 1992; Agnew and Corbridge, 1995; Held, et al., 1999; William Robinson and Harris, 2000). Developing countries have been increasingly, if unevenly, incorporated into these global production networks. This globalization of production has substantially enhanced the compulsory powers of employers in relation to their workers. For workers in developed countries, globalization means that employers are able more credibly to threaten plant relocation and job loss when faced with collective-bargaining situations, and there is strong evidence to suggest that this is increasingly widespread (Bronfenbrenner, 1997;

2000). For workers in developing countries, globalization may imply opportunities for employment which might not otherwise be available, but along with that come the subordination and exploitation entailed in the capitalist labor process (e.g., see Ross, 1997; Kamel and Hoffman, 1999).

In the realm of finance, excess liquidity from consistent US balance-of-payments deficits, the collapse of the Bretton Woods fixed-rate regime and its associated capital controls, the recycling of petrodollars, and the emergence of offshore xenocurrency markets together resulted in breathtaking volumes of foreign exchange trading and speculative international investment which now dwarf the currency reserves of governments and can readily swamp, or leave high and dry, the financial markets of particular nations (Wachtel, 1990; Agnew and Corbridge, 1995; Held, et al., 1999). Responding to short-term differences in perceived conditions of profitability and variations in business confidence between one place and another, as well as speculative guesses about future market fluctuations, these enormous flows are highly volatile. These developments have been consequential, for the emerging historical structures of neoliberal capitalism embody an enhancement – along all four dimensions – of the social powers of capital, especially finance capital, which can effectively preempt expansionary macro-policies aimed at increasing employment or wage levels. Accordingly, the globalization of finance has been accompanied by a resurgence of laissez-faire fundamentalism since the late 1970s, as neoliberal austerity has largely eclipsed the growth-oriented ideology which originally underpinned the postwar world economy (Stephen Gill and Law, 1989; Stephen Gill, 1990: chap. 5; 1995; Wachtel, 1990; Agnew and Corbridge, 1995: chap. 7; Bello, 1994; MacEwan, 1999). This disciplinary power has the effect of prioritizing the interests of investors, who are as a class effectively able to hold entire states/societies hostage. Moreover, the particular interests of the owning class are represented as if they were the general interests of all: "since profit is the necessary condition of universal expansion, capitalists appear within capitalist societies as bearers of a universal interest" (Przeworski, quoted in Paul Thomas, 1994: 153). In this ideological construction, the social and moral claims of working people and the poor are reduced to the pleadings of "special interests" which must be resisted in order to secure the conditions of stable accumulation. Indeed, this is a central part of the ideological justification for the package of austerity policies which the IMF typically imposes on developing countries experiencing financial crisis – the latter itself being largely a result of systemic forces, especially the globalization of finance and its attendant exchange rate instabilities (Bello, 1994; Hahnel, 1999; Tabb, 2001).

Perhaps ironically, then, neoliberalism's resurrection of market fundamentalism has been attendant upon the increasing extensity and intensity of transnational relations. Even as people in locations around the globe are increasingly integrated into transnational social relations, neoliberalism seeks to remove these relations from the public sphere – where they might be subjected to norms of democratic governance – and instead subject them to the power of capital as expressed through the compulsions of the market (Stephen Gill, 2000; Rupert, 2000: chap. 3; Steger, 2002: 43–80). In van der Pijl's apt summary, "The core of the new concept of control which expressed the restored discipline of capital, neoliberalism, resides in raising microeconomic rationality to the validating criterion for all aspects of social life" (van der Pijl, 1998: 129). While Stiglitz (2002b) notes the institutional manifestations of this shift toward "market fundamentalism" and neoliberal austerity, the analytical toolkit of mainstream economics does not enable him to address the underlying dynamics of class-based structures of power, as sketched in the analysis above.

It is important analytically and politically to note the articulation of the structural power of capital with relations of gender and race, as well as the productive, institutional, and compulsory aspects of power which are at work in these, for the world of cheap labor and under-pollution (to paraphrase Lawrence Summers; see Karliner, 1997: 148) in which transnational production is organized is a world which is neither race-nor gender-neutral. The great bulk of workers in export-processing zones (EPZs) – the most labor-intensive nodes of global production chains – are young women (Dicken, 1992: 186; Kamel and Hoffman, 1999: 18, 21–22). Their labor may be culturally constructed as cheap insofar as they are presumed to be under the social umbrella of a male (either father or husband) and therefore not requiring a self-sufficiency wage, and insofar as the gender division of labor marks off "women's work" as "something that girls and women do 'naturally' or 'traditionally'" rather than the expression of hard-won, and more highly rewarded, skill – this latter presumptively an attribute of more masculine employments (Enloe, 1989: 162; see also Pettman, 1996: 167–68). Further, the austerity programs of neoliberalism have a heavy impact on women, intensifying the double burden of gendered work as retrenchment of institutionalized public services puts greater burdens upon households – and therefore feminized domestic labor – for the care of children, the elderly, the sick; even as those same cutbacks affect areas of the gender division of labor, such as education and health care, in which women are concentrated (Pettman, 1996: 168). Economic austerity and a narrowing of options may then compel women to seek employment in export industries and EPZs, or into the informal sector. Moreover, Eurocentrism and racism have generated representations of naturalized poverty among peoples of color in the developing world, attributed to a lack of those things which are presumed to distinguish the more developed (and white) countries – capital, technology, managerial expertise, effective and honest governance, skilled labor, and so forth (Hall, 1996). Racialized discourses of development – understood in terms of providing to the underdeveloped that which is lacking – are manifested in institutions such as the World Bank (Escobar, 1995). Liberalization of, trade with, and investment in the developing world may then appear as the twenty-first century version of the "white man's burden." Bound up with capitalist globalization, then, are ideologies and relations of gender- and race-based domination which effectively interweave the four types of power.

Powers and resistances

The various forms of power bound up with globalizing capitalism generate not only possibilities for domination and exploitation, but also new forms of potential solidarity in resistance to these (Rupert, 2000; 2003). These forms of solidarity have in recent decades taken on an increasingly transnational character. For twenty years or more, there has been resistance to the compulsory adoption of IMF-mandated neoliberal austerity measures in a number of developing countries, with masses of people protesting against privatization, dramatically increased costs for basic services, curtailment of subsidies for staple foods, and so on (Bello, 1994; Katsiaficas, 2001). Articulating the identities of indigenous peoples, Mexican peasants, and global resistors, Subcommandante Marcos has clearly linked the Zapatista struggle against neoliberalism – inaugurated on the very day the North American Free Trade Agreement went into effect (January 1, 1994) – to the 500-year-long history of European colonialism and North American imperialism: "Re-named as 'Neoliberalism' the historic crime in the concentration of privileges, wealth and impunities, democratizes misery and hopelessness" (Zapatistas, 1998: 11). The Zapatistas denounced neoliberalism as the vehicle for commodification of social life and the imposition of a universal model of development which would result in "cultural assimilation and economic annihilation" of alternative ways of life – including their own (Cleaver, 1994).

Inspired by the diverse and dialogical networks of resistance imagined by the Zapatistas, a variety of social movements and activist-oriented nongovernmental organizations (NGOs) – perhaps predominantly but by no means exclusively from the global North[4] – have in recent years coalesced into "a movement of movements" resistant to neoliberal globalization. Among them may be found a wide variety of groups with overlapping emphases: critics of the International Monetary Fund and World Bank and advocates of debt relief for developing countries; groups focused upon global inequality and development; advocates of re-regulation and taxation of global finance capital; groups critical of the heightened power of multinational firms; environmental protection advocates; those critical of the WTO and its agenda of global liberalization; movements of and for small farmers and landless peasants; women's groups and lesbian activists; radical and not-so-radical labor advocates; and anti-capitalist groups motivated by articulations of anarchist and socialist ideologies.[5]

Over the past few years, highly visible mass protests involving tens or hundreds of thousands of people and explicitly targeting capitalist globalization and neoliberalism have occurred in numerous locations around the world. The World Social Forum of Porto Alegre, Brazil – conceived as a grassroots-oriented and democratic alternative coinciding with the annual meetings of the World Economic Forum – drew 10,000 participants to its inaugural meeting in 2001 and perhaps as many as 70,000 in 2002 and up to 100,000 in 2003 (Jennifer Block, 2002; Ehrenreich, 2003; Fisher and Ponniah, 2003). Highlighting the most important factor bringing these various movements and agendas into (at least partial)

---

[4] For example, People's Global Action – a transnational network coordinating localized nodes of resistance to neoliberal globalization since 1998 – includes many of the best-known direct-action groups around the world: the Direct Action Network and the Anti-Capitalist Convergence in North America, the KRRS peasant farmers' movement in India, in Europe Ya Basta (Italy) and Reclaim the Streets (UK), the MST landless peasants' movement of Brazil, and a broad and variegated network of associated groups on every populated continent: see Rupert, 2003. For further evidence of the broadly transnational scope of this movement of movements, see Jaggi Singh, 2001; Bircham and Charlton, 2001: 149–267; Fisher and Ponniah, 2003.
[5] The literatures dealing with globalization and resistance have grown too vast to attempt encapsulation with a single set of references. I have drawn extensively on these literatures, however, in Rupert, 2000; 2003.

alignment, Michael Hardt and Antonio Negri wrote:

> The protests themselves have become global movements, and one of their clearest objectives is the democratization of globalizing processes. This should not be called an anti-globalization movement. It is pro-globalization, or rather it is an alternative globalization movement – one that seeks to eliminate inequalities between rich and poor and between the powerful and the powerless, and to expand the possibilities of self-determination.
>
> (Hardt and Negri, 2001)

Expressing this democratizing impulse, one street protester told the *New York Times*, "There's no magic solution, but we have to struggle and build a more democratic world from the ground up" (quoted in Jacobs, 2002). This project implies reducing the institutional and compulsory powers wielded by the globalizing bloc as part of a process in which structural forms of power might be reconstructed in more popularly enabling and egalitarian forms. Any such process necessarily involves construction of relations of solidarity across meaningful social differences, and thus entails addressing productive forms of power (which generate those meaningful differences) as well.

In its more anarchist inflection, the movement's ends and means are integrally related in a vision of "prefigurative politics" involving decentralized forms of organization and direct democracy in autonomous communities and affinity groups, and direct action (generally eschewing violence against persons) in resistance to systems of hierarchy and exploitation (potentially including capitalism, white supremacy, and masculinism, as well as, of course, the state).[6] Significant as anarchism has been, there are other political visions at work within the global justice movement. Dan LaBotz – longtime labor activist now working with Global Exchange – casts the struggle explicitly in terms of democratic socialism:

> We need to construct a kind of socialism where workers, consumers, and ordinary citizens make the decisions through both direct and indirect democratic processes at all levels . . . The most important thing is our long-range goal, ending corporate control of the economy and political life, and its replacement by a democratic popular power that can protect the planet, ensure human rights, and raise the standard of living in a new world of freedom and peace.
>
> (LaBotz, 2000: 9)

---

[6] On the significance of anarchism within the global justice movement, see Rupert 2003.

Influential Canadian author-activist Naomi Klein (2001a: 82; also 1999) suggests that the movement coalesces around "a radical reclaiming of the commons" – slowing, halting, or reversing tendencies toward privatization and commodification which effectively colonize and consume public space, thereby displacing grassroots processes of democratic deliberation. "There is an emerging consensus," she writes, "that building community-based decision-making power – whether through unions, neighborhoods, farms, villages, anarchist collectives, or aboriginal self-government – is essential to countering the might of multinational corporations" (Klein, 2001b: 312). On the broad terrain of formulations such as these – all of which presuppose a view of the world economy as a sphere of structured social power relations which can and should be reconstructed in more democratic forms – anarchists, socialists, community activists, and autonomist radicals of varying stripe have found sufficient common ground on which to converge for collective acts of resistance.

This nascent movement faces a number of challenges, both internal and external. Within the North American branches of the movement, there are serious divergences about both tactics and strategy (Danaher and Burbach, 2000; Cockburn and St. Clair, 2000; and Yuen, Katsiaficas, and Rose, 2001). One source of tension is the question of cooperation with right-wing anti-globalization forces, their nationalist agendas, and their commitments (implicit or explicit) to white, masculine, heterosexual privilege (see Rupert, 2000). Within the wing of the global justice movement committed to nonviolent direct action, there are significant disagreements about whether destruction of capitalist property (itself the product of more or less violent oppression) constitutes violence and whether nonviolence equates with a self-defeating pacifism. At the broadest level of strategy, disagreements center on reforming, reconstructing, or abolishing global economic institutions in the course of constructing future possible worlds. In these discussions of strategy and tactics, the institutional power of NGOs in the movement has been highly controversial, with many anarchist-inspired activists being bitterly critical of the perceived reformism and institutionalized hierarchical politics of the NGOs (compare Davis, 2001; Barlow and Clarke, 2002: 27–28; Graeber, 2002a; 2002b). Mainstream labor unions in the United States have been ambivalent about the movement, eschewing confrontational direct action and emphasizing the goal of protecting labor rights and attaining "a seat at the table" within global institutions, while maintaining their status of respectability and historically friendly relations with the Democratic Party. US unionists appear to occupy a contradictory ideological position which encompasses both economic nationalism (longstanding and deeply rooted) and emerging tendencies toward transnational solidarity (D. Frank, 1999; Moody, 2000; Rupert, 2000). There are, in short, significant disagreements within the movement about the kinds of global power they are resisting and appropriate forms of counterpower which this resistance requires.

The North American movement has also been challenged by questions concerning its failure to include greater representation from communities of color in the imagination, planning, and execution of its projects (Martinez, 2000; Wong, 2001; Rajah, 2001; Hsiao, 2001). White middle-class activists have been disproportionately represented in the global justice road show, in part because the dull compulsion of the economic renders this mode of peripatetic activism less accessible to those most effectively disadvantaged by existing structures of inequality. As activist Kristine Wong (2001: 222) points out, "Due to the cost of travel and accommodation, as well as the luxury needed to take time off work and family responsibilities, it was less likely that working class people of color would have been able to [participate]." Further, the reliance on confrontational street protests and direct action requires participants to expose themselves to police repression and violence, the significance of which has been historically much more grave for immigrants and people of color. Compounding these issues has been a perceived tendency of mostly white activists to understand the problem in terms of the recruitment of persons of color, in effect extending an invitation to support a project already envisioned, an agenda already formulated. Failure to explicitly address white privilege in the politics of protest – as in social structures more generally – resulted in lost opportunities for transracial solidarity and movement-building, despite broad disaffection with neoliberal capitalism. As one African-American activist explained, many activists of color have been reluctant to "go to a protest dominated by fifty thousand white hippies" (quoted in Martinez, 2000: 77). Racialized forms of productive power reaching into the global justice movement itself, then, have combined with structural power of a racialized division of labor and the institutional and compulsory powers of the state to produce the relative "whiteness" of the North American movement.

Finally, as Himadeep Muppidi suggests (chap. 12 in this volume), the US wing of the movement is often insufficiently attentive to its own position of global power and privilege. Absent a self-conscious critical awareness of their position within structured global inequalities, their representations of globalization and their self-understandings as activists in these struggles may effectively reinforce Western and especially US privilege and thus undermine potential relations of solidarity, reciprocity, and democratizing dialogue with social movements of the postcolonial world. Such lost possibilities for solidarity are vividly reflected in the angry words of R. Geetha, an Indian unionist and women's rights activist: "Who are they [the West] to impose conditions [such as labor standards] on Third World Countries? People are starving here! Why the hell should they tell us what kind of economy we should have?" (quoted in Jaggi Singh, 2001: 48). At the global level, too, the movement confronts structural and productive forms of power which reproduce racialized identities and unequal social positions and complicate attempts to realize potential solidarities in opposition to globalizing capitalism.

These are not, of course, the only obstacles which the movement faces. It is the object of a counterpolitics of both coercion and consent. As Mark Laffey and Jutta Weldes point out (chap. 3 in this volume), the authorities in various cities and countries have responded to the movement's actions with escalating levels of police repression (institutional and compulsory powers). The movement has also faced efforts by globally dominant social forces to disarm it ideologically through representations of "globalization with a human face," corporate responsibility, and the like (see Rupert, 2000: chap. 7). Among the most important agents of these ideological counteroffensives has been the World Economic Forum.

Articulating a hegemonic project: "entrepreneurship in the public interest"

Inspired by Machiavelli's image of power as a centaur – part human and part beast – Gramsci understood political power in terms of an ongoing dialectic of coercion and consent (1971: 169–70), their articulation being variously institutionalized in different times and places according to social circumstances and the history of political struggles. Hegemony – that form of power which relies more upon consent than coercion (although never to the exclusion of the latter) – was understood to be the unstable product of ongoing struggle, "reciprocal siege." In the context of globalizing capitalism, one of the institutional forms through which a hegemonic project has been formulated is the World Economic Forum (WEF).

Evolving out of the European Management Forum which Swiss business professor Klaus Schwab founded in 1971, the WEF has become a membership organization for over 1,000 major international firms, each of which pays substantial annual fees to the forum. The forum explains in its promotional literature why such shrewd business people see this as money well spent: "As a member of the World Economic Forum, you are part of a real Club, and the foremost business and public-interest network in the world" (World Economic Forum, 1997b: 10). In keeping with its program of promoting "entrepreneurship in the public interest," the WEF brings its members together at the annual Davos extravaganza. The Davos meetings offer WEF members "intensive networking in a privileged context allowing for the identification of new business opportunities and new business trends." At Davos, WEF members hobnob with their fellow global capitalists, but also with leaders from political and civil society to whom the forum refers as "constituents" to distinguish them from WEF "members": while paying corporate "members" are entitled to attend WEF events, "constituents" – heads of state and government ministers, academics and policy experts, media figures and cultural leaders from around the world – may attend by invitation only. Thus, the WEF offers its members privileged access to "high-level interaction between political leaders and business leaders on the key issues affecting economic development" on regional and global scales (ibid.).

> The key to Forum activities is direct access to strategic decision-makers, in a framework designed to encourage economic development via private sector involvement. This direct interaction between public and private sector and experts leads to the creation of a partnership committed to improving the state of the world.
>
> (WEF, 1997a)

As Charles McLean, the WEF's director of communications, explained to the *New York Times* (quoted in Barry, 2002), the forum represents "a global town hall of leaders from different segments of society":

> For more than 30 years the World Economic Forum has brought together the major stakeholders in society – business leaders, government leaders, academics, journalists, writers, artists, religious leaders

and representatives of civil society – to tackle humanity's biggest challenges.

(McLean, 2001)

Manifesting in classic form the structural contradiction of capital's privatized social power, the WEF represents itself as being at once a private club and a kind of global public sphere. The forum is an organization in which the various segments of the global power bloc can come together under the leadership of transnational capital to construct a unifying political vision, and present to the rest of the world the interests of global capital in the guise of a universal vision – "entrepreneurship in the public interest."

In recent years the WEF has become increasingly preoccupied with the contentious politics of neoliberal globalization. At the 1996 Davos conclave – well before the emergence of full-blown transnational resistance brought widespread attention to the explosive potential of these issues – the forum's central theme was "sustaining globalization." Forum organizers Klaus Schwab and Claude Smadja suggested that the process of globalization "has entered a critical phase" in which economic and political relationships, both globally and within countries, are being painfully restructured. They acknowledged that these changes are having a devastating impact on large numbers of working people in "the industrial democracies," with heightened mass insecurity resulting in "the rise of a new brand of populist politicians" – the likes of Buchanan, Le Pen, and Haider. They feared that, in the absence of effective measures to address the social circumstances of working people and the weakened ideological legitimacy of global capitalism, the new populisms might continue to gain strength, threaten further progress on the agenda of globalization, and "test the social fabric of the democracies in an unprecedented way." The social forces leading globalization, then, face "the challenge of demonstrating how the new global capitalism can function to the benefit of the majority and not only for corporate managers and investors" (Schwab and Smadja, 1996). In the spirit of this analysis, Schwab addressed the opening session of the 1996 forum: "Business has become a major stakeholder of globalization and has a direct responsibility to contribute to the stability of our global system" (WEF, 1996).

This theme of global capitalists managing the politics of capitalist globalization has continued to hold a special place in the WEF's long-term agenda. Almost a year prior to Seattle, a preemptive vision of

224

"globalization with a human face" was being explicitly constructed as a central theme of the 1999 Davos Forum (this trope was also invoked by President Clinton and Kofi Annan; see Rupert, 2000: chap. 7). Schwab and Smadja struck a note of urgency:

> We are confronted with what is becoming an explosive contradiction. At a time when the emphasis is on empowering people, on democracy moving ahead all over the world, on people asserting control over their own lives, globalization has established the supremacy of the market in an unprecedented way ... We must demonstrate that globalization is not just a code word for an exclusive focus on shareholder value at the expense of any other consideration; that the free flow of goods and capital does not develop to the detriment of the most vulnerable segments of the population and of some accepted social and human standards ... If we do not invent ways to make globalization more inclusive, we have to face the prospect of a resurgence of the acute social confrontations of the past, magnified at the international level.
> (Schwab and Smadja, 1999)

In his opening address, Schwab exhorted members of the global power bloc to "try to define a responsible globality" based on an ethic of "caring for the neighbors in our global village" (Schwab, 1999). The transnational power of corporate capital would not be compromised; rather, the global capitalists of the WEF would ponder the possibility of ruling in a more beneficent fashion in order to legitimize and sustain that power. Such calls for corporate civic leadership have been reiterated in subsequent years (Maitland, 2002).

Despite these hegemonic pretensions, the structured contradiction which underlies the institutional façade of the WEF continually reemerges. In order to maintain the barest credibility of its rhetorical stance of inclusive and open dialog in the face of burgeoning protest movements and increasingly assertive and well-informed critics, with much fanfare and self-congratulation the WEF invited a number of critical individuals and NGOs to participate in its annual meeting in 2001. When Swiss authorities cracked down harshly upon demonstrators attempting to reach Davos in order to voice their criticisms outside the WEF, some of the invited guests inside were unmannered enough to complain to the Swiss government and WEF leadership. "NGOs acting like NGOs and demanding civil liberties and basic democratic rights were not favorably received" (Public Citizen/Global Trade Watch, 2002: 11). Confronted by the criticisms of invited guests – who argued that the exclusivity of "fortress Davos" was the underlying cause of the violence and that the WEF should open itself to civil society groups – Claude Smadja, WEF managing director, responded: "We invite whoever we believe is relevant to open dialogue. We are not the United Nations. We are a private organization" (quoted in Hollingdale, 2001). The experiment, it seems, was not judged to have been a success and such leading lights of the global justice movement as Martin Khor of Third World Network, Walden Bello of Focus on the Global South, representatives of Public Citizen, and others were not invited to return again the following year. The *Financial Times* reported: "The Forum says it is not inviting organizations that contribute only negative views and do not support its 'mission' to narrow global divisions" (de Jonquieres and Yeager, 2002). While the forum claims "a long-standing policy of inclusion when it comes to non-governmental organizations and representatives of civil society" (WEF Press Release, Jan. 5, 2001), Public Citizen estimates that such groups typically account for less than 2 percent of attendees at the annual WEF extravaganza (Public Citizen/Global Trade Watch, 2002: 11). A few less militant or confrontational critics may still be included in WEF deliberations (prominent in 2002 was rock star Bono), but most are relegated to the heavily guarded streets outside, or to alternative venues such as the World Social Forum.

While the WEF has not renounced its hegemonic project of corporate-led "globalization with a human face" – and indeed has now repackaged its brand of public-spirited but privately managed capitalism as a solution to global terrorism – the strategy of inclusion and cooptation of resisters within the WEF itself may have reached its limits. Jean-Christophe Graz has usefully highlighted the structural contradiction within which the WEF is situated, and the implications of this situation for its institutional power: "the separation of transnational elite clubs from the public sphere constitutes both their strength and their weakness," he argues:

> Elite clubs [such as the WEF] do indeed provide informal platforms for networking and delicate economic and political negotiations. They also provide a useful milieu for individuals concerned to bring about the strategic advancement of a cosmopolitan, long-term future of capitalism. Yet their role in the public sphere clashes with the limits of their organizational principles. Divorced from society at large and with no formal devolution of power, paradoxically their influence emphasizes their lack of legitimacy . . . Sooner or later this situation will foster the development of contending forces disputing their very existence.
>
> (Graz, 2003: 322, 337)

While it may not, on its own, achieve a hegemonic global order, the WEF may yet serve as an important institutional site for the political self-organization of global capital, and the development of a strategic vision of globalizing capitalism based upon corporate civic leadership. And the WEF surely has served as a highly visible neon sign advertising the global ambitions of corporate capital, and hence provided a rallying point for the diverse forces which have now come into their own under the banner of the World Social Forum (Teivainen, 2002; Fisher and Ponniah, 2003).

Conclusion

One of the enduring insights of Marxian theory is that the seemingly apolitical economic spaces constructed by liberal capitalism are permeated by structured relations of social power deeply consequential for the (re)production of social life. These powers may be ideologically depoliticized – and thus rendered democratically unaccountable – in liberal representations separating a naturalized and privatized economy from politics. The operation of this economy (and the implicit social powers residing within it) may then be represented as a universal social good, the engine of economic growth, and a generalized prosperity. Critics such as Stiglitz have seen through the false universalism of these latter representations, but have not grounded their critique in an analysis of the structures of capitalism, the social powers they generate, and the resistances which may arise in response to these.

Historical materialism reminds us that social power relations are also processes – dynamic, contradictory, and contestable. As the emergent neoliberal historic bloc has sought to (re)produce its social powers on an increasingly global scale, they have encountered recurrent bouts of more or less explicitly political resistance from a variety of social agents (some explicitly class-identified but many others not) who have challenged neoliberal representations and called into question not just the agenda of neoliberal globalization, but the legitimacy of the social powers underlying it. It is in this context of transnational ideological and political struggle that the stinging institutional critique of an insider such as Stiglitz assumes such significance, and that the World Economic Forum has sought to recast the legitimating narratives of capitalist globalization, upholding private enterprise but in the form of "entrepreneurship in the public interest" – corporate-led "globalization with a human face" and capitalist development as an antidote to terrorism.

227

To the extent that capitalism and its putatively private relations of power organize crucial parts of social life on a transnational scale, the struggles surrounding these relations and their various articulations in sites around the world merit serious study as part of the question of global governance. Critical analyses of class-based powers and their historical interweaving with gendered, raced, and other relations of privilege may shed new light not only on issues of transnational power(s) and global governance but also on possibilities for democratizing projects and the social production of alternative possible worlds.

10 Global civil society and global governmentality: or, the search for politics and the state amidst the capillaries of social power

Ronnie D. Lipschutz

Global civil society exists. Although there remains considerable dispute about whom or what it includes, whether it is international or truly global, and how it is constituted, those agents, actors, organizations, institutions of transnational social and economic exchange and action are there, for all to see (Lipschutz with Mayer, 1996; Wapner, 1996; Keck and Sikkink, 1998; Colas, 2002). My objective in this chapter, therefore, is not to argue for the existence of global civil society (GCS) but, rather, to ask *what* it is. Is GCS a space or locus of sovereign agents or merely a structural effect? Does it wield compulsory power or it is a mere epiphenomenon, a reflection of the state system? Is GCS an institutional phenomenon, the result of the exercise of power by other actors, or is it a productive one, constituted by the social roles and relations growing out of contemporary states and markets? In surveying the growing literature on GCS, one can find supporters of all of these perspectives. This is not wholly surprising, since there is hardly a consensus to be found about the origins of domestic civil societies or their relationship to state and market (see, e.g., Jean Cohen and Arato, 1992).

In this chapter, I propose that global civil society is best understood in terms of institutional and productive power. GCS is generated through productive power, but its major actions rely primarily on institutional power. GCS is a product of *global* liberalism – perhaps globalist liberalism is a better term. By contrast with domestic civil societies in capitalist states, the relationship of GCS to the international system of states and the global economy is a problematic one. As I have asked elsewhere, if

The comments of David Newstone were especially helpful in writing this paper, as were the criticisms and suggestions of Michael Barnett and Bud Duvall in revising it.

there is a *global* civil society, where is the *global* state to which it corresponds? Inasmuch as there is no global state, as such, to "generate" GCS (but see Shaw, 2000), we must explain it by reference to some other structure or process. Alex Colas (2002) argues that GCS is merely "international," and remains linked to national states. Others (including myself in earlier work) argue that emergent forms of global governance constitute a state-like political framework that generates GCS. By contrast, if we adopt the view of the classical political economists – Adam Smith and Karl Marx, among others – and agree that civil society is linked primarily to the market, rather than the state, there is most certainly a globalized economy to which GCS could relate. In this chapter, I adopt a neo-Hegelian approach, and propose a dialectic between developing modes of global political rule and the markets that it shapes and governs. It is here, I will argue, that we must look to account for GCS and where we find its genesis and power. In what follows, I leave the definitional exploration and details of GCS to others (Anheier, Glasius, and Kaldor, 2001; Colas, 2002), and I do not intend to describe or assess those many "behavioral theories" that purport to explain the how, why, when, where, and ends of the actors in GCS (e.g., Keck and Sikkink, 1998; Tarrow, 1998; McAdam, McCarthy, and Zald, 1996). Instead, I problematize GCS as a central and vital element in an expanding global neoliberal regime of governmentality, which is constituted out of the social relations within that regime and which, with and through the capillaries of productive power, helps to legitimize that system of governmentality.

Explanations of GCS can be generally distinguished as either agential or structural. The former tends to see civil society as a realm of free association, independent of states and markets, in which sovereign individuals come together to engage in collective projects (Walzer, 1995). Power, in this scheme of things, appears in compulsory form, as some individuals convince others, through appeals to reason and interest, to join a group project. Civil society organizations (CSOs) then try to wield knowledge and norms, transmitted through the institutional procedures and politics of international regimes, in an effort to influence states and capital. The structural approach regards GCS as a product of the tensions between state and market, the public and private realms, and ethics and morality (Colas, 2002). Here, on the one hand, CSOs seem to emerge from the structural relations between state and market, as a form of social life that is part of neither but emerges to place limits on both. On the other hand, CSOs can also be seen as an effect of productive power, generated as agents struggle to resist the dominating logic of capitalism and the constant efforts of capital to expand the realm of private property. Michel Foucault (1980) pointed out that power was not a commodity that could be accumulated or distributed; rather, it served to constitute the subjects, objects, and relations of everyday life. Such power is exhibited in and through the forms and practices of neoliberal governmentality, although, within that framework, we find the other three types of power being exercised, too.

In this chapter, I argue that GCS is produced by agents resisting the expansion of the market but acting in ways that either unwittingly support the logics of governmentality or deliberately oppose it. The empirical grounding for this argument is to be found in social struggles to regulate the negative effects of global capitalist accumulation or what I call "externalities."[1] As states seek to create attractive environments for foreign investment and international exchange – to become "competition states," in the words of Phil Cerny (2000) and others – they are reluctant to impose social and environmental regulations on capital. In response to this lacuna, regulatory tools are being taken up by a variety of civil society groups and movements, nongovernmental organizations, corporations, and business associations (Cutler, Haufler, and Porter, 1999; Cascio, Woodside, and Mitchell, 1996; Weiner, 1999; Haufler, 2001; Lipschutz, 2002). CSOs are able to exercise some degree of compulsory power over states and their representatives, as documented by Keck and Sikkink (1998), but this pales in comparison to the influence exercised by corporations and capital which, in the United States, at least, operate in a money-friendly environment. Very few CSOs mount structural critiques of the system they are trying to change, inasmuch as this risks charges of radicalism, socialism, and even terrorism. Moreover, even though GCS has been generated out of the structural tensions between state and market, it is too fragmented and diverse to wield significant structural power. Thus, rather than seeking to buttress the state's compulsory and structural power to pressure or force

---

[1] I use the economic term "externality" for both analytical and ironic reasons. First, when "normal" production and economic exchange generate social costs that are not absorbed by the beneficiaries of those activities, a classical externality results. Second, many economists are quick to point out that such social costs are more appropriately subsumed under the category of comparative advantage and market equilibrium. Consequently, the low wages received by workers in Third World factories represent the normal functioning of international supply and demand, rather than a subsidy – or positive externality – to First World consumers.

capital into regulatory compliance, CSOs tend to utilize institutional-ized forms of market power in order to alter consumer behavior and corporate management practices. The flaw in this strategy, as we shall see, arises from the diffuse and decentralized nature of these two forms of power.

I begin this chapter with a discussion of neoliberal governmentality and the theoretical framework that underpins the analysis presented here. I argue that we cannot explain the global proliferation of civil society actors without reference to something that resembles a state. To invert the question posed above: if there is no state, why is there global civil society? The answer has two parts. The first is found in Ellen Meiksins Wood's (1995: chap. 1; 2002) insights into the nature of the public–private divide in capitalist systems; the second, in Foucault's concept of governmentality (1991; see also Dean, 1999). In part 2, I turn to the phenomenon of "politics via markets," that is, the grow-ing tendency of social activists, groups, and organizations to utilize markets in pursuit of political goals (both reflections of institutional power). Here I draw on my research on the proliferation of private and semi-private regimes of global social regulation to illustrate how power remains unexamined and largely ignored by those engaged in the dra-mas of progressive social action. This strategic move reflects GCS's lack of structural power and the fact that, by and large, what are called the "constitutional rules" of neoliberal governmentality are not only not up for debate, they are not even acknowledged to exist (Stephen Gill, 2002; Jayasuriya, 2001).

In part 3, I return to the arguments of Wood and Foucault, and explore the ways in which they help us to understand the relationship between GCS, markets, and the state system. Globalization has done much not only to extend the power and interests of the industrial core, and espe-cially the United States, to all parts of the world. It has also fostered the proliferation and extension of the arms, institutions, and biopolitics of what Martin Shaw (2000) has called the "global state," and Michael Hardt and Antonio Negri have called "empire" (2000). Finally, I con-clude by analyzing the creation and activities of GCS as an effect of power extended into the international-cum-global realm through the offices of the United States and its accomplices in neoliberal globaliza-tion. To understand GCS, in short, requires us to consider how "global" actors are produced in a realm characterized by diffuse forms of power, and why GCS must be recognized as a product of neoliberal globaliza-tion rather than something distinct from it.

Governmentality and the public–private divide

Historically – that is to say, during the apotheosis of the welfare state – the regulation of the economic practices of capitalism and their associated externalities were treated through the agency of what has come to be called the welfare state. The welfare state, in the words of Esping-Anderson (1990), sought to "decommodify" certain aspects of economic and social life, both through the provision of resources and entitlements to certain categories of people and the formulation of "command-and-control regulations" that imposed limits on externality-producing practices by capital. In doing so, the state was taking into the public realm certain "property rights" that had been theretofore regarded as private (Polanyi, 2001; Lipschutz, 2004b). Such internalization did not come cheaply and, according to many, including the advocates and practitioners of what has come to be called neoliberalism, social welfare expenditures represented an inefficient and ineffective allocation of resources. In many countries, it also crowded out private investment, inasmuch as public needs competed for the same pools of capital. Politics, as practiced under these welfare regimes, involved a constant struggle by social forces with both state and capital over the line separating private from public goods.

From a liberal perspective, the boundary between the public and the private is a puzzling one. It is one thing to argue, as did Locke, that private property is the product of one's labor and investment. It is quite another thing, however, to struggle over the privatization of things that are arguably, or customarily, in the public realm (see, e.g., Drahos with Braithwaite, 2003). For example, although human rights apply to individuals, their observance and enforcement by the state can be considered a public good, from both the economic and ethical perspectives. Yet, what corporate codes of conduct (discussed in section 2) do is to *privatize* such rights within a company's commodity chain. Here, institutional power has been used to create private property rights out of a public good.

From a Marxist perspective, the division between public and private and the structural reasons for that distinction are necessary to capitalism and the activities of capital. Justin Rosenberg (1994) and Ellen Wood (1995; 2002) both argue that capitalism represents a separation of the political and the economic, the public and the private, that is historically unique. Political authority over property is hived off into the private sphere, where it is guaranteed by but insulated from the state's compulsory and structural power. In effect, the state's structural power is used to frame the regulations governing both the shape of markets and activities therein, and to create private property rights where none previously existed.

This particular and peculiar organization of market societies, with public and private constituted as distinct realms of authority and activity, relies heavily on civil society to maintain and reproduce the boundary and distinction. Because of competition between capitals and capitalist organizations as well as the uneven distributive outcomes of capitalist accumulation, the threat of an unraveling of the social contract and destabilization of society is always present, as Polanyi (2001) argued. Under conditions of globalized neoliberalism, however, the state is engaged primarily in providing attractive and stable conditions for capital and is less interested in addressing externalities or market failures. It is incumbent upon civil society, therefore, to use its productive power to pressure the state to regulate the sharper edges of the market.

While the precise forms of civil society's productive power vary among states (Dryzek, et al., 2003), it generally takes the form of interest groups, lobbies, and social movements working through political institutions, as it were. But acceptable channels of action available to civil society for this purpose are relatively limited: protests and violence (compulsory power) are rejected by both state and capital as illegal and undermining of investor confidence, while structural restrictions on capital's autonomy are derided as "socialism." Civil society cannot create new political communities with the compulsory and structural power to place limits on capital. The dominant approach, therefore, is to convince capital to agree to place limits on itself (i.e., what Polanyi called "self-regulation"). But this approach has no impact on structure, or the invasion of the public by the private, however, and leaves capital to do pretty much as it pleases.

There are other ways for civil society to exercise power. Drawing on Antonio Gramsci and others, Alex Colas (2002: 43) argues that civil society is the setting from which social movements and political activism originate, "within the context of capitalist modernity." Moreover, he points out, "civil society has historically found expression in two predominant forms – one linked to the private sphere of the capitalist market, the other to the struggles against the all-encroaching power of the state" (ibid.: 47). The former is populated by those organizations and actors who pursue their self-interest through the mechanisms of the

234

market, the latter by those who seek to challenge and change the ethical structures and politics of the state. Although it is tempting to think of the "all-encroaching power of the state" as manifested only in the territorial monopoly of legitimate violence, it is the state's structural power to expand the realm of private property in favor of capital that is the focus of ethical challenges by social movements and where the productive power of civil society is exercised most effectively.

Globalization and the instantiation of neoliberal practices have codified internationally the structural capacity to divide public from private without putting in place a commensurate political authority capable of exercising structural and compulsory power over the expansive tendencies of private actors. Instead, the decentralized organization of markets lends itself only to the creation of weak institutions – that is, international regimes – whose power rests in the stickiness of the bargains around which they have been established (the ease with which such bargains can be broken is evident in the Bush administration's numerous defections from various regimes and conventions). There is little in the way of coordination among these regimes and no centralized direction aside, perhaps, from certain ideological tendencies (Lipschutz, 2003a). What all of these institutions share, however, is governmentalism.

Governmentality, as Michel Foucault put it, is about *management*, about ensuring and maintaining the "right disposition of things" of that which is being governed or ruled. This right disposition "has as its purpose not the action of government itself, but the welfare of the population, the improvement of its condition, the increase of its wealth, longevity, health, etc." (1991: 100; see also Dean, 1999: chap. 1). Anything that challenges this disposition is to be absorbed; anything that disrupts it is to be eliminated. Foucault's notion of governmentality contrasts with his idea of *sovereignty*, which posits the autonomy of the Prince's person and property from that over which he rules. Under sovereignty, power is exercised largely in compulsory and structural terms. Indeed, as Hobbes argued, there can be no limits to the sovereign's power.

Although Foucault wrote only about governmentality within states, with each separate (state) order constituting its own sphere of normality and discipline, the extension of his idea to the international arena is rather straightforward (indeed, there have been incipient forms of governmentality among states for centuries). Global governmentality is more than the sum of national governmentalities; it is more than the state system and its associated organs; it is more than the standard definitions of global governance. It is an arrangement of actors and institutions, of rules and rule, through which the architecture of the global articulation of states and capitalism is maintained. As Mitchell Dean (1999: 172) puts it,

> Neo-liberalism ceases to be a government of society in that it no longer conceives its task in terms of a division between state and society or of a public sector opposed to a private one . . . The market has ceased to be a kind of "fenced-off nature reserve" kept at arm's length from the sphere of public service; instead, the contrivance of markets becomes the technical means for the reformation of all types of provision . . . The point of doing this is . . . to reform institutional and individual conduct so that both come to embody the values and orientations of the market, expressed in notions of the enterprise and the consumer.

Who acts within neoliberal governmentality? The management of human populations and their environments – the exercise of compulsory and institutional power – is the task of both the agencies of government and the populations themselves. The former includes the myriad governmental and international agencies, public and private associations, and even nongovernmental organizations and corporations that populate the global realm, each of which with its own instrumental function as well as normative objectives. Indeed, the riot of global CSOs and social movements, international organizations and associations, transnational corporations and business associations, and even democratic market governments all constitute agents of a global biopolitics seeking to further human progress and welfare. This is not to say these many actors are in coherence with one another in either their activities or objectives. They are, however, engaged increasingly in supporting what Kanishka Jayasuriya (2001) and others (Stephen Gill, 1995; 2002) have described as the instantiation of a global "economic constitutionalism." As Jayasuriya (2001: 452) puts it, "Economic constitutionalism refers to the attempt to treat the market as a constitutional order with its own rules, procedures, and institutions that operate to protect the market order from political interference."

Governmentality is associated with the practice of *biopolitics* which, according to Dean (1999: 99), "is concerned with matters of life and death, with birth and propagation, with health and illness, both physical and mental, and with the processes that sustain or retard the optimization of the life of a population:"

> Bio-politics must then also concern the social, cultural, environmental, economic, and geographic conditions under which humans live, procreate, become ill, maintain health or become healthy, and die. From

this perspective bio-politics is concerned with the family, with housing, living, and working conditions, with what we call "lifestyle," with
public health issues, patterns of migration, levels of economic growth,
and the standards of living. It is concerned with the bio-sphere in which
humans dwell.

(ibid.)

Populations are not composed of sovereign or autonomous individuals,
as normally conceived under liberalism. Rather, they are regarded and
treated as homogeneous collections of people who are molded institutionally into particular categories and forms, who regard themselves
as belonging to these categories and forms, and who act accordingly.
In particular, governmentality produces populations that behave "normally." Individuals comport themselves according to the standards of
"normality" of their specific population. The right disposition of things
is maintained through the standardization of populations within certain defined parameters, the self-disciplining of their own behavior by
individuals conforming to these parameters, and the disciplining function of surveillance and law which seeks to prevent any straying outside those parameters. Taken together, these constrain individuals' practices to a "zone of stability," or "normality." Power is embedded within
the discursive formations that naturalize normality and that motivate
the reproduction of normal populations through associated practices.
This is one of the senses in which, as Foucault puts it (1980: 109–33),
we are the products of power circulating through society in capillary
fashion.

Thus, for example, those with HIV or AIDS are managed as a population with a specific set of characteristics for which treatment is available. The members of this population come to think of themselves and
behave in terms of those characteristics. Normally, within neoliberal
governmentality, medical treatment is obtained through private means:
each patient has a doctor. But private treatment of the disease with
extraordinarily expensive drug "cocktails" excludes a vast fraction of
the affected population, whose illness is regarded as a public (health)
matter. The lack of resources or medicines to normalize these individuals can also be regarded as an externality generated by the expansion of
private ownership of pharmaceuticals (Drahos with Braithwaite, 2003).
This welfare problem can be addressed either by convincing the drug
companies to reduce the price of the cocktails through appeals to "social
responsibility" or through provision of the drugs by states as a public
good recaptured from the private market sphere (see, e.g., Sabin Russell,

237

2003). In the absence of an authoritative center of power to make and enforce a structural change – one that would roll back the boundaries of the private – the productive power inherent in governmentality works to constitute CSOs that, in effect, fill the "power vacuum."

As this example suggests, governmentality poses a number of conceptual as well as practical difficulties where agency and structure are concerned. The first involves the nature of power within governmentality. What generally attracts the greatest scholarly and public attention is the overt display of compulsory power and the search for the impacts of GCS and CSOs on states' decision making and policies. Indeed, this is precisely the nature of Keck and Sikkink's (1998) "boomerang effect," through which transnational activists influence and manipulate states and other actors. Within governmentality, by contrast, what counts is not "getting B to do what A wants, even if B doesn't want to do it" but, rather, "through discursive practices and processes *changing* what B wants to do." To put this another way, social change within a governmental system does not follow simply as a consequence of action, as it is normally understood. Instead, the common understanding of social relations – including relations of property – is discursively transformed in a way that does not directly threaten structural relations between public and private.

A second difficulty associated with governmentality and biopolitics has to do with the processes whereby CSOs are established and how they exercise power. These are, quite clearly, more subtle and complicated than Mancur Olson's (1965) theory of collective action, whereby those who share interests form groups that seek to apply compulsory and institutional power to state agents. Moreover, it would appear that those CSOs of greatest interest to students and scholars of GCS are actually internalized within the system of governmentality that constitutes and subjectifies them. As the example of HIV/AIDS drugs above suggests, the arrangements of rules, regulations, and practices characteristic of contemporary bureaucratic capitalist states *and* global neoliberalism do not and cannot address more than a fraction of the "welfare of populations." Much of the remainder of this function is provided, increasingly, through civil society. That is to say, the activities of CSOs and GCS serve to stabilize and normalize conditions that are seen as threats or disturbances to those conditions of normality. The precise methods of accomplishing these ends, as well as the specific parameters of the ends themselves, are often highly contested, but the overall objective is the same: "optimization of the life of a population" (Dean, 1999: 99; note that no one is in favor of environmental destruction; everyone would like to see people "better off"). In this sense, much of what is often described as opposition and "resistance" – by CSOs, in particular – is better understood as constituting alternative tactics that are integral to governmentality.

Finally, governmentality imposes severe constraints on politics which I conceive of having to do with the exercise of structural power that, in turn, help to "produce" both agents and their social relations. Here, I distinguish between "constitutive" and "distributive" politics (Lipschutz, 1989: 17–20). Constitutive politics has to do with the "rules of the game," that is, the constitution of the structures reflecting the shared ethics of a political community. Distributive politics involves the institutional division of resources or, as Lasswell (1936) put it, "who gets what, when, how." Because the social rules articulated in constitutions are not easily amended, politics generally becomes the struggle for entitlements and the protection of what one already has. Compulsory and institutional power are used to protect or contest given interests although, once or twice in a generation, constitutional "amendments" are made (I am thinking here of both civil rights for African-Americans and marital rights for gays in the United States as examples). Most political decisions are treated as technical and managerial matters, to be considered and addressed by non-elected experts rather than by those who are directly affected (Beck, 2000). Within governmentality, things are much the same. The management of populations is largely technical in nature, because standardized groups behave and respond in standardized ways to standardized policies and stimuli. And these standards are the work primarily of non-elected experts. Individuals within these groups must not diverge significantly from these standards in their behaviors, and there are limits on the degree to which they can contest these standards without being expelled from the group.

The constraints associated with neoliberal governmentality have a critical but somewhat unremarked effect: political agency – that is, the possibility of sovereignty or autonomy – becomes a very difficult task (Epstein, 1995). It is not at all clear that autonomy is ontologically available within neoliberal governmentality, inasmuch as normal behavior is highly prescribed and circumscribed. Indeed, even "resistance" may serve only to reinforce the processes of governmentality, as the demands and actions of dissident movements are absorbed or contained by the agencies and actors operating within the governmental system. While Foucault (1980: 80–81) did not dismiss action, resistance, or revolution as pointless or futile, he did point out that opposition to governmentality may reinforce the very conditions that generate that opposition, for two reasons. First, if an action is deemed threatening enough to society, authorities (including a broad range of state and economic actors) are likely to attempt to manage the agents involved, through institutional power – making the activities illegal – and compulsory power – using the monopoly of violence to suppress the now-illegal activities. Second, actions with goals of regulating or modifying socially damaging practices tend to be absorbed into the governing mechanisms of society, through institutional means.

The power of markets

The particular organization of market societies, with public and private constituted as distinct realms of activity and rule, is hardly "natural" (Rosenberg, 1994; Wood, 2002). In further marking the line between constitutive and distributive politics, and between public and private, the liberal state comes to rely on civil society to maintain and reproduce that boundary. To wit, the maintenance (and expansion) of the private realm mandates limits to activities construed as "political" (Wolin, 1996; Mouffe, 2000), and civil society comes to be the realm within which acceptable collective activities can take place without impinging on institutionalized politics. Indeed, it is incumbent upon civil society make the division appear "natural," which it does discursively through its efforts to prevent the state from intruding on "inappropriate" areas of daily life, especially those involving private property. Given, however, that the state is more interested in providing attractive operating conditions to capital, it may fall to civil society to become more politicized and, through its own regulatory activities, reinforce or reinscribe the separation between the public (politics) and the private (markets). But, as noted above, acceptable forms of action available to civil society for this purpose are relatively limited. Structural power has been largely removed from the agenda through institutional and discursive power, while protests and violence (compulsory power) are rejected by both state and capital as destabilizing and undermining of confidence in the system. What remains?

The refusal of many states to regulate the activities of capital and force it to pay the social costs arising from externalities has led to the generation of a vast number of national and transnational campaigns that utilize lobbying, public pressure, influence, and expertise to impose regulation on capital (Wapner, 1996; Keck and Sikkink, 1998; Tarrow, 1998). The majority of these campaigns seek regulation through markets, seeking to convince individuals to engage in "socially conscious consumption" and businesses to adopt "corporate social responsibility" (Lipschutz with Rowe, forthcoming). In other words, through an elucidation of "real" interests within market settings, GCS seeks to use institutional (market-based) power to influence consumer and corporate behavior as a means of improving labor conditions in factories, reducing environmental effects from industry, and managing international trade in various kinds of goods, such as clothing and coffee (Lipschutz, 2002; 2004b). Consumers come to believe their selective purchasing can induce fear of loss of market share and profits in corporations, who will then internalize social costs.

Many of these campaigns have been successful in terms of these instrumental goals, but they suffer from serious *political* limitations. The most significant of these arises from the ways in which those whose rights are being violated by externalities are treated as objects, rather than subjects, of the campaigns, and are thereby deprived of both structural and productive power (Lipschutz, 2002; 2004a). Moreover, although individual corporations may change their behavior, those individual changes have little or no effect outside the factory walls (Lipschutz, 2002). Under neoliberal conditions, in other words, the only obvious and acceptable means of *regulating* markets – thereby moving the public–private boundary – are based on the *methods* of the market, that is, action articulated through institutional power. As we shall see below, this is the path being taken by many CSOs. Consequently, what appear to be acts by the *sovereign* agents of civil society become, instead, effects of neoliberal governmentality, of an ontology of reason and logic, cause and consequences, separable institutions and "issue areas."

Such limitations are especially evident in apparel industry campaigns. For example, there are at least a dozen civic action and social activism campaigns underway aimed at the Nike Corporation (Connor, 2001). All utilize the implicit threat of a consumer boycott in order to compel Nike to improve health and safety conditions in its 900-odd subcontractors' plants scattered around the world and to ensure that workers are paid at least the minimum wage. These campaigns have generated considerable public attention and Nike has responded energetically, concerned about its market share, its competitiveness, and its image. The company has adopted codes of conduct, contracted out audits of its subcontractors' factories, and permitted independent monitors either to accompany auditors or conduct their own inspections. It has joined the Fair Labor Association and coestablished the Workers' and Communities' Association, as well as taken a number of other steps to improve both conditions of production and its own reputation. And, while there apparently remain significant problems in many, possibly even all, of its subcontractors' operations, a not inconsiderable amount of upward-ratcheting of conditions within the Nike subsystem of global apparel production has taken place (Lipschutz, 2003b). There is also a widely held expectation that, if the company manages to improve conditions in its subcontractors' plants, other corporations, subcontractors, and factory managers will go along in order to remain competitive. Manufacturers will impose standards on their own businesses in order to maintain the good reputation of their brand, to sustain and even increase profit margins, and because it is the "right thing to do" (Fung, O'Rourke, and Sabel, 2001).

There is only limited evidence, however, to indicate that improved conditions do follow such activities. Moreover, not only is the strategy ineffective, it is also seriously flawed. If political conditions in a particular country are generally unfavorable to unions, collective bargaining, and other workers' rights – and this is the case even where countries have ratified relevant International Labour Organisation conventions – improvements in individual plants are not likely to have much impact on labor across the country as a whole (Lipschutz, 2002; 2004a). Amidst all of these activist efforts and corporate codes, virtually no attention has been paid to the constitutive political conditions – that is, the structures of power that states put in place to attract capital and reduce social costs – that led to the demand for social regulation in the first place, to wit, that Northern capital makes substantial profits on the backs of relatively powerless, badly paid, mostly female workers in Southern countries. It is the very fact that labor is badly paid and powerless that makes the host countries so attractive in the first place (and has even led to the reappearance of sweatshops in Los Angeles and New York; see Bonacich and Appelbaum, 2000; Rosen, 2002).

What have been the *constitutive* (as opposed to distributive) political effects of such campaigns? How have they altered either corporation or capitalism in *structural* terms? Are workers in the Nike commodity chain now able to exercise their productive power, that is, to unionize and bargain collectively? Has the public–private boundary been moved? Nike offers improved conditions and higher wages to the workers in its subcontractors' factories, but workers as well as consumers remain fully integrated into the regime of consumption that constitutes contemporary globalization and objectifies those workers and consumers. Workers are still unable to influence or change constitutional arrangements on the factory floor or in society at large. They remain the object of corporate authority (Lipschutz, 2002; 2004a). To put this another way, in host societies as a whole, there has been little in the way of political reform, stronger state regulation, or greater exercise of labor's right to unionize (Lipschutz 2002; 2004a). Capital exercises a form of structural power, authorized by the state, which, at the end of the day, results in little social change. Structures receive a paint job, so to speak, but underneath they are still the same.

What is lacking in these regulatory campaigns is any sense of the political inherent in the very notion of social policy or a recognition of the ways in which *power constitutes not only that which activists seek to change but the activists themselves*. Decisions must be made by those who are affected about what is necessary for the good and just life; that is, they must become autonomous subjects themselves rather than objects dependent on corporate munificence (Polanyi, 2001: chap. 3; Mouffe, 2000). What we find instead are versions of what Sheldon Wolin attacks as "fugitive democracy" (1996), that is, nonpolitical decision-making or "subpolitics" through markets and expertise, or what Chantal Mouffe (2000) calls the "democratic paradox," in which liberalism seriously constrains the political in the name of order and profit.

These outcomes indicate that social regulation and the general relationship between politics and economics, between public and private, are not simply matters that can (or ought) to be left to markets. Regulation of any sort inevitably involves costs imposed on both business and polity, but how such regulation is imposed, and by whom, makes a difference. If companies regulate themselves through codes of conduct, not only can they decide the content of the rules, they are also under no obligation to observe them. The arguments and justifications for regulation – and to whom they are made and why – must come about through politics, which must take place not within or through the market but in the *public* sphere. It is the *ethical* basis of the state's exercise of its power – especially the structural power to constrain the market – that must be changed, and not simply the moral behaviors of individual corporations (Lipschutz with Rowe, forthcoming). Capital is not shy about using its institutional and discursive power to shape markets through state action. Those seeking to put restraints on capital should not be shy about doing so, either. It is only through political action

243

directed to the ethical basis of state power that people and societies will come to recognize and acknowledge the need for social regulations and accept them as a necessary part of global industrialization, development, and economic growth.

To put this another way, under the regime of neoliberal governmentality, compulsory power is deployed by the agents of the state in the service of visible disciplining and punishment, while institutional power serves to keep certain matters off the agenda of distributive politics. CSOs and GCS attempt to bring these matters to public attention in order to get them on the agenda, where they might be incorporated into the normal parameters of governmentality and biopolitics. They do this by trying to illuminate the "true" interests of producers and consumers, and by revealing how present conditions affect those instrumental interests. The hope is that this will induce producers, in particular, to act in a more "socially responsible" way without all the muss and fuss of state-based politics. Yet, all the time, these activities are taking place within a framework of structural power which, ultimately, organizes and maintains the structures of governmentality's agencies, institutions, and practices. The ascendancy of the market lies in the diffuse and invisible nature of the power it exercises, which normalizes behavior within market society and marginalizes behavior outside its confines. There are so many "centers" to this power, however, that there is no possibility of changing all of them.

The power of politics

Foucault's conception of governmentality clarifies and elucidates the problem of autonomy, and helps to locate GCS in world politics. Foucault did not argue that autonomy is impossible but that, at best, it is highly constrained within contemporary liberal social systems as we conventionally understand them. As I noted earlier, in developing the concept of *governmentality*, he proposed that it replaced *sovereignty*. The residue of such sovereignty is to be found in the concept of "consumer sovereignty," the freedom to choose in the market (Lipschutz, 2000; 2001; Milton Friedman, 1962). Global social activism dependent on producer behavior and consumer choice for political effect thus becomes one more manifestation of this very limited freedom.

But all is not lost, as Foucault argued that power is "productive" and not something that can be accumulated for the purposes of compulsion. As he (1980: 119) famously wrote,

> If power were never anything but repressive, if it never did anything
> but say no, do you really think one would be brought to obey it? What
> makes power hold good, what makes it accepted, is simply the fact that
> it doesn't only weigh on us as a force that says no, but that it traverses
> and produces things, it induces pleasure, forms knowledge, produces
> discourse. It needs to be considered as a productive network that runs
> through the whole social body, much more than as a negative instance
> whose function is repression.

On the one hand, power "produces" the subject, in the biopolitical sense,
but the subject that is produced is not as standardized as the parameters of biopolitics might suggest. We are not mere social automatons.
On the other hand, the diffusion of power does allow for what might
be thought of as discursive ruptures or discontinuities in the web of
governmentality. These are small ruptures and are hardly noticeable,
at best, but they represent zones of agency, autonomy, resistance, and
contestation within which forms of sovereign politics can take place
(Lipschutz, 2003a: chap. 6). Such zones might involve "unauthorized"
actions focused on the environment or the mobilization of the weak, or
mass demonstrations that drive presidents from office. Whether peaceful or violent, political action in such zones of agency serves to expose
the contradictions inherent in the increasingly dense web of global governmentality and makes it possible for people to act in spite of that
web. Whether political resistance and contestation can change or overcome governmentality is much less clear. Perhaps new webs can be
spun within these ruptures, webs that are ethically deontological rather
than consequentialist, that is, political in the sense of praxis, rather than
utilitarian and focused primarily on distributive outcomes.

The image of a "web" of governmentality is only a very crude
metaphor, but it begins to suggest something about power: it must be
exercised within the microspaces and capillaries of contemporary life,
in the "spaces of appearance" (Arendt, 1958), and it must be a politics in which not only Habermasian discussion but also group action
are possible. Politics, in the sense I mean it here, has to grow out
of some form of face-to-face praxis, not because place is central (as
many environmentalists have argued; see Lipschutz with Mayer, 1996:
chaps. 7, 8), but because a democratic politics – one involving the
demos – seems to be transformed into biopolitics when larger scales and

numbers are involved. And politics must involve *action*, for it is only then that power becomes productive and politics becomes meaningful (Mouffe, 2000). This suggests a rather different conception of democracy than that commonly held, one that is based in practice rather than platitudes, one whose apotheosis is not the vote but debate and action, as it were (for a more developed version of this argument, see Lipschutz with Rowe, forthcoming).

In *Global Civil Society and Global Environmental Governance* (Lipschutz with Mayer, 1996), I suggested that GCS ought to be viewed not simply as an agglomeration of transnational organizations seeking to regulate and moderate the rougher edges of the international system, thereby participating in governmentality. I also proposed that what was most important about GCS was the *local* politics of groups and activists, focused on specific places but informed by a globalized epistemology. To put this another way, the key to a constitutive politics in which some degree of structural power can be exercised lies in getting people to take action in those places and spaces where they can realize some degree of collective sovereignty and can do so in full awareness that other groups are acting in like fashion in other places and spaces. In this way, people also engender and experience what a democratic politics is meant to be, and they learn what kind of politics goes missing in governmentality.

Such activism is often criticized for being "political," especially when it appears to involve technical or managerial matters. It is criticized for avoiding the vote, defying the law, disrupting normalcy. *Political* is code for an unauthorized politics whose practice creates local ruptures but also teaches people *how* to engage in politics. It shows them *what* is possible, and *how* it can be done. Local face-to-face politics, whether it is focused on the watershed, the urban neighborhood, the disempowered, the oppressed, or the occupied, is not only about the pursuit of shared interests, as collective-action theorists generally describe it (Olson, 1965), or the mobilization of resources, as some social movement theorists would have it (Tarrow, 1998). It is also about *productive* power, about means as well as ends. *People decide and act.* They discover how power functions and how it constrains yet enables action, and, as they act, they assert their political sovereignty and are transformed into sovereign subjects by their action. Examples of such politics can be multiplied manifold, and they are not just manifestations of "friendly, ultra-liberal" towns, such as those one might find along the Northern California coast. Among them are neighborhood associations, environmental justice groups, educational collectives, low-income housing advocates, watershed associations, AIDS activists, renewable energy activists, and, yes, even national liberation and resistance movements. Not all such politics are progressive, nor are they all nonviolent, especially if we take at face value Foucault's dictum that "politics is the continuation of war by other means" (1980: 61). But better politics than war or governmental management.

These are not, to be sure, matters of great power politics. Perhaps such action is best seen as politics in the "capillaries of power," where there is the real possibility of political community through which productive power can be exercised. Such activity represents a form of politics that institutionalized political processes – voting, lobbying, e-mailing representatives – never offer and which is entirely absent from international fora (loci of the famed "democratic deficit"). Action in the microspaces embodies an experience that illuminates the possibilities of politics in all of its raw, elemental form. It is conflictual, disruptive, aggravating but, in terms of praxis, productive. It is not a "solution" to a problem, rather, it is a means of defining the problems to be solved and engaging with those things that ought not to be, but are.

The power of power

The "problem" of accounting for GCS in its many variants and alternatives, as well as explaining its relationship to global governance, arises for several reasons. First, many scholars are more interested in fostering the efficiency and transparency of nongovernmental participation and process. Second, they seek to elucidate and develop mechanisms through which the desires, needs, and interests of those blocked by powerful actors can be fulfilled (Keck and Sikkink, 1998). They are less interested in the normative implications and consequences of how power is exercised and the results of that exercise (which I take to be the goal of political theory). Both are forms of theorizing aptly suited to a liberal worldview, which eschews foundational questions of politics and power and deals with distribution rather than constitution. Such a focus accepts the deployment of power as a given and begs for dispensations from the powerful.

From this view, global civil society is less a "problem" for power than a product of power. It is deeply enmeshed with practices of governmentality and biopolitics. It is a means whereby those matters that cannot or will not be addressed by the agents of the state or interstate institutions will, nonetheless, be dealt with by someone. This view of GCS does not

247

undermine concepts of power so much as it forces us to recognize how particular forms of society and governmentality are constituted and reconstituted, sometimes through the very agency that, at first glance, appears to be a means of opposition and resistance, if not liberation. It also motivates us to ask whether it is possible to (re)create forms of political sovereignty that can function, perhaps, in a counterhegemonic way to challenge the discourses of neoliberalism.

I would argue, by contrast, that a sole concern with distributive issues not only leaves the offending discourses intact but also leads to collaboration with those who exercise domination and institutional power. What is more important in my view is finding ways of challenging and changing the dominant discourses, through a productive engagement in a politics directed toward the structural prerogatives of the state. To mix metaphors, it is not sufficient to focus on the size of the pie's slices, it is necessary to act to change the filling, the crust, and, indeed, the pudding itself.[2] And that is something that the agencies and organizations of global civil society, as they are constituted today, cannot do and will not do.

[2] "Pudding," of course, is a British term for "dessert."

11 Securing the civilian: sex and gender in the laws of war

Helen M. Kinsella

> [T]o fight has always been the man's habit, not the woman's. Law and practice have developed that difference, whether innate or accidental.
> Virginia Woolf, 1938: 9

This chapter examines the productive power of discourses of gender by analyzing a particular institution of global governance – international humanitarian law or the laws of war. I focus on the laws of war for two interdependent reasons. First, the laws of war are a central feature of global governance. They reflect and regulate customs and practices of war among and, less extensively, within states. The laws of war govern both the resort to force (*ius ad bello*) and the use of force (*ius in bello*). Specifically, the laws of war outline the permissible actions for states, militaries, combatants, and non-combatants to take in war according to the formal classification of armed conflicts as international or non-international. As a result, the laws of war are the primary referent for the training and disciplining of those entities and, very recently, the peacekeeping troops of the United Nations (Rowe, 2000).

Yet, second, precisely at the moment that the currency of the laws of war has been generally revalued, and specifically invested with new-found worth for the protection of women, the relationships among power, gender, and the laws of war are scarcely analyzed. The scholarship that does engage in an analysis of gender and the laws of war focuses primarily on the *protection* of women within the law rather than the *production* of women in the law and, importantly, the production of the laws of war themselves.

I thank Lisa Disch and Adam Sitze, as well as Michael Barnett and Bud Duvall, for their incisive comments.

249

By explicitly focusing on the productive power of gender, and its relationship to structural power, I sketch the relations between different forms of power implicated in the laws of war. To presume that power should only be, or can only be, analyzed in its productive mode is to misread the work of Foucault (2000: 337), who is most immediately associated with this mode of theorizing. What he proposes is a "critical investigation of the *thematics* of power," an investigation that is inspired by the disarmingly simple question of "how is power exercised?"

For example, the laws of war rely upon both institutional and structural power in regulating the behavior of individuals – e.g., combatants may not purposely kill civilians. Combatants who do so are considered to be in violation of the laws of war and may be tried for their crimes. Alternatively, attending to institutional and compulsory power illuminates how the very choice of targets upon which combatants may fire results from complicated interactions in which positive law, the vagaries of public opinion, strategic options, and command hierarchies converge.

But, in both cases, these exercises of power also produce that which they seek to regulate – "combatants" and "targets" – for neither of those categories exists outside the law and practices that make them possible. As evidence, witness the intense debates over the proper identification and treatment of the so-called unlawful detainees of Camp X-Ray and the American Taliban, as well as the international outcry over the legality of the bombing of the Afghan wedding party in the ground war in Afghanistan. Significantly, in identifying and defining both "combatants" and "targets," discourses of gender are central. After all, it was the killing of women and children during the bombing that was taken as determinant of the civilian character of the wedding party, as well as of the barbarity of US actions, underscoring the importance of discourses of gender in constituting both "combatants" and "targets."

Therefore, my response to the query that informs this volume – namely, how is power exercised – is to investigate the structural and productive power of sex and sex difference in the laws of war. Accordingly, I write a genealogy of a founding tenet of the laws of war known as the principle of distinction: the injunction to distinguish at all times between combatants and civilians in times of armed conflict. This genealogy considers two crucial moments in the articulation of the principle of distinction – the production of the "combatant" and the "civilian" and the difference between them – as captured in the work of the Dutch diplomat and lawyer Hugo Grotius and in the codification of the 1949

IV Geneva Convention Relative to the Protection of Civilian Persons in Times of War. From this analysis I conclude that discourses of gender do not simply *denote* the difference of combatant and civilian, but *produce* that difference – one that lies at the foundation of the laws of war. Before turning to the writing of this genealogy, however, I first situate my own work in relation to the extant scholarship on gender, power, and the laws of war.

A fundamental axiom of this chapter is that an analysis of gender and the laws of war should not pivot solely on its conception and corresponding treatment of women. Such an analysis considers only how inequities and differences in the conception of women vis-à-vis a comparable norm (most commonly men) affect the conception and treatment of women. To rephrase in the taxonomy of this volume, such an analysis focuses upon structural and institutional power – forms of power that feminists have theorized extensively within standpoint and liberal feminisms, but that arguably inform in principle all feminist theorizing. This is not to minimize the contributions made by Gardam (1992; 1993), specifically on the laws of war, as well as Askin (1997), Copelon (1994), and Charlesworth and Chinkin (2000), among others, who deepened our understanding of the relationship among gender, power, and the laws of war by documenting how the provisions of the law "operate in a discriminatory fashion in relation to women" (ibid.: 15). It is, however, to call for a careful evaluation of the critical purchase of such an approach and to propose a reconfiguration of its critical concepts.

The drawback of an approach that addresses only the protection and treatment of women is that it obscures how gender operates not only to institute difference in the structural relations between men and women, but also to create that difference itself. What I mean by this statement is best clarified by reference to my essay's epigraph: "[T]o fight has always been the man's habit, not the woman's. Law and practice have developed that difference, whether innate or accidental" (Woolf, 1938: 9). Although the impulse is to read Woolf as if she were saying only that men fight and women do not, what I find intriguing about this statement is that a certain ambiguity unsettles its reference to "that difference" developed by law and practice. Is the difference in question here that men *fight* and women *do not*? Or is it that *men* fight and *women* do not? Can it be either without being both? Here it is appropriate to heed Foucault's (2000: 344) insight that "every relationship of power puts into operation differences that are, at the same time, its conditions

251

and its results." Read in these terms, Woolf's statement suggests that analyses of gender, power, and the laws of war must attend not only to the differences created and conceptualized within the laws of war (i.e., combatant vs. civilian), but also to the discourses of gender that produce the differences (i.e., oppositional sex) that serve as the law's referents. We lose this insight when we limit our focus to the *protection* and *treatment* of women within the laws of war. Analyses that engage only structural, institutional, and compulsory power risk overlooking the fully productive power of discourses of gender in constituting the laws of war themselves.

Gender and the laws of war

Let me draw out the context of this claim. In their masterly overview of women, armed conflict, and the law, Gardam and Jarvis (2001: 10) define gender as "the socially constructed roles of women and men ascribed to them on the basis of their sex . . . [which] refers to biological and physical characteristics." Gender is taken as derivative of sex, as a binary difference, rather than generative of it. Gender, in essence, is here the cultural interpretation of sex. The balance of scholarship attending to the laws of war accepts this definition. This lends itself to a focus on sexual violence (primarily rape) as the paradigmatic expression of both the construction of women within the law (as symbols of family honor; as property of their male relatives) and, conversely, of the relative dismissal of women's experiences during war (as rape, for example, was accepted as a traditional and inevitable strategy of war).

Such analyses and corresponding advocacy on the part of feminist scholars and practitioners led to historic shifts in the prosecution of perpetrators and an improvement of protection for women, as well as a reinterpretation of the laws of war to more adequately respond to women's experiences of rape.[1] These are laudable achievements, for they challenge the radical inequalities of institutional and compulsory power within which male sexual violence is strategically facilitated and favored – what feminists have long discussed under the rubric of patriarchy.

---

[1] See the decisions of the UN International Criminal Tribunal for the Former Yugoslavia judgements in the cases of Tadic (1999), Celebici (1998), Furundzija (1998), and Foca (2001); and those of the UN International Criminal Tribunal for Rwanda in the cases of Akayesu (1998) and Musema (2000).

Nonetheless, it behooves us to reconsider the premise upon which such success is gained. If sex and sex difference are understood as an ontological referent for the social or cultural understandings of gender, then sex becomes an incontrovertible ground and reason for the *necessity* of increased protection of women, while gender is said to explain the *paucity* or *neglect* of protection of women. This explanation runs the substantial risk of reifying a conception of women as "always already" victims who are subject to the benevolence or malevolence of their benefactors for presumably immutable anatomical differences. Yet, as Judith Butler (1990: 7) has so precisely detailed, these ostensibly natural facts of sex which are taken to explain displays of protection or predation are themselves produced through discourses of gender which give sex and sex difference meaning.

To fully appreciate the importance of Butler's argument, observe how a continued emphasis of male-on-female sexual violence has made it more difficult to investigate the meanings and consequences of the breadth of sexual violence perpetrated during war – a violence which victimizes men, women, and children and whose purpose includes not only the violation, but also the production of distinct identities. As Zarkov (2001: 69) notes, characterizing men as "never victims of rape and other forms of sexual violence is a very specific, gendered, narrative of war . . . dominant notions of masculinity merge with norms of heterosexuality and definitions of ethnicity and ultimately designate who can and cannot be named a victim of sexual violence." Discourses of gender, interwoven with other discourses of identity, infuse sex and sex differences with specific meaning. It is a specific meaning that we might be tempted to otherwise accept as already *given* solely by sex itself – e.g., men are not raped / rapeable – if it were not for the presence of evidence to the contrary and, in Zarkov's work, the detailing of the sheer force and persistence of a discourse of gender in shaping the visibility, and the meaning, of male rape. This underscores Judith Butler's (1990: 7) most salient point: "gender is not to culture as sex is to nature, gender is also the discursive / cultural means by which 'sexed nature' or 'a natural sex' is produced and established as prediscursive . . . a *politically neutral surface* on which culture acts."

Scholars and activists have long commented upon the contrived roles of women during armed conflicts – "soldiers, saints, or sacrificial lambs" who are "enlisted with or without consent" to wage and witness war (Dombrowski, 1999). Political theorist J. B. Elshtain (1987) invoked the perennial images of a "Just Warrior," the male protector of home and hearth, and a "Beautiful Soul," the female innocent whose purity is to be defended, to represent the symbolic and actual gendering of narratives and practices of war.[2] Stiehm (1982) introduced the now canonical terms of Protector and Protected to capture the fraught and sexed dynamic among those who wield the power of destruction and those dependent upon them to desist or defend from its expression. Women as conscripts or combatants are only provisionally, and frequently at great cost, granted an introduction to the fraternity of fighters within the militarization of masculinity – what Ignatieff (1998: 128) describes as an incitement of "toxic testosterone."

Participation in war, within these analyses, is structured according to a dyad wherein men are regularly positioned as combatants and protectors during war, and women as civilians and protected. Indeed, the putative self-evidence of this remains sufficiently powerful that the recognition of women as active and committed participants/combatants within war requires explicit acknowledgement and, frequently, draws explicit condemnation. This is most clearly captured by the very need to continually establish that women can *also* be combatants and should *also* be allowed to be. As the study undertaken by the International Committee of the Red Cross on women and war concludes, "it is also important to state that women in armed conflicts are *not solely* 'victims' in need of assistance and protection," but are often active and committed participants (Lindsey, 2001: 212; emphasis added). Indeed, one of the purposes of the report conducted under the auspices of the groundbreaking UN Security Council Resolution 1325 on Women and Peace and Armed Conflict is to continue to document and verify the participation of women in combat and as combatants.

Such a resistance to considering women as combatants certainly affects their participation and acceptance – a consequence well articulated by the representative of Jamaica to the Security Council who noted, during a recent discussion on women, peace, and armed conflict, "a narrow definition of who is a soldier or fighter often discriminated against women and girls involved in fighting" (SC/6847, 2000). And, as many have documented, such discrimination prevents demobilized female combatants from receiving appropriate resources after a conflict, and often hinders their successful reintegration within society.

---

[2] This construction is eerily echoed by the envoy from the Russian Federation during the UN Security Council debate on October 24, 2000 (S/PV.4208). He states that: "the words 'women, peace, and security' were a harmonious and natural combination. An unnatural combination was 'women and war' as was 'women and armed conflict.'"

Further, scholars of nationalisms and revolutions call our attention to one of the contradictions of female participation. Depicted as militant virgins simultaneously birthing and defending a nation that may or may not imagine itself male, women are frequently caught within the paradox of forging a new nation and reproducing the old (Pettman, 1996; Yuval-Davis, 1997). Consistently, then, the participation of women in war is conceived of and interpreted primarily in terms of sex and sex difference – the most brutal manifestation of which is the kidnapping of young girls and women for forced sexual and domestic servitude in national militias.

These analyses definitively document the way in which gender acts to demarcate combatants and civilians, but do not necessarily displace an understanding of sex as a prior materiality upon which gender acts. Each underscores the pervasive and persistent inequities of institutional, structural, and compulsory power – indicated by the degree to which women are consistently and categorically conceived of as in need of protection and incapable of protecting. Present, however, in these analyses is a disquieting reliance on the binary opposition of protector/protected to explain the distinctions between combatant and civilian as if it were not only the true or only relation *of* each pair, but a natural analogy *to* each pair. In other words, these binary oppositions (men/women and combatant/civilian) are accepted as given, their prior existence presumed, and they become points of origin for these analyses.

This reifies a dualism of combatant/civilian and protector/protected, whose meaning is constructed as and through opposition, in which an asymmetry of power is rendered intelligible and inevitable in a discourse of gender. Subsequently, this "matching principle" aids the primary and customary assignation of women *as* the paradigmatic "victims" of armed conflict (in particular, of its sexual violence) and not its agents, while reinscribing the binary logic of either one (victims/civilians) or the other (agents/combatants). Ironically, if one of the emphases is to alter the laws of war to accord more accurately and responsively with women's experiences of war, maintaining a binary which is founded on women's exclusion from the primary term, and vulnerability and relative lack of power in the second, will be most difficult. In this respect, advocating the recognition of women as combatants does not *dismantle* the binary logic; it simply reconfigures it. The production of the signal differences – the *difference* of combatant and civilian, the *difference* of protector and protected – remains unexplored and undisturbed. Thus, rather than accept as given, I first open an inquiry into the emergence and articulation of the "combatant" and the "civilian": to ask how a discourse of gender renders that equivocal difference to which Woolf referred as intelligible and (seemingly) inevitable.

The importance of this task is not to be underestimated. As I delineated above, the laws of war are a formidable institution of global governance. The concepts of "combatant" and "civilian" upon which I focus are the foundation of the essential dictate of the modern laws of war – the principle of distinction. The principle of distinction is the injunction to distinguish between combatants and civilians at all times during armed conflicts; it "forms the basis of the entire regulation of war" (Sandoz, Swinarski, and Zimmermann, 1987: 586). Therefore, to consider the relations among gender, power, and the laws of war, it is imperative to return to its most generative concepts, and to do so with full acknowledgement of the *multidimensionality* of power expressed in the relationship of the combatant and the civilian.

Required, then, is no less than a genealogy of the principle of distinction, for, as Foucault (1997: 118) most succinctly stated, a genealogy is a form of history which transforms the "development of the given into a question." A genealogy begins with a careful analysis of the historical articulations of each of these concepts, tracing their graftings at particular moments in which their meanings are created and configured – meanings that we now attribute as essential to their form and function.

In this chapter, I emphasize the emergence and construction of the category and concept of "civilian," for that is the category to which women are most often relegated and the concept by which they are most frequently defined. This does not reinstantiate the belief that to analyze discourses of gender is to analyze the position of women, for, as I demonstrate, discourses of gender will always exceed that reference. Rather, it is because, although the combatant and the civilian are irreducibly codetermined (in that a civilian is that which a combatant is not), the civilian has not been made an equal subject of analysis. I first concentrate explicitly upon the pivotal formation of the concepts and relations of the "combatant" and the "civilian" in the works of Hugo Grotius, works that histories of the laws of war hold as fundamental to our contemporary understandings. Once these are set forth, I turn to an analysis of the 1949 Convention Relative to the Protection of Civilian Persons in Times of War in which the civilian is first made formally a subject of treaty law.

As a final note, I use the term "civilian" advisedly throughout this paper. While "combatant" is part of common parlance from the twelfth century, it was not until the nineteenth century that the civilian, a "nonmilitary man or official," entered into broad use (Oxford English Dictionary, 1989). The locution favored by Grotius and his fellow writers is that those who are to be spared from war are "innocents." This locution informs our present understandings of who shall be spared from war to such a degree that the phrase "guilty civilian" sounds, to us, utterly oxymoronic. The 1949 IV Convention formally refers to "protected persons," while it is in the 1977 Protocols Additional I to the IV Convention that the concept of the "civilian" is invested with a formal definition in the laws of war. I argue that, by tracing the descent of the "civilian" from its earlier manifestations, as an "innocent" and as a "protected person," we can identify the persistent presence of discourses of gender and their integral force in determining the difference of "combatant" and "civilian."

Grotius and the laws of war

The seventeenth-century Dutch lawyer and diplomat Hugo Grotius wrote two highly influential works on the laws of war (*De Jure Pradae* [The Law of Prize and Booty], 1604; *De Jure Belli ac Pacis Libri Tres* [The Laws of War and Peace], 1625 [1925]). Scholars of international law, specifically the laws of war, identify these works as shaping the possibility and substance of the laws of war. As the respected historian of the laws of war Geoffrey Best (1994: 26) states, "no writing has been more determinant of the consideration given to the non-combatant in the modern history of the law of war than Grotius's early seventeenth-century masterwork, the Laws of War." Legal and international relations scholars contend "that the issues that Grotius addressed, the concepts and language he used, even the propositions he advanced, have become part of the common currency of international debate about war in general" (Kingsbury and Roberts, 1990: 26). The immediate impetus of *The Laws of War* was to advocate the establishment and recognition of an order that would moderate and restrain war. How did Grotius imagine its accomplishment? It is here that the analysis of discourses of gender finds its own imperative.

Opening his discussion of the law, Grotius first sets forth the distribution of rights that inform and maintain social order. He proclaims "[b]y generation parents acquire a right over children... [b]ut, if there is a variance in the exercise of these rights the right of the father is given preference on account of the superiority of sex" (Grotius, 1625

[1925]: 231). Essential to the peace and order of domestic society is the proper distribution of power between the sexes. Yet, it is not only domestic order that is founded upon and arises from these hierarchical and gendered relations of power; international order does as well. For the seventeenth-century Dutch, "[h]ome ... was both a microcosm and a permitting condition of a properly governed commonwealth" (Schama, 1997: 386).

Grotius also held that the "maintenance of social order ... is the source of the law so called," and, indeed, "no association of men can be maintained without law" (Grotius, 1625 [1925]: "Prolegomena" 12, 17). For Grotius, then, the source and purpose of the law are to be found in the preservation of the proper social order grounded in the arrangement between the sexes. Reasoning from this recursive relationship, it is fair to say that the peculiar position of women as both subject to and property of men is not simply reflected and regulated in the social order, but also generates the law that governs that social order.

Ever careful to parse the degree of differences within the desired social order, and cognizant of the desirability of peace and the persistence of war, Grotius remains intent upon limiting the authority and right to wage war to those entities identified as public and sovereign. Although it is tempting to deduce from this that the actual pursuit and practice of war should be limited to militaries, armies, and recognizable vested representatives of that sovereign power, it is difficult to find a consistent identification of belligerents or combatants within his work. For one, while the law of nations might restrict the pool of combatants to the above, the law of nature (the dictate of right reason) holds that "no-one is enjoined from waging war" (ibid.: 165).

This tension is complicated by Grotius's position that *all* inhabitants of a country may be warred against, not just "those who actually bear arms, or are the subjects of him that stirs up war" (ibid.: 646). Grotius writes that *"how far* this right to inflict injury extends may be perceived from the fact that the slaughter even of infants and of women is made with impunity and that this is included in the law of war" (ibid.: 648). Since "[n]either sex nor age found mercy," it is established both within the law of nations, evidenced by the practice of nations, and within natural law that the right of killing in war is extensive.

Therefore, Grotius sets himself the task of developing a "remedy" to this "frenzy" of war (ibid.: "Prolegomena" 20). He does so by establishing a mean between "nothing is allowable" and "everything is" (ibid.). This mean derives from the "bidding of *mercy*, if not of justice, that,

258

except for reasons that are weighty and will affect the safety of many, *no action should be attempted whereby innocent persons may be threatened with destruction*" (ibid.: 716). It is this principle that sets the mean and, in turn, regulates the frenzy of war.

Immediately after positing this principle, one which attests to the existence a "more just and better" law, Grotius begins to substantiate its essential precepts. He states: "[t]hat children should always be spared; women, unless they have been guilty of an extremely serious offense; and old men" (ibid.: 734). With this statement, Grotius contravenes the laws of nature and the laws of nations, for each *allows* killing of children, women, and old men since all pose a potential harm and all may claim a potential right of self-defense: "we shall hold to this principle, that by nature every one is the defender of his own rights; that is why hands were given to us" (ibid.: 164). How does he justify his transgression?

For one, quoting Seneca, Grotius straightforwardly states: "let the child be excused by his age, the woman by her sex" (ibid.). At first, it seems that the sex of woman refers literally to the sex *had* by a woman, for not all women are to be spared, only virgins. This is exemplified by the trial of the Midianites that demonstrated that, even in a war so just as to be ordained and fought by God, the virgins were spared. Here discourses of gender differentiate not only between men and women, adults and children, but insofar as they grant to specific women, to virgins, the right of protection they equally differentiate among women. (An analysis of structural power risks obscuring this differentiation among women, and among men, by highlighting the opposition rather than the proliferation of subject positions.)

In continuing to trace Grotius's reasoning, one discovers that it is not simply the lack of sex that sets women apart, to be spared among their kind. Sparing of women during wars is equally grounded in the belief that women cannot "devise wars" (ibid.: 734). Recollect that for Grotius because of "the difference in sex the authority is not held in common but the husband is in the head of the wife . . . [t]he woman under the eye of the man and under his guardianship" (ibid.: 234). And, as Schama (1997: 404) details, in the era in which Grotius lived, women were "formally subject to their husband's legal authority." Consequently, women lack the authority and sovereignty held necessary to devise war within a theory in which "the principal author of war is one whose right has been violated" (Onuma, 1993: 99).

Grotius also argues that wars are to be waged solely for just cause and for just purposes. As formulated, this contention erects another barrier against women as able to authorize or devise wars for, according to Grotius, women are among those who are constitutionally unable to adjudicate between "just and unjust, lawful and unlawful" (Grotius, 1625 [1925]: 497). Drawing from Aristotle, Grotius explains: "alike children, women and men of dull intellect and bad education are not well able to appreciate the distinction" (ibid.). In this phrase, "women" is a problematic middle term – they are either like children or stupid and poorly educated men, or somewhat akin to both. Although the exact analogue may be inconsistent, the consequences are not. Women are incapable of devising war, one grade above animals, akin to children.

Thus, the substantiation of the first principle is as follows. Absent deliberative and sovereign authority, unable to tell just from unjust, and incapable of receiving injury, women are to be spared for they are constitutionally and constitutively incapable of waging war. Women are "innocent" of war, and thus should be spared war, because they lack authority, judgement, and sovereignty. In addition to these definitional deficiencies, women may be spared if they have not *experienced* sex itself.

Now, to dwell on the matter of sex. The power of this configuration of sex, in which differences attributed to materiality of the body are presumed as evident and natural foundations for the opposition of men and women and, in turn, determine the opposition between those who are or are not spared war, is made visible in the central role that temporality plays in the construction of the immunity of children and old men. Grotius posits an analogue between children and women in which the absence of reason, authority, and capacity joins the two. Yet, whereas children may develop, rectifying these deficiencies through education and maturity, women are forever marked as lacking in these regards.[3] Therefore, while children might ever seem the more *"natural"* innocents, in fact it is women who are made innocent as if by *nature*.

It is only women whose innocence is not derived from the sequential and variable attributes of age, choice of religious, pastoral, or artistic occupation, or defined by a range of intellect and education.[4] Old men and children grow in and out of these categories, the cycle of birth,

---

[3] Here the influence of Aristotle comes to the fore. Differences of sex are translated into moral, social, and political distinctions that, in turn, are taken as legitimating, and demonstrating the existence of, putative *biological* differences upon which these social distinctions are premised.

[4] The third group is those who "also should be spared" because they are involved in farming or trade, because "their occupations are solely religious or concerned with letters" or, finally, because they are prisoners of war.

maturity, senility, and death frames their span; women remain forever innocent, forever deficient, because of their sex. What we find in these passages, then, is that in order to enable and stabilize the otherwise inde-terminate distinction between those who may and may not be killed, Grotius turns, in the end, to discourses of gender. In this founding work of the laws of war, discourses of gender establish sex as an ontological basis for distinguishing between the two while, simultaneously, affirm-ing a social and political order within which this understanding of sex is given meaning.

I do recognize that Grotius does begin with the statement that women shall be always spared "*unless* they have been guilty of an extremely serious offense" (ibid.: 734). This makes it tempting to read Grotius's modification of the protection of women as an argument against mine. But, in fact, it underscores the importance of analyzing gender as pro-ductive of sex and sex difference.

Grotius writes that women should not be spared from war if "they commit a crime which ought to be punished in a special manner or unless they take the place of men" (ibid.: 735). This is a radical claim for one who equally holds that women are the "sex which is spared wars" (ibid.: 736). What, then, is the crime for which women ought to be punished in a special manner? Grotius does not say. However, the crime that is given a name, that is, taking the place of *men*, suggests the tenor of the crimes that degrade his defense of women. Moreover, among those who write before him, and upon whom he relies, the serious crime for which women would be specifically punished *is* taking the place of men. For example, Grotius's most favored predecessor, the Italian jurist A. Gentili (1612 [1933]: 256), argues that as a rule the "age of childhood is weak, and so is the sex of women, so that to both an indulgence may be shown." Yet he, like Grotius, makes "an exception of those women who perform duties of men which are beyond the power of the sex in general" (ibid.).[5] What is the substance of this crime that makes its commission so exceptional?

For one, men are "not accustomed to wage war" against women. Quoting the same Roman authorities, both Grotius and Gentili under-score that women are a "sex untrained and inexperienced in war." Due to this, there is little honor to be gained in fighting against such callow foes. Instead, those who do fight women receive only the epitaphs of

---

[5] For Grotius's acknowledgement of his debt, see 1625 [1925], "Prolegomena" 22. See also van der Molen (1968), Borschberg (1994), Meron (1998), and Haggenmacher (1990).

cruelty and savagery and the reputation for inhumanity and impiety, as well as the scorn of those who do not fight women.

Consider, further, how this distinction among men founded upon the pursuit and practice of honor, secured in the sparing of women, differentiates among the commonality of men who wage war. As with the chivalric tradition that precedes Grotius (and which is by no means unfamiliar to him), the honor *of* men is intimately linked to their identity *as* men. It may become good men to respect the strictures on war, but it is also the primary means by which men become good. Women in war confuse and contradict the assignation of men as men – and men as good and just among all other men. Warring women disrupt the order of things. Consequently, taking the place of men must be punished.

Yet, notice how both Grotius and Gentili propose to do so. Grotius simply states that "When Nero in the tragedy calls Octavia a foe, the prefect replies: Does a Woman receive this name?" (Grotius, 1625 [1925]). Likewise, Gentili (1612 [1933]: 257), also quoting Seneca, writes "a woman does not take the name of the enemy," continuing in his own words, "for in so far as women play the part of men they are men and not women." Therefore, Gentili concludes, "if women are guilty, then it will be said that the *guilt* is destroyed rather than woman" (ibid.). Or, as he elaborates, it will be that the "abomination" which is destroyed – not the woman, but her crime of acting like man.

To restate, even when women transgress the boundaries of sex, it is *they* who are rendered suspect and not that boundary itself. It is not woman who receives the name of foe, it is not women who play the part of men, and it is not women who are destroyed – it is the "guilt" and the "abomination" which is so destroyed. Here, both Grotius and Gentili attempt to defend against the evident disruption of the dichotomy of sex that is said to found the social order and, in turn, enable the distinction between those who are and are not "innocent" of war. What this disruption demonstrates, however, is the very plasticity of sex upon which these differences are founded.

1949 Geneva Convention

In the work of Grotius, we see, then, how discourses of gender produce the difference between those who fight and those who do not. The effects of these discourses of gender are not relegated to the past, but echo in our present. It is not that the meanings of "gender" remain the same from the seventeenth to the twentieth century. Rather, discourses of gender persist in producing differences of sex as natural and normal, differences that are then taken as paradigmatic for legislating and legitimating the distinction of "combatant" and "civilian."[6] To demonstrate, I turn now to the 1949 IV Geneva Convention Relative to the Protection of Civilian Persons in Times of War, the purpose of which was to rectify, in light of the past world wars, the neglect of the "civilian" within the laws of war.

The task of the development of the laws of war in 1949 was one similar to that which Grotius set himself in the midst of his contemporary crisis: to regulate and moderate war through the refinement of its rules and requirements while, simultaneously, to produce the distinction between those who fight and those who do not, upon which the possibility of moderation depends. The outlook was no less grim, for, as the judge advocate general of the United States War Department wrote, while humanity itself demands the preservation of the distinction of combatant and civilian, even that distinction is one "more apparent than real" (Nurick, 1945: 680). Only a year earlier, the eminent lawyer H. B. Wheaton decried the very distinction as "illusory" and, as a result, described any efforts to retain its use as "immoral" (ibid.: 681). Echoing this position, the legal scholar Lauterpacht dismissed it as a "hollow phrase" (Rosenblad, 1977: 57).

Nonetheless, the destruction or dissolution of this distinction was said to betray the promise of "civilization" and jeopardize humanity itself. For "barbarity abounds when 'belligerents strike army and civilian population alike without any distinction between the two'" (Best, 1994: 103, quoting the Greek delegate to the preparatory conference). Legal scholar Josef Kunz declared that the two world wars exemplified the "the total crisis of Western Christian culture, a crisis which threatens the very survival of our civilization," for each demonstrated that the "cultured man of the twentieth century is no more than a barbarian under a very superficial veneer of civilization" (1999: 103). To repair the veneer, if

---

[6] I draw my analysis from the final records of the preparatory conferences for the IV Convention and the official Commentaries, produced under the auspices of the International Committee of the Red Cross, which paraphrase and explicate the meanings of the treaties. These documents, often written by the participants in the preparatory conferences, are of utmost significance and importance in interpreting the treaties of the laws of war and are highly "useful for clarifying the intended scope and operation of the provisions" (Gardam and Jarvis, 2001: 258). The Commentaries (Sandoz, Swinarski, and Zimmermann, 1987: xxv) state that "if the interpretation of the texts gives rise to some uncertainty the opinions put forward are *legal* opinions, and not opinions of principle."

not to rehabilitate the man, the necessity of the further development of the laws of war could not be denied. It guaranteed the "survival of our whole civilization" (ibid.).

Thus the question was not how to *distinguish* between combatant and civilian, but how to *produce* the difference between the two. Moreover, because it is the *observance* of this distinction that demarcates civilized nations from their barbarous brethren, men from "savage hordes," and honorable men from dishonorable, this distinction remains the means by which such differences may be indexed and identified (ibid.). Indeed, no better example of the resonance of this claim may be found than in the words of President George W. Bush and his administration in their claim to defend civilization against the existence of lawless violence, of barbarity itself, a primary measure of which is the violation of the principle of distinction or, in the words of President Bush on October 7, 2001, the killing of the "innocent." This barbarous violence is painstakingly contrasted to measures taken by the United States in defense of civilization against "these outlaws and killers of the innocent." Once again, as we saw with Grotius, the laws of war form a pivotal and *productive* dimension of international order. Not only regulating and legislating conduct among (preconstituted) entities, the laws of war constitute the subjects they are said to govern.

The states gathered in 1946 to discuss the future of the laws of war were intimately aware of the formidable transformation of the political landscape. The tactics of terror practiced by both Allied and Axis powers, from aerial and atomic bombings to concentration and internment camps, corrupted any facile distinctions of civilization and barbarism. In the midst of this ruin, the mission of those gathered at the preparatory conferences, some sixty-two delegations from Western, primarily European states, was to instantiate the distinction between those who fought and those who did not and, in so doing, to rehabilitate some measure of civilization itself. This was not an easy proposition.

First, as always, within the structural logic of the law, the identification and determination of the "civilian" were intimately related to the identification and determination of the "combatant." However, as I noted previously, the experiences of the past world wars had convinced most that the clarity and coherency of such determinations were "obsolete," "illusory," "immoral," and "more apparent than real" – assuming that they were ever otherwise. The logic of total war in which all individuals were implicated dominated the discussions in the preparatory conferences

264

requiring that every "enemy national" be treated as a "potential soldier" (Uhler, Coursier, et al., 1958: 232, 372).

Second, the practices of occupation and resistance, as witnessed in both World Wars I and II, forced a controversial reconsideration of the conventional category of "combatant" to provide for the protection and treatment of partisans, or irregulars, upon capture. Underlying this controversy was the fear that any loosening of the standards of organization, appearance, or conduct by which combatants were identified would unfairly benefit irregulars, jeopardize the safety of both regular combatants and civilians, and degrade the standards of conduct, because it would make it *yet more* difficult to distinguish between combatants and civilians. Nonetheless, after much heated debate during the preparatory conference, a less restricted definition of "combatant" was introduced, which rightly acknowledged the participation of partisans, but which further stressed the plasticity of the distinction.

Third, the identification and determination of civilians rested on "much less solid ground" (ibid.: 5). The venerable authors of the ICRC Commentary worriedly wrote regarding the IV Convention: the "wounded and prisoners of war are human beings *who have become harmless*, and the State's obligations toward them are not a serious hindrance to its conduct of the hostilities . . . *civilians have not in most cases been rendered harmless*, and the steps taken on their behalf may be a serious hindrance to the conduct of war" (ibid.). Besides, while one could reasonably assume that the wounded and sick and prisoners of war were identifiable through their military regalia or presence in specific formations of war, civilians were but "an *unorganized mass* scattered over the whole of countries concerned" (ibid.). Thus, the difficulties of identification and determination are compounded by the potential threat posed by this seemingly itinerant mass of individuals.

In responding to these three complicated challenges of identification and determination, one might reasonably assume that the first step would be to define the category under consideration – this was not accomplished. Instead, the formal articles of the IV Convention refer only to the ample concept of "protected persons." "Protected persons" are individuals "taking no active part in the hostilities," including prisoners of war, wounded and sick combatants, detainees and internees, and all others in the hands of the enemy. Article 4 of the 1949 IV Convention attempts to distinguish more clearly among this mix of "protected persons," to elucidate the differences among each of these types and subsequently specify to whom the protections of the IV Convention apply. But as the Commentary on the IV Convention ruefully notes, "the meaning does not stand out very clearly" (ibid.: 45). Thus, Article 4 upon which the identification and determination of "civilian" rest remains irresolute.

The inability to arrive at a coherent definition was a result of the tension between the preservation of state sovereignty to wage war, relatively unhindered by considerations of civilians and conscience, and the recognition of a responsibility to a common humanity. During the preparatory conferences, arguments for the latter were primarily put forth by the USSR and its allies against a coalition led by the United States and United Kingdom. The USSR accused those states that sought to limit the definition and protection of "civilians" as being no less than "enemies of humanity" (Best, 1994: 110). In fact, it was the USSR that decried the scope and definition of "protected persons" found in Article 4, taking it to betray the promise of "conscience and honor of nations, and the traditional standards of conduct generally recognized throughout the civilized world" (Final Record of the Diplomatic Conference of Geneva, 1949: IIB, 376). What precisely were those standards that were generally recognized? What exactly did the civilized world require? It is here that discourses of gender sound again.

Part II, Article 13, of the Geneva Conventions attempts to restore this promise by broadening the definition of those so protected under the IV Convention to *all* populations in countries of conflict. In its short formulation, Article 13 simply states that general protections outlined in Part II cover the "*whole* of the populations of the countries in conflict." In Article 13, nationality and being in the power of the enemy are *no longer* necessary markers for the protections as they were in Article 4. What the Commentaries on the Convention inform us is that the extension of protection to all populations is premised upon binding "belligerents to observe certain restrictions in their conduct of hostilities by erecting protective barriers to shield certain categories of the population who, by definition, take no part in the fighting" (Uhler, Coursier, et al., 1958: 118). Grotius would agree, for temperance in war is the responsibility of those who wage it, while the practice of prudence demands the determination of who shall be spared. He would also assent to the selection of those who shall be spared, as the categories that, by definition, take no part in the fighting are "children, women, old people, the wounded and the sick" (ibid.).

Take note most immediately of two moves. The first is that the extension of protection to *all* populations has just been reduced to *specific* categories. It is not difficult to imagine the consequences of this delimitation of protection to *only* children, women, old people, the wounded, and the sick, for we have too many examples. Most starkly, we see it in the roundup and disappearance of the men from the safe haven of Srebrenica as presumptive combatants regardless of the fact that they were taking no part in the fighting (United Nations, 1998; Carpenter, 2003). However, this is a pattern of presumption common to armed conflicts from Chechnya to Israel–Palestine, and now the United States repeats this selective logic in its requirement that only Muslim men register in the United States.

Further, while this delimitation may have appeared sensible in light of the almost-universal conscription of men during the world wars, it is contradictory on at least two counts. The first is that women *took part* militarily in these wars. In the Soviet Union the participation of women is estimated in excess of 8 percent of the total armed forces – at least 800,000 women in the army, and many thousands in partisan forces. In Greece, Italy, and France, women were active and public partisans and members of resistance movements, while the German and British forces had women working in reserve and support units. Additionally, the status of women as combatants is specifically addressed in the 1949 III Convention Relative to the Treatment of Prisoners of War. In fact, the only time the International Committee of the Red Cross was able to invoke the this Convention was after one of its delegates visited a prisoner-of-war camp in Poland where both men and women were being held. Finally, the logic of total war dispenses with such discrimination between those who fight and those who do not – that is what makes it so horrifying. Total war presumes that *all* are considered combatants. Thus, just as Grotius was bound to do, the Commentaries are compelled to produce a distinction that does not exist before its very institution.

This brings us to the second move. In so instituting this distinction between those who take part in the fighting and those who do not, the Commentaries simultaneously substantiate the definition of the "civilian" never accomplished within the formal articles of the IV Convention, but consistently referred to in the body of the Commentaries. Civilians are those who *"by definition"* "do not bear arms," are "outside the fighting," and "take no active part in the hostilities" (Uhler, Coursier, et al., 1958: 22). Accordingly, civilians are said to be children, women, old people, and the wounded and sick. This is no small triumph, for the essential challenge of the IV Convention was to isolate and identify a category of "civilians" as distinguishable from that of "combatant."

Furthermore, because this distinction is confirmed by the shared "suffering, distress, or weakness" of those who take no part in the fighting, the Commentary's authors' anxious concern over the potential *threat* posed by civilians is easily relieved (ibid.: 119). In terms of their shared suffering, distress, and weakness, there are now three distinct categories of individuals that function as a synecdoche for civilian.

There is a familiar logic of equivalence posited by the Commentaries among these disparate and otherwise distinct categories of individuals. Most immediately it should remind us of Grotius, for it is only women who are said to always already possess these varied attributes (not bearing arms, outside the fighting, weak, suffering, or in distress) as a matter of sex. The others, children, old people, wounded, and sick, all bear these essential attributes as a result of unfortunate circumstances and transient conditions – that is *temporally or chronologically*. And, in fact, the debates in the preparatory conferences were over precise ages by which the categories of children and old people would be known and their "faculties" of judgement and strength could be assessed. There were no corresponding inquiries into the exact criteria by which women would be known; their sex alone (for it is only women that appear to be marked by sex) would be sufficient.

Unlike Grotius, the Commentaries do not argue that women, like children, suffered from diminished powers of reasoning and judgement that render them "innocent" of war. Instead, the Commentaries hold that it is the matter of women's sex itself – defined as reproductive capability and sexual vulnerability. As a result, it is only women out of these other distinct categories (children, old people, wounded, and sick) that both *materialize and stabilize* the distinction of combatant and civilian. In other words, women – like children, old people, and the wounded and sick – are harmless, but unlike children, old men, and the wounded and sick, women pose no *potential* harm. It is only women whose suffering, distress, and weakness, derived from their reproductive capability and sexual vulnerability, are *constant* and natural markers of their very sex and, in turn, of the "civilian."

Most unmistakably, the chorus of appeals to a "warrior's honor," a "proud vision of male identity," as a primary means of protection could only be heard within this orchestration (Ignatieff, 1998). Yet contrary to common presumptions, the very weakness and harmlessness of the "civilian" does not *necessarily* result in an assurance of protection. It certainly did not during World War I or II, nor does it in any of our contemporary wars. As Forsythe (1977: 173) argues, because the "civilian is frequently viewed as nothing: weak . . . old . . . female . . . there is nothing to command respect," and, consequently, combatants have less reason to abide by injunctions to protect and respect civilians. In other words, there is no *necessary* compulsion to do so. Among combatants, protection and respect derive from a sense of collective recognition and collective honor – a sort of ol' boys network of equals, which is absent between combatants and civilians. Moreover, even as women are produced as the paradigmatic civilian, the protections afforded to them are couched in prescriptive rather than prohibitive language. Thus, even if discourses of gender produce the distinction of combatant and civilian, the "civilian" produced is not worthy of much protection at all! Disrupting the presumed correspondence between protection and harmlessness illuminates the multiple dimensions of power at play in producing and protecting the "civilian" – power whose effects are not solely benign.

Thus to accept, as the Commentaries wish us to do, that these interpretations of sex and sex difference offered within are but "normal and natural" is to fail to inquire after the productive discourses of gender which achieve this effect (Uhler, Coursier, et al., 1958: 119). Recognizing that appeals to what is "normal and natural" consolidate and legitimate specific historical and social norms should encourage us to trace what is at stake in the production of these ostensibly natural distinctions. The formulation of the distinction between combatant and civilian draws upon and contributes to a particular vision of a gendered domestic and international order – as we saw most vividly with Grotius, but as is no less evident in the Commentaries and statements quoted above.

There are at least two ways that this is evident. First, in the persistent way in which observance of this distinction sorts states according to degrees of barbarism and civilization, as it did similarly in the work of Grotius. Observance of the distinction, specifically the treatment of women with all due consideration of their sex, remains the hallmark of "every civilized country," whereas transgression conjures the "worst memories of the great barbarian invasions" (Uhler, Coursier, et al., 1958: 205). The recursive relationship between the combatant/civilian distinction and sex and sex difference generates and regulates a particular international order. As the IV Convention and its Commentaries make clear, this international order has as its foundation and future the heterosexual family – the "natural and fundamental group unit of society" (ibid.: 202). It is upon this foundation that an international order can be said to arise.

If it is thought that the attention to women as family is by now out-dated, think again. On October 12, 1999, the director of the International Committee of the Red Cross told the United Nations General Assembly that "when one thinks of 'women,' one also naturally tends to think of the family." Indeed, a large part of postwar reconstruction was occupied with the reconstruction of a highly particular vision of a heterosexual, nuclear family. Postwar states as varied as the USSR, the USA, and the UK shared a singular emphasis on the re-creation of "traditional gender relationships, the familiar and natural order of families, men in public roles, women at home" (Higonnet, et.al., 1987: 41). The promotion and defense of the conventional family, challenged by widespread participation of women in the work of war, shaped postwar policies and politics. In both the United States and France, for example, "the short-lived affirmation of women's independence gave way to a pervasive endorsement of female subordination and domesticity" (May, 1988: 89). Indeed, during the last year of war in Britain, "women auxiliaries were given time off for 'mothercraft' lessons, in order to prepare them for and remind them of their peacetime role" (De Groot and Penistone-Bird, 2000: 15).

These initiatives positioned and governed women as wives and mothers, as sexually available but not sexually adventurous, while instituting men as husbands and providers, the defenders of home and hearth. Therefore, the reconstitution and reaffirmation of the *heterosexual* family the placement of women within that family and in need of male protection, was of utmost importance for a secure domestic order that, in turn, informed the international. Within the ample play of these social and juridical discourses of gender, the salience of reproductive capability and sexual vulnerability as the marker of sex and sex difference is made intelligible. These distinctions of sex that make possible the distinction of combatant and civilian are themselves neither normal nor natural: they are produced by historically particular discourses of gender. And, just as sex and sex difference ensure the self-evidence of the combatant/civilian distinction, so too does that distinction reaffirm the naturalness of sex difference.

Power and the production of difference

My reading of both Grotius and the 1949 IV Convention allows us to recognize how these interpretations of sex and sex differences that each accepts as given, and as paradigmatic of the differences of "combatant" and "civilian," are effects of discourses of gender. This, then, is not only where a genealogy of the laws of war serves its purpose, but also where an understanding of discourses of gender as productive reveals its benefits. We are able to identify both as classic examples of what Wendy Brown (1995: 66) calls instances "in which differences that are effects of social power are neutralized through their articulation as attributes."

Therefore, I maintain my claim that the distinction between combatant and civilian which founds and governs the laws of war and, indeed, contributes to its formative power is an effect of particular, historically rooted formations of sex and sex differences. Further, I argue that this remains true even in the case of the 1997 Protocol I, which formally defines the concept and category of the civilian in the laws of war. The very definition of the civilian in the Protocol draws directly from Article 13 of the IV Convention that, as I just argued, relies upon discourses of gender for its very possibility. As each treaty of the laws of war is responsive such that "every new instrument can only have a purely cumulative or supplementary (but no destructive) effect," by its own terms it would be impossible to negate the continuing influence of the discourses of gender in instituting the possibilities of the distinction itself (Abi-Saab, 1984: 276). The contemporary characterization of women who fight as "de-sexed" is but one indication of the continuing force of gender in the maintenance of this distinction (Lindsey, 2001: 24; UNIFEM, 2003; Farr, 2003).

When the difference of combatant and civilian is legitimated by reference to putatively biological differences of men and women, sexual difference is established not only as a natural fact but as an ontological basis for political and social differences as well. In other words, discourses of gender *produce* the distinctions of sex and sex difference we are now accustomed to identifying as the *ground* of those differences. Consequently, we can see how the very distinction of combatant and civilian is dependent upon, not merely described by, discourses of gender. Thus, understanding the discursive power of gender opens the *entirety* of the laws of war, their structure, their effects, and their role in global governance to analysis – not simply those areas in which women are its explicit subjects. Finally, an analysis of discourses of gender at work in both Hugo Grotius and in the 1949 IV Convention assists us in tracing the ways in which gender is pivotal not only to the establishment of differences of sex and of the civilian, but also to the production and governance of international (civilized) and domestic (familial) orders. Denaturalizing sex and sex difference, while tracing their prodigious effects, certainly opens the possibilities for transformation while,

271

simultaneously, reminding us of the enormous responsibilities entailed in so doing. Indeed, if we are to denaturalize sex and sex difference, thus overturning the foundation of the distinction of combatant and civilian, how shall we reimagine the formulation of this distinction upon which lives depend? How shall we answer who is a civilian; how do we judge, and upon what grounds? Contemplating these questions anew leads us to recognize how an analysis of modes of power necessarily involves an analysis of ethical possibilities, for in seeking to answer them we cannot help but imagine different orders and new forms of governance.

12   Colonial and postcolonial global governance

Himadeep Muppidi

In October 2003, in a memo leaked to the US press, Donald Rumsfeld, the US secretary of defense, claimed that the George W. Bush administration "lack[ed] [the] metrics to know" if it was "winning or losing the global war on terror."[1] Elaborating on this theme, Rumsfeld wondered whether the United States was "capturing, killing or deterring and dissuading more terrorists every day than the madrassas and the radical clerics are recruiting, training and deploying against us." Rumsfeld's comments bring home, quite starkly, the emphasis placed by the Bush administration on "compulsory power" ("capturing, killing or deterring and dissuading...") (table 1.1, p. 12). While this brutally competitive, if quotidian, enterprise does not appear to lack measurable features ("more terrorists everyday than the madrassas and the radical clerics are...deploying"), what seems missing is a broader focus on the interpretive dimension of the United States's "war on terror." Rumsfeld's predominant concern, it seems, is on the measures, the metrics, of the "global war on terror" rather than on its social meanings. What he appears not to be inquisitive about are the global meanings of the war on terror, the underlying social relations, diffuse and direct, productive of these meanings, and whether the United States is "winning or losing the global war on terror" on this interpretive dimension. A focus on the global meanings of the war on terror would draw our attention to the historically broader field of meanings – the productive power – governing

Earlier versions of this paper were presented at the University of Wisconsin-Madison and at the Minnesota International Relations Colloquium of the Department of Political Science, University of Minnesota. I benefited immensely from the comments of participants in both places. I would also like to acknowledge a more specific debt to Mike Barnett, David Blaney, Neta Crawford, Bud Duvall, Orfeo Fioretos, Jonathan Havercroft, Helen M. Kinsella, and Mark Laffey for their feedback on this paper.
[1] See www.usatoday.com/news/washington/executive/rumsfeld-memo.htm.

the conflict. And it is primarily on productive power, those fields of meanings empowering or restraining the capacities to generate compulsory, institutional, and structural powers, that I focus on in this chapter. I discuss below some of the ways in which conceptualizing these fields of meanings as configured on colonial and postcolonial forms offers a useful entry into the politics of global governance.

Ordering the global

In a discipline that has seen, in recent years, a mushrooming of various types of constructivist theories, I begin with the minimal constructivist insight that realities of the global are socially produced. Given the diversity of human beings and political communities in the world, I assume that there are multiple realities of the global: multiple ways of imagining, ordering, and inhabiting our world as a global space. But what would global governance mean in such a multiply imaginable and inhabitable world? How would the different types of power – compulsory, institutional, structural, and productive – come together in the ordering of these worlds? Barnett and Duvall (chap. 1 in this volume) observe that our current conceptualizations of global governance neglect questions of power. The typology they provide rectifies this limitation by, among other things, revealing the different types of power and their possible relationships to global governance. But, though they clarify the multiple types of power that constitute the structures and practices of global governance, they do not explicitly posit any normatively desirable models of global governance.[2] This raises an important question for the study of global governance – what are the normative criteria governing the analysis of global governance – that is answered, to some extent, by the politics of global governance offered in this chapter.

In a world with multiply imaginable globalities, any governance of the global must, I assume, necessarily involve the politics of difference – the negotiation and regulation of difference at the level of imaginations, social powers, identities, and interests. Based on the predominance of authoritarian or democratic processes in shaping the politics of difference, I posit two polar models of global governance: colonial and postcolonial. A colonial global order can be read as one in which anti-democratic and authoritarian processes dominate the politics of difference. Such a politics in a postcolonial order, by contrast, is

---

[2] But see Adler and Bernstein, chap. 13 in this volume.

characterized by the predominance of democratic procedures.[3] While there are many possible indicators of the presence of authoritarian and anti-democratic procedures, I wish to focus here primarily on the presence or absence of a respect for the practices of dissent.

I conceptualize global governance, then, as the meaningful constitution and material realization of a shared imagination of the world, of *the* global, from among multiple possible imaginations of globality. I see this as a necessarily political process that involves different configurations of powers, principles, and practices. My analysis, in this context, seeks to highlight some configurations of powers, principles, and practices that go into the making of colonial and postcolonial orders of global governance. With that aim in mind, I read critically some prominent practices in the contemporary international system in order to show their complicity in the imagination and realization of a colonial or postcolonial order. Though powers of different types – compulsory, institutional, structural, and productive – are constitutive of colonial and postcolonial orders, my analysis will focus primarily on the role of productive power and only secondarily on the other types.

Colonial governance

In recent years, particularly after September 11, 2001, there has been a number of articles in British and American papers and journals advocating a return to a new order of global governance marked by colonial or imperial rule.[4] It is quite easy to read such calls as direct evidence of an Anglo-American desire to institutionalize a new imperial order. Some prominent scholars (e.g., Ikenberry, 2002) have, incorrectly in my view, advanced this line of critique. Differing with such scholars more on their method of analysis than on the spirit behind their criticism, I would argue, on the contrary, that the colonial nature of these calls

---

[3] I do not, obviously, expect actual structures or practices of global governance to fall neatly into one model or another. But I do see these models as useful in making visible the different political effects of historically distinctive configurations of power.

[4] See, for example, Wolf, 2001; Mallaby, 2002b; Cooper, 2002; and Kurtz (2003). Robert Cooper, a British diplomat and adviser to Prime Minister Tony Blair, has explicitly argued for a "new kind of imperialism." Martin Wolf, a columnist for the *Financial Times* (London), builds on some of Robert Cooper's work and Tony Blair's speeches to justify the need for a "new imperialism." Sebastian Mallaby authored a lead article in *Foreign Affairs* (2002b) titled "The Reluctant Imperialist," while Stanley Kurtz (2003) offered a "blueprint" for a "democratic imperialism." For an argument against imperialism, see Ikenberry 2002.

lies not in the stated intentions as much as in a deeper and more insidious neglect of the Other. From my perspective, critics such as Ikenberry are, wittingly or unwittingly, as complicit in a colonial discourse as many of those they criticize. I seek to establish this point by tracing the themes that unite some prominent advocates of a new imperialism. Sebastian Mallaby, an editorial writer for the *Washington Post*, offers a useful entry into some of these resurgent calls for a "new imperialism" (2002b).

Sebastian Mallaby's justification of a "neoimperialism" emerges from his stated concern about the capacity of "dysfunctional" and "failed" states to endanger "orderly" states (ibid.: 6, 3). Arguing that "a new imperial moment has arrived," Mallaby urges the United States to shed its reluctance and to "play the leading role" in instituting a new imperialist order (ibid.: 6). Presuming that any reluctance on its part to embark on a new imperialism can emerge only from instrumental concerns, Mallaby tries to demonstrate the desirability and feasibility of this new, US-led imperialist order.

What is the politics of difference that underlies Mallaby's proposal for global governance? It is clear, from Mallaby's argument, that, within his worldview, "orderly" and "disorderly" states are not equal participants in a global political community where different social actors have reciprocal obligations (ibid.: 3, 2). Turning a political condition (orderliness/disorderliness) into an essentialized state identity, Mallaby's perspective produces the "disorderly," the "failed," and the "poor" as the objects of governance of the "orderly," the successful, and the rich, even going so far as to talk about a new "rich man's burden" (ibid.: 2, 3). The presumption that the disorderliness, dysfunctionality, and poverty of some states are threats to orderly, successful, and rich societies is enough to justify imperialism as the best response to such perceived threats. If there is any reluctance that attaches to the proposed imperialist project, it stems primarily from an instrumental consideration of the costs and benefits from the process. It has little to do with any ethical or normative rejection of the notion of the rich governing the poor or the successful governing those who are seen to have failed. Moreover, even the calculus of costs and benefits that Mallaby relies on has the rich and the "orderly" as its primary subjects and pays little attention to the costs of an imperialist project for the poor and the disorderly.

What understanding of global governance undergirds these proposals? If political participation and dissent are important aspects of any democratic order, then, within Mallaby's perspective, those who are differentiated as poor, dysfunctional, or disorderly possess no such rights. States that lack wealth, order, or functionality are states that are denied democratic rights. Whatever the substantive conception of globality that animates Mallaby, it is not one that requires the democratic consent of those who are to be governed.

Interestingly, Mallaby takes care to distinguish his "neoimperialism" from what he criticizes as the "stale choice" between unilateralism and multilateralism that is constantly cropping up in US foreign policy discussions (ibid.: 6). This is an important distinction to the extent that scholars such as Ikenberry have used precisely the distinction between unilateralism and multilateralism to condemn the "imperial ambition" visible in the Bush administration's new National Security Strategy (2002). Criticizing the new "grand strategy," Ikenberry argues for a return to the older ("realist" and "liberal") grand strategies.

What is interesting about the differences between Mallaby's and Ikenberry's perspectives on global governance is that the latter can only see the compulsory power that drives the unilateralism of the Bush administration as imperial. What is invisible to Ikenberry, the critic of the United States' imperial ambition, is the imperial content of the older grand strategies, particularly in the multilateralism that he recommends as a non-imperial alternative. But Mallaby, the supporter of a "neoimperialism," does not miss the imperial content of the multilateral tradition in US foreign policy. It is for this reason that he argues that what would best promote the new imperialist project are some aspects of the older strategies themselves, particularly that "mix of US leadership and international legitimacy" already manifest in institutions such as the World Bank and the IMF, which "reflect American thinking and priorities yet are simultaneously multinational" (Mallaby, 2002b: 6–7).

It is easy, then, to read the claims of Mallaby as colonial and those of Ikenberry as anti-colonial because they so explicitly demand and reject respectively a "neoimperialism." But this is a fairly limited way, speaking conceptually, of reading those claims. The claims that both make – notwithstanding the support of one and the opposition of another – emerge from a colonial order of global governance not because they invoke or reject imperialism explicitly but primarily because of a deeper silencing of the Other implicit in their discourses.[5] It is obvious that Mallaby's perspective concerns itself very little with either

---

[5] Not surprisingly, I see the nuanced conceptions of power and politics deployed by the Gramscian analysts of American hegemony (Rupert, 2000) as more insightful than the mainstream's uncritical celebration of American "leadership."

the rights of or costs to the poor. But Ikenberry's argument against US imperial ambition is also an instrumental and not a normative one. It is based on the unsustainable nature of an imperial project rather than any ethical objection to imperialism as a specific form of global governance.

Others, more explicit in advocating normatively desirable principles for global governance, are equally culpable on these grounds. In a speech to the Labour Party, Tony Blair (2001), for instance, laid out some worthy political principles – democracy, freedom, and justice – that should, in his view, structure global governance. Depicting and drawing on an expanded conception of freedom (as "not only in the narrow sense of personal liberty but in the broader sense of each individual having the economic and social freedom to develop their potential to the full") and community (as "founded on the equal worth of all"), he declared that "The starving, the wretched, the dispossessed, the ignorant, those living in want and squalor from the deserts of Northern Africa to the slums of Gaza, to the mountain ranges of Afghanistan: they too are our cause. This is a moment to seize" (ibid.). Surely, unlike Mallaby or Ikenberry, this was a leader with a broader conception of freedom and community and one explicitly concerned with the global poor? I would argue, however, that Blair is not too different from them in his colonial orientation toward the global Other.

If we agree, along with Blair, that democracy, freedom, and justice are desirable political principles that should underlie global governance, shouldn't we be finding ways to ensure that "the starving, the wretched, the dispossessed, the ignorant, those living in want and squalor from the deserts of Northern Africa to the slums of Gaza, to the mountain ranges of Afghanistan" somehow have a voice in these deliberations about them? Wouldn't we expect that political participation, the co-constitution of global order by the rich and the starving, by the blessed and the wretched, by the fortunate and the dispossessed, by the ignorant and the educated, would be the first priority of those who sought to "reorder" the globe to facilitate "freedom" and "community"? But some of these constituencies do not have a say in such matters. They are only there as Blair's "cause," as somebody's "moment to seize." A reasonably democratic order – at the global or local level – would make place for a politics that promotes the participation of those who are the objects of a policy. But what we get with Mallaby, Ikenberry, and Blair is global governance without the voice, consent, or participation of those who are to be governed. It is this deeper political disregard for the Others that makes all three complicit in the production of a colonial order of governance.

That colonial order of governance has been prominent from the early days of the George W. Bush administration also. At first sight, the claims advanced by the officials of the Bush administration appear to leave some space for the political resolution of different imaginations of global order. Nicholas Lemann, the Washington correspondent for the *New Yorker*, writes about asking Richard Haass, the director of policy planning for the State Department, whether there was a "successor idea to containment" (2002: 46). Haass observes:

> It is the idea of integration. The goal of US foreign policy should be to persuade the other major powers to sign on to certain key ideas as to how the world should operate: opposition to terrorism and weapons of mass destruction, support for free trade, democracy, markets. Integration is about locking them into these policies and then building institutions that lock them in even more.
>
> (quoted ibid.)

Noteworthy here are a couple of things. First of all, the "key ideas" themselves about "how the world should operate" are more or less set. Politics, then, is not about contesting the US ideas about "how the world should operate" at any fundamental level. It is confined to the question of "persuading" others, primarily major powers, to "sign on." While politics as persuasion is limited to "major powers," even they are not immune from coercive policies. As Haass reminds us, integration is about "locking them" in to certain policies and ensuring that they cannot get out by "lock[ing] them in even more" through institutions. Even in a case involving governance among major powers, the scope of politics is thus narrowly limited to an agreement about already decided "ideas" about "how the world should operate." Once they agree, an "institutionalization" of these policies further restricts the agency of even these major powers. The intense anger generated in the Bush administration over French refusal to go along with the US invasion of Iraq stands as more recent evidence of this attempted institutionalization of US power. Other states that do not "sign on," that seek to escape their "institutionalization" in a US-dominated order have frequently been presented as "outlaw" or "rogue" states that are outside even this limited domain of politics.

Haass points out, for instance, that in the Bush administration's emerging "body of ideas," sovereignty "entails obligations" and also has limits. Governments that fail to meet these obligations of sovereignty – "not to massacre your own people," "not to support terrorism in any way" – lose the "right to be left alone inside [their] territory." "Other governments," Haass asserts, "gain the right to intervene" (quoted ibid.: 45–46). This reconceptualization of national sovereignty is interesting to the extent that sovereignty is not the fundamental right of states anymore but a responsibility defined in some fairly specific, and even potentially commendable, ways. The responsibilities prescribed for the states themselves are not the problem. What is problematic, though, is the presumption that they can come into being through the power of the Bush administration.

But what is the basis of this power? What understandings of the world produce it? On what intellectual and imaginative ground does the Bush administration decide "how the world should operate"? Lemann points out that Professors Bernard Lewis and Fouad Ajami are the "outside experts" on the Middle East – to take one region – who have the "most credibility" within the Bush administration. And what is the advice of these scholars to members of the Bush administration on the Middle East? According to Lemann's source, Lewis presumably counseled the senior foreign policy members that "in that part of the world, nothing matters more than resolute will and force" (ibid.: 47).

I infer from the formulations of Haass and the advice that the Bush administration seems to listen to that other states in the international system – whether France, Iran, Germany, North Korea, Canada, or Iraq – do not really possess the full stature of political subjecthood. They are better understood, following an insightful conceptualization by Scarry (1985: 281–307), in a slightly different context, as objects with varying degrees of responsibility to the "one indispensable nation," the one full subject of the international system, the United States. This colonially imagined order can then be read as possessing at least two features: first, the structuring of the world into the governors and the governed, the subjects of politics and the objects of politics; and, second, the ways in which productive power empowers the subjects of governance but not the objects. I will illustrate the issue of productive power first and then analyze how the putative objects of colonial governance respond to such an order.

The subjects and objects of colonial governance

In 1996, Leslie Stahl, of the CBS television program *60 Minutes*, asked the then US secretary of state Madeleine Albright the following question about economic sanctions against Iraq: "We have heard that over half a million children have died. I mean, that's more than died in Hiroshima. And, you know, is the price worth it?" Faced with that question, Albright responded by saying: "I think this is a very hard choice. But the price – we think the price is worth it." Much of the subsequent outcry over this episode focused on Albright's answer (see Ackerman, 2000). Her willingness to assert that the "price" of the deaths of "half a million children" was worth the continuation of the sanctions against Iraq justifiably attracted a lot of condemnation. I wish, however, to draw attention to a slightly different dimension of this exchange. What I find somewhat more significant than Albright's response is Leslie Stahl's question. I contend that it is in the asking of this question, the fact that such a question can even be posed to Albright, that the productive power of a colonial order is revealed. On my claim, the nature of Albright's answer is really irrelevant. The question is what produces her as capable of offering an acceptable answer; what produces her as acceptable to civilized society in the first place. In that sense, it would not really have made much of a difference if she had claimed that the "price" was *not* "worth it." Productive power, I contend, functions here primarily to make this issue of the deaths of "half a million children" "thinkable" as a legitimate and rational choice in the first place. That such a choice is not ruled out as morally unimaginable or as fundamentally detestable – so reprehensible that that question cannot even be asked – speaks to the power of a colonial order that constantly empowers some actors, such as the United States, as subjects of this colonial order. It is this specific "privilege" that will rarely, if ever, be accorded to a Saddam Hussein. He might be interviewed but he will never be asked, for instance, whether, in his opinion, killing thousands of Kurds was "worth it." That would be "unthinkable," if not morally reprehensible and "evil." But Madeleine Albright and US foreign policy are effortlessly recuperated into the realm of reason and reasonableness by the very posing of this question. One might disagree with their choices – even assert that these policymakers were mistaken – but the underlying assumption of their essential rationality, their fundamental reasonableness, or their basic sanity, is rarely called into question. Colonial governance thus imagines, inhabits, and seeks to realize an order in which some subjects are always already entitled to rationality while others are always already excluded from that privilege.

The imagination and inhabitation of a particular global, however, is not enough to result in its materialization. It is when such imaginations are reciprocated and inhabited by the objects of that imagination that a colonial order will be materialized. That is, it is not enough for some to define others as objects. It is also necessary for those who are objectified thus to reproduce, to live up to, their presumed "responsibilities" as objects of a colonial global order.

I wish to expand on the nature of such "object-responsibilities" by reverting to the insights of Scarry (1985). Offering a very perceptive analysis of the nature of human interaction with the material world of their making, Scarry (ibid.: 281–307) argues that human beings invest otherwise nonsentient objects with a sentience, a certain "object-responsibility." This object-responsibility becomes most visible when objects do not "behave" as we normally expect them to:

> Our behavior toward objects at the exceptional moment when they hurt us must be seen within the context of our normal relations with them. The ongoing, day-to-day norm is that an object is mimetic of sentient awareness: the chair routinely relieves the problem of weight. Should the object prove insufficiently mimetic of awareness, insufficiently capable of accommodating the problem of weight (i.e., if the chair is uncomfortable – an animistic phrase we use to mean if "the person is uncomfortable in the chair"), the object will be discarded or set aside.
>
> (ibid.: 295–96)

Scarry's account of how human beings make the world materially and, in the process of doing so, expect a certain responsibility from the objects of their making is useful in understanding the nature of productive power and governance in colonial global orders. As with humans making the world, political subjects in a colonial order arrogate to themselves the power to remake the world in ways that have little or nothing to do with democratic participation or the consent of others. One can imagine the governed within this system as possessing either no political rights or highly restricted rights of participation. Political objects, then, are expected routinely to be "mimetic of sentient awareness." Just as the chair "relieves the problem of weight" for the human being, political objects in a colonial order are expected to do something similar for the full subjects of that order. It is when such expectations are not met, when such objects "hurt" the subject rather than "accommodate" it that the subject is both suddenly and intensely aware of the object and enraged enough to think of kicking it and/or repairing it. Productive power, then, relates to the materialization of colonial global orders in terms of the systematic production of political objects that are conscious of and routinely deliver, i.e., without breaking down or hurting the political subjects, on their defined responsibilities. Locked into various forms of "institutionalized" and "structural" powers, such objects can be conceptualized as effectively knowing, in the manner of chairs, how to be "mimetic of sentient awareness" and of how to "relieve the problem of weight" for those dominating the global order. It is when such "object-awareness" is lacking that compulsory power might need to be deployed to repair or rebuild the object.

I would suggest that this reading of object-responsibilities allows us to understand much of the Bush administration's rage at "old Europe" and its assumption of "nation-building" tasks in many regions after 9/11. It is precisely in this context of the seeming lack of such a "sentient awareness" that dissent – from states as varied as France, Iran, Turkey, and North Korea – is read not as an assertion of their sovereignty or of their democratic difference on legitimately contested issues but as a sign of their irresponsibility (see Cornwell, 2003; Sciolino, 2003).

But, whatever the limited scope of their responsibility in the eyes of political subjects, political objects are different from material objects in being self-reflexive and in possessing a historically endowed sentient awareness. So looking at the ways in which subaltern actors fail to deliver on their expected responsibilities can allow us an entry into the meanings and practices productive of postcolonial global orders. The disjuncture between the imagination of a colonial order by political subjects and its effective (meaningful and practice-sustaining) reciprocation by political objects offers a rich site for the analysis of some prominent forms of postcolonial politics and resistance. Between the defining of responsibilities by political subjects and their acceptance or rejection by those designated as objects lies a fertile terrain of power, governance, and resistance. Subalterns might not just accept or reject the definition but also misread, misunderstand, appropriate, or rearticulate the carefully defined scope of their putative responsibilities. I offer below a reading on postcolonial lines of some such seemingly "irresponsible" actions on the part of various global subalterns.

Contesting colonial governance

Speaking at the commencement ceremony of the US Coast Guard on May 17, 2000, President Clinton observed that "[g]lobalization [was] tearing down barriers and building new networks among nations and people" (Clinton, 2000). But, he cautioned, there was also a downside to this process. These "new networks" also gave rise to new insecurities. He noted: "The same technology that gave us GPS [global positioning system] and the . . . Internet also apparently empowered a student sitting in the Philippines to launch a computer virus that . . . spread through more than 10 million computers and caused billions of dollars in damage" (ibid.). This combination of a new openness and new insecurities, Clinton warned, signaled a "fateful struggle" between the "forces of integration and harmony" and the "forces of disintegration and chaos" (ibid.).

Listening to President Clinton, one might believe that the Filipino students who unleashed this virus represented the "forces of disintegration and chaos"; that, like the protesters in Seattle and Washington, they were opposed to globalization and this was their way of showing their destructive potential. Or maybe it was just an accident that most Filipinos regretted. But, contrary to such expectations, "half a world away," in the Philippines, what was strongly evident was neither resentment at globalization nor contrition at the damage done by the spread of the computer virus "ILOVEYOU." What was evident was joy and nationalist pride at the global power of the "ILOVEYOU" virus. Some Filipino newspaper columnists diagnosed the virus as a symptom of the technical prowess and ingenuity of Filipino students. Others saw the creator of the program as a "national hero." By unleashing the virus, he had managed, as one prominent columnist noted, to "put the Philippines on the world map" and "proven that the Filipino has the creativity and ingenuity to turn, for better or for worse, the world upside down" (Borjal, 2000).

In emphasizing the Filipino's "creativity and ingenuity to turn . . . the world upside down" "for better or for worse," the columnist draws our attention to the significance of power as technical virtuosity, i.e., power divorced from any obvious normative considerations. It was important, within this perspective, to see and demonstrate, first of all, the technical capacity to exert power itself. What this power was for was not as crucial an issue as the technical demonstration itself. In other words, this is power whose primary aim is the demonstration of its own existence, the control and possession of a certain technique/technology by an actor and therefore the existence and significance of the actor itself. Such a practice acquires meaning in a world in which actors see their political subjectivity as constituted primarily by the possession of vast amounts of technical power. This is the world of superpowers and great powers, a world in which a subaltern can escape object-status only by demonstrating a similar capacity.

It is this imagination that underlies the reactions of various Filipino students who asserted that, while unleashing the virus was "wrong," it was also an "amazing" feat. As another student observed: "Can you imagine, they were able to penetrate the Pentagon? Even though the Philippines is a third-world country, even though we're behind in technology, they were able to do that" (Mydans, 2000). The "even though" of the student testifies to the gap his view of the world takes for granted between the Pentagon and a Third World country, a gap that is "amazingly," if momentarily and spectacularly, bridged by a virus not inappropriately called ILOVEYOU.

Disjunctures between elite and subaltern imaginations are the norm in colonially governed global orders. To take another example, the nuclear tests conducted by India and Pakistan demonstrated a similar disjuncture of imaginations. While many in the First World saw them as heralding a more dangerous world and as increasing global insecurity, many others in the Third World, particularly in India and Pakistan, saw them as desirable demonstrations of technical competence and political agency.

Disjunctures such as these reveal the differential imagining of political agency by subaltern actors in colonial global orders. Subaltern actors, in such orders, often read political agency in terms of actions that disturb and upset the routine object-expectations of the dominant. What is an "irresponsible" action in the eyes of dominant powers is also the very action that brings the subaltern to their visible presence. The Filipinos are joyous about their technologically demonstrated capacity to be "seen" and "heard" in a global colonial order in which they are, otherwise, invisible and mute. Such disruptions of the dominant order, however, are quite often marked by an ambivalence given the implicit desire to be acknowledged in and through a perspective shaded by the vision of the colonizer. These disruptions seek to assert agency by redefining the always already defined responsibilities of the subaltern in a colonial global order. Such redefinitions, undertaken at the level of the dominant meanings, run the risk of not reimagining the overall colonial order, but only repositioning oneself in that colonial order. They are thus, in many ways, quite susceptible to various forms of cooption by the dominant. Indian security policy offers a very good illustration of this tense and risky ambivalence toward the colonizer.

Postcolonial ambivalence

India's 1998 decision to test nuclear weapons is a particularly apt manifestation of a postcolonial state's deep ambivalence toward a colonial order of governance. That decision, taken nearly twenty-five years after India's first test, disrupted the efforts of the existing nuclear weapons states to institutionalize a global nuclear order structured around the NPT (Nuclear Non-Proliferation Treaty) and the CTBT (Comprehensive Test Ban Treaty). The obstruction of the global nuclear order is particularly striking, since India was one of the first countries to propose a CTBT. But what is the source of this policy ambivalence?

The Indian state subscribed to the institutionalization of a global order in which there was a universally shared commitment against conducting nuclear explosions. This, however, was not a discrete commitment but one that was intrinsically related to other powerful understandings of the role of nuclear weapons in the promotion of global insecurity. These other understandings saw the likely use of nuclear weapons as a serious threat to humanity as well as to the peace and stability of the world. What this meant was that global security required the total elimination of nuclear weapons.

The CTBT's ban on nuclear testing was a value that held significance for Indian policymakers because of its power to advance this broader goal of the elimination of nuclear weapons. Without that linkage, India's policymakers argued, a treaty such as the CTBT would only legitimize, as the NPT had done before, an unequal world in which a few states had the right to maintain and refine their nuclear arsenals while others were placed under a mode of governance that ruled out similar rights for them. Such an unequal world was tolerable, in official Indian eyes, only if the nuclear weapons states committed themselves to a time-bound program that eliminated their nuclear arsenals and brought them on a par with the non-nuclear ones. This was what would constitute a really secure world: one in which no one had nuclear weapons or exclusive rights to them. That was the global order, India claimed, that must arise out of the complex set of treaties that were centered on the CTBT, the NPT, the Fissile Material Cut-off Treaty (FMCT), the Chemical Weapons Convention (CWC), and the Biological Weapons Convention (BWC).

The postcolonial understanding of global order was thus one in which all states gave up their right to nuclear weapons so that the world would be a more secure place – at least in terms of weapons of mass destruction. In that sense, India was explicitly committed to a global norm against testing, though this restraint was seen, primarily, as a way of attaining the eventual goal of eliminating nuclear weapons. The CTBT's significance for India lay, then, not merely in its prevention of proliferation but in its ability to promote universal nuclear disarmament. Global security was tied to universal nuclear disarmament and not just to the regime of non-proliferation.

One sign of this alternative imagination of global security lay in the fact that, as I mentioned earlier, India was one of the first countries to suggest the idea of a CTBT, in 1954. India had also continued to campaign consistently for the total elimination of nuclear weapons and signed on to the CWC that, unlike the NPT and the CTBT, was seen as a nondiscriminatory regime. India's international relations were structured, then, into promoting a CTBT that would advance the elimination of nuclear weapons, cap both "vertical" and "horizontal" proliferation, and show a clear path to the eventual elimination of nuclear weapons. But the CTBT that was finally negotiated, in the Indian official view, fell far short of such goals because it only banned further testing. As the Indian minister for external affairs pointed out to the fiftieth session of the UN General Assembly:

> It cannot be argued that the security of a few countries depends on their having nuclear weapons, and that of the rest depends on their not . . . we note that Nuclear Weapon States have agreed to a CTBT only after acquiring the know-how to develop and refine their arsenals without the need for tests . . . The CTBT must contain a binding commitment on the international community, especially the Nuclear Weapon States, to take further measures within an agreed time frame toward the creation of a nuclear weapon free world.
>
> (quoted in Ghose, 1997: 249)

In the absence of any explicit linkages to other commitments about the elimination of nuclear weapons, the CTBT – the very treaty that India had championed consistently – took on a different meaning and significance for Indian policymakers. As the Indian representative to the Conference on Disarmament pointed out, "The CTBT that we see emerging . . . [is] not the CTBT India envisaged in 1954. This cannot be the CTBT that India can be expected to accept" (ibid.: 255).

Far from being a benign commitment, the expectation against nuclear testing became a threatening sign of the growing power of the permanent five members of the UN Security Council to institutional-ize, against the wishes of many, a colonial nuclear order structured around their specific version of global security. The CTBT, in Indian eyes, appeared now as a system of "nuclear apartheid," a regime that was seen as discriminatory in terms of its distribution of "rights" and "duties" between the "nuclear have-lots" and the "nuclear have-nots." The emerging global order thus presented a set of stark choices for Indian policymakers. As Jaswant Singh, India's minister of external affairs at the time, expressed it:

> India's nuclear policy remains firmly committed to a basic tenet: that the country's national security in a world of nuclear proliferation lies *either* in *global disarmament* or in exercise of the *principle of equal and legitimate security for all.*
>
> (1998: 41–42; emphasis added)

As a "threshold" nuclear state that had demonstrated a nuclear capa-bility but had not "weaponized" or asserted an overt nuclear identity, India was ambiguously positioned in the global nuclear order. But as the CTBT was being institutionalized, the legal and diplomatic space for the maintenance of such ambiguous identities became considerably less. This was because the CTBT created two distinct sets of actors with different rights and responsibilities. One set of global actors – the nuclear "have-lots" – did not have to commit themselves to any eventual phas-ing out of nuclear weapons while another set – the nuclear "have-nots" – took on the added obligations of forswearing any further testing.

But what did it signify, in the Indian national imagination, to be a member of one group or the other? Indian policymakers saw themselves becoming an object in the emerging global nuclear order if they did not assert their nuclear subjecthood. If there is anything that a postcolonial imaginary resents and resists strongly, it is the seeming relapse into the position of a colonized object. India's 1998 tests are best read therefore as explicitly *political* acts that testified, as a commentator in *Le Monde* put it, to the "dry assertion of the existence of other visions of the world" (Gire, 1998). The tests were, in many ways, a refusal to quietly accept the position of an object in an emerging global colonial order. But they also signaled an increasing willingness on the part of Indian policymakers to accept full membership in a global order that they themselves had condemned as colonial.

Some later developments in Indo-US relations are crucial in this regard. Though the United States initially responded to the Indian tests by imposing a variety of sanctions, these were followed soon thereafter by extensive talks. One effect of these talks was to promote closer relations between the two states on a range of issues from economic interactions to joint military exercises. There are many ways to understand this sudden warm-up, after years of estrangement, in bilateral relations. One could argue that it was precisely India's demonstrated capacity to disrupt a global order that was being institutionalized without its participation that drove US policymakers quickly to devote greater attention to bilateral relations. More than seven rounds of intense talks between these two states seemed to have been driven by, among other things, a desire to generate some predictability in the nature of Indo-US interactions. Thus, from the perspective of the United States, what was crucial was not so much the demonstrated technical capacity of India to deploy compulsory power, as the need to routinize India's expected responsibilities on the global stage. In other words, the talks were a way to cautiously institutionalize India into the dominant order of global governance precisely because it had demonstrated its capacity to disrupt it.

The dominant manner of that institutionalization involved an attempt to generate and consolidate mutually shared expectations of what each other's roles and responsibilities were. Such actions were matched, on the Indian side, by very demonstrative and demonstrated attempts, in a subsequent crisis with Pakistan, to present itself as a "responsible" nuclear power. What was not fully clear was how radically India's sense of this responsibility differed from or exceeded those imagined and projected for it by the United States. In other words, it was not very clear whether India was planning merely to "sign on" to the key ideas that the United States wanted to lock much of the world into or whether it was going to have a say in what those key ideas were going to be. What was not visible in Indo-US efforts, however, was any effort to reimagine and bring to material existence any noncolonial global nuclear order.

Resistance

Is a politics of difference regarding the global doomed, then, by the historical power of a colonial global order and the poverty of our colonized/colonizing national imaginations? Not necessarily. Those concerned with postcolonial transformations can think about co-constituting the global in ways that are empowered by the national imaginations they inherit but also go beyond its borders in significant ways. Let me illustrate this point with a critique of the dominant and colonial conception of the global on the issue of nuclear security.

Arundhati Roy, the Booker Prize-winning author of *The God of Small Things*, was an important critic of the Indian government's decision to conduct nuclear tests in 1998. Going against the majority of Indian middle-class opinion, she wrote a scathing essay – titled "The End of Imagination" – criticizing the justifications offered by the Indian government. Characterizing the decision as "the final act of betrayal by a ruling class that has failed its people," Roy claimed that the nuclear tests (and the consequent nationalist euphoria) had destroyed an important aspect of India's freedom: its capacity to articulate a different, noncolonial, vision of the global order (1998: 9). She argued that the Indian government's decision should be read not as the defiance of a colonial West but as its own capitulation to the "ultimate coloniser." Nuclear weapons, she asserted passionately, "bury themselves like meat hooks deep in the base of our brains. They are purveyors of madness. They are the ultimate coloniser. Whiter than any white man that ever lived. The very heart of whiteness" (ibid.: 6).

Dismissing the official claims that the tests were a response to "Western Hypocrisy," Roy pointed out that the historical record of "the West" testified more to an arrogance about its compulsory power than to its hypocrisy:

> Exposing Western Hypocrisy – how much more exposed can they be? . . . Colonialism, apartheid, slavery, ethnic cleansing, germ warfare, chemical weapons – they virtually invented it all. They have plundered nations, snuffed out civilizations, exterminated entire populations. They stand on the world's stage stark naked but entirely unembarrassed, because they know that they have more money, more food and bigger bombs than anybody else. They know they can wipe us out in the course of an ordinary working day. Personally, I'd say it is more arrogance than hypocrisy.
>
> (ibid.: 10)

But it was an India that had wanted to be different that had now shown itself to be the real hypocrite. It had "traded" a "moral position" for membership in a colonial order (ibid.).

I offer this brief summary of Roy's critique of India's decision as a good example of an alternative imagination of the global that draws upon but also transcends the limits of the historically given national. There are two things that are particularly striking about this critique. First of all, it was a relatively courageous intellectual stance in terms of the national opposition and ridicule it was bound to – and did – receive within India. Roy had achieved a significant amount of publicity and goodwill just the year before for her literary achievements. Her anti-nuclear position not only risked all that but also invited charges of political naïveté on the part of a literary figure. Second, and most importantly, the criticism is distinctive because it produces an alternative imagination of the global from within a national base. But it does so without allowing the national to colonize our understanding of the possible globals. In other words, Roy's understanding of the global emerges from the national but without becoming subservient to it. The national community does not become the ethical boundary of the imagination or of political practice. Politics does not stop at the water's edge.

Roy begins by criticizing the decision on nationalist grounds. The Indian state has failed to deliver on its claims to the Indian nation and the world. But the claims that it has failed to deliver on are not those that have to do with national security, national power, or some form of national interest. What the Indian state had failed to do was to live up to its moral responsibility to itself and to humanity. Moral responsibility, in this critique, was not something that was to be left to other nations to deliver. It was not something contingent on the capacity of other nations or other people to live up to their responsibilities. It was not a social contract that one state had with others. It was a demand that the national self made on itself. It was a commitment to the nation's own idea of what it was or wanted to be. It is on this level that Roy critiques the Indian state. And when the national self fails to live up to this responsibility Roy threatens secession as one possible, justifiable response:

> If protesting against having a nuclear bomb implanted in my brain is anti-Hindu and anti-national, then I secede. I hereby declare myself an independent, mobile republic. I am a citizen of the earth. I own no territory. I have no flag. I'm female, but have nothing against eunuchs.[6] My policies are simple. I'm willing to sign any nuclear non-proliferation treaty or nuclear test ban treaty that's going. Immigrants are welcome. You can help me design our flag.
>
> (ibid.: 9)

---

[6] This is a reference to the Shiv Sena's (a far-right Indian political party) claim – described early on in the essay – that the nuclear tests proved that "we [Indians] are not eunuchs anymore."

Roy's threat to secede is important not as a practically possible act. It is important, I would argue, as an imaginative claim that forces us to think beyond the moral community of the nation to other valuable forms of political association – possibly to an alternative understanding of the global. Roy thus draws upon the existence of a powerful imagination of the national community to demand more responsible political practices from her state – practices that address the concerns not just of her own national community but also those of other human beings in the world. The national state is thus held responsible not only to those that it sees as its own people, but also to those that it might implicitly produce as Others. The possibility that the states representing these Others might be bankrupt in their moral responsibilities to their own people or to Others is not enough, in Roy's critique, to disown one's own moral responsibility to all of humanity.

But while Roy draws on the existence of a historically powerful imagination of the national self, she does not let it incarcerate her either. Her argument does not privilege her national community as the ultimate boundary of her politics. Such an argument would easily substitute a moral arrogance about one's nation for the military arrogance of others. It would privilege one nation, one configuration of the political self, as the ultimate repository of both good and evil and end up as a colonial moment. But Roy avoids that relapse by her willingness to question the historically received notion of an "authentic India" (ibid.: 15). By problematizing the notion of any fixed or "authentic India," Roy brings home to us the potential limits of any essentialized national communities as empowerers of critical political action. She opens up the imagination to the possibility that the limits of our national boundaries need not be the limits of our political practices or our humanity. Other forms of political association are possible, desirable, and worth striving for. Secession is okay, maybe even desirable if it empowers us to act morally. Treason to one's inherited political community is not the ultimate crime. Failure to deliver on one's moral responsibility to other human beings is. There are therefore other possibilities, "other worlds," "other kinds of dreams," where "failure" is "feasible" and "honourable." And the world, as Roy points out, has "plenty of warriors . . . who go to war each day, knowing in advance that they will fail" (ibid.: 7).

In Roy's critique, as well as those of many other social actors across the world, we can see both the empowering and the limiting aspects of historically inherited national imaginations as they seek to rearticulate the dominant constitutions of the colonial global. Creative political agency lies, then, not in reproducing the national within the colonizer's script of political agency, but in working in and through our historically given interpretations of the national to produce postcolonial orders that are deeply democratic and diverse in their constitution. Other worlds are possible.

As the anti-globalization and anti-war movements in recent years show, the building of these other worlds takes place at many sites and in multiple ways.[7] What is interesting about such efforts is not just how or where they take place but what borders of the historically inherited and geographically and imaginatively incarcerated selves they call into question. Proponents or critics of global governance that do not offer a space for dissensus and difference, that do not encourage a self-reflexivity that engages and seeks to learn from various Others, can be seen as deeply complicit in the production of colonial orders of global governance.

[7] In the context of 9/11, see, for instance, the aims of the advocacy organization "September Eleventh Families for Peaceful Tomorrows," www.peacefultomorrows.org/mission.html. Of relevance also are the imaginings of an alternative global motivating the millions of people all over the world who opposed (and continue to oppose) the US invasion and occupation of Iraq.

13 Knowledge in power: the epistemic construction of global governance

Emanuel Adler and Steven Bernstein

This chapter aims to anchor a normative theory of global governance in a reworked conception of epistemes that accounts for the role of productive power and institutional power in setting the conditions of possibility for good (moral) global governance. We outline our argument in three parts. First, we reintroduce a modified conception of episteme into the international relations (IR) literature to argue that power is a disposition (in the sense of ordering or controlling) that depends on knowledge. Power is also productive in the sense of defining the order of global things, to paraphrase Michel Foucault. In addition, we try to show that power's productive capacity is often followed by the development of formal and informal institutions that play a role in fixing meanings, which are necessary for global governance. Second, we put forward a normative theory of the requirements of global governance that builds on these notions. We argue that global governance rests on material capabilities and knowledge, without which there is no governance, and legitimacy and fairness, without which there is no moral governance. Third, we bring these insights to bear on a brief discussion of the effects of epistemes on emerging pockets of global governance and the possibilities and limits of moving global governance in a more sustainable and just direction. We use international trade and the related legal system to illustrate the above relationship. We also call attention to the fact that, even when thinking about the United States and its use of unprecedented material capabilities vis-à-vis the rest of the world, power, and its effect on global governance, takes a productive form through knowledge and, in particular, epistemes.

"The order of (global) things"

Our argument begins with an attempt to bring the epistemic essence of social relations and political governance back to IR. Doing so leads us to depart somewhat from earlier uses in IR of the "episteme" concept by returning, in part, to Foucault's original formulation of the power/knowledge nexus. To date, IR scholarship has viewed an episteme as either a specific social epistemology of space and authority (Ruggie, 1975; 1993), or the attribute of science-based agents or "epistemic communities" who seek to socially construct policy in their image of truth and principled beliefs (Adler and Haas, 1992). Our reformulation brings back the epistemic dimension to IR as the deepest layer of social knowledge, which, productive of what social reality is, helps constitute the order of global things (Foucault, 1970). If, as Ian Hacking (1999) said, the world does not come classified, rather, people classify it, the epistemic question we reintroduce to the discipline is as follows: what makes people classify their reality the way they do, and how is this related to global governance? Thus, to the related question "what is global governance rooted in?," we answer power, institutions, or both, but only within the social order or social reality that epistemes produce. This means that not only is background knowledge productive of institutions, but also that the essence of global governance is mainly epistemic (Portnoy, 1999: 2). Thus, research on global governance must begin with the background knowledge that people share and selectively attach to material reality.

It is important to clarify at the outset how we use the concept of knowledge in this study. Whereas "knowledge" is the cumulative set of normative, ideological, technical, and scientific understandings that individuals carry in their heads, and that may be stored in books, libraries, and technical plans and technologies, epistemes are the background intersubjective knowledge – collective understandings and discourse – that adopt the form of human dispositions and practices that human beings use to make sense of the world. Narrowly defined, knowledge can become an attribute or a thing that individuals or groups use to achieve some goal or objective over the objections of others. Knowledge can also become a capacity that turns people into experts and courses of action into truthful, appropriate, efficient, or rational policies. Thus understood, one could read the power/knowledge relationship as consistent with compulsory power. We associate the concept of episteme, however, with a second, more encompassing and structural concept: "background knowledge." Like Foucault (1970) and John Ruggie (1975; 1993), we are interested in the background understandings – shaped by general culture, science, and normative understandings – that people use to make sense of the world. Our concept of episteme, however, is more general than Ruggie's (1993) and, we would argue, even more amenable to empirical research than Foucault's. Rather, we take episteme as meaning something akin to what John Searle (1995), following Wittgenstein (1953), has called "the Background," and Pierre Bourdieu has referred to as "habitus" (1977) – intersubjective knowledge that adopts the form of human dispositions and practices.

Episteme thus refers to the "bubble" within which people happen to live, the way people construe their reality, their basic understanding of the causes of things, their normative beliefs, and their identity, the understanding of self in terms of others. Epistemes do not create uniformity of a group or community, but organize their differences around pervasive understandings of reality. Because people live within a plurality of bubbles, each of which is not sealed tight, epistemes may be construed as open fields, which are marked by a plurality of tendencies.[1] More formally, then, an episteme may be considered as one among several possible general ways of interpreting and classifying nature and society, as well as their dynamic, which people can actively and sometimes creatively help transform. By episteme, however, we do not mean mere social imagining; rather, epistemes are social dispositions (ordering collective understandings and discourse), which make the world meaningful. Even though epistemes play a dispositional role in structuring action, nevertheless agents draw upon these dispositions in order to act purposefully. By attaching meanings to material reality, they thus construct social facts (Searle, 1995). As our language of agency should suggest, however, no matter how pervasive and productive an episteme at any historical juncture, the subject never entirely disappears in our conception. As Barnett and Duvall (chap. 1, in this volume) suggest, agents may resist attempts at controlling their behavior and may also have some leeway to change direct or indirect constitutive effects of social relations and discourse. Thus, even when resistance may appear futile or learning slow, the possibility of agency within, or in opposition to, global governance is always present, even if delimited by a prevailing episteme.

[1] We thank Frank Griffiths for this insight.

The following metaphor may help illustrate the "bubble" concept. In the movie *The Truman Show*, a fictional character played by Jim Carrey has lived all of his life within a human-made bubble, without knowing that it was an artificially made world, and that, beyond the bubble, there was the "real world." Within the bubble, Truman went home and to work, interacted with family and friends, played ball, and looked at "the stars" in the sky. One day the bubble burst and Truman finally understood what the viewers knew all along, that what he thought to have been the order of things, indeed, all of his universe – what was, is, and will be – was really only one among many possible "orders of things." Like Truman, individuals and groups act, interact, reason, plan, judge, symbolically represent reality, and have expectations of the future within pervasive interpretative "bubbles." An episteme, thus, "provides the fundamental categories in which thinking [and acting take] place. It establishes the limits of discussion and defines the range of problems that can be addressed" (Wuthnow, 1989: 13). The bubble also determines who is friend and who is foe, but, most importantly, what legitimate power or authority is and means, the validity of knowledge in general, and what validity means, how hierarchical or democratic a system of governance should be, and what we collectively take rationality to be. Unlike Truman, however, people are subject in the real world to a variety of sometimes contradictory dispositions and propensities, which means that people inhabit a plurality of bubbles that are less impermeable than the Truman metaphor might suggest. Moreover, in contrast to Truman, people seldom discover by accident that there may be other ways to classify and order reality, but, rather, actively seek new ways of understanding the world; thus their capacity to adapt and their willingness to learn and to change. The bubble metaphor is useful, however, because it drives home the point that people reason and act within the boundaries of established, albeit dynamic, background knowledge.

Truman's bubble did not just happen to be there, however; in the spirit of compulsion, someone put it there with the aim of controlling events. By this we mean that the relationship between epistemes and power is not merely one of production or constitution of subjectivity by the former. Epistemes themselves, however, are constituted by, and are the products of, social relations and agents, some of which are endowed, by the episteme, with the authority to determine valid knowledge, including knowledge of what good practices and rational behavior mean in particular cultural and historical contexts. Needless to say, this type of authority can sometimes be traced to specific agents, material capabilities, and particular institutions, which is close to the notions of both compulsory power and institutional power. In other words, power can be understood as either an attribute that agents possess and may use as a resource to shape the actions of others, and to affect what agents take to be valid knowledge, or the socially diffuse control of agents by means of previously created rules and institutions. A dual picture of power results, but this duality can be separated only analytically and historically. Accordingly, power means the authority to validate the knowledge on which an episteme is based (and is therefore akin to both institutional power and compulsory power) and the authority, of which epistemes are productive, to construct subjectivity and social facts (and is therefore akin to productive power). In this chapter, however, we are less interested in how epistemes were and are created, and more in their power to construct social reality and enable and delimit agency within them. Institutional power, in turn, enters in this chapter as the expression of epistemes as social mechanisms that help produce subjectivity, as well as agential capacity, at a distance.

It might be objected that epistemes are merely epiphenomenal of hard material capabilities (most commonly associated with compulsory power). We think not for the following two reasons. First, this objection ignores how US power, for example, stems from its being the dominant site of knowledge generation and diffusion with which self and others understand reality. Joseph Nye's instrumentalist concept of "soft" power does not entirely capture this argument, because in Nye's formulation hard and soft power cannot easily be decoupled.[2]

American compulsory and institutional power are neither simply instrumental, nor simply the consequence of a "unique" advantage in market power, ethnic diversity, or free flow of ideas (Canada is equally if

---

[2] Take, for example, the discussion about the dominant position of the United States in benefiting from globalization, in which Keohane and Nye (2000b) dispute the claim of some that globalization can largely be reduced to Americanization. They argue that the American multiethnic culture, large marketplace, and free flow of ideas make it "uniquely adapted as a center of globalization." Thus, "[G]lobalism today is America-centric, in that most of the impetus for the information revolution comes from the United States," which produces a large part of the content of information networks (ibid.: 235). We agree with Keohane and Nye that control of information networks is disproportionately located in American society, which enhances American influence. However, while Keohane and Nye insist that other countries also possess soft power and that it does not accrue to the United States in all areas, one may wonder whether soft power and hard power can be so easily disentangled if in practice soft power accrues to states that are materially powerful.

not more multiethnic, and many countries can claim an equally free flow of ideas). Rather, it derives from a combination of the use of material resources (compulsory power), the control of knowledge for the setting of political agendas (institutional power), and background knowledge (productive power). American power begins with social science discourse and knowledge generated in an American epistemic context, and continues with its application in practice, mainly through economics and business administration and their embeddedness in international organizations, and tacit acceptance by many nongovernmental organizations (NGOs) and other nonstate actors.[3] Thus, US power depends on the diffusion of a global governance episteme, which, to be effective, must take the appearance of being scientific, technical, and universal.

Second, the argument that epistemes are epiphenomenal ignores the requirements of governance, where knowledge is embedded in the power and authority of governing institutions. The 2002 Presidential National Security Directive, for example, adopts a policy of preemption against terrorist networks and rogue states, whether or not legitimated through the United Nations. This directive is not only an expression of overwhelming US military superiority – it begins "the United States possesses unprecedented – and unequaled – strength and influence in the world" (White House, 2002: 1) – but also of its goals, values, ideas and material capabilities (knowledge and power), and normative claims (legitimacy and fairness). For example, it states that victory over terrorism relies on, among other things, the delegitimization of, and creation of a normative taboo against, terrorism, so that it "will be viewed in the same light as slavery, piracy, or genocide; behavior that no government can condone or support and all must oppose" (ibid.: 6). Thus, the directive does not follow simply from present US material capabilities or the "knowledge" of favored "experts" who advise the US government, but also from the prevailing episteme from which the ideas it contains are drawn. Indeed, to the degree that the assertion of US material capability steps outside the bounds of governance enabled by this episteme, its power is arguably diminished.

---

[3] Dezalay and Garth (2002) nicely illustrate this point empirically in their investigation of the role of economics and law, and of economists and lawyers, in the diffusion of dominant epistemic understandings about the management of domestic economies in a world increasingly characterized by globalization and universal human rights. American power is at its zenith, however, when people around the world think and act on the basis of taken-for-granted American understandings of reality.

The epistemic requirements of global governance

In order to study the effect of an episteme on the evolution of global governance, we theorize that global governance rests, on the one hand, on material capability and knowledge and, on the other hand, on legitimacy and fairness (table 13.1). An episteme, at any point in time and place, is the sum of collective understandings and discourse about *material capabilities, knowledge* (normative, ideological, technical, and scientific), *legitimacy* (the acceptance of the right to rule by relevant communities), and *fairness* (which in our account may include notions of accountability, representation, and responsibility). The argument that representation (in other words who gets to participate and how) and responsibility (the obligations to broader society of participants in any governance system)[4] are implicit in a notion of fairness is fairly uncontroversial. We take, however, accountability as part of our understanding of fairness because, from a procedural perspective, without accountability actors may not be able to arrive at, or to know they have arrived at, collective fair practices. We place the above values together in an attempt to capture a bundle of concepts associated with the principled demands communities make on those empowered to take and implement decisions on their behalf. This set of notions, without prejudice to the specific content of procedures and mechanisms in any particular form of governance, reflects commonly asserted requirements of moral governance: that is, that people or communities be represented and treated fairly including a fair distribution of burdens and benefits, and that those who make decisions can be held to account. When we plot these four constitutive elements of order in a 2×2 table, the results are the requirements of global governance; that is, what material capabilities or science alone cannot explain, and what, by themselves, legitimacy and fairness do not produce. Conversely, the absence of these four elements leaves no "order of things" in the sense that Foucault understood social order.

By this we mean *authority, epistemic validity, a conception of good practices, and the institution of rationality.*[5] These are the basic building blocks of governance, the content and meanings of which are constituted by

---

[4] Take the example of medical experts who are called to participate in a government decision about whether to inoculate a population against smallpox to protect against a threat of biological weapons. If their decision is to be fair, it must be based not only on technical knowledge, but also on responsibility for the way knowledge will be used in practice. In other words, a fair decision whether to inoculate in the event of a crisis will have less to do with efficiency or cost-effectiveness than responsibility.

[5] Table 13.1 does not purport to explain outcomes of global governance, let alone predict them. Rather, we use the table as a descriptive taxonomy, in order to suggest the

Table 13.1 *The requirements of global governance*

	Material capability	**Knowledge**
Legitimacy	Authority	Epistemic validity
Fairness	Good practices	Practical reason

culturally and historically contingent, and evolving, epistemes. One should think of epistemes as superimposed on the four cells of table 13.1.

We will use these concepts to better understand how and why we have the institutions we do, what global governance means, and how and why patches or islands of global governance are increasingly based on new kinds of ordering of global things.

By way of example, take the case of epistemic communities. The literature on epistemic communities (Haas, 1992b; Adler and Haas, 1992) has mainly focused on how epistemic communities use scientific knowledge to help frame issues in ways that promote international cooperation. Epistemic communities, however, work within a normative order that grants science the special status it has in the modern world. Seen this way, normative ideas of science – as carried by epistemic communities – are more than just a resource that encourages states to act in ways that are consistent with the specific knowledge in question, for example, mitigating pollution to counter or avoid damage to ecosystems. And the transnational impact of these norms may go beyond helping bring about "policy coordination" between states (Haas, 1992b). Rather, their most far-reaching effect may be the reproduction or transformation of identities and interests, on the basis of which new types of islands of global governance are conceived.

The long-term importance of epistemic communities, thus, lies less in their effect on individuals' beliefs or behavior than in helping reproduce or transform a science-based episteme, upon which present and future generations of political practitioners can draw to know their bearings. Further, as an unintended consequence of the actions of epistemic communities, scientific knowledge becomes socially validated as truth, the power that is used on behalf of this truth acquires social legitimacy, instrumental rationality becomes deeply institutionalized, and efficient practices rather than good practices become the natural order of things.

components of our theory, how they relate to one another, and how from the juxtaposition of these components we arrive at the four normative elements of global governance.

Moreover, the particular manifestation of knowledge in specific issue areas or pockets of governance in turn can select which actors are granted epistemic validity.

Below, we briefly unpack the cells of our table to suggest how that interaction might occur in institutions or pockets of global governance.

Authority

The contemporary debate about the prospects of global governance stems from attempts to understand or explain experienced changes in who makes collective decisions that command authority over political communities and on what authority those decisions are made. In the classic Weberian conception of political authority, coercive *power* or material capability[6] is tightly coupled with *legitimacy*. It is this combination of monopoly of force and legitimacy that provides the reasons why people or a community obey that form of rule and particular rules. Westphalian norms, which root political authority in exclusive territorial spaces, and the gradual consolidation of the means of violence in the hands of state rulers, meant that both coercive force and legitimacy have largely resided in the territorial state in modern times. Since coercive power still largely resides in the state, and only may be moving beyond it slowly, global, regional, or transnational governance, if they are anything new, rest on new bases of authority. Whereas these bases of authority may be backed up by the coercive powers of leading states, the decoupling of coercive force and legitimate rule is the most striking feature of contemporary global governance. The current debate highlights more than ever that authority must rest on legitimacy: "a generalized perception or assumption [among relevant communities] that the actions of an entity are desirable, proper, or appropriate within some socially constructed system of norms, values, beliefs, and definitions" (Suchman, 1995: 574). If legitimacy at its most basic level depends on acceptance of rule or rules by a community with shared values, norms, and beliefs, epistemes constitute the subjectivity about power, legitimacy, and community that is required for political authority.[7]

---

[6] As Barnett and Duvall note in chapter 1 of this book, coercive or material power does not map directly into their taxonomy since they refer to a form of power, not what power is.

[7] For an argument that power, legitimacy, and community are the three essential elements of authority in global governance, see Bernstein, 2002.

302

Epistemic validity

Epistemic validity refers to "legitimate" knowledge, i.e., knowledge that is regarded as valid by a collectivity of subjects. It can mean widely accepted norms, consensual scientific knowledge, ideological beliefs deeply accepted by the collective, and so on. We anchor epistemic validity in a pragmatist philosophical perspective according to which validity rests on deliberation, judgement, and experience of communities that engage in rational persuasion. This is why a useful way to think about epistemic validity is Habermas's (1984) argument that valid knowledge claims are based on comprehensibility, truth, truthfulness, and rightness, which are arrived at pragmatically by communities of the likeminded. Habermas, however, refers to such validity claims as being part of an "ideal-speech situation," to which democratic societies must aspire, if discussion, debate, and social communication in the public sphere are to lead to social progress. If, however, due to culture, history, and social context, people interpret and "classify" reality differently, how can they then trust their knowledge to be true? How can epistemic consensus be achieved across cultures, societies, and polities? These are important questions because, often, political actors consciously use the power of language not only to lie (a primeval practice), or to create confusion between good and bad, but primarily to deliberately subvert the ontological assumptions of social reality, that is, to create a postmodern "tower of Babel." When all intersubjective agreement about reality is lost, claims lose their validity and it is hard to find a source of authority that can rule about what is real and unreal. In court, judges can determine what is legal or illegal, but their claims are based on some basic understandings of social reality. When these basic understandings are threatened, judges may be helpless. For example, think about the repeated and steadfast attempts at Holocaust denial. Or, look at the Temple Mount in Jerusalem in the context of the Middle East conflict. Did the Jewish temple ever exist or not? This is not just a matter of archeology, for every finding can be given a discursive twist and be turned into historical reality or historical "rubbish." This also goes for religious zealots, who, using the latest message from God, are in the business of deconstructing reality. Creating epistemic chaos has thus become a common instrumental means of control and power politics. Epistemic chaos, however, is not sustainable as a form of governance, because authority is not possible without a shared social reality and standards of validity.

Even in the absence of agreement on issues of legitimacy and fair practices beyond the state, epistemic validity may sometimes serve as a proxy for governance. International governance under such circumstances can at most be collective legitimatization among state actors (Claude, 1966). Under such circumstances, the combination of a lack of formal political processes beyond interstate bargaining and the highly technical nature of problems that demand international governance can lead to authority by default appearing to move to technical experts or private authorities as demands[8] for global governance increase (Coleman and Porter, 2000: 380–82). Here the interaction of episteme and experts operates in the way described earlier.

International institutions commonly rely on expert authority in at least three settings. First, experts are called upon to make authoritative interpretations of rules. For example, dispute-resolution panels in trade agreements may rely on trade lawyers and economists rather than judges. Second, experts may develop standards in technical areas, which then may become authoritative either directly or indirectly through recognition of those standards by other institutions (e.g., the World Trade Organization [WTO] recognizing standards from the International Organization for Standardization). Third, experts may gain authority through specialized cause–effect knowledge where their prescriptions gain legitimacy as focal points for cooperation, or the bases of new rules (Haas, 1992b; Adler and Haas, 1992). In all these cases, institutional power will be affected by the way in which experts enter into the construction of rules. Whereas the translation of authoritative knowledge claims into political authority is by no means automatic, when functional authority is granted to experts, purposely or by effect, it may also be a source of legitimacy problems. This problem can be especially acute when governments simply leave technical decisions on complex issues to the private sector to design their own rules (Coleman and Porter, 2000; Cutler, Haufler, and Porter, 1999). Governance may thus be achieved, but without the required moral basis for sustaining authority if it is seen as removed from the state – there is no mechanism in normative political theory that authorizes states to

---

[8] This demand stems primarily from a desire to maintain free global markets – which economic actors view as threatened in the absence of regulation beyond the state. Underlying these demands is a sense that expansion and acceleration of transborder activity have already undermined the political authority of the state. At the same time, mainly non-economic actors are increasing demands for social regulation in areas such as the environment, labor, and human rights and of the global economy more generally.

transfer authority granted to them by citizens. It is not surprising that the same forces that empowered expertise in global governance now understand that their actions disposed them in directions that "advantage some while disadvantaging others" (Barnett and Duvall, chap. 1), and, therefore, have led to increased demands for accountability and democracy.

Good practices

Normative issues cannot be easily escaped if global governance is to be viewed as good and moral – thus, our emphasis on the bundle of notions associated with fairness. The episteme's normative components, therefore, play a critical role with regard to the type of global governance system and processes that will end up developing. At issue here is not only the differing views around the world regarding what stands as good governance, but also the difficulty in applying domestic governance procedures, such as democratic accountability and transparency, to the global level. True, in recent times, there has developed a notion of good (global) practices, most notably within international financial institutions (IFIs) (Woods, 1999). This has led to the development of a discourse of democratic global governance in reference to such institutions (e.g., Keohane and Nye, 2001). The explosion of recent attempts to define good practices and to introduce notions of accountability, responsibility, transparency, and representation to the study of international institutions and global governance is not simply academic. Equally, national, international, and transnational "global governance practitioners" are using similar epistemic materials to make sense of their world, the result of which can be manifested as institutional power.

To take just one important example, the theme of "empowerment" has become a central plank of World Bank policy. The bank's anxiousness to make this goal known within its constituencies and among wider publics is also notable, as evidenced by the theme's prominent play on the World Bank homepage.[9] The four elements of empowerment are "access to information," "inclusion and participation," "accountability," and "local organizational capacity."[10] Woods (1999) has pointed in particular to the new emphasis on the importance of "ownership" of decisions by stakeholders, which means access and accountability to people directly affected. The World Bank Inspection Panel is one

[9] See www.worldbank.org [January 30, 2003].
[10] See www.worldbank.org/poverty/empowerment/index.htm [January 30, 2003].

such attempt to improve accountability, which allows requests from private citizens affected to investigate and review bank programs (Fox, 2000). However, it should also be kept in mind that there remains some disagreement on the specific meaning of good practices, even among IFIs. Compare, for example, International Monetary Fund (IMF) policies and practices, which are highly dependent on expert knowledge in policy-making and confidentiality with governments. This makes the IMF more resistant to wide-ranging reform despite the significant effects of its policies in many countries. Similar language of good governance and transparency is used, but the meaning of these terms refers only in part to its corporate practices and relationships with governments. Instead, good governance in IMF parlance refers primarily to its promotion of what it views as good domestic governance in target states, "by helping countries ensure the rule of law, improve the efficiency and accountability of their public sectors, and tackle corruption" (IMF, 2002).

At the same time, a growing choir around the world, mainly but not limited to those within developing countries, has been asking how it is possible that, if global governance is so "good," their lives have become so much more miserable. Our task here is not to assess progress in global governance, however. Rather, our more limited goal is to describe the components of good global governance, if and when it happens, which we deduce from our understanding of epistemes and their productive power and, by extension, their expression in institutional power. In that context, we find it notable that, despite a sense of lack of progress, many developing country leaders are buying into notions of good governance promoted by the IFIs. The New Partnership for African Development (NEPAD) is a case in point. In the context of NEPAD, leading proponents such as South African president Thabo Mbeki can promote good governance in line with World Bank formulations as part of a deal for increased development assistance, foreign investment, and market access.[11] The most striking feature of NEPAD for our discussion is that it features virtually the same good-governance agenda as that promoted by experts in the IFIs, but within an initiative drawn up by African leaders. The sense of ownership in turn may account for widespread support for the initiative among participating states, at least at the elite level. As Mbeki put it, "We are taking responsibility for the success

[11] Mallaby, 2002a; see also the documentation on NEPAD at www.nepad.org [January 30, 2003].

of the program . . . We can't say it's somebody else's plan. It's our plan" (Mallaby, 2002a).

The productive power of the episteme, "through diffuse social relations," can be seen here at work, albeit partly, for buying into notions of good governance by those who, like Mbeki, demand fairness from the developed countries can be a hollow proposition, or at least only a first step, unless a concept of fairness and right process (Franck, 1990; 1995) has become an integral part of the episteme of global governance. Moreover, that concept must be one that both developed and developing countries borrow from in order to know their bearings.

Whereas some IR scholars are turning to the ideal theory of thinkers such as Habermas and Rawls to uncover what ought to be the basis of fair practices in global governance (e.g., Risse, 2000), notions of fairness are always historically and institutionally bound or informed by an episteme. In this context, debates between Rawlsians and Habermasians over whether right process is a matter of public reason or deliberation seem incongruous with the problem in global governance, which concerns whether different communities or cultures share an episteme (not just normative but also epistemic understandings about how the world works) and enough of a "common lifeworld" (shared experiences of that world) to even enter the possibility of engaging in communicative action of the kind Habermas envisioned.[12]

Practical reason

Closely related to the issue of good practices is practical reason, which, like epistemic validity, relies on a pragmatist reading of rationality that is sensitive to contingent historical and cultural contexts. Practical reason builds on the notion that reasons derive from interpretive and dialogical processes in which intersubjectively validated knowledge and normative understandings of fairness play a major role. Practical reason, for example, concerns the epistemic requirements for democratic practice, which, according to Habermas, requires "discursive validation" and must therefore rest on "good arguments" made under "ideal-speech" conditions where validity claims can be assessed (Habermas, 1979: 178–79). Thomas Risse also addresses the possibility of conditions that approach "an ideal-speech" situation in global governance, where

---

[12] An episteme is antecedent to the shared understandings and experiences that make up a "lifeworld" in the sense Habermas uses the term.

free and equal autonomous actors can challenge validity claims, seek a reasoned communicative consensus about their understandings of the situation and justifications for norms guiding their action, and are open to being persuaded. Governance is viewed as a truth-seeking process, and institutions should be designed to approximate such conditions. Similarly Zürn proposes a "deliberative principle," that "any decision should be backed by arguments committed to values of rationality and impartiality" (2000: 186). Arguments can occur among state representatives themselves, or between them and members of transnational organizations, as well as between them and individual citizens (although the question of who is the relevant community may arise). Nonetheless, any process should involve a situation in which persuasion is possible and common understanding is the goal. The link between epistemic validity and practical rationality is obvious in this regard, as the former is not possible without agreement on the latter.

A dialogical legal approach can go some way to helping with the postmodernization of politics and, thus, to strengthening global governance through reason. As Habermas argues, law can mediate between external facts and legitimate rational discourse and intersubjective understandings. It requires, however, taking law not as a completely functional and reified entity (as Niklas Luhmann [1989] does), but as an entity that remains open to moral and epistemic justification, on the basis of open communication and persuasion. This, for example, means developing institutionalized legal arrangements that can screen the topics and issues in such a way that only morally sound arguments, and arguments that are sound from an epistemic point of view, are accepted as valid and are given international and transnational legitimacy. In other words, dialogical approaches to institutions and the law may help in the establishment of international and transnational legitimate (and thus also illegitimate) arguments. But our earlier discussion suggests this will not be an easy task.

Epistemes and global governance: legalization and trade

Epistemes enable and delimit global governance along the four requirements of global governance outlined in our 2×2 table (table 13.1). We illustrate the practical implications of our theory with two brief examples, the general case of a trend toward legalization and a specific case, governance of international trade.

Legalization

A special issue of the journal *International Organization* from 2000 examined the increasing trend toward legalization in world politics, defined as "a particular form of institutionalization [that] represents the decision in different areas to impose international legal constraints on governments" (Goldstein, et al. 2000: 386). Legalization or "the rule of law" provides a potentially interesting example of a nascent episteme.[13] It is rooted in deep Western civilizational values as well in the discourse of Enlightenment and rationalism. In more recent times, one often hears the "rule of law" being proclaimed as the central defining feature that separates friends and enemies in international relations, and respect for the rule of law as a central criterion by which to judge the behavior of states as responsible internally.

One very concrete implication is to apply this criterion to judge the worthiness of states to receive support from multilateral lending institutions. For example, "good" practices are frequently equated with rule-of-law reform, even to a point that "has led aid providers to act as though law is good and politics is bad" (Upham, 2002: 8). In documenting the evolution of this thinking in the World Bank, Upham notes the close connection between the emphasis on rule of law and particular assumptions about its links to economic growth and the importance of protecting private property rights (epistemic validity), as well as how it informs notions of fairness (good practices) and proper forms of dispute resolution (practical reason). He illustrates with the following quotation from the World Bank website: "Legal and Judicial systems that work effectively, efficiently, and fairly are the backbone of national economic and social development. National and international investors need to know that the rules they operate under will be expeditiously and fairly enforced." The authority of law is also understood to offer the best protection for individuals: "Ordinary citizens need to know that they, too, have the surety and protection that only a competent judicial system can offer."[14] Similar statements, as noted above, characterize the IMF's position on lending.

More broadly, the rule of law (as opposed to other notions of order) is contrasted to anarchy in describing the proper conduct of international

[13] We do not refer, of course, to a general concept of the rule of law, which has been present for some time, but to a more recent understanding that global governance increasingly depends on legally binding rules or soft-law injunctions, and on the diffusion of legal-economic knowledge throughout the system (Dezalay and Garth, 2002).

[14] Both quotations are reproduced in Upham, 2002: 9–10.

relations. There is even an underlying sense in which it identifies the civilized from barbarians. Thus, the criterion of "rule of law" identifies acceptable versus unacceptable forms of governance, privileges a particular kind of knowledge and discourse (rational-legal), and defines insiders and outsiders – those who follow the "rule of law" and those who do not. While legalization is probably not yet institutionalized sufficiently to fully merit the label episteme, imagining such a future is not farfetched, at least in the nonsecurity realm. Even as a nascent episteme, its implications for global governance can be spun out through a couple of illustrative examples.

One example concerns its implications for epistemic validity. Law may empower particular expertise. Even with the best liberal intentions, legitimizing expertise in order to rest governance on sound epistemic foundations always straddles the tenuous line between nondemocratic technocracies in which experts hold power and the benefits or requirements of "objective" or rational discourse and adjudication of claims. For example, recognizing that law may de facto institutionalize power relations, experts can inadvertently play the role of reinforcing that status quo.

Second, and more generally, the effect of a rule-of-law episteme has been to provoke some of the strongest reactions among those labeled as anti-globalization protesters who point to the authority of laws in the European Union and in the WTO. The reaction is often met with bafflement on the part of officials in their "rule-of-law" bubble, who cannot understand a world in which rule of law is a problem. As Miles Kahler has pointed out, however, even in the case of the European Court of Justice, the rule of law "has been directed toward creating the rights of economic citizenship, not building precedents in social or civil rights," a statement that applies to an even greater degree in the WTO (Kahler, 2000: 667–68). The impetus for such legalization comes from corporations and investors who want a stable, transparent, and rule-governed policy environment that they expect to protect them from what they might perceive as arbitrary political or regulatory interference. For them, the requirements of global governance are met. On strictly legal grounds, limited access seems justifiable because the rules are established to govern corporations. But they are not the only community affected by this governance. The practical effect of legalization has been to institutionalize rules and processes in international economic organizations that entrench rights for investors and corporations, with implications for the future direction of global governance that range from enabling and

310

legitimating private authority to limiting the boundary of the community who participates in governance. This is institutional power at work. Nonetheless, the epistemic underpinnings of the institutions thereby created provide resources that the relatively disempowered can utilize, although they are at a distinct disadvantage. For example, by revealing publicly the contradictory tendencies in a rule-of-law discourse that purports to coincide with individual freedom and democratic norms, pressure can build to extend the scope of legalization. Moreover, legalization could extend into the human rights area or incorporate greater accountability for decisions, as occurred domestically when the rule of law became institutionalized in most Western democracies. Whereas productive power is still at work since such arguments would be articulated in the context of extending, not overthrowing the rule of law, our theory suggests that institutions that fail to live up to their normative claims will prompt resistance and be unsustainable in the long term. Moreover, an expanded discourse of legalization empowers societal groups to participate, or at least make claims for a right to participate, more directly in negotiations and judicial proceedings formerly viewed as servicing only the market, because they would subsequently be viewed as part of a broader governing arrangement affecting society as well as the market.

International trade

We focus on international trade, our second example, to illustrate the implications of a legalization episteme, and our theory more broadly, in one major pocket of global governance. Specifically, the Doha Agenda of the WTO, agreed to in late 2001, illustrates how a social episteme operates in the realm of global economic governance, as well as the dynamics of global governance given the requirements we lay out above. Gerald Helleiner put the challenge of global governance that Doha aimed to address very well in a speech to the United Nations Conference on Trade and Development (UNCTAD) in November 2000:

> It will indeed be a major challenge not only substantively to envisage and design appropriate institutional and legal requirements for global economic governance but also to develop effective and legitimate *processes* – processes that are participatory and fair – to move the world toward its required new governance system. If the global rules system is to be "harmonized" through deeper integration among national economies within an agreed overall framework, as most now forecast and many advocate, there must, above all, be full and

> reasonably democratic representation as the rules and framework are created and implemented. There can be "no harmonization without representation."
>
> (Helleiner, 2001: 35)

Superficially, the Doha Agenda was negotiated in the context of demands for a "development" round of trade negotiations owing to increased developing country membership in the WTO. The WTO required a new deal between North and South for reasons that included perceived vulnerabilities of the trade regime and of open markets generally owing to increased market integration and unfinished business from the Uruguay Round, festering disagreements between North and South over the direction of the trade regime and whether it ought to expand its competencies, and a growing unease that the benefits of globalization are not accruing equally to developed and developing countries, especially to the poor in the South. In response, the agenda contains an admittedly ambiguously worded deal offering market access, capacity-building, and technical assistance to the South in exchange for harmonization with the North.

The episteme at work here is well known to observers of the trade regime. A liberal episteme may include the rule of law mentioned above, but more specifically reflects an understanding of the nature of the economy and market that holds efficiency as the highest value, favoring means–end rationality, and a faith in open markets as generators of economic growth and development. While specific policy prescriptions have varied significantly over the history of the regime – from policies that allowed greater leeway for domestic interventions and exceptions characterized as "embedded liberalism" by Ruggie (1982), to more liberalized policies moving in the direction of the "Washington Consensus" (John Williamson, 1990; 1993), to proposed policies that suggest some erosion or limitations of that consensus, drawing on the work of influential critics (e.g., Stiglitz, 1998; 1999) – institutions of world trade have this liberal episteme at the core, with liberal goals beyond reproach. The postwar trade regime has always reflected political compromises only to the degree they create the necessary stability to further the goals of liberalization. (Other major economic institutions including the Organization for Economic Cooperation and Development [OECD][15] and IMF

---

[15] For example, Article 1 of the OECD Convention (1960) commits the organization to policies that aim "to achieve the highest sustainable economic growth . . . and sound economic expansion" of members and nonmembers and "the expansion of world trade on a multilateral, non-discriminatory basis" (OECD, 1973: 48).

similarly take these goals for granted.) The deal in the Doha Agenda is constructed wholly within this "bubble," as its first two paragraphs make clear:

1. The multilateral trading system embodied in the World Trade Organization has contributed significantly to economic growth, development and employment throughout the past fifty years. We are determined, particularly in the light of the global economic slowdown, to maintain the process of reform and liberalization of trade policies, thus ensuring that the system plays its full part in promoting recovery, growth and development. We therefore strongly reaffirm the principles and objectives set out in the Marrakesh Agreement Establishing the World Trade Organization, and pledge to reject the use of protectionism.
2. International trade can play a major role in the promotion of economic development and the alleviation of poverty.

(WTO, 2001)

In terms of fairness and practical reason, the dominant solution is to socialize developing countries through technical assistance into the common institutional framework and set of understandings of the international trade regime. But when what constitutes "fair" trade is a fundamental point of disagreement, this hardly seems a viable solution. As Howse has pointed out, this problem has become especially acute since earlier successes in producing reciprocal tariff reductions have led to increasing attention in the trade regime to domestic policies that are "not necessarily discriminatory in any obvious sense" but that might be viewed as attempts to cheat. Unlike the normative consensus on principles such as most favored nation (MFN) when applied to tariff reductions, there is no "agreed baseline for normal governmental policy-making" (2001: 357) to guide negotiations on subsidies, dumping or "technical" barriers to trade, which dominate post-Doha negotiations.

Here the episteme works to empower particular types of knowledge and expertise to make determinations of fairness, reflecting power differentials within the international trade system. In conjunction with the trend toward legalization noted above, the "rule of law" easily blends into the "rule of lawyers" in the trade regime, and diplomacy is largely replaced by a legal culture in the Western, especially American, tradition (Weiler, 2001: 339). Ironically, this marks a shift even from the GATT system, under which the GATT secretariat, reputedly, frequently drafted decisions for trade panels based on their own ideas of what

313

system stability required, rather than on rigorous treaty interpretation (Howse, 2001: 358, 371). On the substantive side, "normative ambiguity" empowered "trade policy 'experts,' diplomats and bureaucrats in the GATT secretariat [who] played an increasing role in maintaining the system" (ibid.: 358).

A more overtly legal process can have positive and negative consequences. On the positive side, it can level resource differentials. On the negative side, particularly in the context of dispute resolution, it makes compromise difficult given the "win–lose" mentality of the legal profession, as well as the career ambition of lawyers which can lead them to bring disputes to panels because "we can win" (Weiler, 2001: 340). The overriding concern for developing countries is not a legal culture per se, but rather whether such a culture is accessible to them and truly provides a level playing field. Diplomacy is a game many developing countries have experience playing and is well institutionalized in international politics; legalism far less so.

As lawyers become empowered throughout the negotiation and dispute process, trade ministries must scramble to find qualified trade lawyers, and poorer developing countries must sometimes rely on the WTO itself to provide legal services (ibid.: 339). Developing countries simply have few alternatives. An exception that proves the rule is the South Centre based in Geneva. Perhaps the only organization of its kind established by developing country governments to provide intellectual and analytic resources for bargaining on global issues, it has only four full-time analytic staff, three of whom are now engaged on WTO-related issues. Smaller developing countries that have only recently joined the WTO are largely unable to take advantage even of those resources because, for them, technical assistance is required simply to understand the "bible" bloc of WTO agreements, or how to function with limited physical capacity to attend meetings or time to become properly prepared to play an active role. Even more experienced delegations of larger countries that better understand the issues lack the time and resources to make paper submissions, which is an important part of the negotiation process. Owing to its overwhelming workload, South Centre staff produce papers limited at most to commenting on written submissions, with little chance of directing their expertise to broader work on developing negotiating positions. Meanwhile, WTO staff devoted to technical assistance do not have the mandate to assist in making arguments, which leaves even the most able developing countries either subject largely to socialization or on their own to develop arguments to say "no" that will be compelling within the WTO system.[16]

Two kinds of power are actually in operation: first, the power of formal rules negotiated by the members, which is akin to institutional power; second, the power "of a technocratic, epistemic *'eminence grise'* nature," which is productive power (Howse, 2001: 358). The WTO shifted power toward the legal, adding a new layer of judicial authority expected to increase the legitimacy of the organization by ensuring the rule of law would triumph over political considerations.

An ideal-speech situation in the Habermasian sense, under these circumstances, would occur only upon the relinquishing of alternative conceptions of fairness, which may be precisely what negotiations are about. The requirements of fair procedure may demand not simply deliberation or access, but independent ability to develop knowledge consistent with their own community's experience of the world. Only then can procedures be established to adjudicate the claims, which will be difficult given the probability that the issue at stake is precisely the lack of a common lifeworld. Developing countries have found engagement under these circumstances especially difficult given the way dominant epistemes in the trade and economic sphere more generally are entrenched in international institutions.

Helleiner (2001) highlights how this process has operated in institutions of global governance. The weakness of developing country cooperation on research and technical cooperation has meant that "developing country interests have therefore tended to be analysed at greatest length in the multilateral organizations themselves; such analyses are subject to obvious constraints (not least the influence of the industrialized countries within these bodies) from which more independent such work would be free" (2001: 36). Under these circumstances, representation is an important step, but is not enough, nor is accountability or transparency. It is not surprising in this context that a central debate in the context of the Doha Agenda revolves not around capacity-building to implement rules or transfers of resources per se, but around technical assistance – where the real issue is training experts versus empowerment through knowledge. The highly legalized and technical nature of discussion and the sheer volume of meetings all work against developing country representatives' ability to participate or formulate positions independently of the highly institutionalized

---

[16] Interview with a former South Centre official, October 5, 2002.

social episteme. Helleiner is worth quoting at length again in this regard:

> The WTO's *raison d'être* is today seen as the achievement of an agreed set of rules, a "level playing field," for economic transactions within the global economy. It is often presumed, within WTO secretariat and G7 circles, that the universal application of the current rules (and others still to be agreed) will promote development for all; but that is theory or hypothesis rather than reality. Many challenge it . . . and with reason. Even though the WTO charter formally commits it to poverty alleviation and the promotion of sustainable development, these are *not* seen by anyone as primary WTO objectives.
>
> (ibid.: 41–42)

While so far the story of trade just narrated is mainly about power rooted in collective knowledge, our argument is that sustainable global governance also requires legitimacy and fairness. In this case, the importance of creating the possibility of deliberation has been a central focus of many developing countries, academics, and NGOs. A new NGO initiative is worth mentioning in this regard: International Lawyers and Economists Against Poverty (ILEAP). According to its mission statement: "By responding to expressed needs, without any other agendas to promote, through the supply of skilled and highly motivated professionals, it hopes to fill a major 'gap' in the international trading system" (ILEAP, 2001).

Thus, institutional reforms in negotiating and/or adjudication procedures may not offer the largest payoffs in terms of altering power dynamics or improving governance. Proposed reforms include more transparency, increased access for nongovernmental groups, reducing opportunities for strong-arm tactics, enabling greater participation from previously marginalized countries or groups of countries, and streamlining decision-making generally. Whereas these reforms might marginally reduce the ability of major states to utilize compulsory power, productive and institutional power limit what we should expect from such reforms.

Moreover, such reforms alone barely address the normative requirements of global governance. Under such circumstances, dampening the outward expressions of compulsory power can have the ironic consequence of increasing the probability of institutional stalemate or even collapse. Mexican foreign minister Luis Ernesto Derbez, the chair of the 5th WTO Ministerial in Cancun (September 2003), for example, blamed the breakdown of trade talks on entrenched "rhetoric" that prevented movement on core issues (ICTSD, 2003). Our theory suggests that a more fruitful focus for actors disempowered under current institutional arrangements is to emphasize building strategic policy capacity either individually or collectively. This will allow them to articulate and justify their autonomous choices, even given the power dynamics we identify, and thus increase their ability to control their fates and circumstances.

Conclusion

We have argued that understanding power in global governance, as rooted in knowledge and manifested in epistemes, brings back into the discussion of global governance two fundamental bases of global governance that have tended to be ignored or mistreated.

Given our emphasis on knowledge in power, it is worth emphasizing that epistemes that inform global governance are not simply reducible to the material power and interests of dominant states, because they are embedded in institutions and collective understandings of actors who participate in global politics. Thus, even dominant states and leaders may find their own actions or understandings out of sync with them. For example, international economic institutions reflect and promote understandings of the nature of the global economy, which since World War II at least have been largely liberal, although with various degrees of domestic intervention or international management allowed. This episteme persisted despite the waxing and waning of commitments to open markets by major states. Indeed, their own actions and performance would be evaluated in terms of their adherence or consistency with epistemic requirements. The implication is that challenges were not only viewed as illegitimate, but were also largely incomprehensible.

Combining an analytic focus on epistemes with a normative concern over the requirements of global governance also forced us to straddle analytic and normative theory. This undertaking reveals that conceiving a normative critique of global practices and institutions first requires understanding the mechanisms of social constitution and change, which is an analytical endeavor. In other words, when trying to understand the evolution of global governance from a power perspective, normative IR theory requires analytical IR theory, and vice versa. Moreover, bringing in power to a normative or political theory perspective requires broader and multifaceted conceptualizations of power, for example, productive and institutional power. Indeed, we have shown that the concepts of productive power and institutional power are useful in order to unpack the process by which knowledge, practices, institutions, and diffuse control interact in the construction of global governance.

Finally, introducing normative issues, such as fairness, responsibility, and legitimacy to our understanding of power requires a better understanding of what authority means in the context of global governance. Although it will be uncomfortable for many traditional IR scholars, we believe this theoretical straddling is crucial to comprehending the nature and possibilities of global governance.

References

Abbott, Kenneth and Duncan Snidal. 1998. "Why States Act Through Formal International Organizations," *Journal of Conflict Resolution* 42(1):3–32.
  2000. "Hard and Soft Law in International Governance," *International Organization* 54(3):421–56.
Abi-Saab, Georges. 1984. "The Specificities of Humanitarian Law." In Christophe Swinarski (ed.), *Studies and Essays on International Humanitarian Law in Honor of Jean Pictet*, pp. 265–80. Geneva: M. Nijhoff.
Abraham, Kenneth. 1988. "Statutory Intepretation and Literary Theory: Some Common Concerns of an Unlikely Pair." In S. Levinson and S. Mailloux (eds.), *Interpreting Law and Literature: A Hermeneutic Reader*, pp. 115–29. Evanston: Northwestern University Press.
Ackerman, Seth. 2000. "New York Times on Iraq Sanctions: A Case of Journalistic Malpractice," www.fair.org/extra/0003/crossette-iraq.html.
ACLU (American Civil Liberties Union). 2000. *Out of Control: Seattle's Flawed Response to Protests Against the World Trade Organization*. Washington, DC: American Civil Liberties Union.
Adler, Emanuel and Peter M. Haas. 1992. "Conclusion: Epistemic Communities, World Order, and the Creation of a Reflective Research Program," *International Organization* 46:367–90.
Aggarwal, Vinod K. 1995. "Comparing Regional Cooperation Efforts in the Asia-Pacific and North America." In A. Mack and J. Ravenhill (eds.), *Pacific Cooperation: Building Economic and Security Regimes in the Asia-Pacific Region*, pp. 40–65. Boulder: Westview.
Agnew, John A. and Stuart Corbridge. 1995. *Mastering Space: Hegemony, Territory, and International Political Economy*. London: Routledge.
Albin, Cecilia. 2001. *Justice and Fairness in International Negotiation*. New York: Cambridge University Press.
Alvarez, Jose. 2001. "Constitutional Interpretation in International Organizations." In Coicaud and Heiskanen, 2001, pp. 104–54.
Andreas, Peter. 2000. *Border Games: Policing the US – Mexico Divide*. Ithaca: Cornell University Press.

References

Anheier, Helmut, Marlies Glasius and Mary Kaldor (eds.). 2001. *Global Civil Society 2001*. Oxford: Oxford University Press.

Annan, Kofi. 1999a. UN Press Release SG/SM/6938, March 24.

1999b. UN Press Release SG/SM/7136, September 20.

Appadurai, Arjun. 1996. *Modernity at Large: Cultural Dimensions of Globalization*. Minneapolis: University of Minnesota Press.

Arendt, Hannah. 1958. *The Human Condition*. 2nd edn. Chicago: University of Chicago Press.

1959. *The Human Condition*. New York: Anchor Books.

Arrighi, Giovanni. 1994. *The Long Twentieth Century*. London: Verso.

Askin, Kelly Dawn. 1997. *War Crimes Against Women: Prosecution in International War Crimes Tribunals*. The Hague: M. Nijhoff.

Axelrod, Robert. 1984. *The Evolution of Cooperation*. New York: Basic Books.

Ayoob, Mohammed. 1995. *The Third World Security Predicament: State Making, Regional Conflict, and the International System*. Boulder: Lynne Rienner.

Bachrach, Peter and Morton Baratz: 1962. "Two Faces of Power," *American Political Science Review* 56:947–52.

1963. "Decisions and Nondecisions: An Analytic Framework," *American Political Science Review* 57:632–42.

1975. "Decisions and Nondecisions: An Analytic Framework," *American Political Science Review* 57:632–42.

Baldwin, David. 1980. "Interdependence and Power: A Conceptual Analysis," *International Organization* 34(40):471–506.

1989. *The Paradoxes of Power*. New York: Basil Blackwell.

2002. "Power and International Relations." In W. Carlsnaes, T. Risse, and B. Simmons (eds.), *The Handbook of International Relations*, pp. 179–91. Thousand Oaks, CA: Sage.

Baranovsky, Vladimir. 2001. "Humanitarian Intervention: Russian Perspectives." In *Intervention, Sovereignty and International Security*, pp. 12–38. Pugwash Study Group Occasional Papers, 2, 1.

Barlow, M. and T. Clarke. 2002. *Global Showdown*. Toronto: Stoddart.

Barnes, Barry. 1988. *The Nature of Power*. New York: Polity.

Barnett, Michael. 1997. "Bringing in the New World Order: Legitimacy, Liberalism, and the United Nations," *World Politics* 49(4):526–51.

Barnett, Michael and Raymond Duvall. 2005. "Power in International Politics," *International Organization* 59(1) (Winter).

Barnett, Michael and Martha Finnemore. 2004. *Rules for the World: International Organizations in Global Politics*. Ithaca: Cornell University Press.

Barrett, Michèle. 1988. *Women's Oppression Today: Problems in Marxist Feminist Analysis*. London: Verso.

Barro, Robert J. and David Gordon. 1983. "Rules, Discretion, and Reputation in a Model of Monetary Policy," *Journal of Monetary Economics* 12:101–21.

Barry, Dan. 2002. "Appearing in the Role of Evil: The Other Side," *New York Times*, January 31, p. A17.

320

Baumgartner, Tom and Tom R. Burns. 1975. "The Structuring of International Economic Relations," *International Studies Quarterly* 19:126–59.

Bayard, Thomas and Kimberly Ann Elliott. 1994. *Reciprocity and Retaliation in US Trade Policy*. Washington, DC: Institute for International Economics.

Beck, Ulrich. 2000. *What Is Globalization?* Trans. by Patrick Camiller. Cambridge, UK: Polity.

Becker, Elizabeth. 2003. "Bush Aide Threatens to Sue EU," *International Herald Tribune*, January 10, 11.

Beetham, David. 1985. *Max Weber and the Theory of Modern Politics*. New York: Polity.

   1996. *Bureaucracy*. Minneapolis: University of Minnesota Press.

Bello, Walden. 1994. *Dark Victory: The United States, Structural Adjustment, and Global Poverty*. San Francisco: Food First.

Bendor, Jonathan. 1987. "In Good Times and Bad: Reciprocity in an Uncertain World," *American Journal of Political Science* 31:531–58.

Benton, Ted. 1981. "Objective Interests and the Sociology of Power," *Sociology* 15(2):161–84.

Bernstein, Steven. 2001. *The Compromise of Liberal Environmentalism*. New York: Columbia University Press.

   2002. "The Elusive Basis of Legitimacy in Global Governance." Manuscript under review.

Best, Geoffrey. 1994. *War and Law Since 1945*. Oxford: Clarendon.

Bhala, Raj and Kevin Kennedy. 1998. *World Trade Law*. Charlottesville, VA: Lexis Law.

Bhaskar, Roy. 1979. *The Possibility of Naturalism: A Philosophical Critique of the Contemporary Human Sciences*. Atlantic Highlands, NJ: Humanities Press.

Bircham, Emma and John Charlton (eds.). 2001. *Anti-Capitalism: A Guide to the Movement*. London: Bookmarks.

Blair, Tony. 2001. Speech to the British Labour Party conference, October 2, politics.guardian.co.uk/labourconference 2001/story/0,1220,561988,00.html.

Blaney, David and Naeem Inayatullah. 1994. "Prelude to a Conversation of Cultures? Todorov and Nandy on the Possibility of Dialogue," *Alternatives* 19(1):23–51.

   2003. *International Relations and the Problem of Difference*. New York: Routledge.

Blau, Peter. 1964. *Exchange and Power in Social Life*. New York: J. Wiley.

Block, F. 1977. "The Ruling Class Does Not Rule," *Socialist Revolution* 33:6–28.

Block, Jennifer. 2002. "Today, Porto Alegre. Tomorrow . . . ?," *Mother Jones*, February 6, www.motherjones.com/news/feature/2002/02/world_social_forum.html.

Bodansky, Daniel. 2000. "What's So Bad About Unilateral Actions to Protect the Environment." *European Journal of International Law* 11: 339–48.

Boli, John and George M. Thomas. 1999. "INGOs and the Organization of World Culture." In J. Boli and G. M. Thomas (eds.), *Constructing World Culture: International Organizations Since 1875*, pp. 13–49. Stanford: Stanford University Press.

References

Bonacich, Edna and Richard Appelbaum. 2000. *Behind the Label: Inequality in the Los Angeles Apparel Industry.* Berkeley: University of California Press.

Borjal, Art. 2000. "The Filipino Can," *Philippine Star,* May 11, www.philstar.com/datedata/g11-may11/edi2.htm.

Borschberg, Peter. 1994. *Hugo Grotius: "Commentarius in Theses XI."* Berlin: Peter Lang.

Bourdieu, Pierre. 1977. *Outline of a Theory of Practice.* New York: Cambridge University Press.

Bowles, Samuel and Herbert Gintis. 1986. *Democracy and Capitalism.* New York: Basic Books.

Bown, Chad, Hoekman, Bernard and Ozden, Çaglar. 2003. "The Pattern of US Antidumping: The Path from Initial Filing to WTO Dispute Settlement," *World Trade Review* 2(3)(November): 349–71.

Braithwaite, John and Peter Drahos. 2000. *Global Business Regulation.* New York: Cambridge University Press.

Brenner, Johanna. 1993. "The Best of Times, the Worst of Times: US Feminism Today," *New Left Review* 200:101–59.

Brenner, Neil. 1997. "Global, Fragmented, Hierarchical: Henri Lefebvre's Geographies of Globalization," *Public Culture* 10(1):135–67.

Brenner, Neil and Nik Theodore. 2002. "Cities and the Geographies of 'Actually Existing Neoliberalism.'" In N. Brenner and N. Theodore (eds.), *Spaces of Neoliberalism: Urban Restructuring in North America and Western Europe,* pp. 2–32. Oxford, UK: Blackwell.

Brint, Steven. 1994. *In an Age of Experts: The Changing Role of Professionals in Politics and Public Life.* Princeton: Princeton University Press.

Broad, Robin (ed.). 2002. *Global Backlash: Citizen Initiatives for a Just World Economy.* Lanham, MD: Rowman & Littlefield.

Bronfenbrenner, Kate. 1997. "We'll Close!: Plant Closings, Plant-Closing Threats, Union Organizing and NAFTA," *Multinational Monitor* 18(3):8–13.

2000. "Raw Power: Plant-Closing Threats and the Threat to Union Organizing," *Multinational Monitor* (December), www.essential.org/monitor/mm2000/00december/power.html.

Brown, Ashley C. 2001. "Confusing Means and Ends: Framework of Restructuring, Not Privatization, Matters Most," *International Journal of Regulation and Governance* 1(2):115–28.

Brown, Wendy. 1995. *States of Injury: Power and Freedom in Late Modernity.* Princeton: Princeton University Press.

Burley, Anne-Marie. 1993. "Regulating the World: Multilateralism, International Law, and the Projection of the New Deal Regulatory State." In J. Ruggie (ed.), *Multilateralism Matters: The Theory and Praxis of an Institutional Form,* pp. 125–56. New York: Columbia University Press.

Bush, George. 1990. "Address before the 45th Session of the United Nations General Assembly," New York, October 1. In *Public Papers of the Presidents, George Bush, 1990,* vol. II, pp. 1330–34. Washington, DC: Government Printing Office.

322

Bush, Marc and Eric Reinhardt. 2003. "Developing Countries and GATT/WTO Dispute Settlement," *Journal of World Trade* 37(4): 719–35.

Butler, Judith P. 1990. *Gender Trouble: Feminism and the Subversion of Identity*. New York: Routledge.

Butler, Nicole. 2000. "NATO: From Collective Defense to Peace Enforcement." In Schnabel and Thakur, 2000, pp. 273–90.

Butterfield, Greg. 2001. "200,000 Defy Killer Cops: Genoa Street Rage Against Capitalism," July 25, www.iacenter.org/genoa_rage.htm [18 February 2002].

Byers, M. (ed.). 2000. *The Role of Law in International Politics: Essays in International Relations and International Law*. New York and Oxford: Oxford University Press.

Cameron, David R. 1989. "Socialism in an Open Economy: Constraint and Choice in French Economic Policy." Unpublished manuscript, Yale University, New Haven, CT.

1992. "The 1992 Initiative: Causes and Consequences." In A. M. Sbragia (ed.), *Euro-Politics: Institutions and Policymaking in the "New" European Community*, pp. 23–74. Washington, DC: Brookings Institution Press.

Campbell, David. 1992. *Writing Security: United States Foreign Policy and the Politics of Identity*. Minneapolis: University of Minnesota Press.

"The Cancun Challenge." 2003. *The Economist*, September 6.

Caporaso, James. 1978. "Dependence, Dependency, and Power in the Global System: A Structural and Behavioral Analysis," *International Organization* 32(1):13–43.

Carpenter, R. Charli. 2003. "'Women and Children First': Gender, Norms, and Humanitarian Evacuation in the Balkans, 1991–1995," *International Organization* 57(4):661–94.

Cascio, Joseph, Gayle Woodside and Philip Mitchell. 1996. *ISO 14000 Guide: The New International Environmental Management Standards*. New York: McGraw-Hill.

Cassese, Antonio. 1999. "Ex iniura ius oritur: Are We Moving Towards International Legitimation of Forcible Humanitarian Countermeasures in the World Community," *European Journal of International Law* 10:23–30.

Catalinotto, John. N.d. "Left Parties Condemn State Violence: Genoa Struggles Reverberate Throughout Europe," International Action Center, www.iacenter.org/genoa_violence.htm [18 February 2002].

Cerny, Philip G. 2000. "Structuring the Political Arena: Public Goods, States and Governance in a Globalizing World." In R. Palan (ed.), *Global Political Economy: Contemporary Theories*, pp. 21–35. London: Routledge.

Chan, Kenneth S. 1985. "The International Negotiation Game: Some Evidence From the Tokyo Round," *Review of Economics and Statistics* 67(3):456–64.

Chang, Howard. 1995. "An Economic Analysis of Trade Measures to Protect the Global Environment," *Georgetown Law Journal* 83:2131–2213.

Charlesworth, Hilary and Christine Chinkin. 2000. *The Boundaries of International Law: A Feminist Analysis*. Manchester: Manchester University Press.

References

Chayes, Abram and Antonia Handler Chayes. 1993. "On Compliance," *International Organization* 47:175–206.

1995. *The New Sovereignty: Compliance with International Regulatory Agreements.* Cambridge, MA: Harvard University Press.

Chesterman, Simon. 2001. *Just War or Just Peace: Humanitarian Intervention and International Law.* New York: Oxford University Press.

Chevigny, Paul. 1995. *Edge of the Knife: Police Violence in the Americas.* New York: New Press.

Chimni, B. S. 2000. "WTO and Environment: Shrimp–Turtle and EC-Hormone Cases," *Economic and Political Weekly*, May 13, 1752–61.

Chossudovsky, Michel. 2001. "The Quebec Wall: What Lies Behind Free Trade Area of the Americas (FTAA)?," www.iacenter.org/quebec_wall.htm [21 February 2002].

Claude, Inis. 1962. *Power and International Relations.* New York: Random House.

1966. "Collective Legitimization as a Political Function of the United Nations," *International Organization* 20:367–79.

Cleaver, Harry. 1994. "The Chiapas Uprising and the Future of Class Struggle in the New World Order," www.eco.utexas.edu/facstaff/Cleaver/chiapasuprising.html.

Clegg, Stewart. 1989. *Frameworks of Power.* Thousand Oaks, CA: Sage Press.

Clinton, Bill. 2000. "Remarks by the President at the US Coast Guard Academy's 119th Commencement, Cadet Memorial Field, US Coast Guard Academy, New London, Connecticut, May 17, 2000," White House, Office of the Press Secretary, www.pub.whitehouse.gov/uri-res/I2R?urn:pdi://oma_eop_gov_us/2000/5/17/4_text_1.

Cockburn, Alexander and Jeffrey St. Clair. 2000. *Five Days that Shook the World.* London: Verso.

Cohen, G. A. 1979. "Capitalism, Freedom, and the Proletariat." In A. Ryan (ed.), *The Idea of Freedom*, pp. 9–25. New York: Oxford University Press.

Cohen, Jean L. and Andrew Arato. 1992. *Civil Society and Political Theory.* Cambridge, MA: MIT Press.

Coicaud, J. and V. Heiskanen (eds.). 2001. *The Legitimacy of International Organizations.* New York: United Nations University Press.

Colas, Alejandro. 2002. *International Civil Society.* Cambridge: Polity.

Coleman, William D. and Tony Porter. 2000. "International Institutions, Globalization and Democracy: Assessing the Challenges," *Global Society* 14:377–98.

Commission on Global Governance. 1995. *Our Global Neighborhood: The Report of the Commission on Global Governance.* New York: Oxford University Press.

Connor, Tim. 2001. *Still Waiting for Nike to Do It.* San Francisco: Global Exchange, May, www.globalexchange.org/economy/corporations/nike/NikeReport.pdf [30 May 2001].

Cooper, Robert. 2002. "The New Liberal Imperialism," *Observer* (UK), April 7, www.observer.co.uk/Print/0,3858,4388912,00.html.

Copelon, Rhonda. 1994. "Surfacing Gender: Re-engraving Crimes Against Women in Humanitarian War." In A. Stiglmayer (ed.), *Mass Rape: The War*

Against Women in Bosnia-Herzegovina, pp. 197–218. Lincoln: University of Nebraska Press.

Cornwell, Rupert. 2003. "Bush on a Revenge Mission," *Independent* (UK), April 26.

Cox, Robert W. 1992. "Multilateralism and World Order," *Review of International Studies* 18:161–80.

    1994. "Global Restructuring; Making Sense of the Changing International Political Economy." In R. Stubbs and G. Underhill (eds.), *Political Economy in a Changing Global Order*, pp. 45–59. London: Macmillan.

    1996a. "The Global Political Economy and Social Choice." In R. Cox, with T. Sinclair, *Approaches to World Order*, pp. 191–208. Cambridge, UK: Cambridge University Press.

    1996b. "Towards a Posthegemonic Conceptualization of World Order: Reflections on the Relevancy of Ibn Khaldun (1992)." In Robert W. Cox with Timothy J. Sinclair, *Approaches to World Order*, pp. 144–73. Cambridge: Cambridge University Press.

Cox, Robert and Harold Jacobson. 1971. *The Anatomy of Influence*. New Haven: Yale University Press.

Crawford, Neta. 2002. *Argument and Change in World Politics: Ethics, Decolonization, and Humanitarian Intervention*. New York: Cambridge University Press.

Crone, Donald. 1993. "Does Hegemony Matter? The Reorganization of the Pacific Political Economy," *World Politics* 45:501–25.

Cutler, A. Claire, Virginia Haufler and Tony Porter (eds.). 1999. *Private Authority and International Affairs*. Albany: SUNY Press.

Dahl, Robert. 1957. "The Concept of Power," *Behavioral Science* 2:201–15.

Dahl, Robert and Bruce Stinebrickner. 2003. *Modern Political Analysis*, 6th edn. Upper Saddle River, NJ: Prentice Hall.

Danaher, Kevin and Roger Burbach (eds.). 2000. *Globalize This*. Monroe, ME: Common Courage Press.

Davis, James. 2001. "This Is What Bureaucracy Looks Like: NGOs and Anti-Capitalism." In Yuen, Katsiaficas, and Rose, 2001, pp. 175–82.

Dawkins, Kristin, Michelle Thom and Carolyn Carr. N.d. "Information About Intellectual Property Rights No. 1: Property Rights and Biodiversity," www.netlink.de/gen/biopiracy.html [25 February 2002].

de Boissieu, Christian and Jean Pisani-Ferry. 1998. "The Political Economy of French Economic Policy in the Perspective of EMU." In B. Eichengreen and J. Frieden (eds.), *Forging an Integrated Europe*, pp. 49–89. Ann Arbor: University of Michigan Press.

De Cecco, Marcello. 1989. "The European Monetary System and National Interests." In P. Guerrieri and P. C. Padoan (eds.), *The Political Economy of European Integration: States, Markets, and Institutions*, pp. 85–99. Savage, MD: Barnes and Noble.

De Groot, Gerard and Corinna Peniston-Bird (eds.). 2000. *A Soldier and a Woman: Sexual Integration in the Military*. Harlow and New York: Longman.

References

de Jonquieres, Guy and Holly Yeager. 2002. "Davos Goes West," *Financial Times*, January 25.

Dean, Mitchell. 1999. *Governmentality: Power and Rule in Modern Society*. London: Sage.

Deflem, Mathieu. 2000. "Bureaucratization and Social Control: Historical Foundations of International Police Cooperation," *Law and Society Review* 34(3):601–40.

Destler, I. M. and John S. Odell. 1987. *Anti-Protection: Changing Forces in United States Trade Politics*. Washington, DC: Institute for International Economics.

Deudney, Daniel and G. John Ikenberry. 1999a. "The Nature and Sources of Liberal International Order," *Review of International Studies* 25(2): 179–98.

1999b. "Realism, Structural Liberalism, and the Western Order." In E. Kapstein and M. Mastanduno (eds.), *Unipolar Politics: Realism and State Strategies After the Cold War*, pp. 103–37. New York: Columbia University Press.

Dezalay, Yves and Bryant Garth. 2002. *The Internationalization of Palace Wars: Lawyers, Economists, and the Contest to Transform Latin American States*. Chicago: University of Chicago Press.

Dicken, Peter. 1992. *Global Shift*. New York: Guilford.

Digeser, Peter. 1992. "The Fourth Face of Power," *Journal of Politics* 54(4):977–1007.

Diplomatic Conference for the Establishment of International Conventions for the Protection of Victims of War. 1949. Final Record of the Geneva Conventions of 12 August 1949 (International Committee of the Red Cross, Geneva), 1952–60, vols. I–IV.

Dixit, Avinash K. 1996. *The Making of Economic Policy: A Transaction Cost Politics Perspective*. Cambridge, MA: MIT Press.

Djait, Hicham. 1985. *Europe and Islam: Cultures and Modernity*. Berkeley: University of California Press.

Dombrowski, Nicole Ann. 1999. "Soldiers, Saints, or Sacrificial Lambs: Women's Relationship to Combat and the Fortification of the Home Front in the Twentieth Century." In Dombrowski (ed.), *Women and War in the Twentieth Century: Enlisted With or Without Consent*, pp. 2–41. New York: Garland.

Doty, Roxanne. 1996. *Imperial Encounters: The Politics of Representation in North–South Relations*. Minneapolis: University of Minnesota Press.

Downs, George W. and David M. Rocke. 1995. *Optimal Imperfection? Domestic Uncertainty and Institutions in International Relations*. Princeton: Princeton University Press.

Doyle, Michael. 1995. "Liberalism and World Politics." In C. Kegley (ed.), *Controversies in International Relations Theory: Realism and the Neoliberal Challenge*, pp. 81–94. New York: St. Martin's Press.

1997. *Ways of War and Peace*. New York: Norton.

Drahos, Peter, with John Braithwaite. 2003. *Information Feudalism*. London: Earthscan.

Drake, William and Kalypso Nicolaidis. 1992. "Ideas, Interests and Institutionalization: 'Trade in Services' and the Uruguay Round," *International Organization* 46(1):37–100.

Drezner, Daniel W. 2003. "The Hidden Hand of Economic Coercion," *International Organization* 57:643–59.

Dryzek, John S., et al. 2003. *Green States and Social Movements*. Oxford: Oxford University Press.

Duke, Simon, Hans-Georg Ehrhart and Matthias Karadi. 2000. "The Major European Allies: France, Germany and the United Kingdom." In Schnabel and Thakur, 2000, pp. 128–48.

Dunoff, Jeffrey. 1999. "The Death of the Trade Regime," *European Journal of International Law* 10:733–62.

Dworkin, Ronald. 1982. "Law as Interpretation," *Texas Law Review* 60:527–50.
    1986. *Law's Empire*. Cambridge, MA: Harvard University Press.

Earthjustice. 2002. "Three Hundred Citizen Groups Call on Secret World Bank Trade Court to Open Up Bechtel Case Against Bolivia: Case Called a Preview of the Free Trade of the Americas," August 29, www.commondreams.org/news2002/0829-02.htm [2 November 2002].

Eaton, Jonathan. 2003. "Trade and Development: Commercial Policy." Unpublished manuscript, New York University, Department of Economics, spring.

Edelman, Murray. 1988. *Constructing the Political Spectacle*. Chicago: University of Chicago Press.

Ehrenreich, Ben. 2003. "Another World Is Possible," *In These Times*, March 3, p. 17.

Eichengreen, Barry, Jeffry Frieden and Jürgen von Hagen. 1995. "The Political Economy of European Integration: Introduction." In B. Eichengreen, J. Frieden, and J. von Hagen (eds.), *Politics and Institutions in an Integrated Europe*, pp. 1–10. Berlin: Springer.

Elshtain, Jean Bethke. 1987. *Women and War*. New York: Basic Books.

Elster, Jon. 1983. "Exploitation, Freedom, and Justice." In J. R. Pennock and J. Chapman (eds.), *Nomos XXVI: Marxism*, pp. 277–304. New York: New York University Press.
    (ed.). 1998. *Deliberative Democracy*. Cambridge, UK: Cambridge University Press.

Emerson, Richard. 1962. "Power–Dependence Relations," *American Sociological Review* 27:31–41.

Enloe, Cynthia. 1989. *Bananas, Beaches and Bases: Making Feminist Sense of International Politics*. London: Pandora.
    1996. "Margins, Silences, and Bottom Rungs: How to Overcome the Underestimation of Power in the Study of International Relations." In S. Smith, et al. (eds.), *International Theory: Positivism and Beyond*, pp. 186–203. New York: Cambridge University Press.

Epstein, Barbara. 1995. "Why Post-Structuralism Is a Dead End for Progressive Thought," *Socialist Review* 25(2):83–119.

References

Ericson, Richard and Aaron Doyle. 1999. "Globalization and the Policing of Protest: The Case of APEC 1997," *British Journal of Sociology* 50(4):589–608.

Escobar, Arturo. 1995. *Encountering Development: The Making and Unmaking of the Third World*. Princeton: Princeton University Press.

Esping-Anderson, Gøsta. 1990. *The Three Worlds of Welfare Capitalism*. Cambridge: Polity.

Esty, Daniel. 1994. *Greening the GATT: Trade, Environment, and the Future*. Washington, DC: Institute for International Economics.

Esty, Daniel and Damien Geradin (eds.). 2000. *Regulatory Competition and Economic Integration*. New York: Oxford University Press.

"EU: Anti-Globalization Movement Prepares for Genoa Summit." 2001. Agence France Presse, July 11, www.corpwatch.org/news/PND.jsp?articleid=64 [18 February 2002].

FAIR (Fairness & Accuracy in Reporting). 2001. "Police Violence at Genoa – Par for the Course? Media Complacency Helps Normalize Assaults on Demonstrators." Action Alert, July 26, www.fair.org/activism/genoa.html [18 February 2002].

Fairclough, Norman. 1994. *Discourse and Social Change*. Boston: Polity.

Falk, Richard. 1995. *On Humane Governance: Toward a New Global Politics*. Cambridge: Polity.

1999. *Predatory Globalization: A Critique*. Cambridge: Polity.

Farr, Vanessa. 2003. "The Importance of a Gender Perspective to Successful Disarmament, Demobilization, and Reintegration Processes," *Disarmament Forum* 4:25–35.

Fearon, James D. 1998. "Bargaining, Enforcement, and International Cooperation," *International Organization* 52:269–305.

Fehr, Ernst and Simon Gachter. 2000. "Fairness and Retaliation: The Economics of Reciprocity," *Journal of Economic Perspectives* 14(3):159–81.

Ferguson, James. 1994. *The Anti-Politics Machine*. Minneapolis: University of Minnesota Press.

Final Record of the Diplomatic Conference of Geneva. 1949. Vol. IIB.

Finger, J. M., Reincke, U. and Castro, U. 1999. "Market Access Bargaining in the Uruguay Round: Rigid or Relaxed Reciprocity?," World Bank Working Paper 2258. Washington, DC: World Bank.

Finnegan, William. 2002. "Leasing the Rain." *New Yorker*, April 8, www.newyorker.com/fact/content/?020408fa_FACT1.

Finnemore, Martha. 1996. *National Interests in International Society*. Ithaca: Cornell University Press.

2003. *The Purpose of Intervention: Changing Beliefs About the Use of Force*. Ithaca: Cornell University Press.

Finnemore, Martha and Kathryn Sikkink. 1998. "International Norm Dynamics and Political Change." *International Organization* 52(4):887–917.

Fish, Stanley. 1980. *Is There a Text in This Class? The Authority of Interpretive Communities*. Cambridge, MA: Harvard University Press.

328

1982. "Working on the Chain Gang: Interpretation in Law and Literature." *Texas Law Review* 60:551–67.

1989. *Doing What Comes Naturally*. Durham: Duke University Press.

Fisher, William. 1997. "Doing Good? The Politics and Antipolitics of NGO Practices," *Annual Review of Anthropology* 26:439–64.

Fisher, William and Thomas Ponniah. 2003. *Another World Is Possible*. London: Zed Books.

Florini, Ann (ed.). 2000. *The Third Force: The Rise of Transnational Civil Society*. Washington, DC: Carnegie Endowment.

Forsythe, David P. 1997. *Humanitarian Politics: The International Committee of the Red Cross*. Baltimore: Johns Hopkins University Press.

Foucault, Michel. 1970. *The Order of Things: An Archeology of the Human Sciences*. New York: Pantheon.

1980. *Power/Knowledge*. Trans. by Colin Gordon. New York: Pantheon.

1983. "Afterword: The Subject and Power." In H. Dreyfus and P. Rabinow (eds.), *Michel Foucault: Beyond Structuralism and Hermeneutics*, 2nd edn., pp. 202–20. Chicago: University of Chicago Press.

1984. "The Juridical Apparatus." In William Connolly (ed.), *Legitimacy and the State*, pp. 201–22. New York: New York University Press.

1991. "Governmentality." In G. Burchell, C. Gordon, and P. Miller (eds.), *The Foucault Effect: Studies in Governmentality*, pp. 87–104. Chicago: University of Chicago Press.

1995. *Discipline and Punish: The Birth of the Prison*. New York: Vintage.

1997. "Polemics, Politics, and Problematizations: An Interview with Michel Foucault." In Paul Rabinow (ed.), *Ethics: Subjectivity and Truth*, pp. 111–19. Trans. by Robert Hurley et al. New York: New Press.

2000. "The Subject and the Power." In James Faubion (ed.), *Michel Foucault: Power*, pp. 326–48. New York: New Press.

Fox, Jonathan A. 2000. "The World Bank Inspection Panel: Lessons from the First Five Years," *Global Governance* 6(3):279–318.

Franck, Thomas M. 1990. *The Power of Legitimacy Among Nations*. New York: Oxford University Press.

1995. *Fairness in International Law and Institutions*. New York: Oxford University Press.

Frank, D. 1999. *Buy American: The Untold Story of Economic Nationalism*. Boston: Beacon Press.

Frank, Robert H. 1988. *Passions With Reason: The Strategic Role of the Emotions*. New York: W. W. Norton.

Fratianni, Michele and Jürgen von Hagen. 1992. *The European Monetary System and European Monetary Union*. Boulder: Westview.

Frieden, Jeffry A. 1994. "Making Commitments: France and Italy in the European Monetary System, 1979–1985." In B. Eichengreen and J. A. Frieden (eds.), *The Political Economy of European Monetary Unification*, pp. 25–46. Boulder: Westview.

References

Friedman, Milton. 1962. *Capitalism and Freedom*. Chicago: University of Chicago Press.

Friedman, Thomas. 1999. "Senseless in Seattle," *New York Times,* December 1, www.nytimes.com/library/opinion/friedman/120199frie.html.

Fung, Archon, Dana O'Rourke and Charles Sabel. 2001. "Realizing Labor Standards: How Transparency, Competition, and Sanctions Could Improve Working Conditions Worldwide," *Boston Review* 26(1) (February/March), bostonreview.mit.edu/BR26.1/fung.html [15 July 2002].

Furubotn, Eirik G. and Rudolf Richter. 1997. *Institutions and Economic Theory: The Contribution of the New Institutional Economics*. Ann Arbor: University of Michigan Press.

Galanter, Marc. 1974. "Why the 'Haves' Come Out Ahead: Speculations on the Limits of Legal Change," *Law and Society Review* 9:95–160.

Gallie, W. B. 1956. "Essentially Contested Concepts," *Proceedings of the Aristotelian Society* 56:167–98.

Gardam, Judith. 1992. "A Feminist Analysis of Certain Aspects of International Humanitarian Law," *Australian Year Book of International Law* 12:265–78.

1993. "Gender and Non-Combatant Immunity," *Transnational Law and Contemporary Problems* 3:345–70.

Gardam, Judith G. and Michelle J. Jarvis. 2000. "Women and Armed Conflict: The International Response to the Beijing Platform for Action," *Columbia Human Rights Law Review* 32(1):1–65.

2001. *Women, Armed Conflict, and International Law*. Boston: Kluwer Law International.

Garland, David. 2001. *The Culture of Control: Crime and Social Order in Contemporary Society*. Chicago: University of Chicago Press.

Garrett, Geoffrey. 1992. "International Cooperation and Institutional Choice: The European Community's Internal Market," *International Organization* 46:533–60.

Garrett, Geoffrey and Barry R. Weingast. 1993. "Ideas, Interests and Institutions: Constructing the EC's Internal Market." In J. Goldstein and R. O. Keohane (eds.), *Ideas and Foreign Policy: Beliefs, Institutions, and Political Change*, pp. 173–206. Ithaca: Cornell University Press.

Gaventa, John. 1980. *Power and Powerlessness: Quiescence and Rebellion in an Appalachian Valley*. Urbana: University of Illinois Press.

"Genoa G8 and the Aftermath." N.d. *Entremundos*, 2, www.entremundos.org/Newspaper/Archive/Issue2/GenoaG8.htm [18 February 2002].

Gentili, Alberico. 1612 [1933]. *De Jure Belli Libri Tres*. Translated by John C. Rolfe. Oxford, UK: Clarendon.

Ghose, Arundhati. 1997. "Negotiating the CTBT: India's Security Concerns and Nuclear Disarmament," *Journal of International Affairs* 51(1):239–61.

Giddens, Anthony. 1984. *The Constitution of Society: Outline of the Theory of Structuration*. Berkeley: University of California Press.

Gill, Lesley. 2000. *Teetering on the Rim: Global Restructuring, Daily Life, and the Armed Retreat of the Bolivian State*. New York: Columbia University Press.

Gill, Stephen. 1990. *American Hegemony and the Trilateral Commission*. Cambridge, UK: Cambridge University Press.

(ed.). 1993. *Gramsci. Historical Materialism and International Relations*. Cambridge, UK: Cambridge University Press.

1995. "Globalization, Market Civilization, and Disciplinary Neoliberalism," *Millennium* 24(3):399–423.

2000. "Toward a Postmodern Prince? The Battle in Seattle as a Moment in the New Politics of Globalization," *Millennium* 29(1):131–40.

2002. "Constitutionalizing Inequality and the Clash of Globalizations," *International Studies Review* 4(2):47–66.

Gill, Stephen and David Law. 1989. "Global Hegemony and the Structural Power of Capital," *International Studies Quarterly* 33(4):475–99.

Gilpin, Robert. 2002. "A Realist Perspective on International Governance." In D. Held and A. McGrew (eds.), *Governing Globalization: Power, Authority, and Governance*, pp. 237–48. New York: Polity.

Gire, François. 1998. "New Delhi Wished to Create the Irreversible," *Le Monde*, May 22, www.meadev.gov.in/govt/monde.htm.

Glennon, Michael. 2001. *Limits of Law, Prerogatives of Power: Interventionism After Kosovo*. New York: Palgrave Macmillan.

Globalization Challenge Initiative. 2002. "The Threat to Basic Services (Water, Health, and Education): The World Bank Group's Private Sector Development (PSD) Strategy." February 12. www.globalizaction.org/PSD.htm [21 February 2002].

Goldfield, Michael. 1997. *The Color of Politics*. New York: New Press.

Goldstein, Judith, Miles Kahler, Robert O. Keohane and Anne-Marie Slaughter. 2000. "Introduction: Legalization and World Politics," *International Organization* 54:385–89.

Gordenker, Leon and Thomas Weiss. 1996. "Pluralizing Global Governance: Analytical Approaches and Dimensions." In T. Weiss and L. Gordenker (eds.), *NGOs, the UN, and Global Governance*, pp. 17–47. Boulder: Lynne Rienner.

Gowan, Peter. 1999. *The Global Gamble: Washington's Faustian Bid for World Dominance*. London: Verso.

Graeber, David. 2002a. "The New Anarchists," *New Left Review* 13:61–73.

2002b. "Reinventing Democracy." *In These Times*, February 19.

Gramsci, A. 1971. *Selections from the Prison Notebooks*. New York: International Publishers.

Graz, Jean-Christophe. 2003. "How Powerful Are Transnational Elite Clubs? The Social Myth of the World Economic Forum," *New Political Economy* 8(3):321–40.

Gresser, Edward. 2002. "Toughest on the Poor," *Foreign Affairs* November/December:9–14.

References

Grieco, Joseph M. 1990. *Cooperation Among Nations: Europe, America, and Nontariff Barriers to Trade*. Ithaca: Cornell University Press.

1993. "Understanding the Problem of International Cooperation: The Limits of Neoliberal Institutionalism, and the Future of Realist Theory." In D. A. Baldwin (ed.), *Neorealism and Neoliberalism: The Contemporary Debate*, pp. 301–38. New York: Columbia University Press.

1997a. "Realist International Relations Theory and the Study of World Politics." In M. Doyle and G. J. Ikenberry (eds.), *The New Thinking in International Relations Theory*, pp. 163–201. Boulder: Westview.

1997b. "Systemic Sources of Variation in Regional Institutionalization in Western Europe, East Asia, and the Americas." In E. D. Mansfield and H. Milner (eds.), *The Political Economy of Regionalism*, pp. 164–87. New York: Columbia University Press.

Grotius, Hugo. 1625 [1925]. *De Jure Belli ac Pacis Libri Tres: The Laws of War and Peace*. Trans. by F. Kelsey. New York: Carnegie Endowment for International Peace.

Gruber, Lloyd. 2000. *Ruling the World: Power Politics and the Rise of Supranational Institutions*. Princeton: Princeton University Press.

2001. "Power Politics and the Free Trade Bandwagon," *Comparative Political Studies* 34(7):703–41.

Guma, Greg. 2001. "The Empire's Trade Clothes: Saying No to Corporate Tyranny in Quebec City and Beyond," *Toward Freedom: Online Magazine*, March, www.towardfreedom.com/mar01/showdown.htm [21 February 2002].

Guzman, Andrew. 2004. "Global Governance and the WTO," www.law.berkeley.edu//faculty/guzmana/publications.html.

Guzzini, Stefano. 1993. "Structural Power: The Limits of Neorealist Power Analysis," *International Organization* 47(3):443–78.

1998. *Realism in International Relations and International Political Economy*. New York: Routledge.

2000. "The Use and Misuse of Power Analysis in International Theory." In R. Palan (ed.), *Global Political Economy: Contemporary Theories*, pp. 53–66. London: Routledge.

Haas, Peter. 1992a. "Introduction: Epistemic Communities and International Policy Coordination," *International Organization* 46(1):1–35.

(ed.). 1992b. "Power, Knowledge, and International Policy Coordination." *International Organization* special issue 46(1).

Haas, Peter, Robert Keohane and Marc Levy (eds.). 1993. *Institutions for the Earth: Sources of Effective International Environmental Protection*. Cambridge, MA: MIT Press.

Habermas, Jürgen. 1979. *Communication and the Evolution of Society*. Trans. by Thomas McCarthy. Boston: Beacon Press.

1984. *The Theory of Communicative Action*, vol. I. Trans. by Thomas McCarthy. Boston: Beacon Press.

Hacking, Ian. 1999. *The Social Construction of What?* Cambridge, MA: Harvard University Press.

332

Haggard, Stephan. 1995. *Developing Nations and the Politics of Global Integration.* Washington, DC: Brookings Institution Press.

——— 1997. "Regionalism in Asia and the Americas." In E. D. Mansfield and H. V. Milner (eds.), *The Political Economy of Regionalism*, pp. 20–49. New York: Columbia University Press.

Haggenmacher, Peter. 1990. "Grotius and Gentili: A Reassessment of Thomas E. Hollands's Inaugural Lecture." In H. Bull, B. Kingsbury, and A. Roberts (eds.), *Hugo Grotius and International Relations*, pp. 133–76. Oxford: Clarendon Press.

Haglund, David and Allen Sens. 2000. "Kosovo and the Case of the (Not-So) Free Riders: Portugal, Belgium, Canada and Spain." In Schnabel and Thakur, 2000, pp. 181–200.

Hahnel, Robin. 1999. *Panic Rules.* Boston: South End.

Hall, Stuart. 1996. "The West and the Rest: Discourse and Power." In S. Hall, D. Held, D. Hubert, and K. Thompson (eds.), *Modernity*, pp. 184–227. Oxford: Blackwell.

Hall, Stuart, Chas Critcher, Tony Jefferson, John Clarke and Brian Roberts. 1978. *Policing the Crisis: Mugging, the State, and Law and Order.* London: Macmillan.

Handelman, Don. 1995. "Commentary on Heyman," *Current Anthropology* 36:280–1.

Hardt, Michael and Antonio Negri. 2000. *Empire.* Cambridge, MA: Harvard University Press.

——— 2001. "What the Protesters in Genoa Want," *New York Times*, July 20, p. A21.

Harrell-Bond, Barbara. 2002. "Can Humanitarian Work with Refugees Be Humane?," *Human Rights Quarterly* 24:51–85.

Harrison, Glenn W., Thomas F. Rutherford and David G. Tarr. 1995. "Quantifying the Uruguay Round." In W. Martin and L. A. Winters (eds.), *The Uruguay Round and Developing Countries*, pp. 216–52. Washington, DC: World Bank.

Hartz, Louis. 1948. *The Liberal Tradition in America.* New York: Harcourt Brace.

Haufler, Virginia. 2001. *Public Role for the Private Sector: Industry Self-Regulation in a Global Economy.* Washington, DC: Carnegie Endowment for International Peace.

Hay, Colin. 1997. "Divided by a Common Language: Political Theory and the Concept of Power," *Politics* 17(1):45–52.

Hay, Colin and David Marsh. 2000. *Demystifying Globalization.* London: Palgrave.

Hayes, Erin. 1999. "Seeds of Controversy." ABCNews.com, August 2, abcnews.go.com/onair/CloserLook/wnt990802_hayes_story.html [5 November 2002].

Hayward, Clarissa Rile. 2000. *De-Facing Power.* New York: Cambridge University Press.

Heisenberg, Dorothee. 1999. *The Mark of the Bundesbank: Germany's Role in European Monetary Cooperation.* Boulder: Lynne Rienner.

Held, David. 1995. *Democracy and Global Order: From the Modern State to Cosmopolitan Governance.* Stanford: Stanford University Press.

References

Held, David, Anthony McGrew, David Goldblatt, and Jonathan Perraton. 1999. *Global Transformations*. Cambridge: Polity.

Helleiner, Gerald K. 2001. "Markets, Politics and Globalization: Can the Global Economy Be Civilized?," *Journal of Human Development* 2(1) (January):27–46.

Henkin, Louis. 1979. *How Nations Behave: Law and Foreign Policy*, 2nd edn. New York: Columbia University Press.

Henkin, Louis, Ruth Wedgewood, Jonathan Charney, Christine Chinkin, Richard Falk, Thomas Franck and W. Michael Riesman. 1999. "Editorial Comments: NATO's Kosovo Intervention," *American Journal of International Law* 93:824–62.

Herbert, Steve. 1999. "The End of the Territorially Sovereign State? The Case of Crime Control in the United States," *Political Geography* 18(2):149–72.

Herzfeld, Michael. 1993. *The Social Production of Indifference*. Chicago: University of Chicago Press.

Hewson, Martin and Timothy Sinclair. 1999. "The Emergence of Global Governance Theory." In M. Hewson and T. Sinclair (eds.), *Approaches to Global Governance Theory*, pp. 3–22. Albany: SUNY Press.

Higonnet, Margaret R., et al. 1987. *Behind the Lines: Gender and the Two World Wars*. New Haven: Yale University Press.

Hirschman, Albert O. 1945. *National Power and the Structure of Foreign Trade*. Berkeley: University of California Press.

Hirst, Paul. 1998. "Power." In T. Dunne, et al., (ed.), *The Eighty Years' Crisis: International Relations, 1919–1999*, pp. 133–48. New York: Cambridge University Press.

Hollingdale, Michael. 2001 "NGOs Threaten Forum Withdrawal," *SwissInfo*, January 28, www.swissinfo.org.

Howse, Robert. 2001. "The Legitimacy of the World Trade Organization." In Coicaud and Heiskanen, 2001, pp. 355–407.

Howse, Robert and Donald Regan. 2000. "The Product/Process Distinction: An Illusory Basis for Disciplining 'Unilateralism' in Trade Policy," *European Journal of International Law* 11:249–89.

Hsiao, Andrew. 2001. "Color Blind." In Yuen, Katsiaficas, and Rose, 2001, pp. 343–45.

Hudec, Robert. 2000. "Broadening the Scope of Remedies in WTO Dispute Settlement." In F. Weiss (ed.), *Improving WTO Dispute Settlement Procedures: Issues and Lessons from the Practice of Other International Courts and Tribunals*, pp. 345–76. London: Cameron May.

Hurrell, Andrew. 1993. "International Society and the Study of Regimes: A Reflective Approach." In V. Rittberger (ed.), *Regime Theory and International Relations*, pp. 49–72. New York: Oxford University Press.

Hurrell, Andrew and Ngaire Woods (eds). 1999. *Inequality, Globalization, and World Politics*. Oxford: Oxford University Press.

ICTSD (International Centre for Trade and Sustainable Development). 2003. *Bridges Daily Update on the Fifth Ministerial Conference* 6(15), September 15.

Ignatieff, Michael. 1998. *The Warrior's Honor*. New York: Henry Holt.

Ikenberry, G. John. 2001a. *After Victory: Institutions, Strategic Restraint, and the Rebuilding of Order After Major Wars.* Princeton: Princeton University Press.
2001b. "American Grand Strategy in the Age of Terror," *Survival* 43(4):19–34.
2002. "America's Imperial Ambition," *Foreign Affairs* September/October: 44–60.

Ikenberry, G. John and Charles A. Kupchan. 1990. "Socialization and Hegemonic Power," *International Organization* 44(3):283–315.

ILEAP (International Lawyers and Economists Against Poverty). 2001. "Draft Statement of Mission and Principles." Toronto, November.

IMC Global. 2001. Independent Print Media Center, November 28, print. indymedia.org/front.php3?article_id+1047&group=webcast [21 February 2002].

IMF (International Monetary Fund). 2002. "The IMF and Good Governance: A Factsheet," IMF website posted August 31 at www.imf.org/external/np/exr/facts/gov.htm.

Iriye, Akira. 2002. *Global Community: The Role of International Organizations in the Making of the Contemporary World.* Berkeley: University of California Press.

Isaac, Jeffrey. 1987. *Power and Marxist Theory: A Realist View.* Ithaca: Cornell University Press.

Jacobs, Andrew. 2002. "Simple, if Radical, Agendas Lead Thousands to Protest," *New York Times*, February 3, p. 17.

Jacobson, Harold. 1979. *Networks of Interdependence: International Organizations and the Global Political System.* New York: Alfred A. Knopf.

Jayasuriya, Kanishka. 2001. "Globalization, Sovereignty, and the Rule of Law: From Political to Economic Constitutionalism?," *Constellations* 8(4): 442–60.

Johnston, Les. 2000. *Policing Britain: Risk, Security, and Governance.* Harlow: Longman.

Johnstone, Ian. 2003. "Security Council Deliberations: The Power of the Better Argument," *European Journal of International Law* 14(3):437–80.

Jones, Trevor and Tim Newburn. 2002. "The Transformation of Policing? Understanding Current Trends in Policing Systems," *British Journal of Criminology* 42(1):129–46.

Juergensmeyer, Mark. 2000. *Terror in the Mind of God: The Global Rise of Religious Violence.* Berkeley: University of California Press.

Kahler, Miles. 1993. "Multilateralism with Small and Large Numbers." In John Ruggie (ed.), *Multilateralism Matters: The Theory and Praxis of an Institutional Form.* New York: Columbia University Press.
1995. *International Institutions and the Political Economy of Integration.* Washington, DC: Brookings Institution Press.
2000. "Conclusion: The Causes and Consequences of Legalization," *International Organization* 54:661–83.

Kaldor, Mary. 1999. "Transnational Civil Society." In T. Dunne and N. Wheeler (eds.), *Human Rights in Global Politics*, pp. 195–213. Cambridge, UK: Cambridge University Press.

Kaltenthaler, Karl. 1998. *Germany and the Politics of Europe's Money*. Durham: Duke University Press.

Kamel, Rachael and Anya Hoffman (eds.). 1999. *The Maquiladora Reader*. Philadelphia: American Friends Service Committee.

Karawan, Ibrahim. 2000. "The Muslim World: Uneasy Ambivalence." In Schnabel and Thakur, 2000, pp. 215–44.

Karliner, Joshua. 1997. *The Corporate Planet*. San Francisco: Sierra Club Books.

Katsiaficas, George. 2001. "Seattle Was Not the Beginning." In Yuen, Katsiaficas, and Rose, 2001, pp. 29–36.

Katzenstein, Peter (ed.). 1996. *The Culture of National Security*. New York: Columbia University Press.

Keck, Margaret E. and Kathryn Sikkink. 1998. *Activists Beyond Borders: Advocacy Networks in International Politics*. Ithaca: Cornell University Press.

Kendall, Gavin and Gary Wickham. 1999. *Using Foucault's Methods*. Thousand Oaks, CA: Sage.

Kennedy, David. 1994. "A New World Order: Yesterday, Today, and Tomorrow," *Transnational Law and Contemporary Problems* 4(4):1–47.

1998. "A New World Order: Yesterday, Today, and Tomorrow," *Transnational Law and Contemporary Problems* 4(4):1–47.

Keohane, Robert O. 1984. *After Hegemony: Cooperation and Discord in the World Political Economy*. Princeton: Princeton University Press.

1986. "Reciprocity in International Relations," *International Organization* 40(1):1–27.

1989. "Closing the Fairness–Practice Gap," *Ethics and International Affairs* 3:101–16.

1990. "International Liberalism Reconsidered." In J. Dunn (ed.), *The Economic Limits to Modern Politics*, pp. 165–94. New York: Cambridge University Press.

1997. "International Relations and International Law: Two Optics," *Harvard International Law Journal* 38: 487–502.

2001. "Governance in a Partially Globalized World," *American Political Science Review* 95(1):1–14.

2002a. "Accountability and Global Governance." Unpublished manuscript, February.

2002b. *Power and Governance in a Partially Globalized World*. London and New York: Routledge.

Keohane, Robert and Joseph Nye. 1977. *Power and Interdependence*. Boston: Little, Brown.

2000a. "Introduction." In J. Nye and J. Donahue (eds.), *Governance in a Globalizing World*, pp. 1–44. Washington, DC: Brookings Institution Press.

2000b. *Power and Interdependence*. 3rd edn. New York: Longman.

2001. "The Club Model of Multilateral Cooperation and Problems of Democratic Legitimacy." In R. Porter, et al. (eds.), *Efficiency, Equity, and Legitimacy: The Multilateral Trading System at the Millennium*, pp. 264–94. Washington, DC: Brookings Institution Press.

Kingsbury, Benedict and Adam Roberts. 1990. "Introduction: Grotian Thought in International Relations." In H. Bull, B. Kingsbury, and A. Roberts (eds.), *Hugo Grotius and International Relations*. Oxford: Clarendon Press, pp. 1–64.

Klabbers, Jan. 2001. "Changing Image of International Organizations." In Coicaud and Heiskanen, 2001, pp. 221–55.

Klein, Naomi. 1999. *No Logo*. New York: Picador.

2001a. "Reclaiming the Commons," *New Left Review* 9:81–89.

2001b. "The Vision Thing." In Yuen, Katsiaficas, and Rose, 2001, pp. 311–18. Reprinted from *The Nation*, June 10, 2000.

Knight, W. Andy, S. Neil MacFarlane, and Thomas G. Weiss. 2001. "What Is Our Niche?," *Global Governance* 7(1):1–9.

Knorr, Klaus. 1973. *Power and Wealth: The Political Economy of International Power*. New York: Basic Books.

Koh, Harold. 1997. "Why Do Nations Obey International Law?," *Yale Law Journal* 106:2599–2659.

Komesar, Neil. 1995. *Imperfect Alternatives: Choosing Institutions in Law, Economics and Public Policy*. Chicago: University of Chicago Press.

2002. *Law's Limits: The Rule of Law and the Supply and Demand of Rights*. New York: Cambridge University Press.

Koremenos, Barbara. 2001. "Loosening the Ties that Bind: A Learning Model of Agreement Flexibility," *International Organization* 55(2):289–325.

Koremenos, Barbara, Charles Lipson and Duncan Snidal. 2001. "The Rational Design of International Institutions," *International Organization* 55(4): 761–99.

Koreniewicz, Roberto Patricio and William C. Smith. Forthcoming. "Transnational Social Movements, Elite Projects, and Collective Action from Below in the Americas." In L. Fawcett and M. Serrano (eds.), *Regionalism and Governance in the Americas*. New York: Palgrave.

Koskenniemi, Martti. 1989. *From Apology to Utopia*. London: Coronet Books.

2002. *The Gentle Civilizer of Nations: The Rise and Fall of International Law, 1870–1960*. New York: Cambridge University Press.

Krasner, Stephen D. 1985. *Structural Conflict: The Third World Against Global Liberalism*. Berkeley: University of California Press.

1991. "Global Communications and National Power: Life on the Pareto Frontier," *World Politics* 43:336–66.

Kratochwil, Friedrich. 1989. *Rules, Norms and Decisions: On the Conditions of Practical and Legal Reasoning in International Affairs*. New York: Cambridge University Press.

2000. "How do Norms Matter?" In Byers, 2000, pp. 35–68.

Kreps, David. 1990. "Corporate Culture and Economic Theory." In J. E. Alt and K. A. Shepsle (eds.), *Perspectives on Positive Political Economy*, pp. 90–143. Cambridge, MA: Harvard University Press.

Krisch, Nico. 2003. "More Equal than the Rest? Hierarchy, Equality and US Predominance in International Law." In M. Byers and G. Nolte (eds.), *United*

States Hegemony and the Foundations of International Law, pp. 135–75. Oxford, UK: Oxford University Press.

Kritsiotis, Dino. 2000. "The Kosovo Crisis and NATO's Application of Armed Force Against the Federal Republic of Yugoslavia," *International and Comparative Law Quarterly* 49 (April): 330–59.

Kruse, Thomas. 2001. "Bolivia Under Martial Law," April 8, www.coli.unib.de/p̂ietsch/stop-war/PineSGI4101000410113764102381 1-100000.html [20 February 2002].

2002. "Bechtel Versus Bolivia: The Next Battle in the 'Water War,'" Public Citizen, www.citizen.org/cmep/Water/cmep_Water/reports/bolivia/articles.cfm?ID=8114 [2 November 2002].

Kunz, Josef L. 1999. "The Chaotic Status of the Laws of War." In J. Gardam (ed.), *Humanitarian Law*. Dartmouth: Ashgate.

Kurtz, Stanley. 2003. "Democratic Imperialism: A Blueprint," *Policy Review* 118, www.policyreview.org/apr03/kurtz_print.html.

Kydland, Finn E. and Edward C. Prescott. 1977. "Rules Rather than Discretion: The Inconsistency of Optimal Plans," *Journal of Political Economy* 85:473–91.

LaBotz, Dan. 2000. "Moving for Global Justice," *Against the Current*, www.igc.org/solidarity/atc.

Lacher, Hannes. 2002. "Making Sense of the International System: The Promises and Pitfalls of the Newest Marxist Theories of International Relations." In Rupert and Smith, 2002, pp. 147–64.

Lake, David A. 1999a. *Entangling Relations: American Foreign Policy in Its Century*. Princeton: Princeton University Press.

1999b. "Global Governance: A Relational Contracting Approach." In A. Prakash and J. Hart (eds.), *Globalization and Governance*, pp. 31–53. New York: Routledge.

Lasswell, Harold. 1936. *Politics: Who Gets What, When, How*. New York: P. Smith.

Lasswell, Harold and Abraham Kaplan. 1950. *Power and Society: A Framework for Political Inquiry*. New Haven: Yale University Press.

Latham, Robert. 1999. "Politics in a Floating World." In M. Hewson and T. Sinclair (eds.), *Approaches to Global Governance Theory*, pp. 23–53. Albany: SUNY Press.

Lawrence, Robert. 2003. *Crimes and Punishments: An Analysis of Retaliation Under the WTO*. Washington, DC: Institute of International Economics.

Legro, Jeff. 1997. "Which Norms Matter? Revisiting the 'Failure' of Internationalism," *International Organization* 51(1):31–64.

Lemann, Nicholas. 2002. "The Next World Order," *New Yorker*, April 1:42–48.

Lincoln, Bruce. 1994. *Authority: Construction and Corrosion*. Chicago: University of Chicago Press.

Lindsey, Charlotte. 2001. *Women Facing War: ICRC Study on the Impact of Armed Conflict on Women*. Geneva: International Committee of the Red Cross.

Lipietz, Alain. 1989. *Towards a New Economic Order: Post-Fordism, Ecology and Democracy*. Cambridge: Polity.

Lipschutz, Ronnie. 1989. *When Nations Clash: Raw Materials, Ideology and Foreign Policy*. New York: Ballinger/Harper & Row.

2000. *After Authority: War, Peace, and Global Politics in the Twenty-First Century*. Albany: SUNY Press.

2001. "Who You Callin' 'Hegemonic'? Or, What Kind of Democracy Do You Want With Those Markets?" Paper presented at 2001 Hong Kong Convention of International Studies, July 26–28, 2001, Hong Kong.

2002. "Doing Well by Doing Good? Transnational Regulatory Campaigns, Social Activism, and Impacts on State Sovereignty." In J. Montgomery and N. Glazer (eds.), *Challenges to Sovereignty: How Governments Respond*, pp. 291–320. New Brunswick, NJ: Transaction.

2003a. *Global Environmental Politics: Power, Perspectives and Practice*. Washington, DC: CQ Press.

2003b. "Regulation for the Rest of Us? Global Social Activism, Corporate Citizenship, and the Disappearance of the Political," University of California eScholarship Repository, repositories.cdlib.org/cgirs/CGIRS-2003-1/.

2004a. "Constituting Political Community: Globalization, Citizenship, and Human Rights." In A. Brysk and G. Shafir (eds.), *People out of Place*, pp. 29–52. London: Routledge.

2004b. "Sweating It Out: NGO Campaigns and Trade Union Empowerment," *Development in Practice*, February, 197–209.

Lipschutz, Ronnie with J. Mayer. 1996. *Global Civil Society and Global Environmental Governance: The Politics of Nature from Place to Planet*. Albany: SUNY Press.

Lipschutz, Ronnie with James K. Rowe. Forthcoming. *Regulation for the Rest of Us? Globalization, Governmentality, and Global Politics*. London: Routledge.

Lose, Lars. 2001. "Communicative Action and the World of Diplomacy." In K. Fierke and K. E. Jorgensen (eds.), *Constructing International Relations: The Next Generation*, pp. 179–201. Armonk, NY: M. E. Sharpe.

Ludlow, Peter. 1982. *The Making of the European Monetary System*. London: Butterworth.

Luhmann, Niklas. 1989. *Ecological Communication*. Cambridge: Polity.

Lukes, Steven. 1974. *Power: A Radical View*. Houndmills: Macmillan Education.

Macdonell, Diane. 1984. *Theories of Discourse: An Introduction*. Boston: Blackwell.

MacEwan, Arthur. 1999. *Neoliberalism or Democracy?* London: Zed Books.

Macey, Jonathan. 2003. "Regulatory Globalization as a Response to Regulatory Competition," *Emory Law Journal* 52:1353–79.

MacIntyre, Alisdair. 1985. *Whose Justice? Whose Rationality?* London: Duckworth.

Maitland, Alison. 2002. "Companies Pledge Better Corporate Citizenship," *Financial Times*, February 4.

Malcolm, Noel. 2003. "Hobbes' Theory of International Relations." In N. Malcolm (ed.), *Aspects of Hobbes*, pp. 432–56. Oxford, UK: Oxford University Press.

References

Mallaby, Sebastian. 2002a. "Mbeki and Wolfensohn Are in Consensus," *International Herald Tribune*, September 24 (originally printed in *Washington Post*, September 24).

2002b. "The Reluctant Imperialist: Terrorism, Failed States, and the Case for American Empire," *Foreign Affairs* March/April:2–7.

Manning, Peter K. 2000. "Policing New Social Spaces." In J. W. E. Sheptycki (ed.), *Issues in Transnational Policing*, pp. 177–200. London and New York: Routledge.

Mansbach, Richard W. and John A. Vasquez. 1981. *In Search of Theory: A New Paradigm for Global Politics*. New York: Columbia University Press.

Martin, Lisa L. 1992a. *Coercive Cooperation: Explaining Multilateral Economic Sanctions*. Princeton: Princeton University Press.

1992b. "Interests, Power, and Multilateralism," *International Organization* 46:765–92.

Martinez, E. 2000. "Where Was the Color in Seattle?" In K. Danaher and R. Burbach (eds.), *Globalize This!*, pp. 74–81. Monroe, ME: Common Courage Press.

Marx, Karl. 1977. *Capital*, vol. I. New York: Vintage.

Maskus, Keith. 2000. "Intellectual Property Issues for the New Round." In J. Schott (ed.), *The WTO After Seattle*, pp. 137–58. Washington, DC: Institute for International Economics.

Mastanduno, Michael. 1999. "Preserving the Unipolar Moment: Realist Theories and US Grand Strategy After the Cold War." In E. Kapstein and M. Mastanduno (eds.), *Unipolar Politics: Realism and State Strategies After the Cold War*, pp. 138–81. New York: Columbia University Press.

Matheson, Michael. 2000. "Justification for the NATO Air Campaign in Kosovo," *Proceedings of the 94th Annual Conference of the American Society of International Law*, p. 301.

May, Elaine Tyler. 1998. *Homeward Bound: American Families in the Cold War Era*. New York: Basic Books.

McAdam, Doug, John D. McCarthy and Meyer N. Zald. 1996. *Comparative Perspectives on Social Movements: Political Opportunities, Mobilizing Structures, and Cultural Framings*. Cambridge, UK: Cambridge University Press.

McCahery, Joseph, William Bratton, Sol Piocciotto, Colin Scott (eds.). 1996. *International Regulatory Competition and Coordination*. Oxford and New York: Clarendon Press and Oxford University Press.

McCalla, Robert B. 1996. "NATO's Persistence After the Cold War," *International Organization* 50(3)(Summer): 445–75.

McCulloch, Neil, L. Alan Winters and Xavier Cirera. 2001. *Trade Liberalization and Poverty: A Handbook*. London: Center for Economic Policy Research.

McDougal, Myres and Harold Lasswell. 1959. "The Identification and Appraisal of Diverse Systems of Public Order," *American Journal of International Law* 53:1–29.

McGinnis, John and Mark Movsiean. 2000. "The World Trade Constitution: Reinforcing Democracy Through Trade," *Harvard Law Review* 114:511–606.

McLean, Charles. 2001. "The Case for Davos," *International Herald Tribune*, February 13.

McMichael, Philip. 1997. "Rethinking Globalization: The Agrarian Question Revisited," *Review of International Political Economy* 4(4):630–62.

McNamara, Kathleen R. 1998. *The Currency of Ideas: Monetary Politics in the European Union*. Ithaca: Cornell University Press.

Mearsheimer, John J. 1994–95. "The False Promise of International Institutions," *International Security* 19:5–49.

2001. *The Tragedy of Great Power Politics*. New York: Norton.

Melitz, Jacques. 1988. "Monetary Discipline and Cooperation in the European Monetary System: A Synthesis." In F. Giavazzi, S. Micossi and M. Miller (eds.), *The European Monetary System*, pp. 51–79. Cambridge, UK: Cambridge University Press.

Memorandum of Understanding on the Conservation and Management of Marine Turtles and Their Habitats of the Indian Ocean and South-East Asia. 2001. www.wcmc.org.uk/cms/.

Meron, Theodor. 1998. *War Crimes Law Comes of Age: Essays*. Oxford: Clarendon Press and New York: Oxford University Press.

Milgrom, Paul R., Douglass C. North and Barry R. Weingast. 1990. "The Role of Institutions in the Revival of Trade: The Medieval Law Merchant, Private Judges, and the Champagne Fairs," *Economics and Politics* 2:1–23.

Milgrom, Paul and John Roberts. 1992. *Economics, Organization and Management*. Englewood Cliffs, NJ: Prentice-Hall.

Mitchell, Ronald B. 1994. *Intentional Oil Pollution at Sea: Environmental Policy and Treaty Compliance*. Cambridge, MA: MIT Press.

Mitrany, David. 1966. *A Working Peace System*. Chicago: Quadrangle Books.

Mittal, Anuradha and Peter Rosset. 2001. "Genetic Engineering and the Privatization of Seeds," *Dollars and Sense Magazine* March/April, www.thirdworldtraveler.com/Transnational_corps/GE_ Privatization_Seeds.html [25 February 2002].

Moody, Kim. 2000. "Global Capital and Economic Nationalism," *Against the Current*, www.igc.org/solidarity/atc/87Moody.html.

Moore, Mike. 2001. "Promoting Openness, Fairness and Predictability in International Trade for the Benefit of Humanity." Speech to the Inter-Parliamentary Union meeting on international trade, Geneva, June 8, www.wto.org/wto/english/news_e/spmm_e/spmm64_e.htm [5 July 2001].

Moravcsik, Andrew. 1998. *The Choice for Europe: Social Purpose and State Power from Messina to Maastricht*. Ithaca: Cornell University Press.

Morrow, James D. 1994. "Modeling the Forms of International Cooperation: Distribution Versus Information," *International Organization* 48:387–423.

Mouffe, Chantal. 2000. *The Democratic Paradox*. London: Verso.

Murphy, Craig. 1984. *Emergence of the NIEO Ideology*. Boulder: Westview.

References

1994. *International Organizations and Industrial Change*. New York: Oxford University Press.

Mydans, Seth. 2000. "National Pride over a Virus in the Philippines," *New York Times*, May 12, p. C1.

Neumann, Iver. 1999. *Uses of the Other: "The East" in European Identity Formation*. Minneapolis: University of Minnesota Press.

Neumann, Iver and Jennifer Welsh. 1991. "The Other in European Self-Definition: An Addendum to the Literature on International Society," *Review of International Studies* 17:327–48.

Newman, Robert. 2000. "When the Death Star of the WTO Exploded with the Protests in Seattle, GATS was the Hatch-Pod in Which Darth Vader Made His Escape," *Guardian*, November 11, access.lowtech.org/freepeople/gats.html [20 February 2002].

Nichols, Philip. 1996. "Trade Without Values," *Northwestern University Law Review* 90:658–719.

Nurick, Lester. 1945. "The Distinction Between Combatant and Noncombatant in the Law of War," *American Journal of International Law* 39(4):680–97.

Nye, Joseph. 1990. "Soft Power." *Foreign Policy* 80 (Fall):153–71.

2002. *The Paradox of American Power: Why the World's Only Superpower Can't Go It Alone*. New York: Oxford University Press.

2004. *Soft Power: The Means to Success in World Politics*. New York: Public Affairs.

Oatley, Thomas. 1997. *Monetary Politics: Exchange Rate Cooperation in the European Union*. Ann Arbor: University of Michigan Press.

Oatley, Thomas and Robert Nabors. 1998. "Redistributive Cooperation: Market Failure, Wealth Transfers, and the Basle Accord," *International Organization* 52:35–54.

OECD (Organization for Economic Cooperation and Development). 1973. *OECD: History, Aims, Structure*, 2nd edn. Paris: OECD.

Ohmae, Kenichi. 1990. *The Borderless World: Power and Strategy in the Interlinked Economy*. London: Collins.

Olson, Mancur. 1965. *The Logic of Collective Action: Public Goods and the Theory of Groups*. Cambridge, MA: Harvard University Press.

O'Malley, Patrick and D. Palmer. 1996. "Post-Keynesian Policing," *Economy and Society* 25(2):137–55.

Onuma, Yasuaki. 1993. "On War." In Yasuaki Onuma (ed.), *A Normative Approach to War: Peace, War, and Justice in Hugo Grotius*. Oxford: Clarendon Press and New York: Oxford University Press.

Ostry, Sylvia. 2002. "The Uruguay Round North–South Grand Bargain, Implications for Future Negotiations." In D. Kennedy and J. Southwick (eds.), *The Political Economy of International Trade Law: Essays in Honor of Robert E. Hudec*, pp. 285–300. New York: Cambridge University Press.

Oye, Kenneth A. 1986. "Explaining Cooperation Under Anarchy: Hypotheses and Strategies." In K. A. Oye (ed.), *Cooperation Under Anarchy*, pp. 1–24. Princeton: Princeton University Press.

Packenham, Robert. 1973. *Liberal America and the Third World*. Princeton: Princeton University Press.

Padoa-Schioppa, Tommaso. 1986. "Lessons from the EMS." Lecture at the European University Institute, February 20. Reprinted in Banca d'Italia, *Economic Bulletin* 2.

Palast, Greg. 2001. "The World Bank's Former Chief Economist's Accusations Are Eye-Popping – Including How the IMF and US Treasury Fixed the Russian Elections," *Observer* (UK), October 10. www.globalexchange. org/wbimf/observer101001.html [20 February 2002].

Panitch, Leo. 1996. "Rethinking the Role of the State." In J. H. Mittelman (ed.), *Globalization: Critical Reflections*, pp. 83–116. Boulder: Lynne Rienner.

Paris, Roland. 1997. "Peacebuilding and the Limits of Liberal Internationalism," *International Security* 22(2):54–89.

2002. "International Peacebuilding and the 'Mission Civilisatrice,'" *Review of International Studies* 28(4):637–56.

Parisi, Francesco and Nita Ghei. N.d. "The Role of Reciprocity in International Law." George Mason University Law and Economics Research Paper No. 02–08, www.law.gmu.edu/faculty/papers/docs/02–08.pdf.

Paulus, Andreas L. 2001. *Die Internationale Gemeinschaft im Volkerrecht*. Munich: Verlag C. H. Beck.

Peck, Jamie and Adam Tickell. 1994. "Searching for a New Institutional Fix: The *After*-Fordist Crisis and the Global–Local Disorder." In A. Amin (ed.), *Post-Fordism: A Reader*, pp. 280–315. Oxford, UK: Blackwell.

2002. "Neoliberalizing Space." In N. Brenner and N. Theodore (eds.), *Spaces of Neoliberalism: Urban Restructuring in North America and Western Europe*, pp. 33–57. Oxford, UK: Blackwell.

Petras, James and Morris Morley. 1990. *US Hegemony Under Siege: Class, Politics and Development in Latin America*. London: Verso.

Pettman, Jan Jindy. 1996. *Worlding Women*. London: Routledge.

Pierson, Paul. 2000. "Limits of Design: Explaining Institutional Origins and Change," *Governance* 13(4):475–99.

Polanyi, Karl, 2001. *The Great Transformation*, 2nd edn. Boston: Beacon Press.

Pollack, Mark A. 1997. "Delegation, Agency, and Agenda Setting in the European Community," *International Organization* 51:99–134.

2003. *Engines of Integration*. New York: Oxford University Press.

Portnoy, Brian. 1999. "Building the 'Missing Pillar'? Multilateralism, Extraterritoriality, and Cooperation in International Antitrust." Paper presented to CASPIC MacArthur Scholar's Conference, University of Chicago.

Posner, Theodore and Timothy Rief. 2000. "Homage to a Bull Moose: Applying Lessons of History to Meet the Challenges of Globalization," *Fordham International Law Journal* 24:481–518.

Postema, Gerald. 1987. "Protestant Interpretation and Social Practices," *Law and Philosophy* 6:283–319.

References

Prakash, Aseem and Jeffrey Hart. 1999. "Globalization and Governance: An Introduction." In A. Prakash and J. Hart (eds.), *Globalization and Governance*, pp. 2–11. New York: Routledge.

Price, Richard. 1998. "Reversing the Gun Sights: Transnational Civil Society Targets Land Mines," *International Organization* 52(3):575–612.

Pruzin, Daniel. 2003. "Three More Latin American Countries Defect from G-21 Alliance on Farm Trade," *International Trade Reporter* 20 (BNA) 1685, October 16.

Public Citizen/Global Trade Watch. 2002. *Davos World Economic Forum: Pricey Corporate Trade Association Loses Its Camouflage.* Washington, DC: Public Citizen.

Puchala, Donald J. and Raymond F. Hopkins. 1981. "International Regimes: Lessons from Inductive Analysis." In S. Krasner (ed.), *International Regimes*, pp. 61–91. Ithaca: Cornell University Press.

Raiffa, Howard. 1982. *The Art and Science of Negotiation.* Cambridge, MA: Harvard University Press.

Rajah, Colin. 2001. "Where Was the Color at A-16?" In Yuen, Katsiaficas, and Rose, 2001, pp. 237–40.

Rawls, John. 1971. *A Theory of Justice.* Cambridge, MA: Harvard University Press.

Raz, Joseph. 1990. "Introduction." In J. Raz (ed.), *Authority*, pp. 6–11. New York: Cambridge University Press.

Richardson, James L. 1997. "Contending Liberalisms: Past and Present," *European Journal of International Relations* 3(1):5–34.

Rieff, David. 1999. "A New Age of Liberal Imperialism," *World Policy Journal* 1(7) (Summer): 1–10.

Rights and Democracy. 2001. "Hughes Report: A Wake-up Call about Summit Policing." News Release, August 7, www.ichrdd.ca/english/commdoc/prelease/hughesReport.html [18 February 2002].

Riker, William H. 1980. "Implications from the Disequilibrium of Majority Rule for the Study of Institutions," *American Political Science Review* 74:432–46.

Risse, Thomas. 2000. "Let's Argue!: Communicative Action in World Politics," *International Organization* 54:1–39.

Roberts, Adam. 1999. "NATO's Humanitarian War," *Survival* 41(3):102–23.

Robinson, Ronald. 1972. "Non-European Foundations of European Imperialism: Sketch for a Theory of Collaboration." In R. Owen and B. Sutcliffe (eds.), *Studies in the Theory of Imperialism*, pp. 117–42. London: Longman.

Robinson, William and Jerry Harris. 2000. "Towards a Global Ruling Class," *Science and Society* 64(1):11–54.

Rosen, Ellen I. 2002. *Making Sweatshops: The Globalization of the US Apparel Industry.* Berkeley: University of California Press.

Rosenau, James. 1995. "Governance in the Twenty-First Century," *Global Governance* 1(1):13–43.

Rosenau, James N. and Ernst-Otto Czempiel (eds.). 1992. *Governance Without Government: Order and Change in World Politics.* Cambridge: Cambridge University Press.

Rosenberg, Justin. 1994. *The Empire of Civil Society*. London: Verso.

Rosenblad, Esbjorn. 1977. *International Humanitarian Law*. Geneva: Henry Dunant Institute.

Rosendorff, B. Peter and Helen V. Milner. 2001. "The Optimal Design of International Trade Institutions: Uncertainty and Escape," *International Organization* 55:829–57.

Ross, Andrew (ed.). 1997. *No Sweat*. London: Verso.

Rowe, Peter. 2000. "Maintaining Discipline in United Nations Peace Support Operations: The Legal Quagmire for Military Operations," *Journal of Conflict and Security Law* 5(1):45–62.

Roy, Arundhati. 1998. "The End of Imagination," *Frontline* (India), August 1–14, vol. XV, No. 16, www.flonnet.com/fl1516/15160040.htm. Page numbers are from the special publication of this essay by *Frontline* (India). Chennai: Kasturi and Sons.

Rubinstein, Ariel. 1982. "Perfect Equilibrium in a Bargaining Model," *Econometrica* 50:97–109.

Ruggie, John Gerard. 1975. "International Responses to Technology: Concepts and Trends," *International Organization* 29:557–83.

1982. "International Regimes, Transactions, and Change: Embedded Liberalism in the Postwar Economic Order," *International Organization* 36(2): 379–415.

1993. "Territoriality and Beyond: Problematizing Modernity in International Relations," *International Organization* 47:139–74.

Ruggie, John and Friedrich Kratochwil. 1986. "International Organization: A State of the Art on an Art of the State," *International Organization* 40(4): 753–76.

Rupert, Mark. 1995. *Producing Hegemony: The Politics of Mass Production and American Global Power*. Cambridge, UK: Cambridge University Press.

1998. "(Re)Engaging Gramsci," *Review of International Studies* 24:427–34.

2000. *Ideologies of Globalization: Contending Visions of a New World Order*. New York: Routledge.

2003. "Anti-Capitalist Convergence? Anarchism, Socialism and the Global Justice Movement." In M. Steger (ed.), *Rethinking Globalism*, pp. 121–35. Lanham, MD: Rowman & Littlefield.

Rupert, Mark and Hazel Smith (eds.). 2002. *Historical Materialism and Globalization*. New York: Routledge.

Russell, Bertrand. 1986. "The Forms of Power." In S. Lukes (ed.), *Power*, pp. 19–27. New York: New York University Press.

Russell, Sabin. 2003. "AIDS-Hit Nation to Battle Epidemic: South Africa Shifts to Ambitious Plan for Drug Distribution," *San Francisco Chronicle* November 20:1.

Russett, Bruce and John O'Neal. 2001. *Triangulating Peace: Democracy, Interdependence, and International Organizations*. New York: Norton.

Sampson, Gary. 2000. "Trade, Environment and the WTO: The Post-Seattle Agenda 24." Washington, DC, and Baltimore: Overseas Development Council and Johns Hopkins University Press.

Sandoz, Yves, Christophe Swinarski, and Bruno Zimmermann, eds. 1987. *Commentary on the Additional Protocols of 8 June 1977 to the Geneva Conventions of 12 August 1949*. Geneva: International Committee of the Red Cross and M. Nijhoff.

Sands, Philippe and Pierre Klein. 2000. *Bowett's Law of International Institutions*. 5th edn. London: Sweet & Maxwell.

Sanger, David. 2001. "A Grand Trade Bargain," *Foreign Affairs* 80(1):65–76.

Sarooshi, Danesh. 1999. *The United Nations and the Development of Collective Security: The Delegation by the UN Security Council of Its Chapter VII Powers*. New York: Oxford University Press.

Scarry, Elaine. 1985. *The Body in Pain: The Making and Unmaking of the World*. Oxford: Oxford University Press.

Schachter, Oscar. 1977. "The Invisible College of International Lawyers." *Northwestern Law Review* 72:217–26.

1989. *International Law in Theory and Practice*. Recueil des Cours, Hague Academy Lectures. Norwell, MA: M. Nijhoff.

Schama, Simon. 1997. *An Embarrassment of Riches: An Interpretation of Dutch Culture in the Golden Age*. New York: Vintage.

Schattschneider, E. E. 1960. *The Semi-Sovereign People: A Realist's View of Democracy in America*. New York: Holt, Rinehart and Winston.

Schein, Edgar. 1996. "Culture: The Missing Concept in Organization Studies," *Administrative Studies Quarterly* 41:229–40.

Schelling, Thomas. 1960. *The Strategy of Conflict*. Cambridge, MA: Harvard University Press.

Schnabel, A. and R. Thakur (eds.). 2000. *Kosovo and the Challenge of Humanitarian Intervention*. New York: United Nations University Press.

Scholte, Jan Aart. 1997. "The Globalization of World Politics." In J. Baylis and S. Smith (eds.), *The Globalization of World Politics: An Introduction to International Relations*, pp. 13–30. Oxford, UK: Oxford University Press.

Schwab, Klaus. 1999. "Finding the Right Balance: Opening Address to Annual Meeting." Davos, World Economic Forum. live99.weforum.org/opening_ksc.asp.

Schwab, Klaus and Claude Smadja. 1996. "Start Taking the Backlash Against Globalization Seriously," *International Herald Tribune*, February 1.

1999. "Globalization Needs a Human Face," *International Herald Tribune*, January 28.

Sciolino, Elaine. 2003. "'Pragmatic' Chirac Faces US Wrath," *New York Times*, April 25.

Scott, James C. 1998. *Seeing Like a State: How Certain Schemes to Improve the Human Conditions Have Failed*. New Haven: Yale University Press.

Scott, Joan Wallach. 1999. *Gender and the Politics of History*. Revised edn. New York: Columbia University Press.

Scott, John. 2001. *Power*. New York: Polity.

Searle, John. 1995. *The Construction of Social Reality*. New York: Free Press.

"Secretive 'Sirenes': Maintaining Public Order and State Security." 1996–97. Fortress Europe?, circular letter, December/January, www.fecl.org/circular/4904.htm [20 February 2002].

Sell, Susan. 2003. *Private Power, Public Law: The Globalization of Intellectual Property Rights*. New York: Cambridge University Press.

Sell, Susan and Prakash, Aseem. 2004. "Using Ideas Strategically: The Contest Between Business and NGO Networks in Intellectual Property Rights," *International Studies Quarterly* 48(1):143–75.

Sen, Amartya. 1992. *Inequality Reexamined*. Oxford, UK: Oxford University Press.

1999. *Development as Freedom*. New York: Alfred A. Knopf.

Sewell, James P. and Mark B. Salter. 1995. "Panarchy and Other Norms for Global Governance: Boutros-Ghali, Rosenau, and Beyond," *Global Governance* 1(4):373–82.

Shaffer, Gregory. 1999. "United States: Import Prohibition of Certain Shrimp and Shrimp Products," *American Journal of International Law* 93(2):507–14.

2000. "WTO Blue-Green Blues: The Impact of US Domestic Politics on Trade–Labor, Trade–Environment Linkages," *Fordham International Law Journal* 24 (November–December):608–51.

2001. "The World Trade Organization Under Challenge: Democracy and the Law and Politics of the WTO's Treatment of Trade and Environment Matters," *Harvard Environmental Law Review* 25:1–93.

2003a. *Defending Interests: Public–Private Partnerships in WTO Litigation*. Washington, DC: Brookings Institution Press.

2003b. "How to Make the WTO Dispute Settlement System Work for Developing Countries: Some Proactive Strategies," ICTSD, www.ictsd.org/pubs/ictsd_series/resource_papers/DSU_2003.pdf.

Shaw, Martin. 2000. *Theory of the Global State*. Cambridge, UK: Cambridge University Press.

Sheptycki, J. W. E. 2000. "The 'Drug War': Learning from the Paradigm Example of Transnational Policing." In J. W. E. Sheptycki (ed.), *Issues in Transnational Policing*, pp. 201–28. London: Routledge.

Shore, Cris and Susan Wright. 1997. "Policy: A New Field of Anthropology." In Cris Shore and Susan Wright (eds.), *Anthropology of Social Policy: Critical Perspectives on Governance and Power*, pp. 3–41. New York: Routledge.

Shultz, Jim. 2001. "An Open Letter to Mr. Riley Bechtel," December 18, www.globalizaction.org/Bechtel.htm [21 February 2002].

Simma, Bruno. 1999. "NATO, the UN and the Use of Force: Legal Aspects," *European Journal of International Law* 10(1):1–22.

Singh, Jaggi. 2001. "Resisting Global Capitalism in India." In Yuen, Katsiaficas, and Rose, 2001, pp. 47–52.

Singh, Jaswant. 1998. "Against Nuclear Apartheid," *Foreign Affairs* September/October:41–52.

Sklair, Leslie. 2001. *The Transnational Capitalist Class*. Oxford: Blackwell.

References

Slaughter, Anne Marie. 2000. "Governing Through Government Networks." In Byers, 2000, pp. 177–205.

Smith, Jay. 2003. "WTO Dispute Settlement: The Politics of Procedure in Appellate Body Rulings," *World Trade Review* 2(1):65–100.

Smith, Paul. 1997. *Millennial Dreams: Contemporary Culture and Capital in the North*. London: Verso.

Smith, Steve. 1996. "Positivism and Beyond." In S. Smith, K. Booth and M. Zalewski (eds.), *International Theory: Positivism and Beyond*, pp. 11–44. New York: Cambridge University Press.

Spaventa, Luigi. 1980. "Italy Joins the EMS: A Political History." Occasional paper no. 32, Johns Hopkins University, Bologna Center.

Starr, Paul. 1992. "Social Categories and Claims in the Liberal State." In M. Douglas and D. Hull (eds.), *How Classification Works: Nelson Goodman Among the Social Sciences*, pp. 154–79. Edinburgh: Edinburgh University Press.

State watch. 2001a. "Public Order Policing in Europe: Policy Backlash Expected." June, www.statewatch.org/news/2001/jun/publicorder.htm [18 February 2002].

——— 2001b. "The 'Enemy Within': EU Plans the Surveillance of Protestors and the Criminalization of Protests." August. www.statewatch.org/news/2001/aug/12poreport.htm [20 February 2002].

——— 2001c. "Proposal to Create EU Para-Military Police Units to Counter Protests." October, www.statewatch.org/news/2001/oct/01paramilitary.htm [19 February 2002].

Steger, Manfred. 2002. *Globalism: The New Market Ideology*. New York: Rowman & Littlefield.

Steinberg, Richard. 2002. "In the Shadow of Law or Power? Consensus-Based Bargaining and Outcomes in the GATT/WTO," *International Organization* 56(2):339–74.

Steiner, George. 1961. *The Death of Tragedy*. London: Faber and Faber.

Stiehm, Judith Hicks. 1982. "The Protected, the Protector, and the Defender," *Women's Studies International Forum* 5(3/4):367–76.

Stiglitz, Joseph E. 1998. "More Instruments and Broader Goals: Moving Toward the Post-Washington Consensus." World Institute for Development Economics Research, United Nations University, Annual Lecture 2, Helsinki, January 7.

——— 1999. "Whither Reform? Ten Years of the Transition." Keynote Address of the World Bank Annual Bank Conference on Development Economics, Washington, DC, April 28–30.

——— 2002a. "A Fair Deal for the World," *New York Review of Books*, 49 (May 23): 24–28.

——— 2002b. *Globalization and Its Discontents*. New York: W. W. Norton.

Stokes, Susan. 2001. *Mandates and Democracy: Neoliberalism by Surprise in Latin America*. Cambridge, UK: Cambridge University Press.

Suchman, Mark C. 1995. "Managing Legitimacy: Strategic and Institutional Approaches," *Academy of Management Review* 20:571–610.

Sunstein, Cass. 1996. *Legal Reasoning and Political Conflict*. New York: Oxford University Press.

Sutcliffe, Bob. 2001. *100 Ways of Seeing an Unequal World*. London: Zed Books.

Tabb, William K. 2001. *The Amoral Elephant: Globalization and the Struggle for Social Justice in the Twenty-First Century*. New York: Monthly Review.

Tarrow, Sidney. 1998. *Power in Movement: Social Movements and Contentious Politics*, 2nd edn. Cambridge, UK: Cambridge University Press.

Taylor, Ian. 1999. *Crime in Context: A Critical Criminology of Market Societies*. Cambridge: Polity.

Taylor, Michael. 1987. *The Possibility of Cooperation*. New York: Cambridge University Press.

Teivainen, Teivo. 2002. "The World Social Forum and Global Democratization: Learning from Porto Alegre," *Third World Quarterly* 23(4):621–32.

Third World Traveler. 2000. "Global Resistance to Structural Adjustment Programs." Sonoma County Peace Press, June/July, www.thirdworldtraveler. com/Structural_Adjustment/GlobalResist_StrucAdjust.htm [20 February 2002].

Thomas, Caroline. 1999. "Where Is the Third World Now?," *Review of International Studies* 25(Special Issue):225–43.

Thomas, Paul. 1994. *Alien Politics: Marxist State Theory Retrieved*. London: Routledge.

"Three Protesters Shot at EU Summit." 2001. CNN.com, June 16. europe.cnn. com/2001/WORLD/europe/06/16/eu.protests [19 February 2002].

Tinbergen, Jan. 1965. *International Economic Integration*. Amsterdam and New York: Elsevier.

Toope, Stephen. 2000. "Emerging Patterns of Governance and International Law." In Byers, 2000, pp. 91–108.

True, Jacqui. 1999. "Expanding Markets and Marketing Gender: The Integration of the Post-Socialist Czech Republic," *Review of International Political Economy* 6(3):360–89.

Tsebelis, George. 1990. *Nested Games: Rational Choice in Comparative Politics*. Berkeley: University of California Press.

Tsoukalis, Loukas. 1989. "The Political Economy of the European Monetary System." In P. Guerrieri and P. C. Padoan (eds.), *The Political Economy of European Integration: States, Markets, and Institutions*, pp. 58–84. Savage, MD: Barnes and Noble.

Turtle Land Restoration Network v. Donald Evans. 2002. 284 F.3d 1282.

Uhler, Oscar M., Coursier, Henri, et al. 1958. *Geneva Convention Relative to the Protection of Civilian Persons in Time of War: Commentary*. Trans. by Ronald Griffin and C. W. Dumbleton. Geneva: International Committee of the Red Cross.

UNDP (United Nations Development Programme). 2003. *Making Global Trade Work for People*. London: Earthscan.

References

UNIFEM. 2003. "Gender-Aware Disarmament, Demobilization, and Reintegration (DDR): A Checklist," www.womenwarpeace.org/issues/ddrenglish.pdf.

United Kingdom House of Commons. 1999. Hansard Debates for 30 June 1999, pt. 15, Column 314, www.publications.parliament.uk/pa/cm199899/cmhansrd/vo990630/debtext/90630-15.htm [27 February 2002].

United Nations. 1998. *Report of the Secretary-General Pursuant to General Assembly Resolution 53/35.* New York: United Nations.

 2000. *Millennium Report of the Secretary-General of the United Nations.* www.un.org/millennium/sg/report.

United States Public Law 101–169. 1989. Section 609. 21 November.

Upham, Frank. 2002. "Mythmaking in the Rule of Law Orthodoxy." Working Paper 30. Washington, DC: Carnegie Endowment for International Peace.

van der Molen, Gesina H. J. 1968. *Alberico Gentili and the Development of International Law: His Life, Work and Times.* 2nd revised edn. Leiden: A. W. Sijthoff.

van der Pijl, Kees. 1984. *The Making of an Atlantic Ruling Class.* London: Verso.

 1998. *Transnational Classes and International Relations.* London: Routledge.

Vasquez, John. 1998. *The Power of Power Politics: From Classical Realism to Neotraditionalism.* New York: Cambridge University Press.

Verhofstadt, Guy. 2002. "Towards Ethical Globalization," *OECD Observer* 231/232(May):4.

Verzola, Roberto. 1998. "Second Opinion," *The Journal*, November 17, www.geocities.com/Eureka/Plaza/5712/obet/pirates/html [26 September 2002].

Wachtel, Howard M. 1990. *The Money Mandarins.* Armonk, NY: M. E. Sharpe.

Wallach, Lori and Michelle Sforza. 1999. *Whose Trade Organization?* Washington, DC: Public Citizen/Global Trade Watch.

Wallerstein, Immanuel. 1998. "The New World Disorder: If the States Collapse, Can the Nations Be United?" In A. Paolini, A. Jarvis and C. Reus-Smit (eds.), *Between Sovereignty and Global Governance: The United Nations, the State and Civil Society*, pp. 171–85. New York: Palgrave.

Waltz, Kenneth N. 1979. *Theory of International Politics.* New York: McGraw-Hill.

 1999. "Globalization and Governance," *PS Online*, December.

Walzer, Michael. 1995. "The Concept of Civil Society." In Walzer (ed.), *Toward a Global Civil Society*, pp. 7–28. Providence, RI: Berghahn Books.

Wapner, Paul. 1996. *Environmental Activism and World Civic Politics.* Albany: SUNY Press.

Weber, Max. 1947. *The Theory of Social and Economic Organization.* Translated by A. M. Henderson and Talcott Parsons. New York: Free Press.

 1949. "'Objectivity' in Social Science and Social Policy." In Weber, *The Methodology of the Social Sciences*, pp. 50–112. Trans. and edited by E. Shils and H. Finch. New York: Free Press.

 1978a. "Bureaucracy." In H. H. Gerth and C. W. Mills (eds.), *From Max Weber: Essays in Sociology.* New York: Oxford University Press.

1978b. "The Social Psychology of the World Religions." In H. H. Gerth and C. W. Mills (eds.), *From Max Weber: Essays in Sociology*. New York: Oxford University Press.

Weber, Steve. 2000. "International Organizations and the Pursuit of Justice in the World Economy," *Ethics and International Affairs* 14:99–118.

Weeks, John. 2001. "Globalize, Global-ize, Global Lies: Myths of the World Economy in the 1990s." In R. Albritton, et al. (eds.), *Phases of Capitalist Development: Booms, Crises, and Globalizations*, pp. 263–82. London: Palgrave.

WEF (World Economic Forum). 1996. "Creative Impatience Can Manage Problems of Globalization," February 1, www.weforum.org/frames/press/am96/pr10ph.htm.

1997a. "About the World Economic Forum." Geneva: World Economic Forum.

1997b. "Committed to Improving the State of the World." Geneva: World Economic Forum.

Weidlich, Thom. 2002. "Executive Life; Call Him to Ease the Pain of Tax Bite," *New York Times*, April 7, Section 3, p. 16.

Weiler, J. H. H. 2001. "The Rule of Lawyers and the Ethos of Diplomats: Reflections on WTO Dispute Settlement." In R. Porter, et al. (eds.), *Efficiency, Equity, and Legitimacy: The Multilateral Trading System at the Millennium*, pp. 334–50. Washington, DC: Brookings Institution Press.

Weiner, Jarrod. 1999. *Globalization and the Harmonization of Law*. London: Pinter.

Weiss, Rick. 1999. "Monsanto's Gene Police Raise Alarm on Farmers' Rights, Rural Tradition," *Washington Post*, February 3, p. 1A, www.biotech-info.net/traditions.html [26 September 2002].

Wellens, Karel. 2002. *Remedies Against International Organizations*. New York: Cambridge University Press.

Weller, Marc. 1999. *The Crisis in Kosovo, 1989–1999: From the Dissolution of Yugoslavia to Rambouillet and the Outbreak of Hostilities*. Cambridge, UK: Documents and Analysis Publishing.

Wendt, Alexander. 1992. "Anarchy Is What States Make of It: The Social Construction of Power Politics," *International Organization* 46(2):391–425.

1998. "On Constitution and Causation in International Relations," *Review of International Studies* 24:101–18.

1999. *Social Theory of International Politics*. New York: Cambridge University Press.

White, N. D. 2000. "The Legality of Bombing in the Name of Humanity," *Journal of Conflict and Security Law* 5:27–43.

White House. 2002. *The National Security Strategy of the United States of America*. Washington, DC: White House.

Wichterich, Christa. 2000. *The Globalized Woman: Reports from a Future of Inequality*. London: Zed Books.

Wilkenson, Riorden and Steve Hughes (eds.). 2003. *Global Governance: Critical Perspectives*. New York: Routledge.

Williams, Michael C. 1996. "Hobbes and International Relations," *International Organization* 50(2):213–36.

References

Williamson, John. 1990. "The Progress of Policy Reform in Latin America." *Policy Analyses in International Economics*, no. 28, pp. 1–33. Washington, DC: Institute for International Economics.
    1993. "Democracy and the 'Washington Consensus.'" *World Development* 21:1329–36.
Williamson, Oliver E. 1985. *The Economic Institutions of Capitalism*. New York: Free Press.
Wittgenstein, Ludwig. 1953. *Philosophical Investigations*. Oxford, UK: Blackwell.
Wolf, Martin. 2001. "The Need for a New Imperialism," *Financial Times* (UK), October 9.
Wolin, Sheldon. 1996. "Fugitive Democracy." In S. Benhabib (ed.), *Democracy and Difference*, pp. 31–45. Princeton: Princeton University Press.
Wong, Kristine. 2001. "The Showdown Before Seattle: Race, Class and the Framing of a Movement." In Yuen, Katsiaficas, and Rose, 2001, pp. 215–24.
Wood, Ellen Meiksins. 1995. *Democracy Against Capitalism: Renewing Historical Materialism*. Cambridge, UK: Cambridge University Press.
    2002. *The Origin of Capitalism: A Longer View*. London: Verso.
Woods, Ngaire. 1999. "Good Governance in International Organizations," *Global Governance* 5:39–61.
    2003. "Order, Justice, the IMF and the World Bank." In R. Foote, J. Gaddis, and A. Hurrell (eds.), *Order and Justice in International Relations*, pp. 80–102. Oxford: Oxford University Press.
Woolf, Virginia. 1938. *Three Guineas*. Harmondsworth: Penguin.
Wrong, Dennis. 1988. *Power: Its Forms, Bases, and Uses*. Chicago: University of Chicago Press.
WTO (World Trade Organization). 1998. *Trading into the Future*, 2nd edn. Geneva: World Trade Organization.
    1998a. "United States – Import Prohibition of Certain Shrimp and Shrimp Products: Report of the Appellate Body." WT/DS58/AB/R, October 12.
    1998b. "United States – Import Prohibition of Certain Shrimp and Shrimp Products: Report of the Panel." WT/DS58/R, May 15.
    2001. "Ministerial Declaration." Fourth ministerial conference, Doha. WT/MIN(01)/DEC/1, November 14.
WTO Focus. 1999. "WTO Organizes 'Geneva Week' for Non-Resident Delegations." 43 (November): 16.
Wuthnow, Robert. 1989. *Communities of Discourse*. Cambridge, MA: Harvard University Press.
Yarbrough, Beth V. and Robert M. Yarbrough. 1992. *Cooperation and Governance in International Trade: The Strategic Organizational Approach*. Princeton: Princeton University Press.
Young, Oran. 1994. *International Governance: Protecting the Environment in a Stateless Society*. Ithaca: Cornell University Press.
Yuen, Eddie, George Katsiaficas, and David Burton Rose (eds.). 2001. *The Battle of Seattle: The New Challenge to Capitalist Globalization*. New York: Soft Skull Press.

Yuval-Davis, Nira. 1997. *Gender and Nation.* London: Sage.

Zabusky, Stacia. 1995. *Launching Europe: An Ethnography of European Cooperation in Space Science.* Princeton: Princeton University Press.

Zacher, Mark and Richard Matthews. 1995. "Liberal International Theory: Common Threads, Divergent Strands." In C. Kegley (ed.), *Controversies in International Relations Theory: Realism and the Neoliberal Challenge,* pp. 107–50. New York: St. Martin's Press.

Zakaria, Fareed. 2003. *The Future of Freedom: Illiberal Democracy at Home and Abroad.* New York: Norton.

Zapatistas. 1998. *Documents from the 1996 Encounter for Humanity and Against Neoliberalism.* New York: Seven Stories Press.

Zarkov, Dubravka. 2001. "The Body of the Other Man: Sexual Violence and the Construction of Masculinity, Sexuality, and Ethnicity in the Croatian Media." In C. Moser and F. Clark (eds.), *Victims, Perpetrators or Actors,* pp. 69–82. London: Zed Books.

Zhang, Yunling. 2000. "China: Whither the World Order After Kosovo?" In Schnabel and Thakur, 2000, pp. 117–27.

Zoll, Daniel. 2000. "Soaking the Poor: SF's Bechtel Wants the Bolivian People to Pay for Its Bad Water Investment," December 13, www.ratical.org/co-globalize/waterBolivia.html [2 November 2002].

Zürn, Michael. 2000. "Democratic Governance Beyond the Nation-State: The EU and Other International Institutions," *European Journal of International Relations* 6:183–221.

Index